Digital Commercial Law

Digital Commercial Law

Private Law in the Age of Tokens, Platforms, and Automation

CHRISTOPHER K. ODINET
and
ANDREA TOSATO

OXFORD
UNIVERSITY PRESS

OXFORD
UNIVERSITY PRESS

Oxford University Press is a department of the University of Oxford. It furthers the University's objective of excellence in research, scholarship, and education by publishing worldwide. Oxford is a registered trade mark of Oxford University Press in the UK and in certain other countries.

Published in the United States of America by Oxford University Press
198 Madison Avenue, New York, NY 10016, United States of America.

Library of Congress Cataloging-in-Publication Data
Names: Odinet, Christopher K. author | Tosato, Andrea author
Title: Digital commercial law : private law in the age of tokens, platforms, and automation / Christopher K. Odinet, Andrea Tosato.
Description: New York : Oxford University Press, 2026. |
Includes bibliographical references and index.
Identifiers: LCCN 2026002465 (print) | LCCN 2026002466 (ebook) |
ISBN 9780197758625 hardback | ISBN 9780197758632 epub |
ISBN 9780197758649 updf | ISBN 9780197758656 online
Subjects: LCSH: Commercial law—Technological innovations | Digital currency—Law and legislation | Blockchains (Databases)—Law and legislation | Contracts—Technological innovations | Property—Technological innovations | Security (Law) | Bailments | Electronic commerce—Law and legislation
Classification: LCC K1005 .O33 2026 (print) | LCC K1005 (ebook)
LC record available at https://lccn.loc.gov/2026002465
LC ebook record available at https://lccn.loc.gov/2026002466

DOI: 10.1093/9780197758656.001.0001

Printed by Marquis Book Printing, Canada

The manufacturer's authorized representative in the EU for product safety is Oxford University Press España S.A. of Parque Empresarial San Fernando de Henares, Avenida de Castilla, 2 – 28830 Madrid (www.oup.es/en or product.safety@oup.com). OUP España S.A. also acts as importer into Spain of products made by the manufacturer.

Note to Readers

This publication is designed to provide accurate and authoritative information in regard to the subject matter covered. It is based upon sources believed to be accurate and reliable and is intended to be current as of the time it was written. It is sold with the understanding that the publisher is not engaged in rendering legal, accounting, or other professional services. If legal advice or other expert assistance is required, the services of a competent professional person should be sought. Also, to confirm that the information has not been affected or changed by recent developments, traditional legal research techniques should be used, including checking primary sources where appropriate.

(Based on the Declaration of Principles jointly adopted by a Committee of the American Bar Association and a Committee of Publishers and Associations.)

Contents

Acknowledgments

Like many in our generation of legal scholars, we came of age during a period of extraordinary technological disruption. We were both young lawyers when Bitcoin first appeared in early 2009, amid the chaos of the global financial crisis. At the time, neither of us could have imagined that this mysterious so-called *cryptocurrency*, created by an anonymous figure known only as Satoshi Nakamoto, would present private law with its greatest challenge since the rise of telecommunications networks and the internet, nor that it would shape the trajectory of our academic careers so profoundly.

Our individual paths to this project were different, yet strikingly convergent. Both of us had been trained in classical doctrinal analysis, steeped in the rich intellectual heritage of the private law of contract, property, tort, and restitution. Most remarkably, each of us brings dual legal education to this collaboration: One of us was born and raised in Italy's civil law system, with extensive grounding in its Roman law roots, while the other hails from Louisiana, one of the few mixed civil/common law jurisdictions in the United States. Despite these civil law foundations, however, we have both spent much of our academic careers within the common law world: both now in the United States, though one began in the United Kingdom.

From the outset, our scholarship has focused on the normative aims and key tenets of private law. We have studied the interface between contract and property, the complex architecture of commercial transactions, the challenges posed by voluntary exchanges involving intangible assets, and the intricacies of cross-border business relationships. This is the sophisticated, doctrinal work that has underpinned any functioning legal system for millennia but has, in recent decades, been overshadowed by public law topics that capture broader attention. It was from this perspective that we watched the digital asset revolution unfold. From Bitcoin's origins through the explosive growth of Ethereum, the initial coin offering (ICO) boom, the rise of decentralized finance, and the crypto collapses that followed, we became troubled by a dangerous imbalance in the legal community's approach to these innovations.

As we will explain fully in the Introduction (Chapter 1), the predominant narrative among legislators, regulators, lawyers, and academics was almost exclusively focused on regulatory questions. Should Bitcoin be treated as a currency, payment instrument, or commodity? Are ICOs issuances of securities?

What anti-money laundering requirements should apply to cryptocurrency exchanges? These were undoubtedly important issues, yet we found ourselves increasingly concerned that this regulatory preoccupation was obscuring fundamental matters, including whether digital assets constitute personal property and, more broadly, the private law framework that governs their commercial circulation.

These concerns crystallized into action around 2018. In what would become the intellectual inception point of this book, we both served on the Uniform Law Commission and American Law Institute joint committee and explored whether the Uniform Commercial Code needed updating for the digital age. Here, we found ourselves thrust into heated debates about the fundamental nature of digital assets. What should have been straightforward discussions about commercial law quickly devolved into passionate arguments that revealed profound misunderstandings about basic principles of property and contract law.

We watched, in astonishment, as sophisticated lawyers and industry participants, with decades of experience, made assertions that flew in the face of centuries-old private law doctrine. Most troubling was the belief that clever contracts and code could override the various mandatory rules of property, contract, secured transactions, and bankruptcy—what we call the "flexibility fallacy." Equally unsettling were arguments that the *numerus clausus* principle was obsolete in the digital age and that private ordering could spawn property rights that would bind unaware third parties. Crucially, these were not abstract theoretical propositions but practices that lawyers and market participants were already embedding into major digital asset platforms, with potentially catastrophic consequences that ultimately materialized. In those rooms, we first recognized the urgent need for rigorous scholarly writing on these topics, planting the seeds for this book.

Our collaboration traces back to the 2022 American Bar Association Business Law Section spring conference in Atlanta. Over lunch, at a small Lebanese restaurant, while discussing the then-nascent problem of stablecoin insolvency, we discovered our shared anxiety about these fundamental misunderstandings plaguing the digital assets ecosystem. Despite different institutional backgrounds and areas of expertise, we found ourselves consistently aligned in our conviction that this rapidly evolving landscape could not be properly understood or regulated without a full appreciation of its private law bedrock. Thus began a years-long joint effort to reconcile technological innovation and enduring commercial law principles. The spectacular failures that began to emerge later in 2022, from the collapse of Terra/Luna to the infamous FTX bankruptcy, reinforced our resolve, confirming that many of these disasters could be traced to grave mistakes about established contract and property law doctrines. These concerns define the dual purpose of this book: to clarify how traditional legal principles apply to new technologies, and to advance normative arguments for an approach to digital asset governance that properly balances public regulation with private law foundations.

In undertaking such an ambitious project, we have incurred enormous debts to countless individuals who have shaped our thinking, challenged our assumptions, and improved our theses. While we could never adequately thank everyone who contributed to this endeavor, we attempt to acknowledge at least some of our most significant (nondischargeable) creditors here.

We begin by expressing our profound gratitude to the visionary leaders at the Uniform Law Commission and American Law Institute who had the foresight to recognize that emerging technologies demanded significant legal reform. Undertaking a comprehensive revision of the UCC to address digital assets required considerable courage, given the political controversies that would surround the project. Their willingness to open the UCC revision process to unprecedented public scrutiny and participation created the laboratory in which many of our ideas were tested and refined. The intellectual rigor of those proceedings, the willingness of participants to engage with difficult questions, and the collaborative spirit that characterized even the most contentious debates taught us invaluable lessons. We specifically thank Eleanor Barrett, Amelia H. Boss, Thomas J. Buiteweg, Stephen Y. Chow, Neil B. Cohen, Deanne Dissinger, Henry Deeb Gabriel, Larry T. Garvin, Teresa Wilton Harmon, Steven L. Harris, Stephanie A. Heller, Thomas S. Hemmendinger, William H. Henning, Charles W. Mooney Jr., Juliet Moringiello, Benjamin Orzeske, Sandra M. Rocks, Tim Schnabel, Stephen L. Sepinuck, Ed Smith, Sandra S. Stern, Steven O. Weise, Diane Wood, and Candace M. Zierdt.

Our international law reform work has been equally formative in shaping this project. We thank our colleagues at the International Institute for the Unification of Private Law (UNIDROIT), particularly those involved in the Digital Assets and Private Law project. The comparative perspective that this work provided enriched our understanding immeasurably and helped us to see both the universality of certain fundamental issues and the importance of contextual factors in their resolution. We specifically note the contributions of Louise Gullifer, Charles W. Mooney Jr., Steven O. Weise, Neil B. Cohen, Hideki Kanda, Jason Grant Allen, Reghard Brits, Hubert de Vauplane, Thiebald Cremers, Marek Dubovec, David Fox, Matthias Haentjens, Hannah Yee-Fen Lim, Philipp Paech, Nina-Luisa Siedler, Luc Thévenoz, Jeffrey Wool, Mimi Zou, Dora Neo, Ignacio Tirado, Anna Veneziano, Giulia Previti, Hamza Hameed, and all the members of the UNIDROIT Secretariat. Similarly, our work with the Hague Conference on Private International Law (HCCH) has deepened our appreciation for how digital assets challenge traditional concepts of jurisdiction and applicable law. In this arena, we thank Gérardine Goh Escolar, Matthias Lehmann, Juliano Alves

Pinto, Teresa Rodríguez de las Heras Ballell, Sandra Rocks, and all the members of the HCCH Permanent Bureau.

Throughout this project, we have been blessed with extraordinary colleagues who have provided extensive comments and critiques on various chapters and ideas. These conversations took place in faculty workshops, academic conferences, bar association meetings, and informal discussions that stretched over many years. We particularly thank the scholars whose work and insights have shaped our thinking: David Abrams, Kristen D. Adams, Tom Baker, LaToya Baldwin Clark, Carl S. Bjerre, Vanessa Casado-Perez, Neil B. Cohen, Nestor Davidson, Rashmi Dyal-Chand, Joshua Fairfield, Pamela Foohey, Sarah Green, Louise Gullifer, David Hoffman, Thomas Keijser, Bob Lawless, Adam Levitin, John Lovett, Charles W. Mooney Jr., Juliet Moringiello, Felix Mormann, Timothy Mulvaney, Nizan Geslevich Packin, Jennifer Payne, Carla Reyes, Marc Roark, Jeanne Schroeder, Christopher Serkin, Nadav Shoked, Joseph William Singer, David Skeel, Daniel Walters, Kevin Werbach, and Burcu Yüksel Ripley. We also benefited enormously from the perspectives of practitioners who work daily with these issues and helped us understand key practical implications, including but certainly not limited to Andrew Hinkes, Patrick Augustus Guida, Mary Gilmore-Maurer, Urszula McCormack, Teresa Harmon, Stephanie A. Heller, Norman M. Powell, and Stephen A. Keen.

We particularly acknowledge those who disagreed with our conclusions, as their challenges forced us to sharpen our arguments and consider perspectives we might otherwise have overlooked. The adversarial nature of academic discourse, one of scholarship's great strengths, pushed us to think more deeply about our assumptions and articulate our positions more clearly. All errors and shortcomings remain our own.

We are also deeply grateful to those scholars who provided us with crucial mentorship and encouragement during the early stages of this work, when it was far from clear that the private law analysis of digital assets would find a receptive audience in either academic or policy circles. To that end, first we must pause to acknowledge Professor Juliet Moringiello of the Widener University Commonwealth Law School, whose passing occurred during the late stages of the writing of this book. Her pioneering scholarship on commercial law and digital property helped establish the intellectual foundations upon which much of our work builds. To our readers, you will see her name and imprint throughout these pages. But Professor Moringiello's contributions to the field extended far beyond her groundbreaking academic writings. She was instrumental in bridging the worlds of legal scholarship and practical law reform, serving with distinction on multiple Uniform Law Commission drafting committees and helping to shape the 2022 UCC amendments that feature prominently in our analysis—in fact, she was the vice chair of the drafting committee. Perhaps most importantly, she was a mentor of extraordinary generosity, who understood that scholarship flourishes through collaboration and who dedicated herself to nurturing emerging voices in commercial law.

Her commitment to bringing rigorous private law analysis to emerging technologies, combined with her tireless efforts to connect academic insights with real-world commercial needs, exemplified the kind of scholarship we aspire to in this book. The legal academy lost a brilliant scholar, and we both lost a mentor and a friend.

We are equally indebted to Professor Charles W. Mooney Jr., known to all as Chuck. His mastery of commercial law has molded not only our work but the entire field for decades. Chuck served as reporter for the 2001 UCC Article 9 revisions, and he again stepped in to complete the 2022 UCC Amendments following the untimely passing of Steven L. Harris. His influence extends internationally through his leadership in UNIDROIT and the United Nations Commission on International Trade Law (UNCITRAL), where he has shaped several important instruments, including the Geneva Securities Convention and the Model Law on Secured Transactions.

Chuck uniquely combines rigorous doctrinal analysis with creative problem-solving, understanding both what the law is and what evolving markets need. Strong in his convictions and formidable in debate, he remains fair, open to new ideas, and willing to reconsider his positions. Beyond his own scholarship, he has tirelessly fostered the next generation of commercial law scholars, offering detailed feedback and supporting junior academics seeking tenure-track positions. For one of us in particular, Chuck has been not merely a mentor but an essential guide through the transition from UK to US legal academia and the complexities of participating in the UCC drafting process—a debt that can never be fully repaid.

We must also acknowledge our extraordinary coauthors on prior articles that form the foundation for several chapters in this book. We are particularly indebted to Kara Bruce for her sophisticated analysis of bankruptcy and consumer protection; to R. Wilson Freyermuth for his deep knowledge of real estate finance and secured transactions; to the late Juliet Moringiello for her pioneering work on the intersection of property law and emerging technologies; to Diane Lourdes Dick for her innovative scholarship on corporate law and insolvency; and to Giuliano G. Castellano for his brilliant understanding of financial regulation. We are profoundly grateful not only for their permission to incorporate and build upon our joint work but also for their enthusiastic support of this broader project.

Our research assistants provided extraordinary support throughout this project. They not only helped with the mundane tasks of cite-checking and source verification but also provided substantive insights that markedly improved our analysis. We are particularly grateful to Harper Beasley, Richard Berner, Zach Brown, Maya George, Madison Hall, Jordan Jenquin, Blaine Kaplani, Martin Kiernan, Michael Kohn, Purabi Kunwar, Zachary Manuel, Evan McKay, John M. Miles, Matthew Norton, Michael O'Rear, Tripper Warlick, Lucas Wetsch, and Nick Yost. Relatedly, for his extensive editorial expertise, we thank Michael Waters, editorial advisor to the law journals at the University of Oklahoma, for his hard work, patience, and talent.

We also extend our appreciation to the institutions that have supported this work. Our respective law schools (both present and past) provided generous research support, as well as the collegial environment that encourages ambitious scholarship. Their libraries and support staff were instrumental in helping bring this project to the finish line. We are particularly grateful to the deans and our faculty colleagues (present and former) at the University of Iowa College of Law, the University of Pennsylvania Carey Law School, the Southern Methodist University Dedman School of Law, the University of Georgia School of Law, l'Université Paris 1 Panthéon-Sorbonne, SciencesPo, and the Texas A&M University School of Law.

The publishing and editorial teams at Oxford University Press, notably our excellent project editor Jacqueline Ridberg Larabee, deserve special thanks for their patience and their commitment to the highest standards of scholarly publication. The complexity of our subject matter and the rapid evolution of both technology and law created numerous challenges. Their professionalism and expertise proved essential in bringing this project to completion.

We specifically acknowledge the anonymous reviewers whose detailed comments improved this book immeasurably. The peer review process, at its best, represents a great strength of academic publishing, and we were fortunate to encounter reviewers who provided genuinely constructive criticism. They forced us to clarify nebulous arguments, support controversial claims, and consider alternative perspectives we had not adequately addressed.

Finally, we must acknowledge the unwavering support of our spouses, whose patience, understanding, and encouragement sustained us throughout the years it took to complete this project. Academic writing, particularly collaborative scholarship of this scope, demands countless hours of research, writing, Zoom meetings, phone calls, and revisions that inevitably encroach upon family time and personal commitments. They not only tolerated the late nights, weekend work sessions, and extended periods of distraction that this project required but actively encouraged us to pursue this ambitious undertaking even when the path forward seemed uncertain. One of us is deeply grateful to his father for his wisdom and support, to his sister and her family for their encouragement, and to Eleonora and Matilde for their love and patience. The other thanks his husband Dub Lee for all his love, encouragement, support, and always excellent cooking.

This work would not have been possible without all of you.

PART I

1
Introduction

Digital assets are everywhere. From Bitcoin and stablecoins to non-fungible tokens (NFTs) and tokenized real estate, these new forms of digital property have burst onto the commercial landscape, promising to revolutionize how we transact, invest, and store value. Yet, while regulators race to oversee this emerging market and headlines buzz with tales of crypto fortunes and scandals, a crucial dimension has been overlooked—the basic private law framework governing these assets. In this book, we introduce and then develop the idea of *digital commercial law*—the body of rules determining who owns digital assets, how they can be transferred, what happens when they are held by custodians, and why attempts to circumvent or reinvent private law through smart contracts and distributed ledgers often fail. Our aim in the pages that follow is to bring clarity to these fundamental questions and to help lawyers, judges, and policymakers better understand and shape the future of commercial transactions in the digital age.

* * *

But before we get to the core contribution, a little history and character development are necessary. It all started in October 2008, amidst the turmoil of the global financial crisis, when an individual or group using the pseudonym "Satoshi Nakamoto" published a whitepaper titled *Bitcoin: A Peer-to-Peer Electronic Cash System*.[1] This document theorized a distributed ledger technology (DLT) network—commonly referred to as a blockchain—which would enable the creation and maintenance of a decentralized digital currency, free from reliance on central banks. The timing was significant: just a month earlier, the collapse of Lehman Brothers, a major investment bank, had starkly exposed the vulnerabilities of centralized financial systems. In early 2009, Nakamoto's vision materialized with the launch of Bitcoin.

For the first three years, Bitcoin remained largely a niche phenomenon. It was primarily a computer science project that attracted programmers, individuals

[1] Satoshi Nakamoto, Bitcoin: A Peer-to-Peer Electronic Cash System (Oct. 31, 2008), https://bitcoin.org/bitcoin.pdf.

Digital Commercial Law. Christopher K. Odinet and Andrea Tosato, Oxford University Press.
 DOI: 10.1093/9780197758656.003.0002

associated with previous digital currency attempts,[2] cypherpunks,[3] and crypto-anarchists.[4] Much of the early community interaction and development took place on online forums, particularly the *BitcoinTalk* forum, where enthusiasts, including the pseudonymous Satoshi Nakamoto, actively discussed and refined the Bitcoin protocol.[5] During this period, Bitcoin's price was highly volatile but remained very low, fluctuating from nearly zero in 2009 to just a few cents by 2010, and reaching approximately $5 by the end of 2011.[6] Nevertheless, the seeds were being planted for Bitcoin's use as a medium of exchange and store of value, with the first real-world transaction occurring in 2010 when Bitcoins were exchanged for tangible goods.[7]

Legal scholars, lawmakers, regulators, and the judiciary were slow to engage with Bitcoin in its early days. Between 2009 and 2012, very little scholarship addressed this new type of digital asset, mostly in the form of short contributions or student notes.[8] This early literature primarily considered Bitcoin for its potential use as a currency.[9] These writings largely focus on its implications for criminal activities,[10] gambling,[11] and, to a much lesser extent, financial regulation.[12]

[2] *See* David Chaum, *Blind Signatures for Untraceable Payments*, *in* ADVANCES IN CRYPTOLOGY 199 (David Chaum, Ronald L. Rivest & Alan T. Sherman eds., 1983); ARVIND NARAYANAN, JOSEPH BONNEAU, EDWARD FELTEN, ANDREW MILLER & STEVEN GOLDFEDER, BITCOIN AND CRYPTOCURRENCY TECHNOLOGIES: A COMPREHENSIVE 18 (2016).

[3] *See* Craig Jarvis, *Cypherpunk Ideology: Objectives, Profiles, and Influences (1992–1998)*, 6 INTERNET HISTORIES 315 (2022), https://www.tandfonline.com/doi/epdf/10.1080/24701475.2021.193 5547; Eric Hughes, A Cypherpunk's Manifesto (Mar. 9, 1993), https://www.activism.net/cypherpunk/manifesto.html; THOMAS RID, RISE OF THE MACHINES: A CYBERNETIC HISTORY (2016); Enrico Beltramini, *Against Technocratic Authoritarianism: A Short Intellectual History of the Cypherpunk Movement*, 5 INTERNET HISTORIES 101 (2020), https://www.resistance.money/class/readings/against.pdf.

[4] Timothy C. May, The Crypto Anarchist Manifesto (1988), https://www.activism.net/cypherpunk/crypto-anarchy.html; Timothy C. May, The Cyphernomicon (Sept. 10, 1994), https://nakamotoinstitute.org/static/docs/cyphernomicon.txt.

[5] NARAYANAN, BONNEAU, FELTEN, MILLER & GOLDFEDER, *supra* note 2, at 170–71.

[6] *See Bitcoin Price History*, COINMARKETCAP, https://coinmarketcap.com/currencies/bitcoin/historical-data/(last visited Feb. 22, 2025).

[7] *See* Benjamin Wallace, *The Rise and Fall of Bitcoin*, WIRED (Nov. 23. 2011), https://www.wired.com/2011/11/mf_bitcoin/.

[8] A HeinOnline search of the Law Journal Library collection returns thirty-six results for articles including the word "bitcoin" between 2009 and 2013. *See, e.g.*, Reuben Grinberg, *Bitcoin: An Innovative Alternative Digital Currency*, 4 HASTINGS SCI. & TECH. L.J. 159 (2012); Nikolei Kaplanov, *Nerdy Money: Bitcoin, the Private Digital Currency, and the Case Against Its Regulation*, 25 LOY. CONSUMER L. REV. 111 (2012); Daniel Smith, *More Money, More Problems: The Bitcoin Virtual Currency and the Legal Problems That Face It*, 3 CASE W. RES. J.L. TECH. & INTERNET 427 (2012); Ruoke Yang, *When Is Bitcoin a Security Under U.S. Securities Law*, 18 J. TECH. L. & POL'Y 99 (2013); Robert Stokes, *Virtual Money Laundering: The Case of Bitcoin and the Linden Dollar*, 21 INFO. & COMM. TECH. L. 221 (2012).

[9] *See* Grinberg, *supra* note 8; Kaplanov, *supra* note 8; Yang, *supra* note 8.

[10] *See* Jared A. Kleiman, *Beyond the Silk Road: Unregulated Decentralized Virtual Currencies Continue to Endanger U.S. National Security and Welfare*, 4 NAT'L SEC. L. BRIEF, no. 1, 2013, at 59; Stokes, *supra* note 8.

[11] *See* Grinberg, *supra* note 8; Smith, *supra* note 8.

[12] See, for example, Grinberg, *supra* note 8; Kaplanov, *supra* note 8.

Lawmakers similarly showed almost no interest in Bitcoin, except as a possible instrument for malfeasance.[13] Concerns that this new and poorly understood technology might facilitate illicit activities and possibly destabilize the financial system were unsurprising, especially after the Great Financial Crisis.[14] Conspicuously absent was any analysis of Bitcoin and its underlying technology from a private law perspective: specifically, whether these tokens constituted personal property (and if so, of what kind), as well as what sort of rules would apply to their transfer, use as collateral, or bailment.

In 2013, Bitcoin experienced its first significant bull run, starting the year at $13 per token and spiking up to $1,100 in December.[15] Concurrently, Ripple Labs launched its eponymous blockchain network and cryptocurrency (XRP) with the aim of enabling real-time cross-border transactions.[16] In the same year, Vitalik Buterin published the Ethereum Whitepaper proposing a blockchain network capable of running "smart contracts"—computer programs capable of executing complex computational operations—rather than merely transferring tokens from one participant to another, which was the limitation of Bitcoin at the time.[17] This wave of developments, however, was not without setbacks. In February 2014, Mt. Gox, then the largest Bitcoin exchange, collapsed after losing approximately 850,000 bitcoins (worth about $450 million at the time) to hacking.[18]

As DLT networks and digital assets gained prominence, US regulatory agencies cautiously entered this space. In March 2013, the Financial Crimes Enforcement Network (FinCEN), a bureau within the US Department of the Treasury charged with safeguarding the financial system from illicit use and combating money laundering, issued interpretive guidance on applying Bank Secrecy Act rules to virtual currencies.[19]

[13] In the United States, see *Combating Transnational Organized Crime: International Money Laundering as a Threat to Our Financial Systems: Hearing Before the Subcomm. on Crime, Terrorism, and Homeland Security of the H. Comm. on the Judiciary*, 112th Cong. (2012), https://www.congress.gov/112/chrg/CHRG-112hhrg72786/CHRG-112hhrg72786.pdf. In the United Kingdom, see *Home Affairs Committee – Ninth Report: Drugs: Breaking the Cycle*, WWW.PARLIAMENT.UK (Dec. 3, 2012), https://publications.parliament.uk/pa/cm201213/cmselect/cmhaff/184/18402.htm.

[14] *See generally* HILARY J. ALLEN, DRIVERLESS FINANCE: FINTECH'S IMPACT ON FINANCIAL STABILITY (2022).

[15] *Bitcoin [Price Index]*, COINDESK, https://www.coindesk.com/price/bitcoin/ (click on "All" button) (last visited Mar. 16, 2025).

[16] Andrey Sergeenkov, *What Is Ripple (XRP)?*, FORBES: DIGITAL ASSETS (Oct. 27, 2024), https://www.forbes.com/sites/digital-assets/article/what-is-ripple-xrp/.

[17] Vitalik Buterin, *Ethereum Whitepaper [2014]*, ETHEREUM.ORG, https://ethereum.org/en/whitepaper/ (last updated Feb. 12, 2025).

[18] Robert McMillan, *The Inside Story of Mt. Gox, Bitcoin's $460 Million Disaster*, WIRED (Mar. 3, 2014), https://www.wired.com/2014/03/bitcoin-exchange/.

[19] Fin. Crimes Enf't Network, Dep't of the Treasury, Guidance No. FIN-2013-G001, Application of FinCEN's Regulations to Persons Administering, Exchanging, or Using Virtual Currencies (Mar. 18, 2013), https://www.fincen.gov/sites/default/files/shared/FIN-2013-G001.pdf.

The following year, the Commodity Futures Trading Commission (CFTC) asserted its jurisdiction over Bitcoin when its chairman testified before Congress, classifying it as an asset within the agency's purview.[20] This declaration was soon followed by enforcement actions against several entities engaged in spot and leveraged trading of digital assets.[21] One of these actions involving the prominent crypto platform Bitfinex deserves particular attention.

In 2016, the CFTC sanctioned Bitfinex for enabling leveraged trading of cryptocurrencies without complying with the Commodities Exchange Act's regulatory obligations.[22] Notably, this action exposed a variety of transactions occurring on this platform, including the lending of cryptocurrencies among users, the use of these assets as collateral, and custodial arrangements in omnibus accounts between Bitfinex and its users with end-of-day netting. In its action, however, the CFTC largely overlooked crucial private law issues, such as the users' rights and obligations, the allocation of ownership rights between users and the platform, and the creation and perfection of security interests. The agency only briefly contemplated whether an "actual delivery" of cryptocurrency was possible. This action showed a significant disconnect. On the one hand, the CFTC was keen to intervene in the cryptocurrency space; on the other, the agency lacked a comprehensive understanding of the rights and obligations defining user-platform relationships. This knowledge gap would prove problematic years later when several exchanges, all operationally similar to Bitfinex, collapsed and entered bankruptcy.

The Securities and Exchange Commission (SEC) initially approached the cryptocurrency space with caution. Its first significant action came in 2013 with charges against Trendon Shavers for defrauding investors in a Bitcoin-based Ponzi scheme.[23] By 2017, however, the SEC had fully entered the fray, asserting that certain transactions involving digital assets could be classified as investment contracts pursuant to the *Howey* test.[24] The SEC's position was exemplified in a settlement with Bitcoin Investment Trust and SecondMarket, Inc. over alleged violations of the Securities Exchange Act of 1934.[25]

[20] *Testimony of Chairman Timothy Massad Before the U.S. Senate Committee on Agriculture, Nutrition & Forestry*, Commodity Futures Trading Comm'n (Dec. 10, 2014), https://www.cftc.gov/PressRoom/SpeechesTestimony/opamassad-6.

[21] Coinflip, Inc., No. 15-29 (Commodity Futures Trading Comm'n Sept. 17, 2015); TeraExchange LLC, No. 15-33 (Commodity Futures Trading Comm'n Sept. 24, 2015); BFXNA Inc., No. 16-19 (Commodity Futures Trading Comm'n June 2, 2016).

[22] BFXNA Inc., No. 16-19.

[23] SEC v. Shavers, No 4:13-CV-416 (E.D. Tex. Aug. 6, 2013).

[24] U.S. Securities and Exchange Commission, *Report of Investigation Pursuant to Section 21(a) of the Securities Exchange Act of 1934: The DAO*, Release No. 81207 (July 25, 2017) (available at https://www.sec.gov/litigation/investreport/34-81207.pdf).

[25] Press Release, SEC, SecondMarket, Inc. and Bitcoin Investment Trust (BIT) Settle Charges Relating to Unlawful Redemptions of BIT Shares During a Continuous Distribution (July 11, 2016), https://www.sec.gov/files/litigation/admin/2016/34-78282-s.pdf.

While regulatory agencies were defining their roles, law enforcement took decisive action against illicit activities involving digital currencies. In May 2013, the US Department of Justice shut down Liberty Reserve, a Costa Rica-based digital currency service, on charges of money laundering and operating an unlicensed money transmitter business. This operation, involving cooperation from seventeen countries, was described as the largest international money laundering prosecution in history at that time.[26] Later in October of that year, the Federal Bureau of Investigation (FBI) seized the Silk Road, an online black market known for facilitating illegal drug transactions using Bitcoin. The agency arrested Ross Ulbricht, the site's founder, on charges including narcotics trafficking, computer hacking, and money laundering, marking a significant crackdown on the illicit use of cryptocurrencies.[27] Concurrently, the Internal Revenue Service (IRS) also weighed in, classifying virtual currencies as property for federal taxation purposes.[28]

Between 2013 and 2016, a growing number of legal scholars started to explore DLT and digital assets in greater depth. While attention to taxation and criminal law persisted,[29] there was a significant shift toward examining the financial regulation challenges posed by blockchain technology and virtual currencies. The peer-to-peer nature of these networks, the absence of central banks, disintermediation, and pseudonymity attracted particular scrutiny, as did the potential for blockchain networks to compete directly with traditional financial infrastructure.[30] Some approached this technology optimistically, envisioning interesting

[26] Press Release, U.S. Att'ys Off., S. Dist. of N.Y., Manhattan U.S. Attorney Announces Charges Against Liberty Reserve, One of World's Largest Digital Currency Companies, and Seven of Its Principals and Employees for Allegedly Running a $6 Billion Money Laundering Scheme (May 28, 2013), https://www.justice.gov/usao-sdny/pr/manhattan-us-attorney-announces-charges-against-liberty-reserve-one-world-s-largest.

[27] Press Release, U.S. Att'ys Off., S. Dist. of N.Y., Manhattan U.S. Attorney Announces Seizure of Additional $28 Million Worth of Bitcoins Belonging to Ross William Ulbricht, Alleged Owner and Operator of "Silk Road" Website (Oct. 25, 2013), https://www.justice.gov/usao-sdny/pr/manhattan-us-attorney-announces-seizure-additional-28-million-worth-bitcoins-belonging.

[28] I.R.S. Notice 2014-21, 2014-16 I.R.B. 938, https://www.irs.gov/pub/irs-drop/n-14-21.pdf.

[29] *See, e.g.*, Lawrence Trautman, *Virtual Currencies; Bitcoin & What Now After Liberty Reserve, Silk Road, and Mt. Gox?*, 20 RICH. J.L. & TECH., article no. 13, issue no. 4, 2014, https://jolt.richmond.edu/files/2021/12/Virtual-Currencies-Bitcoin-What-Now-After-Liberty-Reserve-Silk.pdf; Lawrence J. Trautman, *Cybersecurity: What About U.S. Policy?*, 2015 U. ILL. J.L. TECH. & POL'Y 341.

[30] *See, e.g.*, Aaron Wright & Primavera De Filippi, Decentralized Blockchain Technology and the Rise of *Lex Cryptographia* (Mar. 12, 2015), https://wgig.org/igf/cms/wks2015/uploads/proposal_background_paper/SSRN-id2580664.pdf; Kevin V. Tu & Michael W. Meredith, *Rethinking Virtual Currency Regulation in the Bitcoin Age*, 90 WASH. L. REV. 271 (2015); Douglas W. Arner, Janos Barberis & Ross P. Buckley, *The Evolution of FinTech: A New Post-Crisis Paradigm*, 47 GEO. J. INT'L L. 1271 (2016); Carla L. Reyes, *Moving Beyond Bitcoin to an Endogenous Theory of Decentralized Ledger Technology Regulation: An Initial Proposal*, 61 VILL. L. REV. 191 (2016); Mark Edwin Burge, *Apple Pay, Bitcoin, and Consumers: The ABCs of Future Public Payments Law*, 67 HASTINGS L.J. 1493 (2016); Chris Brummer, *Disruptive Technology and Securities Regulation*, 84 FORDHAM L. REV. 977 (2015); Primavera De Filippi, *Bitcoin: A Regulatory Nightmare to a Libertarian Dream*, 3 INTERNET POL'Y REV., no. 2, 2014, https://policyreview.info/articles/analysis/bitcoin-regulatory-nightmare-libertarian-dream.

opportunities, but the majority viewed it with skepticism, if not as an outright threat to financial stability. Only a handful of scholars investigated the private law questions posed by this new technology, including the legal nature of digital assets, their use in commercial transactions, and their implications in bankruptcy proceedings, with the works of Joshua Fairfield, Juliet Moringiello, and Jeanne Schroeder standing out for their foresight and insightfulness.[31]

The year 2017 ushered in a new phase of explosive growth for DLT networks and digital assets. Bitcoin surpassed $13,700 per token,[32] while Ethereum's Ether climbed from $8 to over $700 by year's end.[33] During this period, several other notable permissioned and permissionless networks were created or gained traction. These included Hyperledger Fabric (launched in 2015 but widely adopted in 2017), R3's Corda (released in 2016, with significant growth in 2017–2018), Stellar (founded in 2014, with major developments in 2017), EOS (launched in 2018), and Cardano (launched in 2017).[34]

This surge in activity was largely driven by the proliferation of initial coin offerings (ICOs), a novel fundraising mechanism that gained significant traction in 2017. In an ICO, project developers create ("mint") their own tokens, typically on the Ethereum network, using smart contracts.[35] These tokens are then sold to the public with the promise of either an ownership stake in the venture or access to future services. Distinct and independent from Ether but recorded on the same Ethereum ledger, these tokens purportedly confer various rights within their respective project ecosystems.[36] The ICO approach allows software developers to raise capital quickly and directly from a global pool of investors, bypassing traditional venture capital routes. Although ICOs have gained significant attention (including from investors), the actual legal

[31] Jeanne L. Schroeder, *Bitcoin and the Uniform Commercial Code*, U MIAMI BUS. L. REV., Spring 2016, at 1; Joshua A. T. Fairfield, *BitProperty*, 88 S. CAL. L. REV. 805 (2015) (building on earlier work at Joshua A. T. Fairfield, *Virtual Property*, 85 B.U. L. REV. 1047 (2005); Joshua A. T. Fairfield, *Smart Contracts, Bitcoin Bots, and Consumer Protection*, 71 WASH. & LEE L. REV. ONLINE 35 (2014); *see also* Chelsea Deppert, *Bitcoin and Bankruptcy: Putting the Bits Together*, 32 EMORY BANKR. DEV. J. 123 (2015); Michael Abramowicz, *Cryptoinsurance*, 50 WAKE FOREST L. REV. 671 (2015); Lorena Yashira Gely-Rojas, *Cryptocurrencies and the Uniform Commercial Code: The Curious Case of Bitcoin*, 8 U. P.R. BUS. L.J. 129 (2016); Juliet M. Moringiello, *False Categories in Commercial Law: The (Ir) Relevance of (In)Tangibility*, 35 FLA. ST. U. L. REV. 119 (2007); Christopher K. Odinet, *BitProperty and Commercial Credit*, 94 WASH. U. L. REV. 649 (2017).

[32] *Bitcoin [Price Index]*, *supra* note 15.

[33] *Ethereum [Price Index]*, COINDESK, https://www.coindesk.com/price/ethereum/ (click on "All" button) (last visited Mar. 16, 2025).

[34] DELOITTE CTR. FOR FIN. SERVS., DELOITTE INSIGHTS: EVOLUTION OF BLOCKCHAIN TECHNOLOGY: INSIGHTS FROM THE GITHUB PLATFORM (2017), https://www2.deloitte.com/content/dam/insights/us/articles/4107_GitHub-blockchain/4107_Github-blockchain.pdf.

[35] *See* Shaanan Cohney, David Hoffman, Jeremy Sklaroff & David Wishnick, *Coin-Operated Capitalism*, 119 COLUM. L. REV. 591 (2019).

[36] WILLIAM MOUGAYAR, THE BUSINESS BLOCKCHAIN: PROMISE, PRACTICE, AND APPLICATION OF THE NEXT INTERNET TECHNOLOGY 30–32 (2016).

entitlements granted by holding these various tokens remained speculative and underdeveloped.

Concurrently, the first stablecoins started to gain traction. Originally created in 2014, Tether (USDT)—a token designed to maintain a 1:1 peg with the US dollar, backed by reserves held by its issuer—saw its supply grow from $10 million to $2.8 billion in 2017.[37] Similarly, MakerDAO launched its DAI stablecoin on the Ethereum network in December 2017.[38] Unlike Tether, DAI maintained its dollar peg through a complex system of smart contracts, representing a decentralized and automated approach to stablecoin issuance. By offering tokens with price stability in an otherwise volatile market, stablecoins became a cornerstone of the DLT ecosystem, facilitating trading and enabling more complex financial operations within the space.

NFTs also gained mainstream attention on the Ethereum network during these years. NFTs are uniquely identifiable tokens within a specific DLT network that can be transferred and programmed through smart contracts.[39] Projects like CryptoKitties, Decentraland, and CryptoPunks achieved widespread popularity between 2017 and 2018. Moreover, NFTs catalyzed the concept of tokenization—the practice of representing both tangible assets, such as rare cars and paintings, and intangible assets, such as digital art or intellectual property rights, as tokens on a DLT network.[40] Proponents argued that these tokenized assets could then be traded more efficiently, purportedly enabling the transfer of ownership and other property rights in the linked assets with unprecedented ease, transparency, and liquidity, all thanks to the underlying blockchain technology.

Unsurprisingly, this rapid expansion attracted wild speculation and fraudulent activities and exposed security vulnerabilities. High-profile incidents included the 2016 DAO hack, resulting in a $50 million theft,[41] and the Parity wallet freeze in 2017, which locked up $300 million worth of Ether.[42] The ICO boom also spawned numerous scams and failed projects. A 2018 Ernst & Young

[37] *Transparency*, TETHER, https://tether.to/en/transparency/ (last visited Mar. 16, 2025).

[38] MAKERDAO, THE MAKER PROTOCOL: MAKERDAO'S MULTI-COLLATERAL DAI (MCD) SYSTEM (2023 rev.) (white paper), https://makerdao.com/whitepaper/White%20Paper%20-The%20Maker%20Protocol_%20MakerDAO%E2%80%99s%20MultiCollateral%20Dai%20(MCD)%20System-FINAL-%20021720.pdf.

[39] Robyn Conti, *What Is an NFT? Non-Fungible Tokens Explained*, FORBES (May 10, 2024), https://www.forbes.com/advisor/investing/cryptocurrency/nft-non-fungible-token/.

[40] Juliet M. Moringiello & Christopher K. Odinet, *The Property Law of Tokens*, 74 FLA. L. REV. 607 (2022); Steven L. Schwarcz, *Next-Generation Securitization: NFTs, Tokenization, and the Monetization of "Things,"* 103 B.U. L. REV. 967 (2023); Christopher K. Odinet & Andrea Tosato, *The Intersection of NFTs and Structured Finance*, 103 B.U. L. REV. 1005 (2023).

[41] Klint Finley, *A $50 Million Hack Just Showed That the DAO Was All Too Human*, WIRED (June 18, 2016), https://www.wired.com/2016/06/50-million-hack-just-showed-dao-human/.

[42] Alex Hart, *$300 Million in Cryptocurrency Was Lost Yesterday*, THE GUARDIAN (Nov. 8, 2017), https://www.theguardian.com/technology/2017/nov/08/cryptocurrency-300m-dollars-stolen-bug-ether#:~:text=The%20lost%20%24300m%20follows,that%20devops199%20triggered%20by%20accident.

report estimated that more than 10 percent of ICO proceeds were lost to hackers, while many projects collapsed without delivering on their promises.[43]

Despite these risks, the sector saw substantial capital inflow. Venture capital investments in blockchain startups surged from $1.04 billion in 2017 to $4.1 billion in 2018, and further to $7.5 billion in 2019.[44] The talent pool expanded rapidly, with blockchain-related job postings increasing 386 percent in 2017 and a further 33 percent in 2018.[45] Deloitte's 2019 survey showed 83 percent of respondents saw compelling blockchain use cases, up from 74 percent in 2018, indicating growing demand for blockchain expertise.[46] In this landscape, major technology companies, financial institutions, and startups alike competed fiercely for blockchain talent.

With such a momentous increase in activities on DLT networks, US regulatory agencies scrambled to respond. In 2017, as cryptocurrency prices soared, FinCEN took action against BTC-e, one of the largest digital currency exchanges at the time, and its operator, Alexander Vinnik, for alleged money laundering and operating an unlicensed money services business.[47] Two years later, FinCEN issued new interpretive guidelines, reaffirming that persons involved in transmitting convertible virtual currencies (CVCs) would be considered "money service businesses" subject to registration and compliance. Notably, these guidelines considered a wide range of CVC activities, including various types of exchanges, wallets, kiosks, and anonymizing services.[48] Collectively, these enforcement actions and accompanying regulatory guidelines revealed the challenges FinCEN faced in regulating a space characterized by the absence of traditional financial intermediaries.

The CFTC likewise intensified its regulatory efforts. In 2017, the agency publicly reaffirmed its "general anti-fraud and manipulation enforcement authority

[43] Anna Irrera, *More Than 10 Percent of $3.7 Billion Raised in ICOs Has Been Stolen—Ernst & Young*, REUTERS (Jan. 22, 2018), https://www.reuters.com/article/business/more-than-10-percent-of-37-billion-raised-in-icos-has-been-stolen-ernst-yo-idUSKBN1FB1NO/.

[44] CB INSIGHTS, THE BLOCKCHAIN REPORT 2020 (Mar. 2020), https://www.cbinsights.com/research/report/blockchain-report-2020/.

[45] Guy Berger, *Introduction* to LINKEDIN 2018 U.S. EMERGING JOBS REPORT (Dec. 13, 2018), https://economicgraph.linkedin.com/research/linkedin-2018-emerging-jobs-report.

[46] DELOITTE DEV., DELOITTE INSIGHTS: DELOITTE'S 2019 GLOBAL BLOCKCHAIN SURVEY (2019), https://www2.deloitte.com/content/dam/insights/us/articles/2019-global-blockchain-survey/DI_2019-global-blockchain-survey.pdf.

[47] Press Release, Fin. Crimes Enf't Network, FinCEN Fines BTC-e Virtual Currency Exchange $110 Million for Facilitating Ransomware, Dark Net Drug Sales (July 27, 2017), https://www.fincen.gov/news/news-releases/fincen-fines-btc-e-virtual-currency-exchange-110-million-facilitating-ransomware.

[48] Fin. Crimes Enf't Network, FinCEN Guidance No. FIN-2019-G001, Application of FinCEN's Regulations to Certain Business Models Involving Convertible Virtual Currencies (May 9, 2019), https://www.fincen.gov/sites/default/files/2019-05/FinCEN%20Guidance%20CVC%20FINAL%20508.pdf.

over virtual currency cash markets as a commodity in interstate commerce."[49] This stance was judicially endorsed in 2018 when, in *CFTC v. McDonnell*, the Eastern District of New York ruled that Bitcoin is a commodity under the Commodities Exchange Act.[50] The CFTC's jurisdiction was further cemented in the case of *In re My Big Coin*, where a federal court explicitly upheld the agency's authority in pursuing an enforcement action concerning fraud involving a prospective cryptocurrency.[51] Concurrently, the CFTC approved the Chicago Mercantile Exchange and the CBOE Futures Exchange to start trading self-certified Bitcoin futures contracts, marking a significant step in cryptocurrencies' integration into traditional financial markets.[52]

During these years, the SEC emerged as the most proactive US regulatory agency in this space. In July 2017, the SEC issued the DAO Report, asserting that, under the long-established *Howey* test, many digital asset offerings—including ICOs—could be classified as sales of investment contracts, thus requiring compliance with federal securities laws.[53] This position was reinforced through a series of strategic enforcement actions against token issuers,[54] culminating in the 2019 release of the SEC Framework for Investment Contract Analysis of Digital Assets.[55] However, the SEC's actions were not without controversy. Industry participants and even some SEC commissioners, notably Hester Peirce,[56] criticized the agency's guidelines as ambiguous and technologically unsophisticated. Crucially, the SEC's approach entirely overlooked private law issues by failing to draw distinctions between transactions in which the respective rights and obligations fundamentally differed for the parties involved from one type of digital asset transaction to another.

[49] Commodity Futures Trading Commission, Understand the Risks of Virtual Currency Trading, CFTC, https://www.cftc.gov/LearnAndProtect/AdvisoriesAndArticles/understand_risks_of_virtual_currency.html (last visited Apr. 29, 2025).

[50] CFTC v. McDonnell, 287 F. Supp. 3d 213 (E.D.N.Y. 2018).

[51] CFTC v. My Big Coin Pay, Inc., 334 F. Supp. 3d 492 (D. Mass. 2018); *see also* CFTC v. Gelfman Blueprint, Inc., No. 17-cv-7181 (S.D.N.Y. filed Sept. 21, 2017).

[52] Press Release, Commodity Futures Trading Comm'n, CFTC Statement on Self-Certification of Bitcoin Products by CME, CFE and Cantor Exchange (Dec. 1, 2017), https://www.cftc.gov/PressRoom/PressReleases/pr7654-17.

[53] Report of Investigation Pursuant to Section 21(a) of the Securities Exchange Act of 1934: The DAO, Exchange Act Release No. 81207 (July 25, 2017), https://www.sec.gov/litigation/investreport/34-81207.pdf.

[54] *See, e.g.*, *In re* Munchee Inc, Securities Act Release No 10445 (Dec. 11, 2017), https://www.sec.gov/files/litigation/admin/2017/33-10445.pdf; *In re* Tomahawk Exploration LLC, Securities Act Release No 10530 (Aug. 14, 2018), https://www.sec.gov/files/litigation/admin/2018/33-10530.pdf; *REcoin Group Foundation, et al.: Litigation Release No. 24081*, U.S. Sec. & Exch. Comm'n (Mar. 26, 2018), https://www.sec.gov/enforcement-litigation/litigation-releases/lr-24081; *PlexCorps, et al.: SEC Emergency Action Halts ICO Scam: Litigation Release No. 24079*, U.S. Sec. & Exch. Comm'n (Dec. 1, 2017), https://www.sec.gov/enforcement-litigation/litigation-releases/lr-24079.

[55] *Framework for "Investment Contract" Analysis of Digital Assets*, U.S. Sec. & Exch. Comm'n (July 5, 2024), https://www.sec.gov/corpfin/framework-investment-contract-analysis-digital-assets.

[56] Hester Peirce, *Speech: How We Howey*, U.S. Sec. & Exch. Comm'n (May 9, 2019), https://www.sec.gov/news/speech/peirce-how-we-howey-050919.

The financial regulatory landscape was further developed in 2018, as various state securities regulators began launching enforcement actions against public offerings of tokens to investors under state blue sky laws.[57] This "finreg"-focused approach continued with the Office of the Comptroller of the Currency (OCC) allowing national banks to provide cryptocurrency custody services in 2020.[58]

Governmental and nongovernmental organizations also reacted to the emergence of DLT networks and digital assets. Here again, the primary emphasis came from entities focused on financial regulation. The International Monetary Fund and the Financial Stability Board undertook projects exploring how these novel technologies called into question the existing paradigm. With a few notable exceptions, most organizations focused on private law did not show similar interest. For example, in 2017, the United Nations Commission on International Trade Law (UNCITRAL) chose not to pursue work exploring private law issues raised by DLT networks, digital assets, and smart contracts in favor of a project on the international effects of judicial sales of ships.[59] By contrast, in 2018, the Uniform Law Commission (ULC) and the American Law Institute (ALI) formed a study committee to investigate whether the UCC should be reformed to address new technologies.

These developments across the regulatory and law reform spectrum drew a large cohort of legal scholars determined to investigate DLT networks and digital assets in depth. The vast majority of the literature produced between roughly 2017 and 2019 continued to examine this space through the lens of financial regulation. One line of scholarship focused on the regulation of DLT networks per se.[60] Another investigated the impact of cryptocurrencies and other digital assets

[57] *See, e.g.*, Emergency Cease and Desist Order, *In re* Bitconnect, No. ENF-18-CDO-1754 (Tex. State Sec. Bd. Jan. 4, 2018), https://www.ssb.texas.gov/sites/default/files/BitConnect_ENF-18-CDO-1754.pdf; Press Release, Letitia James, N.Y. State Att'y Gen., Attorney General James Directs Unregistered Crypto Lending Platforms to Cease Operations In New York, Announces Additional Investigations (Oct. 18, 2021), https://ag.ny.gov/press-release/2021/attorney-general-james-directs-unregistered-crypto-lending-platforms-cease.

[58] Authority of a National Bank to Provide Cryptocurrency Custody Services for Customers, OCC Interpretive Letter No. 1170 (July 22, 2020), https://www.occ.gov/topics/charters-and-licensing/interpretations-and-actions/2020/int1170.pdf.

[59] U.N. Comm'n on Int'l Trade Law, Rep. of the U.N. Comm'n on Int'l Trade Law, 51st Sess., ¶¶ 247–48, 252, U.N. Doc. A/73/17 (2018), available at https://docs.un.org/en/A/73/17%20.

[60] *See, e.g.*, Kevin Werbach, *Trust, but Verify: Why the Blockchain Needs the Law*, 33 Berkeley Tech. L.J. 487 (2018); Carla L. Reyes, *Conceptualizing Cryptolaw*, 96 Neb. L. Rev. 384 (2017); Lawrence J. Trautman, *Bitcoin, Virtual Currencies, and the Struggle of Law and Regulation to Keep Peace*, 102 Marq. L. Rev. 447 (2018); Primavera De Filippi & Aaron Wright, Blockchain and the Law: The Rule of Code (2018); Dirk A. Zetzsche, Ross P. Buckley, Janos N. Barberis & Douglas W. Arner, *Regulating a Revolution: From Regulatory Sandboxes to Smart Regulation*, 23 Fordham J. Corp. & Fin. L. 31 (2017); Primavera De Filippi & Samer Hassan, *Blockchain Technology as a Regulatory Technology: From Code Is Law to Law Is Code*, 21 First Monday, no. 12, 2016, https://firstmonday.org/ojs/index.php/fm/article/view/7113/5657; Dirk A. Zetzsche, Ross P. Buckley & Douglas W. Arner, *The Distributed Liability of Distributed Ledgers: Legal Risks of Blockchain*, 2018 U. Ill. L. Rev. 1361; Albert C. Lin, *Herding Cats: Governing Distributed Innovation*, 96 N.C. L. Rev. 945 (2018).

on traditional finance, expressing concerns about systemic risk and stability.[61] Another focused on ICOs and the parallels with initial public offerings of securities.[62] However, private law issues continued to attract limited attention,[63] except for the relationship between legal contracts and smart contracts[64] and the impact of decentralized autonomous organizations on the law of business entities.[65]

Between 2020 and 2022, the DLT ecosystem experienced another quantum leap in adoption and commercial activity. Catalyzed partly by the global pandemic and subsequent stay-at-home mandates, the uptake of DLT networks and digital assets accelerated dramatically.[66] Bitcoin and Ether reached unprecedented peaks, as did the protocol tokens of emerging networks like Solana, Cardano, and Polkadot. Stablecoins proliferated in number and circulation, with their total supply ballooning to $150 billion, becoming a cornerstone of the digital asset ecosystem.[67] Concurrently, NFTs evolved from niche digital collectibles to high-value assets, commanding record prices at prestigious auction houses.[68] Tokenization expanded its reach, encompassing assets from real estate to luxury watches, fine wines, precious metals, and intellectual property rights.[69]

[61] Robert C. Hockett & Saule T. Omarova, *The Finance Franchise*, 102 CORNELL L. REV. 1143 (2017); William Magnuson, *Regulating Fintech*, 71 VAND. L. REV. 1167 (2018); Chris Brummer & Yesha Yadav, *Fintech and the Innovation Trilemma*, 107 GEO. L.J. 235 (2019); Saule T. Omarova, *New Tech v. New Deal: Fintech as a Systemic Phenomenon*, 36 YALE J. ON REG. 735 (2019); Lawrence J. Trautman & Alvin C. Harrell, *Bitcoin Versus Regulated Payment Systems: What Gives*, 38 CARDOZO L. REV. 1041 (2017); Hilary J. Allen, *$=Euro=Bitcoin?*, 76 MD. L. REV. 877 (2017); Dan Awrey & Kristin van Zwieten, *The Shadow Payment System*, 43 J. CORP. L. 775 (2018); William Magnuson, *Financial Regulation in the Bitcoin Era*, 23 STAN. J.L. BUS. & FIN. 159 (2018); Carol Goforth, *Securities Treatment of Tokenized Offerings Under U.S. Law*, 46 PEPP. L. REV. 405 (2019).

[62] *See, e.g.*, Cohney, Hoffman, Sklaroff & Wishnick, *supra* note 35; Dirk A. Zetzsche, Ross P. Buckley, Douglas W. Arner & Linus Fohr, *The ICO Gold Rush: It's a Scam, It's a Bubble, It's a Super Challenge for Regulators*, 60 HARV. INT'L L.J. 267 (2019).

[63] Notable exceptions are Kevin V. Tu, *Perfecting Bitcoin*, 52 GA. L. REV. 505 (2018); Eric D. Chason, *How Bitcoin Functions as Property Law*, 49 SETON HALL L. REV. 129 (2018); Ronald J. Mann, *Reliable Perfection of Security Interests in Crypto-Currency*, 21 SMU SCI. & TECH. L. REV. 159 (2018).

[64] Kevin Werbach & Nicolas Cornell, *Contracts Ex Machina*, 67 DUKE L.J. 313 (2017); Jeremy M. Sklaroff, *Smart Contracts and the Cost of Inflexibility*, 166 U. PA. L. REV. 263 (2017); James Grimmelmann, *All Smart Contracts Are Ambiguous*, 2 J.L. & INNOVATION 1 (2019); J. G. Allen, *Wrapped and Stacked: 'Smart Contracts' and the Interaction of National and Formal Language*, 14 EUR. REV. CONT. L. 307 (2018).

[65] Usha R. Rodrigues, *Law and the Blockchain*, 104 IOWA L. REV. 679 (2019); Carla L. Reyes, *If Rockefeller Were a Coder*, 87 GEO. WASH. L. REV. 373 (2019); Lynn M. Lopucki, *Algorithmic Entities*, 95 WASH. U. L. REV. 887 (2018); Carla L. Reyes, Nizan Geslevich Packin & Benjamin P. Edwards, *Distributed Governance*, 59 WM. & MARY L. REV. ONLINE 1 (2017–2018); Shawn Bayern, *Are Autonomous Entities Possible?*, 114 NW. U. L. REV. ONLINE 23 (2019).

[66] Hadar Y. Jabotinsky & Roee Sarel, *How the COVID-19 Pandemic Affected the Cryptocurrency Market*, CLS BLUE SKY BLOG, https://clsbluesky.law.columbia.edu/2021/03/26/how-the-covid.

[67] *Total Stablecoin Supply*, THE BLOCK, https://www.theblock.co/data/decentralized-finance/stablecoins (click on "All" button for 2022 data) (last visited Mar. 16, 2025).

[68] *See, e.g.*, *Beeple's Opus*, CHRISTIE'S, https://www.christies.com/features/Monumental-collage-by-Beeple-is-first-purely-digital-artwork-NFT-to-come-to-auction-11510-7.aspx (last visited Oct. 7, 2024).

[69] Schwarcz, *supra*, note 40; *see also* Odinet & Tosato, *Structured Finance*, *supra* note 40.

Decentralized finance (DeFi) projects multiplied, introducing a variety of "staking"[70] and lending mechanisms. Platforms such as Celsius and Voyager exemplified this trend, offering yields on cryptocurrency deposits that far outstripped traditional financial products, sometimes exceeding 20 percent annually.[71] Buoyed by this surge of activity, cryptocurrency exchanges and custodial services experienced exponential growth. Global giants such as Binance, Coinbase, and Kraken consolidated their market dominance, while newcomers like FTX rapidly ascended to prominence, collectively serving as critical on-ramps for the burgeoning digital asset market.[72]

This exuberance came to an abrupt halt in 2022 with the arrival of the so-called crypto winter. As central banks around the world tightened monetary policy to curb inflation, liquidity rapidly drained from digital asset markets. To paraphrase Warren Buffett, when the tide went out, it became clear that many had been swimming without trunks. The illusion of boundless prosperity, disintermediation, and democratization quickly unraveled, exposing widespread fraud, hollow projects, and incompetent management. Bitcoin and Ether plummeted, while smaller protocol tokens were all but obliterated.[73] Entire networks collapsed, with Terra/Luna's implosion standing out as particularly catastrophic, wiping out nearly $60 billion in market value virtually overnight.[74] Many stablecoins depegged from their fiat counterparts, leaving holders with worthless tokens.[75] The NFT market, previously buoyant, saw floor prices crash to near zero for many collections.[76] Exchanges and lending platforms, once considered rising giants, crumbled under the pressure. Voyager, Celsius, and Genesis filed for bankruptcy, while the spectacular fall of FTX, once valued at $32 billion, sent shockwaves through the entire crypto ecosystem. Digital asset markets did not begin to stabilize until the second quarter of 2023, but by then,

[70] *See What Is Crypto Staking and How Does It Work?*, Binance Acad. (Aug. 14, 2024), https://academy.binance.com/en/articles/what-is-staking.

[71] MacKenzie Sigalos, *A Tax Write-Off May Be Possible for Bitcoin Lost to Lending Platforms Like Celsius*, CNBC, https://www.cnbc.com/2022/07/06/tax-writeoff-possible-for-bitcoin-lost-to-lending-sites-like-celsius.html (July 6, 2022).

[72] Jonathan Ponciano, *Billionaire Bankman-Fried's FTX Launches $2 Billion Crypto Fund Amid Venture's Massive Deal Boom*, Forbes, https://www.forbes.com/sites/jonathanponciano/2022/01/14/billionaire-bankman-frieds-ftx-launches-2-billion-crypto-fund-amid-ventures-massive-deal-boom/ (Jan. 14, 2022).

[73] Frank Holmes, *Bitcoin Is Marked Down as "Crypto Winter" Wipes Out Billions in Market Value*, U.S. Global Investors, https://www.usfunds.com/resource/bitcoin-is-marked-down-as-crypto-winter-wipes-out-billions-in-market-value/ (July 25, 2022).

[74] Krisztian Sandor & Ekin Genc, *The Fall of Terra: A Timeline of the Meteoric Rise and Crash of UST and LUNA*, CoinDesk, https://www.coindesk.com/learn/the-fall-of-terra-a-timeline-of-the-meteoric-rise-and-crash-of-ust-and-luna (May 11, 2023).

[75] *See* Andrea Tosato, Diane Lourdes Dick & Christopher K. Odinet, *Debt Tokens*, 173 U. Pa. L. Rev. 1103, 1122–32 (2025).

[76] *NFT Crash and Crypto Winter 2022*, MyArtBroker, https://www.myartbroker.com/investing/articles/nft-crash-and-crypto-winter-2022 (Dec. 7, 2022).

the damage was profound—not just in terms of value destruction, but also to the credibility of the entire sector.

As the digital asset market experienced this intense boom-and-bust cycle, US regulatory agencies intensified their efforts to establish oversight. FinCEN and the CFTC maintained their regulatory approaches while expanding enforcement actions. FinCEN issued updated guidance on virtual currency business models in 2021,[77] while the CFTC brought significant cases against BitMEX, Tether, and, notably, against Ooki DAO, marking its first action against a decentralized autonomous organization.[78] The Office of Foreign Assets Control (OFAC) also adopted a more aggressive stance, exemplified by its sanctions against Tornado Cash, a cryptocurrency mixer, in August 2022.[79]

During this period, the SEC emerged as the most active regulator under Chairman Gary Gensler's leadership. The agency intensified its enforcement efforts by pursuing various token sales as unregistered securities offerings under the *Howey* test, including against Kik, Telegram, and Ripple, as well as against certain issuers of NFTs.[80] Moreover, the SEC brought actions alleging certain token sales constituted issuances of debt securities under the *Reves* test, notably against DMM and Kraken for their yield products.[81] The agency also moved against well-established platforms, such as Coinbase and OpenSea, asserting that numerous secondary market token transactions

[77] *FinCEN Issues Guidance on Virtual Currencies and Regulatory Responsibilities*, Fin. Crimes Enf't Network (May 18, 2021), https://www.fincen.gov/news/news-releases/fincen-issues-guidance-virtual-currencies-and-regulatory-responsibilities.

[78] Press Release, Commodity Futures Trading Comm'n, Federal Court Orders BitMEX to Pay $100 Million for Illegally Operating a Cryptocurrency Trading Platform and Anti-Money Laundering Violations (Aug. 10, 2021), https://www.cftc.gov/PressRoom/PressReleases/8412-21; Press Release, Commodity Futures Trading Comm'n, CFTC Orders Tether and Bitfinex to Pay Fines Totaling $42.5 Million (Oct. 15, 2021), https://www.cftc.gov/PressRoom/PressReleases/8450-21; Press Release, Commodity Futures Trading Comm'n, CFTC Imposes $250,000 Penalty Against bZeroX, LLC and Its Founders and Charges Successor Ooki DAO for Offering Illegal, Off-Exchange Digital-Asset Trading, Registration Violations, and Failing to Comply with Bank Secrecy Act (Sept. 22, 2022), https://www.cftc.gov/PressRoom/PressReleases/8590-22. *See* Carla L. Reyes, Nizan Geslevich Packin & Benjamin P. Edwards, *Distributed Governance*, 59 Wm. & Mary L. Rev. Online 1 (2017-2018).

[79] Press Release, U.S. Dep't of the Treasury, U.S. Treasury Sanctions Notorious Virtual Currency Mixer Tornado Cash (Aug. 8, 2022), https://home.treasury.gov/news/press-releases/jy0916.

[80] Press Release, U.S. Sec. & Exch. Comm'n, SEC Charges Issuer With Conducting $100 Million Unregistered ICO (June 4, 2019), https://www.sec.gov/news/press-release/2019-87; Press Release, U.S. Sec. & Exch. Comm'n, SEC Halts Alleged $1.7 Billion Unregistered Digital Token Offering (Oct. 11, 2019), https://www.sec.gov/news/press-release/2019-212; Press Release, U.S. Sec. & Exch. Comm'n, SEC Charges Ripple and Two Executives with Conducting $1.3 Billion Unregistered Securities Offering (Dec. 22, 2020), https://www.sec.gov/news/press-release/2020-338.

[81] Press Release, U.S. Sec. & Exch. Comm'n, SEC Charges Decentralized Finance Lender and Top Executives for Raising $30 Million Through Fraudulent Offerings (Aug. 6, 2021), https://www.sec.gov/news/press-release/2021-145; Press Release, U.S. Sec. & Exch. Comm'n, Kraken to Discontinue Unregistered Offer and Sale of Crypto Asset Staking-As-a-Service Program and Pay $30 Million to Settle SEC Charges (Feb. 9, 2023), https://www.sec.gov/news/press-release/2023-25.

involved securities trading.[82] Furthermore, the SEC proposed expanding its interpretation of "exchange" to potentially encompass providers of software for decentralized exchanges like Uniswap.[83] While the SEC secured several litigation victories,[84] it also encountered significant judicial setbacks, most notably in the Ripple case and, more recently, in its action against Coinbase.[85] Moreover, its aggressive stance faced industry pushback, with critics arguing the SEC was overreaching and creating uncertainty through "regulation by enforcement."[86]

Concurrently, legislators sought to intervene more decisively. At the federal level, several bills were introduced, including the Stablecoin TRUST Act and the Lummis-Gillibrand Responsible Financial Innovation Act, both of which aimed to create a comprehensive regulatory framework for digital assets.[87]

At the state level, various laws were enacted, ranging from requiring cryptocurrency businesses to obtain state licenses as money transmitters[88] to introducing new corporate forms for DAOs (as in Wyoming)[89] to establishing specialized regulatory regimes, such as New York's BitLicense.[90] Crucially, despite encountering some resistance, a few states began adopting the 2022 revisions to the UCC jointly proposed by the Uniform Law Commission and the American Law Institute. The revisions introduced a new private law framework for the circulation of certain digital assets.

[82] Press Release, U.S. Sec. & Exch. Comm'n, SEC Charges Coinbase for Operating as an Unregistered Securities Exchange, Broker, and Clearing Agency (June 6, 2023), https://www.sec.gov/news/press-release/2023-102.

[83] *See generally* U.S. Securities Exchange Commission Release No. 34-94062, (Jan. 26, 2022); *see also* Uniswap Labs, *Response to Wells Notice*, Uniswap Blog (Mar. 2025), https://blog.uniswap.org/wells-notice-response.pdf.

[84] SEC v. Kik Interactive Inc., 492 F. Supp. 3d 169 (S.D.N.Y. 2020); SEC v. Telegram Group Inc., 448 F. Supp. 3d 352 (S.D.N.Y. 2020).

[85] SEC v. Ripple Labs, Inc., No. 20 Civ. 10832 (S.D.N.Y. July 13, 2023); SEC v. Coinbase, Inc., No. 23 Civ. 4738 (S.D.N.Y. July 13, 2023).

[86] *See SEC Crypto Enforcement Actions Under Gary Gensler Reach 10-Year High*, COINTELEGRAPH (Jan. 24, 2024), https://cointelegraph.com/news/sec-enforcement-actions-gary-gensler [https://perma.cc/5UVJ-RUKC].

[87] *S.5340–Stablecoin TRUST Act of 2022*, CONGRESS.GOV, https://www.congress.gov/bill/117th-congress/senate-bill/5340 (last visited Mar. 18, 2025); *S.4356 - Lummis-Gillibrand Responsible Financial Innovation Act*, CONGRESS.GOV, https://www.congress.gov/bill/117th-congress/senate-bill/4356 (last visited Mar. 18, 2025). Of the thirty-nine bills introduced in Congress between 2019 and 2023, fifteen were focused on the financial regulatory treatment of the digital asset market and its participants.

[88] *See* Joseph Jasperse, *50-State Review of Cryptocurrency and Blockchain Regulation*, WHARTON SCH., UNIV. OF PENN.: STEVENS CTR. FOR INNOVATION IN FIN. (Feb. 2023), https://stevenscenter.wharton.upenn.edu/publications-50-state-review/.

[89] *Legislation—2021: SF0038—Decentralized Autonomous Organizations*, STATE OF WYO., 68TH LEGISLATURE, https://www.wyoleg.gov/Legislation/2021/SF0038 (last visited Mar. 18, 2025); *Virtual Currency Business Licensing*, N.Y. STATE DEP'T OF FIN. SERVS., https://www.dfs.ny.gov/virtual_currency_businesses (last visited Mar. 18, 2025).

[90] *See* N.Y. COMP. CODES R. & REGS. tit. 23, § 200 (2015).

In 2021, the executive branch also recommended increased regulatory oversight. The President's Working Group on Financial Markets released a report examining the risks and regulatory gaps associated with stablecoins.[91] This was followed in 2022 by President Biden's Executive Order on Ensuring Responsible Development of Digital Assets, which called for a comprehensive approach to cryptocurrency regulation, signaling a more coordinated federal strategy.[92] Notably, both reports focused almost exclusively on regulatory concerns, disregarding private law implications.

The flurry of market developments and regulatory activity catalyzed a robust response from legal academia. Once again, the predominant focus remained on public law aspects, particularly financial regulation. Scholars continued to examine the potential disruption of traditional financial systems by DLT networks and digital assets, while also subjecting the actions of regulatory bodies, especially the SEC, to intense scrutiny. This analysis often culminated in proposals for alternative regulatory frameworks, reflecting the complex interplay between innovation and existing legal structures.

During this period, a body of private law scholarship finally began to take shape. This emerging discourse coalesced around three primary lines of inquiry. The first strand pursued a systematic examination of DLT networks and digital assets, grappling with fundamental questions about their status as personal property, the rules governing their circulation, and the applicable laws in cross-border transactions.[93] The second line of research scrutinized transactions involving digital assets in which participants' expectations diverged from legal realities, as evidenced in various tokenization projects and instances in which tokens were used as collateral.[94] The third avenue of exploration delved into the legal implications of custodial relationships in the digital asset space, a topic of particular relevance in light of high-profile exchange insolvencies such as FTX

[91] PRESIDENT'S WORKING GRP. ON FIN. MKTS., REPORT ON STABLECOINS (2021). https://home.treasury.gov/system/files/136/StableCoinReport_Nov1_508.pdf.

[92] Ensuring Responsible Development of Digital Assets, Exec. Order No. 14067, 87 Fed. Reg. 141 (Mar. 14, 2022), https://www.govinfo.gov/content/pkg/FR-2022-03-14/pdf/2022-05471.pdf.

[93] *See, e.g.*, Kelvin F. K. Low & Eliza Mik, *Pause the Blockchain Legal Revolution*, 69 INT'L & COMP. L.Q. 135 (2020); Moringiello & Odinet, *supra* note 40; Francesca C. Villata, *Cryptocurrencies and Conflict of Laws*, *in* BLOCKCHAIN AND PRIVATE INTERNATIONAL LAW (Andrea Bonomi, Matthias Lehmann & Shaheeza Lalani eds., 2023).

[94] Shaanan Cohney & David A. Hoffman, *Transactional Scripts in Contract Stacks*, 105 MINN. L. REV. 319 (2020); Heather Hughes, *Blockchain and the Future of Secured Transactions Law*, 3 STAN. J. BLOCKCHAIN L. & POL'Y 21 (2020); R. Wilson Freyermuth, Christopher K. Odinet & Andrea Tosato, *Crypto in Real Estate Finance*, 75 ALA. L. REV. 93 (2023); Odinet & Tosato, *Structured Finance*, *supra* note 40; Juliet M. Moringiello & Christopher K. Odinet, *NFTs, Property Rights, and Realty in* THE CAMBRIDGE HANDBOOK OF LAW AND POLICY FOR NFTS 275 (Nizan Geslevich Packin ed., 2024); Juliet M. Moringiello & Christopher K. Odinet, *Blockchain Real Estate and NFTs*, 64 WM. & MARY L. REV. 1131 (2023).

and Genesis.[95] Despite these valuable contributions, it is noteworthy that the volume of private law scholarship remained relatively modest compared to the extensive body of literature focused on the financial regulatory aspects of digital assets.

Throughout the past fifteen years, DLT networks and digital assets have experienced remarkable growth in adoption and functionality. This journey, far from smooth or linear, has been characterized by cyclical patterns of euphoric peaks followed by precipitous contractions. Yet each downturn has been followed by a new zenith, surpassing previous highs in monetary value, user base, and the range of applications. As of 2024, it appears largely uncontroversial that DLT networks and digital assets have secured a lasting place in our digital landscape. However, this does not preclude future failures; indeed, many projects and even entire networks may yet collapse. Nonetheless, market participants have demonstrably embraced this technology for its utility as a store of value, a medium of exchange, a platform for decentralized code execution, and a means of digitally representing and transferring assets. This enduring appeal suggests that DLT networks and digital assets will continue to play a significant role in shaping the future of commercial transactions.

Yet, the tumultuous emergence of DLT networks and digital assets has created an urgent imperative for lawmakers and legal scholars to engage with this new technology. The basic question—what the Germans would aptly describe as a *Grundfrage*—is whether the current body of rules and principles is adequate to address this innovation or whether it requires modifications, additions, or even a complete overhaul. This inquiry is, of course, a recurring motif throughout legal history, akin to a playful dance between innovation and jurisprudence. From ancient times to the present day, each era's innovations—be they ships, printing presses, steam engines, or the internet—have compelled a reassessment of existing legal frameworks, challenging jurists to reconcile established principles with the exigencies of technological progress.

There is, however, a notable imbalance in the current approach of lawmakers and legal scholars to DLT networks and digital assets. The predominant focus has been on examining and addressing this new technology through the lens of public law, with particular emphasis on financial regulation, and to a lesser extent, criminal law and taxation. Taken in the aggregate, the prevailing discourse has centered on regulatory concerns: determining which activities enabled by this technology should be permitted or prohibited, identifying the appropriate regulatory bodies, and establishing the requisite compliance frameworks. This

[95] *See, e.g.*, Matthias Haentjens, Tycho De Graaf & Ilya Kokorin, *The Failed Hopes of Disintermediation: Crypto-Custodian Insolvency, Legal Risks and How to Avoid Them*, 2020 Sing. J. Legal Stud. 526; Dirk Zetzsche, Julia Sinnig & Areti Nikolakopoulou, *Crypto Custody*, 19 Cap. Mkts. L.J. 207 (2024).

approach typically explores questions of market integrity, consumer protection, systemic risk, and the prevention of illicit activities. In contrast, little attention has been given to the private law aspects of DLT networks and digital assets—particularly in areas such as contract, property, commercial law, and bankruptcy—leaving the respective rights and obligations of parties engaged in the novel transactional structures emerging within these decentralized systems underexplored.

As with most complex sociolegal phenomena, there is no single explanation for this imbalance. As systems theory demonstrates, legal developments are shaped by a multitude of interconnected social, economic, and technological factors.[96] Nonetheless, we hypothesize a few of these reasons.

First, Bitcoin, the first DLT network to emerge, had the declared aim of creating a currency alternative to those issued by sovereign entities. While subsequent DLT networks and digital assets have diversified and expanded in their applications, many of the most significant use cases are financial in nature—offering digital representations of value, disintermediated payment instruments, vehicles for capital raising, and mechanisms to facilitate cross-border transactions. Consequently, from its inception, this technology has naturally drawn intense scrutiny from regulatory bodies and scholars specializing in financial regulation.

Second, this technology emerged in the aftermath of the 2008 financial crisis and matured through subsequent economic turbulences, including the European sovereign debt crisis, the 2015–2016 Chinese market volatility, and the COVID-19 pandemic. These events, particularly the lingering impact of the Great Recession, heightened concerns about the fragility of traditional financial systems and their vulnerability to black swan events. In the eyes of some observers, the specter of systemic risk found new forms in cryptocurrencies, stablecoins, NFTs, tokenizations, and DeFi. This perceived threat has naturally drawn significant attention from institutions and researchers specializing in financial regulation.

Third, private law, once a cornerstone of legal scholarship, has seen its prominence wane in recent decades. Lacking uniformity across jurisdictions and legal cultures, this contraction has been especially sharp in the United States. Anecdotally, it is sometimes said that the "important" legal issues of the day lie elsewhere, particularly the interpretation of the Constitution. Another explanation sometimes heard among law professors is that private law and commercial law in particular are stale subjects with little new developments, and, in any event, merely state law issues.

[96] *See generally* Niklas Luhmann, Law as a Social System (Klaus A. Ziegert trans., 2004).

Whatever the explanation, the imbalance between public and private law analysis regarding DLT networks and digital assets has profound and far-reaching implications. The dearth of private law scrutiny creates a chasm in knowledge and understanding. Fundamental questions are shrouded in doubt: Are digital assets personal property that can be owned, possessed, or controlled? What rules govern their transfer, and can ownership pass from someone without a legitimate title? Does altering the state of a digital asset on a DLT network affect its ownership, and if so, under what conditions? How should conflicts be resolved when multiple parties claim ownership of the same digital asset? What are the requirements to create and perfect a security interest in digital assets offered as collateral? Can these assets embody ownership rights in other things—such as a payment receivable, a copyright, a digital artwork, or even physical objects like a car or a statue? And what rules apply to the various forms of bailment when digital assets are deposited with an exchange, entrusted to another party, or locked into a smart contract?

This lacuna is not merely theoretical. When parties enter transactions with uncertain rights and obligations, expectations are frustrated, disinformation proliferates, and confidence erodes, leading to failed deals and unfulfilled bargains. Such uncertainty gives rise to misaligned incentives, wasted resources, and increased transaction costs—all typical of market failures. The absence of legal clarity also invites unnecessary litigation, as parties are forced to resolve disputes ex post through the courts rather than relying on definite rules *ab initio*. Moreover, this ambiguity hampers innovation and creates a fertile ground for fraud and manipulation, as bad actors exploit the gaps in legal understanding to their advantage.

In the realm of DLT networks and digital assets, the absence of a comprehensive private law analysis risks misguided and ineffective regulatory interventions. Without a clear understanding of the fundamental nature of the activities and entities they seek to govern, regulators may develop frameworks that are ill-suited and counterproductive to their intended purposes. This issue has already manifested itself in notable ways. A prime example is the regulatory debate surrounding stablecoins. Initial discussions polarized around two main views: one arguing that stablecoin issuers were essentially creators of private money and should be regulated as banks or money market funds; others contending that stablecoins were securities falling under SEC jurisdiction. However, this debate was recalibrated following the collapse of prominent stablecoins, such as TerraUSD. These events revealed that stablecoin issuers employed diverse business models, creating a nexus of rights and obligations vis-à-vis their holders that neither of the proposed regulatory frameworks neatly fits. This misalignment stemmed from a fundamental problem: The regulatory debate had developed without a complete understanding of the private law underpinnings of the activity in question.

Similar challenges are emerging in other areas of the DLT and digital asset ecosystem. The tokenization of assets, the use of digital assets as collateral, and the legal treatment of smart contracts all raise complex questions about ownership, security interests, and enforceability. These issues underscore the critical need for a nuanced, well-informed understanding of private law realities as a prerequisite for effective regulatory responses. Without this foundation, regulatory efforts risk being disconnected from the actual mechanics and implications of the technologies and practices they aim to oversee.

* * *

We embarked on this project on the basis of two converging experiences: our observations of the public–private law imbalance surrounding DLT networks and digital assets, and our firsthand involvement in legislative and law reform initiatives in the United States and internationally.

Our journey began around 2018 when the ULC and ALI convened a joint committee to explore whether amendments to the UCC were necessary in response to the momentous rise of several emerging technologies, including DLT networks and digital assets.[97] The committee held public meetings—both in person and remotely—that engaged a wide-ranging constituency, including American Bar Association advisors, and hundreds of observers from academia, law firms, national and international agencies, trade associations, technology companies, and representatives of intergovernmental law reform organizations.

This extensive consultation process revealed that blockchains, smart contracts, cryptocurrencies, stablecoins, and other digital assets had spawned novel transactional structures, practices, and business models. In particular, the private law framework governing the ownership transfer of these digital assets and their use as collateral was riddled with legal uncertainties. Similarly, there was great confusion surrounding transactions in which digital assets—primarily NFTs—were purported to represent ownership or other proprietary rights in tangible and intangible assets, as well as monetary obligations arising from sources such as the sale of goods, the provision of services, and the extension of loans.

Understanding the urgency of these issues, the ULC and ALI decided to update the UCC. From 2020 to 2022, amid the global COVID-19 emergency, a joint ULC/ALI committee wrote and refined proposed amendments through an iterative process of drafting, public scrutiny, and revision.[98] The shift to

[97] *See* U.C.C. & Emerging Technologies 1–3 (Am. L. Inst. & Unif. L. Comm'n, Draft for Approval July 2022), https://perma.cc/U5MZ-MXPC.

[98] The interim drafts of the Drafting Committee are available at *UCC, 2022 Amendments to*, Unif. L. Comm'n, https://www.uniformlaws.org/viewdocument/archive-committee-55?CommunityKey=1457c422-ddb7-40b0-8c76-39a1991651ac&tab=librarydocuments (last visited Mar. 18, 2015).

virtual meetings necessitated by the pandemic amplified participation and democratized access, fostering unprecedented engagement from observers both within the United States and internationally. This expanded reach enriched the process, which transparently incorporated suggestions and criticisms from a diverse pool of industry participants, academics, practitioners, and judges.[99] The final 2022 UCC Amendments were adopted by the ALI in April 2022[100] and by the ULC shortly thereafter in July.[101]

We had the privilege of participating in this reform process as academic observers, with one of us closely involved in developing core concepts that would shape the new UCC Article 12 on Controllable Electronic Records. Our initial enthusiasm for engaging at the intersection of traditional commercial law and the rapidly evolving world of digital assets was soon tempered by what we witnessed. To our astonishment, stakeholders—including seasoned lawyers and in-house counsel for major market participants—frequently made assertions about digital assets that fundamentally contradicted cardinal principles of private law. In time, we came to see that these were not mere oversights, but rather profound misconceptions.

Some of the most egregious examples showed a complete disregard for *numerus clausus*—the legal principle that property law recognizes only a closed list of property rights, ensuring transactions remain transparent and predictable.[102] Equally concerning was the limited appreciation for the significance of classifying digital assets within established categories of personal property. Relatedly, there was a staggering misapplication of the concept of *possession*, with many participants casually extending this notion to intangible digital assets. We also observed fanciful assertions about the process of *reifying*[103] personal property into digital assets through tokenization.[104] We were disconcerted by the complete disregard for the doctrine of privity when contractual obligations are transferred alongside digital assets.[105] Finally, responses either demonstrated a fundamental misunderstanding of how UCC Article 9 applies to digital assets as

[99] *See* U.C.C. & EMERGING TECHNOLOGIES 1–2.

[100] *See ULC Approves ALI Joint Project on UCC and Emerging Technologies*, AM. L. INST. (July 15, 2022), https://www.ali.org/news/articles/ulc-approves-ali-joint-project-ucc-and-emerging-technologies.

[101] *See* U.C.C. AMENDMENTS (AM. L. INST. & UNIF. L. COMM'N, 2022), https://www.uniformlaws.org/HigherLogic/System/DownloadDocumentFile.ashx?DocumentFileKey=d5bcf850-366f-b4b5-e7d6-6749ba2382c6.

[102] Thomas W. Merrill & Henry E. Smith, *Optimal Standardization in the Law of Property: The Numerus Clausus Principle*, 110 YALE L.J. 1 (2000); Yun-chien Chang & Henry E. Smith, *The Numerus Clausus Principle, Property Customs, and the Emergence of New Property Forms*, 100 IOWA L. REV. 2275 (2015); Francesco Parisi, *Entropy in Property*, 50 AM. J. COMP. L. 595 (2002).

[103] *See* FINANCIAL COLLATERAL 14 (Matthias Haentjens ed., 2020).

[104] Moringiello & Odinet, *supra* note 40, at 615.

[105] Winterbottom v. Wright (1842) 152 Eng. Rep. 402 (Exch.).

collateral, or relied on overly simplistic analogies that compared these complex transactions to pawnshop dealings.

The common thread uniting all these misconceptions is what we started to describe as the flexibility fallacy. By this, we mean the fundamental error in assuming that private law rules and standards—particularly those in property law—are infinitely malleable and can be reshaped at will. This misguided notion appeared to stem from three interconnected convictions. First was the belief in the absolute supremacy of contractual agreements and terms of service, erroneously assuming they can override all legal principles, including mandatory rules, and bind not just contracting parties but also third parties entirely extraneous to the arrangement in question. Second was a dangerous blurring of the property–contract law divide, manifesting in the erroneous belief that all property rules can be rewritten or reshaped by mere contractual agreement.

Both of these two convictions fundamentally clash with what Thomas Merrill and Henry Smith describe as the driving divergence between property and contract law—specifically, property law's distinctive information-cost function.[106] As they explain, while contract law can accommodate highly customized arrangements between identified parties, property law necessarily leans toward standardization and bright-line rules because property rights bind large and indefinite numbers of third parties who must process information about those rights. If packages of property rights come in too many forms and without easy-to-understand rules, parties will be more hesitant to transact and more due diligence will be required before property can change hands.

Third and finally was the conviction that DLT networks and other digital asset technologies could somehow transcend legal boundaries, viewing technological capabilities as a source of rights and obligations divorced from traditional legal frameworks—a grotesque caricature of Lawrence Lessig's "code is law"[107] thesis. These misguided understandings failed to recognize that while technology can indeed create new methods of transacting and storing value, it cannot arbitrarily rewrite the underlying principles of private law. Indeed, the notion that technological systems can simply contract around information-cost constraints ignores the numerus clausus principle (a topic we explore in greater depth in Chapter 2 in this book). The numerus clausus principle holds that the law limits the available forms of property interests to a finite menu of standardized options precisely to reduce the information costs imposed on third parties. As Merrill and Smith explain, just as nineteenth-century courts rejected attempts to create novel types of property interests that would increase third-party information costs, modern

[106] *See* Thomas W. Merrill & Henry E. Smith, *The Property/Contract Interface*, 101 Colum. L. Rev. 773, 790–91 (2001).

[107] Lawrence Lessig, Code and Other Laws of Cyberspace 6 (1999).

courts should be skeptical of efforts to use private agreements or technological systems to create entirely new forms of property rights that deviate from traditional standardized categories.[108] Thus, the flexibility fallacy that we observed in those meetings and interactions fails to appreciate that the standardization of property rights serves crucial notice and coordination functions that simply cannot and should not be contracted around in a free-wheeling fashion.

But what alarmed us most during these meetings was not merely how misguided these ideas were but, rather, the vehemence with which they were proffered and their widespread acceptance within the digital assets community. We soon realized that this cavalier attitude towards established private law principles was being actively implemented in the design and operation of numerous digital asset firms, including crypto exchanges, lending platforms, DeFi intermediaries, stablecoin issuers, and various other entities operating in this space. In our assessment, the flexibility fallacy creates significant risks for users, investors, and the broader digital asset ecosystem—risks that, as we will explore later in this book, have already materialized in several instances. More profoundly, building on such unstable legal foundations threatens to undermine the very innovations that the digital assets industry desires to advance.

Despite these challenges, the drafting committee successfully completed its work, formulating a new UCC framework for the transfer of ownership and the use of digital assets as collateral, as well as the tokenization of certain receivables. This body of rules (which we will explain more fully in Part I of this book) is primarily contained in the new Article 12 and revised Article 9. It is designed to be technology-neutral and consistent with established private law principles. These new rules bring legal certainty to DLT networks and digital assets, providing a stable foundation for stakeholders to operate and innovate with confidence.

Over the past two years, bills incorporating these changes have been introduced in legislatures across several states. As of this writing, twenty-five states have adopted the amendments, with more likely to follow. However, this process has been uncharacteristically bellicose for UCC amendments. The controversy reflects both the imbalance between public and private law in this space, and the widespread misconceptions about the private law framework governing digital assets.

In March 2023, South Dakota Governor Kristi Noem vetoed a bill that would have implemented the 2022 UCC Amendments, describing her action as a stand against an "attack on economic freedom."[109] Governor Noem even appeared on national television, suggesting that the proposed amendments surreptitiously

[108] Merrill & Smith, *supra* note 102.

[109] Press Release, Gov. Kristi Noem, Gov. Noem Vetoes Attack on Economic Freedom (Mar. 10, 2023), https://news.sd.gov/news?id=news_kb_article_view&sysparm_article=KB0039891.

paved the way for a US central bank digital currency (CBDC) to be used as a federal monitoring tool.[110] Concurrently, organizations like the Heartland Institute amplified these concerns, producing dubious "fact sheets" for lawmakers across several states. In Florida, Governor Ron DeSantis went as far as signing a bill that purported to ban the use of a federal CBDC within the state by expressly excluding it from the scope of the UCC.

This entirely unfounded criticism starkly illustrates the confusion between public and private law, as it fundamentally misconstrues the nature and function of the UCC as state-level private law. First, the 2022 UCC Amendments neither have the authority nor the intent to establish a CBDC in the United States. If federal legislation were enacted in this space, it would have primacy over any conflicting provision in a state's UCC.[111] The 2022 UCC Amendments simply include a barebones ruleset for CBDCs issued by foreign states so that private parties holding or owning these digital assets may have a uniform legal framework across all fifty states. Second, an express exclusion of CBDCs from the scope of the UCC does not have the effect of a ban; rather, it results in these assets being governed by the common law rules for intangibles or money.

Another misguided criticism targets the exclusion of cryptocurrencies, such as Bitcoin, from the 2022 UCC Amendments' revised definition of "money."[112] While it is true that the amendments do not classify cryptocurrencies as "money," this choice was not intended to penalize or hinder digital assets but rather to accommodate them more effectively within the UCC framework. In Article 12, the drafters introduced the new category of controllable electronic records.[113] This new category type is specifically tailored to facilitate trading and collateralizing digital assets like cryptocurrencies and NFTs. By contrast, UCC rules for money are designed for tangible banknotes that are exchanged in person and, thus, are entirely ill-suited for digital assets. Moreover, it is important to note that both money and controllable electronic records are UCC-defined categories, with functions limited to the application of this statute—any meaning within the UCC has no bearing outside of this commercial law framework.

However, our direct involvement with private law reform projects in the realm of DLT networks did not end with the 2022 UCC Amendments. Between 2022 and 2024, we individually served as reporters for a ULC's study

[110] *See* Carla L. Reyes, *Emerging Technology's Unfamiliarity with Commercial Law*, 119 Nw. U. L. Rev. Online 31 (2024); Carla L. Reyes & Andrea Tosato, *Crypto's Future Is at Stake in a Dispute over Commercial Law's Definition of Money*, Barron's (Apr. 7, 2023), https://www.barrons.com/articles/crypto-commercial-laws-definition-of-money-5fbd8fe4.

[111] U.S. Const. art. VI, cl. 2; *see also* U.C.C. § 9-109(c)(1) (Am. L. Inst. & Unif. L. Comm'n, 2022).

[112] See Jesse Hamilton, *Florida's DeSantis Waging Toothless Campaign Against Digital Dollars, Lawyers Say*, CoinDesk (May 19, 2023), https://www.coindesk.com/policy/2023/05/17/floridas-desantis-waging-toothless-campaign-against-digital-dollars-lawyers-say.

[113] U.C.C. § 12-102(1).

committee investigating the use of tokens and related crypto devices in real estate transactions[114] and a drafting committee for the Virtual Currency Customer Protection Act.[115] Internationally, we contributed to the drafting committee for the UNIDROIT Principles on Digital Assets and Private Law,[116] as well as the Hague Conference projects on Private International Law rules for Digital Assets and Central Bank Digital Currencies.[117]

These experiences corroborated and reinforced our insights from the 2022 UCC Amendments process. The legal approach to DLT networks and digital assets remains heavily skewed toward public law, with the focus disproportionately placed on financial regulation. Even when grappling with strictly private law matters, it is almost impossible to escape being drawn into regulatory debates, such as whether a given transaction constitutes an issuance of securities or whether registration with a particular agency is required. Furthermore, when confronting complex issues at the intersection of contract, property, bailment, secured transactions, and bankruptcy law, the flexibility fallacy emerges in full force—with a pervasive attitude that all challenges can be resolved through adroit contractual arrangements, terms of service, and "immutable" computer coding. These ongoing misconceptions underscore the urgent need for a granular and exhaustive examination of the private law dimension of DLT networks and digital assets.

* * *

To truly understand the *why* of this project, one has to see the digital asset economy as more than just gambling at the crypto casino. While investing in speculative crypto assets like the worldwide billionaire Elon Musk's favored Dogecoin[118] and high-profile scandals like that involving the insolvent crypto exchange giant FTX and Sam Bankman-Fried[119] have dominated headlines, the underlying technologies and innovations driving this sector have far-reaching

[114] *Use of Tokens or Other Similar Products in Real Property: Transactions Committee*, Unif. L. Comm'n (2022), https://perma.cc/T6NW-6VUF.

[115] Uniform Law Commission, *New Study and Drafting Committees*, Uniform Law Comm'n, https://www.uniformlaws.org/discussion/new-study-and-drafting-committees (last visited Apr. 29, 2025).

[116] *Digital Assets and Private Law*, UNIDROIT, https://www.unidroit.org/work-in-progress/digital-assets-and-private-law/ (last visited Mar. 19, 2025).

[117] *See First Meeting of the HCCH-UNIDROIT Digital Assets and Tokens Joint Project Takes Place in The Hague*, UNIDROIT (June 12, 2023), https://www.unidroit.org/first-meeting-of-the-hcch-unidroit-digital-assets-and-tokens-joint-project-takes-place-in-the-hague/; *Central Bank Digital Currencies Project (CBDCs Project)*, HCCH, https://www.hcch.net/de/projects/legislative-projects/cbdcs (last visited Mar. 19, 2025).

[118] Kevin Roose, *He's a Dogecoin Millionaire. And He's Not Selling.*, N.Y. Times (Sept. 13, 2021), https://www.nytimes.com/2021/05/14/technology/hes-a-dogecoin-millionaire-and-hes-not-selling.html.

[119] Cailtin Ostroff & Corinne Ramey, *Sam Bankman-Fried and the FTX Collapse: What to Know as the Trial Gets Going*, Wall St. J. (Oct. 3, 2023), https://www.wsj.com/finance/regulation/sam-bankman-fried-trial-ftx-explained-17aaa89f.

implications that reach beyond crypto trading and various related machinations. Rather, it is the advent of a new technology—one that has emerged over the past fifteen years and has transformative potential.

This innovation consists of networks—centralized or decentralized, permissioned or permissionless—that record and support digital assets (*rectius*, data entries) with which individuals can engage directly, without the need for intermediaries, through software that can be programmed to operate completely autonomously.

Today, this technology takes the form of DLT networks, fungible and NFTs, and smart contracts. In the future, it may evolve into new implementations with added functionality. Yet, we believe that the core elements of this novel digital architecture have become a permanent fixture of the commercial landscape. To frame our discussion accurately and to clarify our focus, throughout this book, we aim to avoid talking about crypto and, instead, to speak of property and other legal rights in electronic form—to be more specific, we are talking about *digital assets*. We view the digital asset economy, which is underpinned by the transformative technology we described above, as representing a shift in how we operationalize and administer various kinds of transactions.

To be sure, it is important to be clear about what the digital asset economy is *not*. It is not a new way of doing ownership or other property rights. That's the hype. But the reality is that the technology underpinning digital asset creation, transfer, and management has the potential to make a variety of existing transactions easier, cheaper, more widely available, and more secure.

Based on this technological premise, our book explores what we term *digital commercial law*—the body of rules and principles governing commercial transactions that involve these new digital assets. Our analysis adopts a private law lens concentrating primarily on issues within contract, property, reification, bailments, and bankruptcy law. This investigation proceeds in layers of increasing complexity, beginning with foundational issues, such as the legal nature of digital assets as personal property and moving on to transactional structures like ownership transfers, secured transactions, and custodial arrangements. It culminates in the examination of sophisticated multilateral operations that simultaneously engage multiple branches of commercial law, such as the issuance and redemption of stablecoins or the tokenization of bankruptcy claims on digital platforms.

This project has three primary aims. First, we seek to redress the imbalance between public and private law approaches to DLT networks and digital assets. The current legal discourse heavily emphasizes public law considerations—particularly financial regulation aimed at preserving market stability and protecting investors—while largely overlooking crucial private law dimensions. This neglect leaves key private law questions unanswered, creating uncertainty that hampers business, frustrates party expectations, and increases the likelihood of litigation. Our work addresses these gaps, aiming to foster legal certainty, support innovation, and mitigate the risks of fraud. Moreover, we seek to restore the crucial interplay between private and public law, with the hope that future regulatory interventions are built on a lucid understanding of the rights, obligations, and property interests involved in the transactions in question.

Second, we aim to denounce and dispel the "flexibility fallacy"—a widespread misconception that contractual arrangements and software code can boundlessly reshape private law rules. In this effort, we seek to restore the bright line that has historically demarcated the realms of contract and property law. In the domain of DLT networks and digital assets, this line has been blurred. Similar to how Roman surveyors carefully delineated urban boundaries, this work seeks to examine and clarify the distinction between contract and property law, while acknowledging the complex interplay between these two fundamental areas of private law. To be sure, our purpose is not to declare certain transactions inherently impossible, but rather to demonstrate that private ordering solutions must operate within—not override—fundamental private law tenets. Throughout this book, we expose the futility of attempting to circumvent mandatory rules and foundational property law concepts through crude contractual arrangements. Simultaneously, we show that many of the objectives sought by market participants can indeed be achieved, but only by embracing, rather than circumventing, the tools offered by existing private law frameworks.

Our third aim is to make a compelling case for reinvigorating private law scholarship and education in the twenty-first century. The complex questions raised by DLT networks and digital assets reveal that private law is not, as some suggest, an ossified and antiquated field. Rather, it is a dynamic and sophisticated body of rules and principles that, when properly understood and applied, provides essential tools to govern contemporary commercial relationships. Through this lens, we hope to spark renewed interest in private law's development and teaching in the digital age, highlighting its enduring relevance in an era of rapid technological innovations.

Part I of this book contains four chapters. Following this introduction, the remaining three chapters examine three pressure points in the digital asset space that have proved a persistent source of difficulty for courts, lawyers, and market participants. Chapter 2 explores the *legal nature of digital assets*—specifically addressing what they are from a conceptual standpoint. This analysis delves into whether digital assets constitute personal rights, merely enforceable between individuals and created by contract, or property rights that are opposable against the world. The differing conceptualizations impact ownership, transferability, and legal protections afforded to digital assets. Chapter 3 addresses the concept of *tokenization*, which involves digitally embedding real-world or digital asset rights in uniquely coded tokens. This chapter delves into how tokenization intersects with property and contract rights, and its role in various business models within the digital asset ecosystem. Chapter 4, in turn, shifts to discussing the concept of *custody*, analyzing the services offered by digital asset firms for storing and transacting client holdings. This discussion highlights the multiplicity of ways that firms custody digital assets and the distinct bailment law concepts (carrying enormous real-world consequences) that divide these arrangements.

With the foundation laid and these three pressure points identified, the stage is set for Parts II and III. The discussion of legal nature, tokenization, and custody (all three private law concepts) in Part I provides the lens through which readers of Parts II and III can understand the private law and private ordering breakdowns in the digital asset marketplace. Part II focuses on the simpler ways that these breakdowns manifest themselves through an exploration of NFTs in creative works in Chapter 5 and the deployment of digital assets and commercial law in bankruptcy claims trading in Chapter 6.

In Part III, we present more complex problems where multiple aspects and layers of custody and tokenization, as well as related private law concepts, are intertwined. The discussion here delves into two of the most prominent and controversial aspects of the crypto asset landscape: *the tokenization of interests in real estate markets* and *the use of stablecoins as private money*. Part III serves as a capstone because these two case studies encapsulate the broader themes of this book. In the real estate context, the false notion of private law's limitless flexibility has been overstated to an extreme degree, and the convoluted private ordering has had the perverse effect of creating more transaction costs while largely retaining existing ones that the use of digital asset technology was intended to reduce. Meanwhile, public law approaches have dominated discussions of stablecoins, while private law considerations have been largely overlooked despite obvious breakdowns in private ordering.

Finally, in the Conclusion, we offer our call to action while offering a hopeful outlook for the future of digital commercial law. We argue that a more balanced approach to regulating digital assets is not only possible but essential for this emerging field. This balance can be achieved through concerted efforts across multiple fronts: the judiciary, as courts grapple with novel questions of digital commercial law; legislatures, as they craft laws that bridge traditional commercial principles and digital innovation; and crucially, law schools, which bear the responsibility of educating the next generation of lawyers. By fostering a more holistic understanding of digital assets that encompasses both public regulatory frameworks and private law principles, we can restore equilibrium to the legal landscape. This balanced approach will not only harmonize public and private law considerations but also provide clear guidance for the future of commercial transactions in the digital age.

2
Digital assets as property

2.1 Introduction

In Part I, we analyze three cornerstones of digital commercial law: the legal nature and commercial circulation of digital assets,[1] the use of digital assets as representations of ownership and other proprietary rights in other assets (a concept known as *tokenization*), and, finally, the custody of digital assets. This ground level investigation addresses foundational private law issues—issues that are prerequisites to decoding the complex digital asset transactions and business models that we examine in Parts II and III of this book.

We begin with what we described in the introduction as the *Grundfrage*: the fundamental question—is it possible to own digital assets as a form of property? Relatedly, if the answer is yes, how do they fit within existing property taxonomies? And what rules should govern their circulation in commerce?

The *Grundfrage* is far from academic. Every day, market participants execute millions of transactions worth billions of dollars, relying on an uncertain patchwork of traditional legal frameworks awkwardly adapted to this new technology.[2] The practical implications are both immediate and far-reaching. When digital assets are stolen through hacks or fraud, courts must grapple with whether they constitute "property" that can be recovered through traditional remedies such as conversion and replevin.[3] When these assets are pledged as collateral in lending arrangements—a market that reached into the billions in 2024—lenders need clarity on how to perfect and enforce their security interests against both the borrower and third parties.[4] When major crypto platforms such as FTX, Celsius, and Genesis become insolvent, bankruptcy courts must navigate complex questions about whether customers' digital asset deposits belong to the debtor's

[1] Various portions of this chapter are drawn, in whole or in part, from Andrea Tosato & Christopher K. Odinet, *Digital Assets and the Property Question*, Fla. L. Rev. (forthcoming 2026), https://papers.ssrn.com/sol3/papers.cfm?abstract_id=5151907 [hereinafter Tosato & Odinet, *Property Question*]. Any reproductions are made with the express permission of the authors.

[2] *Crypto Trading Volume Tracker*, CoinCodex, https://coincodex.com/trading-volume/ (last visited Feb. 14, 2025).

[3] *See, e.g.*, Ox Labs, Inc. v. BitPay, Inc., No. CV 18-5934 (KSX), 2020 WL 1039012 (C.D. Cal. Jan. 24, 2020); Temurian v. Piccolo, No. 18-cv-62737, 2019 WL 1763022 (S.D. Fla. Apr. 22, 2019).

[4] *See generally Lending Protocols*, DeFiLlama, https://defillama.com/protocols/lending (last visited Feb. 14, 2025); *see also* Zack Pokorny, *The State of Crypto Lending*, Galaxy Research (Apr. 14, 2025), https://www.galaxy.com/insights/research/the-state-of-crypto-lending/.

Digital Commercial Law. Christopher K. Odinet and Andrea Tosato, Oxford University Press.
 DOI: 10.1093/9780197758656.003.0003

estate or else constitute separately owned property that should be returned to account holders.[5] Even routine business matters, from recording digital assets on balance sheets to determining their tax treatment, hinge on their fundamental legal characterization.[6] And the stakes of these questions have only grown as institutional investors, banks, and payment processors have entered the digital asset ecosystem, bringing with them the need for clear legal frameworks that can support sophisticated commercial arrangements.[7]

Thus, the *Grundfrage* is a first-order question because its answer defines the scope of digital commercial law itself. If digital assets cannot be owned, or if ownership is possible for only a narrow subset of them, then the ambit of digital commercial law would be severely circumscribed. Conversely, if digital assets can be personal property, understanding how they fit within the broader framework of property law provides crucial insights into their legal treatment.

2.2 The growth of digital asset markets and the *Grundfrage*

We begin our examination by surveying the remarkable evolution of digital asset markets. Understanding this trajectory provides essential context for analyzing the questions surrounding their legal nature and commercial circulation. It is a short but intense history, spanning fifteen years, marked by exponential growth in value, volumes, and complexity. What began in 2009 as a cypherpunk experiment in digital cash has since blossomed into a complex ecosystem worth almost $4 trillion as of December 2024.[8]

Cryptocurrencies have led the charge in this remarkable growth story. Bitcoin, which first traded for mere pennies, has seen its market capitalization climb to nearly $2 trillion in 2025, commanding the lion's share of the crypto market. Stablecoins—digital assets designed to maintain "a stable price relative to a specified asset"[9]—have experienced their own dramatic ascent, expanding

[5] *See In re* Celsius Network LLC, 644 B.R. 276, 280 (Bankr. S.D.N.Y. 2022); *In re* FTX Trading Ltd., No. 22-11068, 2024 WL 4562675 (Bankr. D. Del. Oct. 23, 2024); *In re* Genesis Glob. Holdco, LLC, 652 B.R. 618, 623 (Bankr. S.D.N.Y. 2023); *see also* Kara Bruce, Christopher K. Odinet & Andrea Tosato, *Bankrupt Crypto Organizations*, N.C. L. Rev. (forthcoming 2026), https://papers.ssrn.com/sol3/papers. cfm?abstract_id=5115277.

[6] *See Accounting for and Disclosure of Crypto Assets: Accounting Standards Update 2023-08*, FASB: Fin. Acct. Standards Bd. (Dec. 2023), https://www.fasb.org/page/PageContent?pageId=/projects/recentlycompleted/accounting-for-and-disclosure-of-crypto-assets.html; *see also* I.R.S. Notice 2014-21, 2014-16 I.R.B. 938.

[7] U.S. Dep't of the Treasury, Fin. Stability Oversight Council, *Report on Digital Asset Financial Stability Risks and Regulation* (2022), https://home.treasury.gov/system/files/261/FSOC-Digital-Assets-Report-2022.pdf.

[8] *Total Cryptocurrency Market Capitalization*, CoinGecko, https://web.archive.org/web/20241206082925/https://www.coingecko.com/en/global-charts (last visited Dec. 6, 2024).

[9] *See* Kara J Bruce, Christopher K. Odinet & Andrea Tosato, *The Private Law of Stablecoins*, 54 Ariz. St. L.J. 1073 (2022).

from a modest $5 billion in early 2020 to over $200 billion in circulation today.[10] The market for non-fungible tokens (NFTs) has traced an equally dramatic, if more volatile, trajectory. NFT valuations surged from $82 million in 2020 to an astounding $17.6 billion in 2021, though in subsequent years, a significant contraction followed this meteoric rise.[11]

Within this bustling ecosystem, a fundamental distinction has emerged between two categories of digital assets. The first comprises assets like Bitcoin, Ethereum, and Solana that market participants trade for their intrinsic value and technological utility.[12] The second encompasses digital assets that derive their value from purportedly representing rights in other assets or claims against third parties—a concept known as *tokenization*, which we discuss in more depth in Chapter 3 and elsewhere in this book.

The velocity and complexity of digital asset circulation have evolved in lockstep with their increasing value. Early Bitcoin transactions in 2009–2010 were peer-to-peer and sporadic, taking minutes or hours to settle.[13] Over time, centralized exchanges have emerged as crucial trading venues, processing and finalizing millions of transactions worth trillions daily.[14] Most recently, decentralized exchanges have come to the fore, enabling highly complex automated and fully disintermediated transactions for a variety of digital assets, with daily trading volumes regularly exceeding $30 billion.[15]

The demographics of digital asset market participants have also evolved dramatically. Originally a niche movement comprising technologists, cryptographers, and crypto-anarchists,[16] this cohort has expanded to encompass institutional investors, traditional financial institutions, and retail traders.[17]

[10] Brian McGleenon, *Total Stablecoin Market Cap Tops $200 Billion as Onchain Lending Yields Surge*, The Block (Dec. 9, 2024), https://www.theblock.co/post/329947/stablecoin-market-cap-200-billion-usd.

[11] Ryan Browne, *Trading in NFTs Spiked 21,000% to More Than $17 Billion in 2021, Report Says*, CNBC (Mar. 10, 2022, 1:00 AM), https://www.cnbc.com/2022/03/10/trading-in-nfts-spiked-21000 percent-to-top-17-billion-in-2021-report.html.

[12] *See* Jocelyn Blake, *Exploring the Intrinsic Value of Bitcoin: Insights from Metcalfe's Law and Production Costs*, Bitget (Dec. 12, 2024), https://www.bitget.com/news/detail/12560604426 149; Emi Lacapra, *Why Does Ethereum Have an Intrinsic Value?*, Cointelegraph (Apr. 24, 2022), https://cointelegraph.com/explained/why-does-ethereum-have-an-intrinsic-value.

[13] Arvind Narayanan, Edward Felten, Joseph Bonneau, Steven Goldfeder & Andrew Miller, Bitcoin and Cryptocurrency Technologies: A Comprehensive Introduction 23–25 (2016).

[14] *See* Adam J. Levitin, *Not Your Keys, Not Your Coins: Unpriced Credit Risk in Cryptocurrency*, 101 Tex. L. Rev. 877, 889 (2023).

[15] *Top Decentralized Exchanges Ranked by 24H Trading Volume*, CoinGecko, https://web.archive.org/web/20241220230720/https://www.coingecko.com/en/exchanges/decentralized (last visited Dec. 20, 2024).

[16] Craig Jarvis, *Cypherpunk Ideology: Objectives, Profiles, and Influences (1992–1998)*, 6 Internet Histories 315 (2022), https://www.tandfonline.com/doi/epdf/10.1080/24701475.2021.1935547.

[17] *See* Kara Bruce, Christopher K. Odinet & Andrea Tosato, *DAOs in Financial Distress*, *in* Foundations of Decentralized Organizations: Blockchain and the Future of Corporate Law (Kevin Werbach, Eva Micheler & Bianca Kremer eds., forthcoming 2026) (on file with authors).

At present, major financial institutions, including BlackRock, Fidelity, and Franklin Templeton, offer digital asset services, while payment giants such as PayPal, Stripe, and Visa facilitate cryptocurrency transactions for hundreds of millions of users.[18]

Sovereign approaches to digital assets have traced an arc from prohibition to selective embrace. China's 2017 ban on cryptocurrency trading and initial coin offerings marked an early restrictive stance, followed by similar measures in Russia and India.[19] However, this trajectory has shifted significantly. El Salvador and the Central African Republic both adopted Bitcoin as legal tender in 2021 and 2022, respectively.[20] Argentina now accepts Bitcoin for tax payments.[21] In the United States, political discourse has increasingly centered on digital assets' potential role in monetary policy, with recent proposals even suggesting the establishment of sovereign Bitcoin reserves.[22] In turn, even countries that initially opposed cryptocurrencies have moderated their stance, with Russia and China markedly softening their positions.

These empirical data might lead to the seemingly compelling yet ultimately incomplete conclusion that digital assets must be capable of being legally owned. Indeed, the growing market capitalization, increasing trading volumes, and expanding institutional adoption could be interpreted as dispositive, if not conclusive, evidence that digital assets are eligible subject matter for property. After all, why would countless individuals, corporations, and governments commit substantial resources toward assets that exist beyond the realm of legal property?

This pragmatic reasoning has a certain allure. However, as the nineteenth-century British philosopher and jurist Jeremy Bentham lucidly explained, property is a right distinct from the physical object to which it relates, and this right "is entirely the creature of law."[23] Property exists through the recognition and protection afforded by legal systems, and its nature is determined by the framework governing it. While the pervasive trading of digital assets indicates a societal

[18] Tosato & Odinet, *Property Question*, *supra* note 1, n.2.

[19] Law Libr., Libr. of Congress, Regulation of Cryptocurrency Around the World: November 2021 Update (2021), https://www.loc.gov/item/2021687419/.

[20] Ryan Browne, *Central African Republic Adopts Bitcoin as Legal Tender*, CNBC (Apr. 28, 2022), https://www.cnbc.com/2022/04/28/central-african-republic-adopts-bitcoin-as-legal-tender.html. Interestingly, El Salvador reversed itself in February 2025. Katarina Hall, *El Salvador Walks Back Its Bitcoin Law*, Reason (Feb. 3, 2025), https://reason.com/2025/02/03/el-salvador-walks-back-its-bitcoin-law/.

[21] Andrés Engler, *Argentina's Mendoza Province Now Accepts Cryptocurrencies for Tax Payments*, CoinDesk (Aug. 29, 2022), https://www.coindesk.com/policy/2022/08/29/argentinas-mendoza-province-now-accepts-cryptocurrencies-for-tax-payments.

[22] David Feliba, *US States Lead in Strategic Bitcoin Reserve Creation — Will Trump Deliver on His BTC Promise?*, Cointelegraph (Feb. 12, 2025), https://cointelegraph.com/news/us-states-lead-strategic-bitcoin-reserve-creation-will-trump-deliver-his-btc-promise.

[23] 1 Jeremy Bentham, Theory of Legislation 138 (Boston, Weeks, Jordan & Co., R. Hildreth trans., 1840), https://babel.hathitrust.org/cgi/pt?id=hvd.hwx2m2&seq=142.

expectation that they can be owned—a consideration particularly relevant in common law jurisdictions where custom and practice have historically shaped property rights[24]—such behavior alone cannot determine their legal classification as objects of property.

Thus, to answer our *Grundfrage*, it is necessary to investigate the relevant property law framework and, pursuant to its principles and rules, determine whether digital assets can be owned. Moreover, this assessment should consider the differences across legal traditions and jurisdictions in this area of the law. But, before we set off, we wish to make clear that what follows is not a vacuous scholastic exercise in legal theory; rather, this discussion has profound practical implications. As Henry Smith has observed, "property is the platform for the rest of private law"[25] and serves, to quote Joseph Singer, as "the infrastructure of a free and democratic society."[26] Property law provides stability.[27] Therefore, understanding how digital assets fit within the schema of property law offers essential insights for determining the legal regime governing their commercial circulation, which is their voluntary transfer, use as collateral in secured transactions, holding in trust, devolution by will, and treatment in insolvency.

2.3 Digital assets as property

Common law and civil law systems have developed distinct conceptions of personal property.[28] Even among jurisdictions that belong to the same legal tradition, there can be meaningful variations despite shared foundations. These differences have resulted in substantively divergent frameworks for determining whether an asset can be owned, particularly in civil law systems, where more rigid codified rules often apply.[29]

[24] *See* Frederick Pollock, The Genius of the Common Law (2008).

[25] Henry E. Smith, *Property as the Law of Things*, 125 Harv. L. Rev. 1691 (2012); *see also* Eric R. Claeys, *Exclusion and Private Law Theory: A Comment on Property as the Law of Things*, 125 Harv. L. Rev. F. 133, 134 (2012).

[26] Joseph William Singer, *Property as the Law of Democracy*, 63 Duke L.J. 1287, 1303 (2014).

[27] Abraham Bell & Gideon Parchomovsky, *A Theory of Property*, 90 Cornell L. Rev. 531, 552 (2005); *see also* Eduardo Moisés Peñalver & Sonia K. Katyal, *Property Outlaws*, 155 U. Pa. L. Rev. 1095, 1098 (2007).

[28] *See generally* Yaëll Emerich, Conceptualising Property Law: Integrating Common Law and Civil Law Traditions (2018); Anna di Robilant, *Property: A Bundle of Sticks or a Tree?*, 66 Vand. L. Rev. 869 (2013).

[29] Regarding digital assets, see Kelvin F. K. Low & Megumi Hara, *Cryptoassets and Property*, *in* Research Handbook on European Property Law 146 (Sjef van Erp & Katja Zimmermann eds., 2024). For example, Australia, Canada, England, New Zealand, Singapore, and the United States all have common law traditions under which their property law frameworks share a common lineage (yet present not-insubstantial differences). Even more starkly, among civilian systems, there are significant differences between the Germanic and Francophone systems. *See* George L. Gretton, *Ownership and its Objects*, 71 Rabels Zeitschrift für ausländisches und internationales Privatrecht (RabelsZ) [Rabel J. Compar. & Int'l Priv. L.] 802 (2007), https://doi.org/10.1628/0033725

Historically, common law systems have developed a fluid rather than rigidly defined property law framework.[30] As Carol Rose aptly notes, "[O]ver time, the straightforward common law crystalline rules [of property law] have been muddied repeatedly by exceptions and equitable second-guessing."[31] Nestor Davidson observes that property law "has always had its equitable adjustments to counterbalance the perceived benefits of formalism's purported certainty," reflecting an understanding that emphasizes contingency, pluralism, and property's "social function."[32]

This flexibility has eased the challenge of accommodating novel types of assets that advances in technology and the sciences have generated at an increasingly accelerated pace. Indeed, over the past fifty years, assets such as know-how, transferable state licenses,[33] emission allowances,[34] milk quotas,[35] frozen sperm,[36] domain names,[37] and genetically modified plant cells[38] have all been brought within the realm of personal property with relative ease.

When confronted with the question of whether a new type of asset can be owned, Canadian property law scholar Bruce Ziff argues that common law courts have generally adopted two approaches.[39] The first is the *attributes* approach. As explained by Ziff, judges "search for a strong family resemblance.

07782419462; Simon Douglas & Ben McFarlane, *Defining Property Rights*, *in* PHILOSOPHICAL FOUNDATIONS OF PROPERTY LAW 219 (James Penner & Henry E. Smith eds., 2014). Kelvin F. K. Low, *Bitcoins as Property: Welcome Clarity?*, 136 LAW Q. REV. 345 (2020); J. E. Penner, *The "Bundle of Rights" Picture of Property*, 43 UCLA L. Rev. 711 (1996); J. E. PENNER, THE IDEA OF PROPERTY IN LAW (1997); Ben McFarlane & Simon Douglas, *Property, Analogy and Variety*, 42 OXFORD J. LEGAL STUD. 161 (2022); David Fox, *Cryptocurrencies in the Common Law of Property*, *in* CRYPTOCURRENCIES IN PUBLIC AND PRIVATE LAW 139 (David Fox & Sarah Green eds., 2019); Johan David Michels & Christopher Millard, *The New Things: Property Rights in Digital Files?*, 81 CAMBRIDGE L.J. 323 (2022).

[30] Tara K. Righetti & Joseph A. Schremmer, *Waste and the Governance of Private and Public Property*, 93 U. COLO. L. REV. 609 (2022).

[31] Carol M. Rose, *Crystals and Mud in Property Law*, 40 STAN. L. REV. 577, 578 (1988).

[32] Nestor M. Davidson, *New Formalism in the Aftermath of the Housing Crisis*, 93 B.U. L. REV. 389, 395 (2013).

[33] *See* Saulnier v. Royal Bank of Can., 2008 SCC 58, [2008] 3 S.C.R. 166 (Can.); Anthony Duggan, *In the Wake of the Bingo Queen: Are Licenses Property?*, 47 CANADIAN BUS. L.J. 225 (2009).

[34] Armstrong DLW GmbH v. Winnington Networks Ltd. [2012] EWHC (Ch) 10 (Eng.).

[35] Swift v. Dairywise Farms Ltd. (No. 1) [2000] 1 WLR 1177, [2000] 1 All. E.R. 320 (Eng.).

[36] Yearworth v. North Bristol NHS Trust [2009] EWCA (Civ) 37 (Eng.).

[37] *See* Emke v. Campana, LLC, No. CIV A 306-CV-1416-L, 2007 WL 2781661 (N.D. Tex. Sept. 25, 2007); CRS Recovery v. Laxton, 600 F.3d 1138, 1143 (9th Cir. 2010); Jubber v. Search Mkt. Direct, Inc. (*In re* Paige), 413 B.R. 882, 918 (Bankr. D. Utah 2009); Sprinkler Warehouse v. Systematic Rain, 880 N.W.2d 16, 22 (Minn. 2016); *see also* Nicholas Nugent, *Masters of Their Own Domains: Property Rights as a Bulwark Against DNS Censorship*, 19 COLO. TECH. L.J. 43 (2021); Daniel Hancock, *You Can Have It, but Can You Hold It?: Treating Domain Names as Tangible Property*, 99 KY. L.J. 185 (2011); Frederick M. Abbott, *On the Duality of Internet Domain Names: Propertization and Its Discontents*, 3 N.Y.U. J. INTELL. PROP. & ENT. L. 1 (2013);.

[38] Nathan A. Busch, *Jack and the Beanstalk: Property Rights in Genetically Modified Plants*, MINN. INTELL. PROP. REV., Dec. 2002, at 1, https://scholarship.law.umn.edu/cgi/viewcontent. cgi?article=1381&context=mjlst.

[39] BRUCE ZIFF, PRINCIPLES OF PROPERTY LAW 60–61 (7th ed. 2018).

The quest is to find a normative basis for recognition internal to (immanent in) the law of property, thereby expanding the field of ownership in a way that preserves the coherence of the law of property."[40] This method aligns with the traditional view of property law as the law of things, meaning property as a right in a thing (an "in rem right") enforceable against others.[41]

The second is the *functional* approach. Courts assess whether a particular type of asset can be owned by considering "how property, as a tool of social life, should be used."[42] Such an "approach recognizes that property is not an acontextual entity that demands conceptual purity, but a purposive concept, to be used to meet social needs."[43] This method is conceptually proximate to the theories of Hohfeld,[44] legal realists[45] and, more recently, the progressive property theorists,[46] according to whom property law should be conceptualized as a bundle of rights and other relations between persons in respect of things.

[40] *Id.* at 60–61; *see* Paul Babie, *Of Crocodiles and Cryptocurrency: Or, Property Is a Relationship Between Persons in Respect of Things, and Why It Matters*, OXFORD FACULTY OF L. BLOGS (Feb. 15, 2023), https://blogs.law.ox.ac.uk/blog-post/2023/02/crocodiles-and-cryptocurrency-or-property-relationship-between-persons-respect.

[41] A "unique thing about property law is the fact that it protects rights against the world rather than rights against particular individuals, as is the case with contract law." Joseph William Singer, Essay, *Democratic Estates: Property Law in a Free and Democratic Society*, 94 CORNELL L. REV. 1009, 1021 (2009) [hereinafter Singer, *Democratic Estates*]; *see also* 1 JOHN AUSTIN, LECTURES ON JURISPRUDENCE OR THE PHILOSOPHY OF POSITIVE LAW 380 (3d ed. London, John Murray, 1869) (for a nineteenth-century exposition of this theory of property at common law); William Swadling, *Property: General Principles*, *in* ENGLISH PRIVATE LAW ¶ 4.07 (Andrew Burrows ed., 3d ed. 2013) (providing the traditional position in English law); Jane B. Baron, *Radical Contingency and the Bundle of Rights*, *in* RESEARCH HANDBOOK ON PROPERTY, LAW AND THEORY 169 (Chris Bevan ed., 2024); Smith, *supra* note 25, at 1691.

[42] Babie, *supra* note 40.

[43] *Id.* For a collection of recent property theory scholarship across a spectrum, see David A. Dana & Nadav Shoked, *Property's Edges*, 60 B.C. L. REV. 753 n.21 (2019).

[44] Wesley Newcomb Hohfeld, *Some Fundamental Legal Conceptions as Applied in Judicial Reasoning*, 23 YALE L.J. 16, 28–59 (1913).

[45] *See, e.g.*, Felix S. Cohen, *Transcendental Nonsense and the Functional Approach*, 35 COLUM. L. REV. 809, 815 (1935) ("The circularity of legal reasoning in the whole field of unfair competition is veiled by the 'thingification' of *property*.").

[46] *See, e.g.*, Gregory S Alexander, Eduardo M. Peñalver, Joseph W. Singer & Laura S. Underkuffler, *A Statement of Progressive Property*, 94 CORNELL L. REV. 743 (2009); Timothy M. Mulvaney, *Progressive Property Moving Forward*, 5 CALIF. L. REV. CIR. 349, 351 (2014); Hanoch Dagan, Essay, *Pluralism and Perfectionism in Private Law*, 112 COLUM. L. REV. 1409 (2012); Jedediah Purdy, *A Freedom-Promoting Approach to Property: A Renewed Tradition for New Debates*, 72 U. CHI. L. REV. 1237, 1258–60 (2005); Gregory S. Alexander, *The Social-Obligation Norm in American Property Law*, 94 CORNELL L. REV. 745 (2009) [hereinafter Alexander, *The Social-Obligation Norm*]; Eduardo M. Peñalver, *Land Virtues*, 94 CORNELL L. REV. 821 (2009) [hereinafter Peñalver, *Land Virtues*]; Eduardo M. Peñalver, *Property as Entrance*, 91 VA. L. REV. 1889 (2005) [hereinafter Peñalver, *Property as Entrance*]; Singer, *Democratic Estates*, *supra* note 41; Singer, *Democracy*, *supra* note 26; Joseph William Singer, *The Ownership Society and Takings of Property: Castles, Investments and Just Obligations*, 30 HARV. ENVTL. L. REV. 309 (2006); Joseph William Singer, *After the Flood: Equality & Humanity in Property Regimes*, 52 LOY. L. REV. 243 (2006); ERIC T. FREYFOGLE, ON PRIVATE PROPERTY: FINDING COMMON GROUND ON THE OWNERSHIP OF LAND (2007); John A. Lovett, *Progressive Property in Action: The Land Reform (Scotland) Act 2003*, 89 NEB. L. REV. 739 (2011); Nestor M. Davidson & Rashmi Dyal-Chand, *Property in Crisis*, 78 FORDHAM L. REV. 1607 (2010); Christopher K. Odinet, *Of Progressive Property and Public Debt*, 51 WAKE FOREST L. REV. 1101 (2016).

Consistent with this flexible approach to novel forms of property, common law courts have grappled with the issue of whether digital assets can constitute personal property without excessive difficulty. However, the analytical rigor and exhaustiveness of these decisions vary markedly, with a notable divergence between US courts and those of other common law jurisdictions.

2.3.1 Under the common law outside the United States

In Australia,[47] England and Wales,[48] Hong Kong,[49] New Zealand,[50] and Singapore,[51] courts have all concluded that digital assets can be the subject matter of property. The vast majority of these decisions, in our view, have explicitly embraced the attributes approach, with courts finding particular guidance in the analytical indicia set forth in the 1965 *National Provincial Bank Ltd. v. Ainsworth* case, decided by the House of Lords in the United Kingdom.[52]

[47] Comm'r of the Austl. Fed. Police v. Bigatton [2020] NSWSC 245 (Austl.); Chen v. Blockchain Glob Ltd (2022) 66 VR 30 (Austl.); *In re* Blockchain Tech Pty Ltd [2024] VSC 690 (Austl.).

[48] Vorotyntseva v. Money-4 Ltd. [2018] EWHC 2596 (Ch), [13]; Shair.Com Glob. Digit. Servs. Ltd. v. Arnold, 2018 CanLII 1512, [15] (Can. B.C. S.C.); A.A. v. Persons Unknown & Ors., Re Bitcoin [2019] EWHC 3556 (Comm); Ion Sci. Ltd. v. Persons Unknown, [2020] EWHC (Ch) (Dec. 21 2020) (unreported), at [11]; Fetch.AI Ltd. v. Persons Unknown Category A [2021] EWHC 2254 (Comm), [9]; Mr. Dollar Bill Ltd. v. Persons Unknown [2021] EWHC 2718 (Ch), [10]; Wang v. Darby [2021] EWHC 3054 (Comm), [55]; Danisz v. Persons Unknown [2022] EWHC 280 (QB), [13]; D'Aloia v. Persons Unknown [2022] EWHC 1723 (Ch); Tulip Trading Ltd. v. Bitcoin Ass'n for BSV [2023] EWCA Civ. 83, [24]. Under English law, see also *Law Com No. 256: Digital Assets: Consultation Paper*, U.K. LAW COMM'N (July 28, 2022), https://perma.cc/M7HH-YU9U, and UK JURISDICTION TASKFORCE, LEGAL STATEMENT ON CRYPTOASSETS AND SMART CONTRACTS (Nov. 2019), https://technation.io/wp-content/uploads/2019/11/6.6056_JO_Cryptocurrencies_Statement_FINAL_WEB_111119-1.pdf.

[49] *See* Nico Constantijn Antonius Samara v. Stive Jean Paul Dan, [2022] HKCFI 1254, [36]-[39]; *see also In re* Gatecoin Ltd., [2023] HKEC 1223, [59] (stating that crypto is a "property" in Hong Kong and is capable of forming the subject matter of a trust).

[50] Ruscoe v. Cryptopia Ltd (in Liq) [2020] NZHC 728, [2020] 2 NZLR 809.

[51] *See* CLM v. CLN [2022] SGHC 46; B2C2 Ltd. v. Quoine Pte. Ltd. [2019] SGHC (I) 03, [2019] 4 SLR 17 at [142]; Quoine Pte. Ltd. v. B2C2 Ltd. [2020] SGCA (I) 02, [2020] 2 SLR 20 at [144]; Janesh s/o Rajkumar v. Unknown Person ("CHEFPIERRE") [2022] SGHC 264 (deciding that an NFT could be "property" for an interim injunction); Bybit Fintech Ltd. v. Ho Kai Xin & Others, SGHC 199 [2023] [hereinafter ByBit] (deciding that a stablecoin could be "property" capable of being held on trust).

[52] Nat'l Provincial Bank Ltd. v. Ainsworth [1965] AC 1175 (HL) 1247–48. This analytical framework has also been embraced in extrajudicial initiatives dealing with the question of whether digital assets can be owned. *See Law Com No. 256*, *supra* note 48; UK JURISDICTION TASKFORCE, *supra* note 48. It should be noted that courts have also addressed two additional conceptual hurdles in applying property law to digital assets: first, whether they constitute mere information (which traditionally cannot be appropriated), and second, whether public policy considerations militate against their recognition as property. Both issues have been resolved in favor of treating digital assets as property. *See* Ruscoe v. Cryptopia Ltd (in Liq) [2020] NZHC 728, [117]–[133] (concluding that cryptocurrencies are not mere information); A.A. v. Persons Unknown & Ors., Re Bitcoin [2019] EWHC 3556 (Comm) [57]–[59] (finding no public policy grounds for excluding Bitcoin from the ambit of property). It should be noted that the Ainsworth indicia have been the subject strong criticism by KEVIN GRAY & SUSAN FRANCIS GRAY, ELEMENTS OF LAND LAW 97 (5th ed. 2009).

In his oft-cited dictum, Lord Wilberforce outlined four essential, though not exhaustive, criteria for an asset to qualify as the subject matter of property: "it must be definable, identifiable by third parties, capable in its nature of assumption by third parties, and have some degree of permanence or stability."[53]

This analytical framework has proven remarkably adaptable across various types of digital assets. For instance, the New Zealand High Court and the Australian Supreme Court of Victoria have held that cryptocurrencies satisfy all four *Ainsworth* indicia.[54] Similarly, the Singapore High Court reached analogous conclusions regarding NFTs in *CLM v. CLN* and *Rajkumar v. Unknown Person*, while in *Bybit Fintech Ltd v. Ho Kai Xin*, the court extended this reasoning to stablecoins.[55] English courts have similarly developed their jurisprudence through the Ainsworth framework. In *AA v. Persons Unknown*, the High Court applied the criteria to Bitcoin, affirming its classification as property under English law.[56] Likewise, in *Osbourne v. Persons Unknown*, the High Court recognized NFTs as property, implicitly aligning its reasoning with the *Ainsworth* indicia.[57]

In Canada, courts across multiple provinces have addressed whether digital assets can be the object of property rights with varying approaches. Early decisions from the British Columbia Supreme Court in *Shair.Com* and *Copytrack* apodictically treated cryptocurrencies as property without providing theoretical analysis.[58] This trend continued in Nova Scotia's *QuadrigaCX* proceedings and Alberta's digital asset forfeiture cases.[59] By contrast, in *Cicada 137 LLC v. Medjedovic*, the Ontario Superior Court eschewed classifying digital assets as property. Justice Myers adopted a cautious approach, finding it sufficient for the case that the tokens represented invested value subject to control, while explicitly reserving the broader question of their property status for future development.[60]

[53] Nat'l Provincial Bank Ltd. v. Ainsworth [1965] AC 1175 (HL) 1247–48.

[54] *See* In re Blockchain Tech Pty Ltd [2024] VSC 690 (Austl.); Ruscoe v. Cryptopia Ltd (in Liq) [2020] NZHC 728; CLM v. CLN [2022] SGHC 46.

[55] Janesh s/o Rajkumar v. Unknown Person ("CHEFPIERRE") [2022] SGHC 264; ByBit, *supra* note 51.

[56] A.A. v. Persons Unknown & Ors., Re Bitcoin [2019] EWHC 3556 (Comm).

[57] *Id.*; Osbourne v. Persons Unknown [2023] EWHC 39 (Ch).

[58] *See* Shair.Com Glob. Digit. Servs. Ltd. v. Arnold, 2018 CanLII 1512, [13]–[17] (B.C. S.C.); Copytrack Pte. Ltd. v. Wall, 2018 CanLII 1709 (Can. B.C.S.C.). *See also* Janis Sarra & Louise Gullifer, *Crypto-Claimants and Bitcoin Bankruptcy: Challenges for Recognition and Realization*, 28 INT'L INSOLVENCY REV. 233, 246–48 (2019).

[59] *See* Re Quadriga Fintech Solutions Corp., 2019 NSSC 65 (Can.); Edmonton Police Serv. v. 2A Fresh Bitcoin, 2023 ABQB 513 (Can.).

[60] Cicada 137 LLC v. Medjedovic, 2022 ONSC 369, [24] (Can.).

2.3.2 Under American law

In the United States, the analysis of digital assets as property is complicated by the interplay between federal and state law. Property law falls within the jurisdiction of states as a general matter,[61] with federal law providing overarching regulatory frameworks in areas such as securities, commodities, taxation, bankruptcy, anti-money laundering, and interstate commerce.[62] Both federal and state courts have recognized digital assets as subject matter of property, albeit through disparate analytical approaches that privilege practical outcomes and pragmatism over theoretical clarity and doctrinal coherence.

At the federal level, this recognition has emerged primarily through bankruptcy proceedings, enforcement actions, and limited agency guidance. Bankruptcy courts have consistently treated digital assets as property of the estate, as exemplified in *In re Celsius Network, In re Voyager Digital Holdings, In re Genesis Global Holdings*, and *In re FTX Trading*, where the analysis centered on whether customer-deposited cryptocurrencies belonged to the debtor's estate.[63] Similarly, in criminal forfeiture and regulatory enforcement contexts, federal courts have readily accepted digital assets as property capable of seizure or transfer restriction.[64] The Securities and Exchange Commission, the Commodity Futures Trading Commission, and other regulatory agencies have further cemented this position by implicitly recognizing a variety of digital assets as personal property in their enforcement actions.[65] As far back as 2014,

[61] *See generally* SHELDON F. KURTZ, HERBERT HOVENKAMP, CAROL NECOLE BROWN & CHRISTOPHER K. ODINET, CASES AND MATERIALS ON AMERICAN PROPERTY LAW (7th ed. 2019) (expounding the largely state-based law of property in the United States).

[62] *See* Bd. of Regents of State Colls. v. Roth, 408 U.S. 564, 577 (1972); *see also* Logan v. Zimmerman Brush Co., 455 U.S. 422, 430 (1982).

[63] *In re* Celsius Network LLC, 647 B.R. 631, 637 (Bankr. S.D.N.Y. 2023); *In re* Voyager Digital Holdings, Inc., No. 22-10943 (MEW), 2022 WL 3146796, at *3 (Bankr. S.D.N.Y. Aug. 5, 2022); *In re* Genesis Glob. Holdco, LLC, 658 B.R. 31, 52 (Bankr. S.D.N.Y. 2024); *In re* FTX Trading Ltd., No. 22-11068 (JTD), 2024 WL 3191668, at *1, *13 (Bankr. D. Del. June 26, 2024); *see also In re* BlockFi Inc., No. AP 23-1144 (MBK), 2023 WL 6148151 (D.N.J. Sept. 20, 2023) (examining property rights in crypto lending relationships); *see In re* Cred Inc., 658 B.R. 783 (Bankr. D. Del. 2024) (analyzing ownership of pledged bitcoins); *see generally In re* Three Arrows Capital, 647 B.R. 440 (Bankr. S.D.N.Y. 2022) (Chapter 15 proceeding addressing cross-border digital asset recovery); *see In re* Hector DAO, Ch. 15 Case No. 3:24-BK-16067, Adv. No. 25-01200-MBK (D.N.J. June 17, 2024) (Chapter 15 proceeding classifying a decentralized autonomous organization [DAO] as eligible for bankruptcy protection).

[64] United States v. Ulbricht, 31 F. Supp. 3d 540 (S.D.N.Y. 2014); *see also* United States v. 50.44 Bitcoins, No. CV ELH-15-3692, 2016 WL 3049166, at *3 (D. Md. May 31, 2016).

[65] The CFTC has carried out a series of enforcement actions that progressively expanded its oversight of digital assets as commodities and implicitly recognized them as personal property. *See* CFTC v. McDonnell, 287 F. Supp. 3d 213 (E.D.N.Y. 2018) (explicitly characterizing virtual currencies as commodities); CFTC v. My Big Coin Pay, Inc., 334 F. Supp. 3d 492 (D. Mass. 2018); Sec. & Exch. Comm'n v. Binance Holdings Ltd., 738 F. Supp. 3d 20, 31–33 (D.D.C. 2024). The SEC has similarly developed its approach through enforcement actions focused on securities law violations yet implicitly treating the underlying digital assets as property. *See* SEC v. Terraform Labs Pte. Ltd., 708

the Internal Revenue Service has considered cryptocurrencies to be a form of property.[66]

State courts have likewise generally concluded that digital assets are the subject matter of property. However, they have largely eschewed the *Grundfrage*, adopting instead a pragmatic stance that appears to espouse, at least implicitly, the functional approach to property. For the most part, they have recognized digital assets as personal property almost as a *fait accompli* based on their widespread commercial circulation and social adoption, focusing primarily on remedial considerations.

This functional approach is particularly evident in cases involving conversion claims, fraudulent transfers, and other traditional property-based causes of action. In *Temurian v. Piccolo*, for instance, the Florida court readily recognized cryptocurrencies as property to enable recovery in a fraud case, while in *Ox Labs v. BitPay*, conversion claims involving Bitcoin were adjudicated on the premise of its property status.[67] Similarly, in *Archer v. Coinbase*, the court accepted that cryptocurrencies could theoretically be subject to conversion claims, thereby implicitly reinforcing their status as property.[68] More recent cases have continued this trend while grappling with increasingly complex arrangements, such as in *Lee v. Binance* and *Coinbase v. Bielski*, where courts have had to navigate the intersection of property rights with custodial relationships and platform obligations.[69]

A more principled framework for analyzing whether digital assets can constitute property might perhaps be extrapolated from *Kremen v. Cohen*.[70] In this 2003 decision, the US Court of Appeals for the Ninth Circuit, applying California law, confronted the then-novel question of whether domain names could be recognized as property. Drawing from California precedent establishing that

F. Supp. 3d 450 (S.D.N.Y. 2023) (stablecoins); *see* SEC v. AriseBank, No. 3:18-CV-186-M, 2018 WL 10419828 (N.D. Tex. Mar. 9, 2018) (treating cryptocurrency as property subject to receivership); *see* SEC v. Ripple Labs Inc., 682 F. Supp. 3d 308 (S.D.N.Y.); *see* SEC v. Telegram Group Inc., 448 F. Supp. 3d 352 (S.D.N.Y. 2020) (examining property rights in prefunctional tokens); SEC v. Kik Interactive Inc., 492 F. Supp. 3d 169, 173 (S.D.N.Y. 2020).

[66] *See* I.R.S. Notice 2014-21, 2014-16 I.R.B. 938.

[67] Temurian v. Piccolo, No. 18-CV-62737, 2019 WL 1763022, at *3, n.1 (S.D. Fla. 2019); Ox Labs Inc. v. BitPay, Inc., 848 F. App'x 795, 796 (9th Cir. 2021); Currier v. PDL Recovery Grp., No. 14-12179, 2018 WL 4057394, at *2 (E.D. Mich. 2018); *see also* Nibi, Inc. v. John Doe, No. 5:24-cv-06184 (N.D. Cal. filed Aug. 30, 2024); Krishna Okhandiar v. John Duff III, No. 2:23-cv-01409 (D. Nev. filed Sept. 10, 2023); Eric Schiermeyer v. Wright Thurston, No. 2:23-cv-00589 (D. Utah filed Aug. 31, 2023).

[68] Archer v. Coinbase, Inc., 53 Cal. App. 5th 266, 275–78 (2020).

[69] Coinbase, Inc. v. Bielski, 599 U.S. 736 (2023); *see also* Tiger Mines N. Y., Inc. v. Tether Holdings Ltd., No. 1:24-cv-5905, 2024 WL 3635177 (S.D.N.Y. filed Aug. 2, 2024) (addressing property rights in frozen digital assets); Vandelay Indus. TM LLC v. Bitwise Hold 10 Priv. Index Fund, LLC, No. 653436/2024 (N.Y. Sup. Ct. filed July 8, 2024) (examining property interests in managed cryptocurrency fund).

[70] Kremen v. Cohen, 337 F.3d 1024 (9th Cir. 2003).

property encompasses "every intangible benefit and prerogative susceptible of possession or disposition,"[71] the court developed a three-part test that echoes the *Ainsworth* indicia: "First, there must be an interest capable of precise definition; second, it must be capable of exclusive possession or control; and third, the putative owner must have established a legitimate claim to exclusivity."[72]

We believe that digital assets such as cryptocurrencies, NFTs, and stablecoins appear particularly amenable to analysis under the *Kremen* framework. As data entries in distributed ledger systems, these assets typically satisfy the first part of the test. Each cryptocurrency token, NFT, or stablecoin unit has exact, mathematically defined properties and quantities. The second requirement of exclusive possession or control is generally achieved through cryptographic mechanisms, such as public–private key pairs, that afford their holders the ability to enjoy the benefits of these assets. Through the lens of Hohfeld's legal framework, this control represents a "privilege" that confers on keyholders the liberty to use and transfer the asset, while creating in all others a correlative "no-right" to prevent or interfere with such activities.[73] Finally, legitimate claims to exclusivity can be established through the technological architecture of the relevant protocols—whether through proof-of-work mining, proof-of-stake validation, or smart contract execution that creates or transfers tokens according to predetermined parameters. These protocol-level mechanisms create verifiable and transparent records that document the creation of each digital asset and all subsequent transfers, thereby providing objective evidence to support claims of exclusivity under traditional property frameworks.

This judicial recognition of digital assets as property in the United States, though largely driven by practical imperatives, also finds theoretical support in legal scholarship—albeit from a relatively small cohort of scholars who have engaged with the fundamental property law questions rather than regulatory concerns. Juliet Moringiello provided an early theoretical foundation, arguing that "the idea of tangibility as tangibility has no relevance to property law" because courts have historically adapted possession and control concepts to novel types of assets, regardless of their physical manifestation.[74] As she points out, the conceptual leap from determining possession of a wild fox to establishing control over a domain name is a small one, given courts' centuries-long history of refashioning possession concepts to accommodate new forms of property rights. Shawn Bayern similarly suggested that the inherent flexibility of common law enables it to specifically accommodate cryptocurrencies within existing

[71] *Id.* at 1030.
[72] *Id.*
[73] *See* Hohfeld, *supra* note 44, at 28–59.
[74] Juliet M. Moringiello, *False Categories in Commercial Law: The (Ir)relevance of (In)tangibility*, 35 FLA. ST. U. L. REV. 119, 164 (2007).

property frameworks.[75] Joshua Fairfield subsequently developed a more comprehensive theory for this position, leveraging a functional view of property that emphasizes social recognition over formal categorization. He posited that "when digital assets are treated by owners as personal property, the law of personal property should apply"—an approach that has proved particularly prescient as digital assets have gained widespread market acceptance.[76]

2.4 The classification of digital assets within property

Once it is established that digital assets can be owned, the next crucial step in determining the private law regime governing their commercial circulation is to classify these assets within existing property law categories. This is necessary because legal systems do not craft bespoke regimes for each novel invention that emerges. Rather, they operate through general and abstract categories of property into which novel assets must be subsumed. As Judge Frank Easterbrook observed in rejecting calls for specialized "cyberlaw," there was never a "Law of the Horse" despite horses' centrality to nineteenth-century life and commerce.[77] The general principles of property, tort, and contract law adequately governed transactions involving horses.[78]

The classification exercise we undertake here involves principles that vary substantially between common law and civil law systems. Moreover, even jurisdictions belonging to the same legal tradition often diverge in their approach, despite their shared roots. In common law jurisdictions, the categorization of personal property has traditionally been framed by the *summa divisio* between *choses* in possession and *choses* in action.[79] This foundational distinction was famously described by the nineteenth-century English jurist Lord Justice Edward Fry in the following terms: "[A]ll personal things are either in possession or action. The law knows no tertium quid between the two."[80]

[75] *See* Shawn Bayern, *Dynamic Common Law and Technological Change: The Classification of Bitcoin*, 71 Wash. & Lee L. Rev. Online 22 (2014).

[76] *See* Joshua Fairfield, *BitProperty*, 88 S. Cal. L. Rev. 805 (2015) [hereinafter Fairfield, *BitProperty*]; Joshua Fairfield, *Tokenized: The Law of Non-Fungible Tokens and Unique Digital Property*, 97 Ind. L.J. 1267 (2022) [hereinafter Fairfield, *Tokenized*]; *see also* Joshua A. T. Fairfield, *Virtual Property*, 85 B.U. L. Rev. 1047 (2005) (earlier work developing foundation ideas about virtual property more broadly); *see also* Christopher K. Odinet, *BitProperty and Commercial Credit*, 94 Wash. U. L. Rev. 649 (2017).

[77] Frank H. Easterbrook, *Cyberspace and the Law of the Horse*, 1996 U. Chi. Legal F. 207.

[78] *See* Lawrence Lessig, *The Law of the Horse: What Cyberlaw Might Teach*, 113 Harv. L. Rev. 501 (1999) (engaging with and partially challenging Easterbrook's position).

[79] *See In re* Morales, 403 B.R. 629 (Bankr. N.D. Iowa 2009).

[80] Colonial Bank v. Whinney [1885] 30 Ch D 261, 285 (Eng.).

This binary classification has historically carried profound implications for the commercial circulation of assets. Choses in possession encompass all property rights in relation to things that are susceptible to physical taking. These rights are typically transferred through a combination of intention and delivery of the thing. Owners enjoy robust remedies against interfering third parties and various good faith purchase exceptions. Choses in action, by contrast, include property rights "which can only be claimed or enforced by action, and not by taking physical possession."[81] They transfer through assignment, remain strictly subject to the *nemo dat quod non habet* rule, and provide their holders with a narrower set of remedies.[82]

The scope of choses in possession has remained uncontroversial.[83] However, the boundaries of choses in action have been the subject of sustained scholarly debate since the late nineteenth century.[84] Initially, disagreements concerned whether the category should be confined to rights of action in contract and debt or extended to other intangible rights such as causes of action in tort, equitable interests, and intellectual property rights.[85] In recent decades, these definitional challenges have resurfaced as courts have grappled with novel intangible assets such as milk quotas, carbon emission allowances, telecommunications licenses, and rights over hunting estuarine crocodiles.[86]

Digital assets present the latest challenge to this traditional dichotomy.[87] Mirroring the approach to the *Grundfrage*, we first survey the treatment of this issue in other common law jurisdictions and then turn to the position in the United States.

[81] Torkington v. Magee 2 [1902] 2 K.B. 427, 430 (Eng.); *see also* Robert Stevens, *Crypto Is Not Property*, 139 LAW Q. REV. 615 (2023).

[82] *See also* RESTATEMENT (FOURTH) OF PROPERTY § 1.1 (Tentative Draft No. 5, 2024).

[83] *See* Swadling, *supra* note 41; *see also* W. H. HASTINGS KELKE, AN EPITOME OF PERSONAL PROPERTY LAW 2 (3d ed. 1910).

[84] *See also* W. S. Holdsworth, *The History of the Treatment of "Choses" in Action by the Common Law*, 33 HARV. L. REV. 997 (1928) (tracing the early history of choses in action in English and American law); Kevin Sobel-Read, Glen Anderson & Jaakko Salminen, *The Critical Role of Choses in Action: A Call for Harmonization Across Common Law Jurisdictions*, 45 FORDHAM INT'L L.J. 513 (2022).

[85] See the scholarly debate in T. Cyprian Williams, *Terms Real and Personal in English Law*, 4 LAW Q. REV. 394 (1888); Howard W. Elphinstone, *What Is a Chose in Action?*, 9 LAW Q. REV. 311 (1893); Charles Sweet, *Choses in Action*, 11 LAW Q. REV. 238 (1895); T. C. W. [T. Cyprian Williams], *Is a Right of Action in Tort a Chose in Action?*, 10 LAW Q. REV. 143 (1894); Frederick Pollock, *What Is a Thing?*, 10 LAW Q. REV. 318 (1894). For modern analysis of this debate, see SARAH WORTHINGTON, EQUITY 58–62 (2d ed. 2006).

[86] *See* Sobel-Read, Anderson & Salminen, *supra* note 84.

[87] This challenge was aptly illustrated by the Singaporean Court of Appeal in Quoine Pte. Ltd. v. B2C2 Ltd., [2020] SGCA (I) 02, [2020] 2 SLR 20 at [144], which noted the appeal of classifying cryptocurrencies as property while acknowledging the complexities involved in determining the precise nature of such property.

2.4.1 Under the common law outside the United States

In common law jurisdictions other than the United States, an uncontroversial consensus has emerged that digital assets cannot qualify as choses in possession. This is based on the view that possession requires tangibility.[88] To quote Thomas Merrill: "Possession is limited to tangible objects, that is, things that have physical dimensions."[89]

By contrast, the possible classification of digital assets as choses in action has sparked considerable debate. One view, grounded in Blackstone's classical conception, maintains that choses in action require the right holder to have an actual cause of action against another person.[90] Digital assets almost invariably fail to satisfy this criterion—this is particularly evident with cryptocurrencies in decentralized networks such as Bitcoin and Ethereum, but it also applies to many other digital assets, such as NFTs, that purport to create enforceable rights against specific persons.

Proponents of this view argue that digital assets belong in a *tertium quid*—a third category of personal property distinct from both choses in possession and choses in action—on the basis that they exist independently of the law as data objects.[91] Such supporters trace the origins of this third category to the UK Privy Council's decision in *Attorney-General of Hong Kong v. Nai-Keung*,[92] which concerned export quotas, and suggest it encompasses not only digital assets but also milk quotas and EU carbon emissions allowances.[93] This perspective calls for the development of a new body of rules tailored to this third category, either through judicial action or statutory intervention. Notably, this thesis has gained significant traction in recent years, receiving judicial endorsement in England and Hong Kong,[94] as well as support from influential law reform bodies[95] and commentators.[96]

[88] Thomas W. Merrill, *Ownership and Possession*, *in* LAW AND ECONOMICS OF POSSESSION 25 (Yun-Chien Chang ed., 2015); H. E. Smith, *The Elements of Possession*, *in* LAW AND ECONOMICS OF POSSESSION, *supra*, at 65; D. R. Harris, *The Concept of Possession in English Law*, *in* OXFORD ESSAYS IN JURISPRUDENCE 69 (A. G. Guest ed., 1961). For a discussion of the academic literature on possession, see João Marinotti, *Possessing Intangibles*, 116 NW. U. L. REV. 1227, 1252–54 (2022). We note that although courts could theoretically redefine possession to eliminate the tangibility requirement, they have not yet done so.

[89] Merrill, *supra* note 88, at 25.

[90] 2 WILLIAM BLACKSTONE, COMMENTARIES *396–97.

[91] *See Law Com No. 412: Digital Assets: Final Report*, U.K. LAW COMM'N ¶¶ 2.52–53, 3.3, 3.25–30, 3.36–58, 3.65–69, 4.1–5 (June 27, 2023), https://perma.cc/3FE6-Q76T; UK JURISDICTION TASKFORCE, *supra* note 48, at [57].

[92] Att'y-Gen. of Hong Kong v. Nai-Keung [1987] 1 WLR 1339 (PC), at 1342; Swift v. Dairywise Farms Ltd. (No. 1) [2000] 1 WLR 1177 (Eng.); Armstrong v. Winnington Networks Ltd., [2013] EWHC (Ch) 156.

[93] *See Law Com No. 412*, *supra* note 91.

[94] *See* A.A. v. Persons Unknown & Ors., Re Bitcoin [2019] EWHC 3556 (Comm); Tulip Trading Ltd. v. Bitcoin Ass'n for BSV [2023] EWCA Civ. 83, [24]; *In re* Gatecoin Ltd. (In Liq.) [2023] 3 HKC 401 [47], [56]–[59].

[95] *See* UK LAW COMM'N, *supra* note 48; UK JURISDICTION TASKFORCE, *supra* note 48, at [57].

[96] Fox, *supra* note 29, at 139; Michels & Millard, *supra* note 29.

An alternative view rejects the necessity of a *tertium quid*, arguing instead that digital assets can and should be accommodated within the existing category of choses in action.[97] Advocates for this approach believe that courts should develop the commercial circulation regime for digital assets by carefully adapting established principles governing choses in action. This thesis builds upon the English legal historian Sir William Holdsworth's historical analysis, which revealed choses in action as a residual category that has progressively expanded beyond its original conception of mere rights enforceable through court action.[98] This broader conception has gained particular traction in Australia, where it is now settled law,[99] and courts across multiple jurisdictions have begun applying it to digital assets, though often without extensive doctrinal analysis.[100]

What is striking about this debate on whether digital assets are choses in action or a *tertium quid* is that it has stifled deeper investigations into the legal rules governing their commercial circulation. Indeed, the preoccupation with classification has impeded the development of a coherent framework for how property law applies to these assets in commercial transactions. This narrow framing has left fundamental questions largely unexplored, including the precise subject matter of the property right, the mechanisms by which title passes, and the applicability of the *nemo dat* rule and its exceptions. Yet these issues are essential to resolving even basic property disputes. Consequently, significant uncertainty persists in these jurisdictions regarding whether a good faith purchaser acquires valid title to a digital asset obtained through deceit or misrepresentation, raising, in turn, concerns about the finality of transactions. Similarly, the creation and perfection of security interests in digital assets remain unsettled. Moreover, the absence of clear rules governing priority conflicts has left undefined how competing claims should be resolved, particularly in insolvency proceedings or in disputes involving multiple claimants asserting proprietary rights over the same asset.

2.4.2 Under American law

In the United States, the classification of digital assets within property has attracted limited attention. Unlike other common law jurisdictions, there has

[97] Low, *supra* note 29.

[98] 7 W. S. Holdsworth, A History of English Law 515–23 (2d ed. 2018) (1914); *see also* Holdsworth, *supra* note 84, at 997–1030.

[99] In Australia, the High Court held unambiguously that choses in action are not limited to rights enforceable by a court in *Nat'l Trs Ex's and Agency Co of Australasia Ltd v. Fed Comm'r of Tax'n* (1954) 91 CLR 540 (Austl.); *see also Commonwealth v. WMC Resources Ltd* (1998) 194 CLR 1 at [180] (Austl.).

[100] In England, Fetch.AI Ltd. v. Persons Unknown Category A [2021] EWHC 2254 (Comm), [9]; in New Zealand, Ruscoe v. Cryptopia Ltd (in Liq) [2020] NZHC 728, [2020] 2 NZLR 809. Most recently in Australia, *In re* Blockchain Tech Pty Ltd [2024] VSC 690 (Austl.).

been no debate regarding whether they are choses in possession or choses in action. Courts have not engaged with this issue, and commentators have only addressed it tangentially, on specific and narrow grounds rather than as a fundamental property law question.

We believe this relative silence can be attributed to three interrelated developments in US property law that differentiate it markedly from that of other common law jurisdictions. First, the orientation of American scholars in this field has traditionally centered on land and real estate, with much of the theoretical discourse focused on normative debates about property rights, ownership, and societal functions.[101] Consider, for example, Guido Calabresi and A. Douglas Melamed's seminal 1972 article, which presents a unified framework for understanding how legal systems protect entitlements.[102] The authors introduce three key methods of protection: property rules, liability rules, and inalienability rules. While the authors indeed use both real and personal property examples to make their argument, the former dominate the analysis and carry the heaviest weight throughout the article. The article's most extensive and detailed applications center on real property (particularly in its extended discussion of pollution and nuisance law), the "Guidacres" eminent domain example, and various land use conflicts between neighbors.[103] In contrast, while personal property examples appear throughout the article—including discussions of bodily integrity, theft, and transferable rights—these tend to be briefer, less detailed and used more for supplementary explanation.

Similarly, Harold Demsetz's 1967 paper lays out a foundational economic theory explaining how and why property rights have emerged and evolved in society.[104] His article argues that property rights develop primarily to help people internalize externalities when the benefits of doing so exceed the costs. In developing this theory, Demsetz works through his key theoretical concepts, including externalities, negotiation costs, and the internalization of benefits and costs, through land ownership. His most extensive example examines the evolution of Native American land rights. By contrast, his treatment of personal property is notably less prominent. Examples involving personal property (such as corporate shares, patents, or primitive tools and weapons) appear more briefly, often in footnotes or near the paper's end. Indeed, his emphasis on real property is deliberate rather than coincidental—Demsetz explicitly states that land ownership provides a "particularly useful example" for developing his theory.

[101] *See also* Lovett, *supra* note 46, at 743–53.

[102] Guido Calabresi & A. Douglas Melamed, *Property Rules, Liability Rules, and Inalienability: One View of the Cathedral*, 85 Harv. L. Rev. 1089, 1089–92 (1972).

[103] *Id.* at 1106–08, 1115–24.

[104] Harold Demsetz, *Toward a Theory of Property Rights*, 57 Am. Econ. Rev. (Special Issue) 347 (1967).

Coming into the modern era, the work of prominent progressive property theorists of the last few decades has also tended to lean more heavily in the direction of real property. In his important article titled *Democratic Estates: Property Law in a Free and Democratic Society*, Joseph Singer explores property law through the lens of land and real estate, using examples of land ownership, transfer, and regulation to illustrate broader legal and philosophical concepts about property rights.[105] His analysis systematically examines how real property interactions reflect social relationships, democratic values, and the complex legal frameworks that govern land ownership and use. Gregory Alexander's article on *The Social-Obligation Norm in American Property Law* also primarily uses land as the focal point for illustrating the social-obligation norm in property law.[106] It discusses land-related doctrines like eminent domain, land reform, and environmental and historical preservation. The emphasis is on the societal responsibilities of landowners and the community's interest in land use and distribution. Personal property is referenced more sparingly.

Relatedly, Eduardo Peñalver's important work also tends to focus on real property, such as in *Land Virtues*, which discusses land's complexity, memory, and its unique role in human flourishing.[107] In *Property as Entrance*, Peñalver develops a critique of property as both an *exit* and *entrance* mechanism, primarily through analysis of real property's role in community formation—particularly highlighting how territorial spaces such as homes, neighborhoods, and separatist enclaves shape social interactions.[108]

Similarly, the works of leading so-called exclusionary or information cost theorists,[109] Thomas Merrill and Henry Smith, have relied heavily on the example of real property. In his seminal work, *Property and the Right to Exclude*, Merrill demonstrates a clear preference for using real property examples, particularly land, to illustrate its theoretical arguments.[110] The recurring hypothetical of "Blackacre" serves as the primary vehicle for explaining how exclusion rights operate and relate to other property rights.[111] While the article acknowledges personal property through examples such as books and financial instruments, these receive significantly less attention and typically appear as brief illustrations rather than points of sustained analysis. Similarly, in Smith and Merrill's influential coauthored work, *Optimal Standardization in the Law of Property*, the focus is again on real property—particularly estates in land—as the primary

[105] Singer, *Democratic Estates*, *supra* note 41, at 1020–21.

[106] Alexander, *The Social-Obligation Norm*, *supra* note 46, at 775–79.

[107] Peñalver, *Land Virtues*, *supra* note 46, at 828–30.

[108] Peñalver, *Property as Entrance*, *supra* note 46, at 1940–44.

[109] *See* Lovett, *supra* note 46, at 746; *see also* Jane B. Baron, *The Contested Commitments of Property*, 61 Hastings L.J. 917, 918, 924–27 (2010).

[110] *See* Thomas Merrill, *Property and the Right to Exclude*, 77 Neb. L. Rev. 730, 740–43 (1998).

[111] *Id.* at 740–44.

lens for understanding the numerus clausus principle.[112] Personal property appears mainly as a foil to show how property rights can be even more restricted, with the authors noting that "personal property is restricted to fewer available forms of ownership than real property."[113] And again, in their piece titled *What Happened to Property in Law and Economics?*, Smith and Merrill primarily examine real property (particularly land) to illustrate the traditional in rem conception of property as a right to exclude and secure investment.[114] Through historical references to Blackstone and Smith, as well as to Coase's land-dispute examples, the discussion emphasizes the security and standardization benefits tied to land ownership.

That is not to say that personal property has not been explored at all. Indeed, it has, but often with far less prominence. In Richard Posner's *Utilitarianism, Economics, and Legal Theory*, personal property examples are more prominently featured and discussed in greater detail compared to real property examples.[115] The personal property scenarios involving diamond necklaces, babies in the adoption market, and body parts (organs) are used to explore complex ethical issues and the boundaries of wealth maximization theory. These examples are particularly provocative and are designed to challenge conventional moral intuitions by pushing the implications of economic analysis to controversial limits. In contrast, the real property examples, such as pollution affecting residential property values, are generally more straightforward and used to illustrate conventional market transactions or externality problems. Posner uses personal property cases to a greater extent because they allow him to explore ethically complex issues, such as the commodification of human constituents (e.g., body parts or identity), which test the limits of economic efficiency as a normative guide for legal rules. Real property discussions, while still significant, are comparatively more conventional and less ethically provocative.

Consider also Margaret Jane Radin's powerful article *Property and Personhood*, which advances the theory that certain property becomes so fundamentally connected to human identity that it warrants enhanced legal protection.[116] While Radin employs both personal and real property examples to make

[112] Thomas W. Merrill & Henry E. Smith, *Optimal Standardization in the Law of Property: The Numerus Clausus Principle*, 110 YALE L.J. 1, 12–15 (2000).

[113] *Id.* at 17. The article's treatment of personal property is largely confined to a single extended hypothetical about a watch and observations about the limitations on creating servitudes in personal property. *See id.* at 27–33, 18–19.

[114] Thomas W. Merrill & Henry E. Smith, *What Happened to Property in Law and Economics?*, 111 YALE L.J. 357, 360–64, 386–88.

[115] *See* Richard A. Posner, *Utilitarianism, Economics, and Legal Theory*, 8 J. LEGAL STUD. 103 (1979).

[116] Margaret Jane Radin, *Property and Personhood*, 34 STAN. L. REV. 957, 957–59 (1982).

this argument, these two categories serve distinct roles in her analysis. Personal property examples such as wedding rings, family heirlooms, and personal effects appear frequently as accessible illustrations of her core concept. However, real property (particularly the home) provides the substantive foundation for her most significant legal arguments. Radin uses residential property to demonstrate how her theory operates within existing legal frameworks, particularly in Fourth Amendment case law, landlord-tenant law, zoning regulations, and eminent domain. Though personal property examples help readers grasp the property–personhood connection intuitively, real property examples do the analytical heavy lifting, which we think understandably reflects both the greater frequency of real property disputes in courts and real property's central role in generating the legal doctrine through which Radin develops her theory.

To be sure, none of this is surprising or blameworthy. The emphasis on real property in the property law literature aligns with the common law tradition's historical focus on land rights. This focus comes from the law's feudal origins, where land ownership was the primary source of wealth, power, and social status. As such, legal doctrines were developed to protect landowners' interests and to regulate the transfer and use of land. Moreover, land has always held unique legal significance due to its immobility, permanence, and economic value, necessitating complex rules to govern its use and inheritance.

To see this historical emphasis on land even more clearly, one need look no further than the many modern property law casebooks used in American law schools—all of which overwhelmingly prioritize real property over personal property.[117] These textbooks dedicate extensive coverage to topics such as estates in land, land use regulations, servitudes, landlord-tenant law, and conveyancing, while offering far less treatment of personal property issues like possession, finders' rights, and bailments.[118] The disproportionate focus suggests that land remains the central organizing principle of property law, perpetuating the notion that legal complexity and importance are primarily associated with real estate. Consequently, students are trained to view property law through the lens of

[117] *See* James Charles Smith, Edward J. Larson & Alejandro Camacho, Property: Cases and Materials 143–61, 166–85, 416–38, 485–555, 607–90, 697–733, 755–82, 789–840 (3d ed. 2013); John G. Sprankling & Raymond R. Coletta, Property: A Contemporary Approach 98–134, 135–43, 150–58, 407–34, 543–662, 666–716, 716–60, 765–80, 783–855, 901–23, 925–79 (3d ed. 2015); Joseph William Singer, Bethany R. Berger, Nestor M. Davidson & Eduardo Moises Penalver, Property Law: Rules, Policies, and Practices 3–39, 283–328, 333–409, 513–56, 556–74, 662, 687, 809–902, 907–1011, 1013–91, 1141–1262 (6th ed. 2014); Kurtz, Hovenkamp, Brown & Odinet, *supra* note 61, at 209–72, 287–377, 437–96, 507–652, 679–834, 863–918, 923–49, 1083–1185, 1217–92, 1307–30, 1355–1426.

[118] *See* Smith, Larson & Camacho, *supra* note 117, at 79–95, 102–06, 121–34, 139–43, 305–14, 755–82; Sprankling & Coletta, *supra* note 117, at 161–67, 174–91, 198–203, 212–30, 237–308; Singer, Berger, Davidson & Penalver, *supra* note 117, at 30–136, 141–46, 150–58, 171–236, 329–33; Kurtz, Hovenkamp, Brown & Odinet, *supra* note 61, at 8–49, 50–79, 117–77, 272–87, 426–37.

land ownership, reinforcing a hierarchy in which personal property is secondary and consequently less legally significant.

Thus, with few notable exceptions,[119] this focus has left personal property relatively understudied, often treated as a secondary concern in both academic discourse and judicial development. Meanwhile, intellectual property has evolved as a largely autonomous field, with its own community of scholars and distinct theoretical frameworks.[120] Consequently, the theoretical property law dimensions of digital assets are of interest only to the few scholars positioned at the intersection of personal property theory, commercial law, and technological innovation.

Second, when American legal scholars have engaged with personal property law, they have concentrated on the practical incidents of ownership, possession, control, transfer, and use as collateral.[121] For example, Juliet Moringiello argues in her innovative 2007 article *The (Ir)relevance of (In)tangibility* that the legal system's persistent focus on tangibility compared to intangibility in commercial law creates "false categories unrelated to significant legal distinctions" that "hinder the ability of commercial law to expand to adequately accommodate electronic assets."[122] Instead of fixating on whether an asset is tangible or intangible, she contends that courts and lawmakers should concentrate on "the relationships between the persons claiming rights in those assets and the assets themselves."[123] This pragmatic approach is particularly evident in her critique of how courts have struggled with electronic assets such as domain names, where she argues they have become unnecessarily "confounded" by intangibility (i.e., things that "cannot easily be grabbed"[124]) rather than focusing on fundamental property relationships and the practical ability to control and transfer these assets.

Similarly, Joshua Fairfield has argued in his insightful 2015 work *BitProperty* that property is fundamentally about information and its transfer, rather than rigid doctrinal categories based on physical tangibility.[125] Rather than fixating

[119] *See* Marinotti, *supra* note 88; Moringiello, *supra* note 74, at 121; Fairfield, *BitProperty*, *supra* note 76; Odinet, *supra* note 67, at 688; Joshua A. T. Fairfield, Owned: Property, Privacy, and the New Digital Serfdom (2017).

[120] *See generally* U.S. Intellectual Property Law and Policy (Hugh C. Hansen ed., 2006); Amanda Reid, S. Sean Tu & Jessica M. Kiser, Fundamentals of United States Intellectual Property Law: Copyright, Patent, and Trademark (8th ed. 2024).

[121] *See* Moringiello, *supra* note 74, at 119; Fairfield, *BitProperty*, *supra* note 76; Fairfield, *Tokenized*, *supra* note 76; Jeanne L. Schroeder, *Bitcoin and the Uniform Commercial Code*, 24 U. Miami Bus. L. Rev. 1, 14, 27–28, 43 (2016); Odinet, *supra* note 67, at 688. One recent exception to this trend is João Marinotti's 2022 article, which "critiques the pragmatic, flexible approach" described above. *See* Marinotti, *supra* note 88, at 1229–30, 1252.

[122] Moringiello, *supra* note 74, at 119.

[123] *Id.* at 133.

[124] *Id.* at 156–57.

[125] Fairfield, *BitProperty*, *supra* note 76, at 811.

on traditional property categories, Fairfield examines the practical incidents of digital property ownership, analyzing the mechanics of transfer through tokenization and sidechains, the role of possession and control in creating ownership claims, the potential use of digital assets as collateral, and the critical function of information rights and verification in maintaining property systems. Along those lines, in 2016, Jeanne Schroeder observed the need for a fundamentally pragmatic, policy-oriented approach to digital assets that prioritizes functional outcomes over rigid taxonomies.[126] She explicitly rejects formalistic approaches, arguing that "the conflation of possession with physical custody of tangible things, if ever justified in the past, is hopelessly unsophisticated and increasingly unworkable in the 21st century."[127]

The pragmatic orientation found in the scholarly work of these legal academics mirrors the general movement in American twentieth-century legal thought toward flexible, policy-oriented frameworks and away from rigid common law taxonomies. While the distinction between choses in possession and choses in action remains part of American common law, these categories have receded from prominence in both judicial reasoning and scholarly writing. Indeed, the last significant legal scholarship on the chose in action category was during the first quarter of the twentieth century—largely led by Walter Cook and Samuel Williston—with the animating focus being issues involved in the assignment of debts.[128]

Notably, the few US scholars who have considered whether digital assets are choses in action or a *tertium genus* have ultimately suggested that it is a fruitless analytical approach. Discussing Bitcoin, Shawn Bayern observed that it "is not a contract or a bailment. Indeed, it is probably not a *chose* in action of any kind because it represents no claim against others.... In a meaningful sense, it is something new."[129] However, rather than dwelling on this classification conundrum, Bayern advocated for a functional approach. In his view, traditional categories should be given limited attention, focusing instead on practical outcomes: "a bitcoin is an important economic right to many who participate in the network. It is clearly proper to criminalize its theft. It matches parties' expectations if

[126] Schroeder, *supra* note 121, at 14, 27–28, 43.

[127] *Id.* at 27.

[128] *See, e.g.*, Walter Wheeler Cook, *The Alienability of Choses in Action*, 29 HARV. L. REV. 816 (1916) [hereinafter Cook, *Alienability*]; Samuel Williston, *Is the Right of an Assignee of a Chose in Action Legal or Equitable?*, 30 HARV. L. REV. 97 (1916); Walter Wheeler Cook, *The Alienability of Choses in Action: A Reply to Professor Williston*, 30 HARV. L. REV. 449 (1917) [hereinafter Cook, *A Reply*]; Holdsworth, *supra* note 84; Paul Bruton, *The Requirement of Delivery as Applied to Gifts of Choses in Action*, 39 YALE L.J. 837 (1930); L. L. Briggs, *The Assignment of Choses in Action*, 49 J. ACCT. 330 (1930); Kevin Sobel-Read, *Recalibrating Contract Law: Choses in Action, Global Value Chains, and the Enforcement of Obligations Outside of Privity*, 93 TUL. L. REV. 1 (2018). For a notable, more modern exception, *see* Sobel-Read, Anderson & Salminen, *supra* note 84.

[129] Bayern, *supra* note 75, at 34.

bitcoin is treated as intangible, moveable personal property. Contracts involving bitcoins should be enforced."[130]

Third, this functional approach to property law has ushered in new categories for personal property in the United States that have structurally curtailed the significance of the *summa divisio* between choses in possession and choses in action. This new taxonomy finds its primary expression in the regime established by the Uniform Commercial Code (UCC) for a wide range of commercial transactions, including sales, leases, negotiable instruments, documents of title, investment securities, and security interests. At its core, the UCC establishes a distinctly American framework of personal property categories—including goods, accounts, payment intangibles, investment property, and intangibles—that, while bearing traces of the traditional chose distinction, operates largely independently from these historical classifications.[131] In the United States, the crucial question is whether and how digital assets fit within these UCC categories and their corresponding regimes. Common law treatment, and consequently the potential classification of digital assets as choses in action, plays a consequential but residual role confined to those areas where the UCC does not apply.

2.5 Commercial circulation regime of digital assets in American law

The preceding analysis has shown that the classification of digital assets within property differs markedly in the United States compared with other common law jurisdictions. This divergence reflects both the more functional orientation of US property law and the prominent role of the categories codified in the UCC. In this section, we focus on two fundamental aspects of this framework: the voluntary transfer of ownership of digital assets, and their use as collateral in secured transactions. We defer our discussion of two related but distinct issues to subsequent chapters—specifically, the use of digital assets to represent property rights in other assets (Chapter 3) and the custody of digital assets (Chapter 4).

2.5.1 Prior to the 2022 UCC Amendments

Our examination is divided into two periods: before and after the 2022 UCC Amendments. This chronological organization sharply illuminates the

[130] *Id.*

[131] See, e.g., UCC § 9-102(a)(44).

developmental trajectory of US personal property law in relation to digital assets. We begin with the period from 2009 to 2022, during which time courts and scholars grappled with applying existing state common law principles and UCC categories to this entirely novel type of intangible.

(a) Transferring ownership of digital assets

From the early days of the Bitcoin network, the commercial circulation of digital assets has predominantly occurred through arrangements in which parties agreed to exchange these assets for money, other digital assets, or alternative forms of consideration. In the United States, as the Constitution does not grant the federal government general authority over private property transfers, these transactions largely fall within the domain of state law.

Market participants have always referred to the trading of tokens as "sales." However, this colloquialism has no dispositive effect in law. Across almost all fifty states, local enactments of UCC Article 2 govern sale contracts, defined as agreements in which a seller transfers title to "goods" to a buyer for a price.[132] Crucially, under this statute, "goods" means "all things . . . which are movable at the time of identification to the contract for sale other than the money in which the price is to be paid, investment securities . . . and things in action."[133] Therefore, whether a contract for the transfer of ownership of digital assets is a "sale" depends on whether these assets are "movable" and not "things in action."

The difficulty with this somewhat formalistic assessment is that UCC Article 2 does not define either of these terms. Regarding the former, historically, all things that are neither real estate nor fixtures of real estate have been classified as movables.[134] As such, it would appear relatively uncontroversial to include digital assets in this category. By contrast, determining whether digital assets are "things in action" is more problematic.

Because Article 2 does not define this concept, attention must turn to the common law as it supplements the UCC whenever not displaced by its provisions.[135] Logically, this issue—whether digital assets constitute things in action and thus fall outside the scope of "goods"—should have been the prompt for analyzing the classification of digital assets within US property law categories. Yet, as discussed in Section 2.4.2, US property law scholarship and jurisprudence

[132] There is an exception, however, in Louisiana, where the Civil Code governs the law of sales, rather than Article 2. *See* LA. CIV. CODE ANN. art. 2439–2659 (2024).

[133] U.C.C. § 2-105.

[134] *See Property*, BLACK'S LAW DICTIONARY (12th ed. 2024).

[135] U.C.C. § 1-103(b) (AM. L. INST. & UNIF. L. COMM'N, 2022) ("Unless displaced by the particular provisions of [the Uniform Commercial Code], the principles of law and equity . . . supplement its provisions.").

largely abandoned the systematic examination of the distinction between choses in action and choses in possession during the latter half of the twentieth century.

Against this backdrop of legal uncertainty, prior to the 2022 UCC Amendments, practitioners and commentators generally concluded that transfers of ownership in digital assets fell outside Article 2's scope, despite the absence of judicial decisions directly addressing this issue and limited scholarly examination. Instead, these transactions were understood to be governed by state law rules applicable to the assignment of intangibles.[136]

We agree that this was the correct interpretation of the pre-2022 legal framework. In our view, whether digital assets are "things in action" or some novel tertium genus does not alter the conclusion that transactions for their transfer fall outside Article 2. If one believes that digital assets are things in action, they are outside the definition of "goods" and thus beyond the confines of Article 2. But even if one espouses the view that digital assets are not things in action but rather encompassed in a novel tertium genus, bringing transactions for their transfer under Article 2 would not be doctrinally sound.

Article 2 is ontologically founded on the premise that the object of sale contracts is corporeal things over which a person can have physical dominion.[137] This is especially noticeable regarding the concepts of "possession" and "delivery" which are cornerstones of this statute and assume that the parties are dealing with tangible things. Even if one redefined the category of things in action to exclude digital assets, this would not have overcome the inherent incompatibility of Article 2 with intangibles. Notably, this was the reasoning that led courts and commentators to repeatedly rebuke calls to bring transactions involving data, digital images, and other intangibles under Article 2.[138]

While the exclusion of digital asset transfers from Article 2 was doctrinally correct, subjecting these transactions to the law governing assignments of intangibles presented three grave problems. First, this body of rules varies considerably across states, being largely dominated by local case law rather than uniform statutory rules.[139] Imposing such legal fragmentation on digital asset

[136] Kate Allass, *Cryptoassets: A Guide on Key Legal Issues*, Farrer & Co (Feb. 12, 2020), https://www.farrer.co.uk/news-and-insights/cryptoassets-a-guide-on-key-legal-issues2/; *What Sort of Property Is a Cryptoasset?*, Norton Rose Fulbright (Feb. 2021), https://www.nortonrosefulbright.com/en/knowledge/publications/26ade77a/what-sort-of-property-is-a-cryptoasset.

[137] According to U.C.C. § 2-105(1), "goods" are defined as "all things (including specially manufactured goods) which are movable at the time of identification to the contract for sale." U.C.C. § 2-105(1).

[138] *See* Michael L. Rustad & Elif Kavusturan, *A Commercial Law for Software Contracting*, 76 Wash. & Lee L. Rev. 775 (2019).

[139] *See* David Frisch, *§ 1-103:69 Assignments*, *in* 1 Lawrence's Anderson on the Uniform Commercial Code § 1-103:69 (3d ed. Dec. 2024 update), Westlaw ANDR-UCC § 1-103:69; *see also* Howard O. Hunter, *§ 19:41 Procedural and Substantive Distinction*, *in* Modern Law of Contracts (Mar. 2025 update), Westlaw MODCON § 21:2.

markets, which are inherently borderless and require velocity in trading, was especially problematic. This lack of uniformity created significant friction in cross-border transactions and impeded the development of standardized trading practices, as market participants had to navigate potentially conflicting rules across different jurisdictions.

Second, state rules for the assignment of intangibles were developed primarily to govern receivables—monetary claims against specific persons. These rules focused on issues of enforceability and defenses between creditors and debtors,[140] making them conceptually ill-suited for digital assets that exist as self-contained data objects rather than claims against identifiable parties. Moreover, states largely ceased developing these rules independently in the 1960s, when the transactions involving most receivables were subsumed under UCC Article 9.[141]

Third, and most problematically, common law rules for intangible assignments across all states shared one crucial feature: the strict application of the *nemo dat* principle without any good faith purchaser exception.[142] This meant that anyone acquiring a digital asset would need to verify the complete chain of title back to its creation, such as a block reward for mining or its original minting. The implications of this rule were severe. Every transaction carried a potential lawsuit—specifically, the risk of being unwound if any defect was discovered in the chain of title, no matter how remote.[143] A purchaser could never be certain of acquiring an asset free from competing claims, even when acting in good faith and paying full value. The only exception was acquiring assets directly from their creator or original recipient. Given the pseudonymous nature of digital asset markets, the high velocity of trading, and the complex web of transactions typical in these markets, such verification was not only practically impossible but fundamentally at odds with the operation of the market. This legal uncertainty posed an existential threat to the development of digital asset markets and severely limited their potential for mainstream adoption.

(b) Collateralizing digital assets

While the commercial circulation of digital assets initially centered on outright transfers, by the mid-2010s, market participants began exploring their potential as collateral in secured lending arrangements. This development accelerated

[140] Cook, *Alienability*, *supra* note 128; Williston, *supra* note 128; Cook, *A Reply*, *supra* note 128.

[141] After two decades of state-by-state statutory "fixes" throughout the 1940s and 1950s aimed at addressing legal uncertainly, these issues were largely resolved with the adoption of Article 9 of the Uniform Commercial Code. Article 9 provides clear rules governing the assignment of accounts and other payment rights: U.C.C. §§ 9-109(a)(3), -309(3), -310(a), -318(a)-(b), -404, -406(d).

[142] Restatement (Fourth) of Property § 1.1 (Am. L. Inst., Tentative Draft No. 5, 2024).

[143] This is often referred to as the problem of "merchantability." *See* 17 Robert S. Hunter, Estate Planning & Administration in Illinois § 48:12 (vol. 17, Ill. Prac. Series, 4th ed. 2007).

rapidly with the rise of centralized exchanges offering margin trading and specialized lending platforms deploying increasingly sophisticated mechanisms to collateralize digital assets. As these secured lending practices became more prevalent and complex, legal scholars recognized the urgency of determining the applicable legal framework.

In the United States, as with transfers of ownership, secured transactions fall within the domain of state law, with UCC Article 9 serving as the primary source of rules across all fifty states. Article 9 applies to "a transaction, regardless of its form, that creates a security interest in personal property or fixtures by contract" with a security interest defined as "an interest in personal property or fixtures which secures payment or performance of an obligation."[144]

Article 9 is not built on traditional common law categories of personal property, such as choses in possession and choses in action. Instead, it establishes its own taxonomy of collateral types, including goods, investment property, instruments, documents, chattel paper, accounts, and deposit accounts.[145] For each of these categories, Article 9 articulates distinct rules governing the creation of security interests (attachment), their effectiveness against third parties (perfection), and their relative ranking when multiple creditors claim interests in the same collateral (priority).[146] On the whole, this statute establishes a functional framework applicable to all secured transactions generally, while also incorporating bespoke rules tailored to the unique characteristics and practices of different collateral types. It balances theoretical elegance with commercial pragmatism.[147]

The Article 9 taxonomy was originally developed in the 1950s and has been periodically amended to accommodate emerging asset classes and commercial practices. Unsurprisingly, prior to the 2022 UCC Amendments, this architecture did not include any classification specifically designed for digital assets. As a result, digital assets fell within the residual category of "general intangibles"—a catch-all designation that has historically served as the default for novel intangible assets, from intellectual property rights to franchise agreements.[148]

[144] U.C.C. § 9-109(a)(1) (Am. L. Inst. & Unif. L. Comm'n, 2022) (scope provision); U.C.C. § 1-201(b)(35) (Am. L. Inst. & Unif. L. Comm'n, 2022) (definition of security interest).

[145] U.C.C. § 9-102(a) (definitions).

[146] U.C.C. § 9-317.

[147] *See* 1–2 Grant Gilmore, Security Interests in Personal Property (1965); Grant Gilmore, *The Secured Transactions Article of the Commercial Code*, 16 Law & Contemp. Probs. 27 (1951).

[148] "General intangible" means any personal property, including things in action, other than accounts, chattel paper, commercial tort claims, deposit accounts, documents, goods, instruments, investment property, letter-of-credit rights, letters of credit, money, and oil, gas, or other minerals before extraction. The term includes payment intangibles and software. *See* Schroeder, *supra* note 121, at 9–15, 19–21 (explaining why digital assets, including Bitcoin, would not fit in the categories of UCC Article 9 "money" and "deposit accounts").

As a result, prior to the 2022 UCC Amendments, the regime for the use of digital assets as collateral could be summarized as follows. For creation (attachment) of a security interest, three requirements had to be met: the secured party had to give value, the debtor needed rights in the collateral, and the parties had to enter into an authenticated security agreement describing the collateral.[149] Regarding perfection, secured parties had only one option: filing a financing statement in the appropriate public registry.[150] Unlike with certain other types of collateral, Article 9 did not provide alternative perfection methods such as possession or control.[151] As for priority, the general rule of "first-to-file-or-perfect" governed competing claims, meaning that the first secured party to either file a financing statement or otherwise perfect their security interest through another available method had priority over subsequent secured parties.[152] Moreover, security interests would automatically attach to digital assets received as proceeds of original collateral and remain perfected.

Thus, prior to the 2022 UCC Amendments, the framework for using digital assets as collateral was both clear and well understood.[153] Market participants could rely on long-standing Article 9 principles for their secured transactions. The system accommodated blanket liens on all present and future digital assets of a debtor, permitted straightforward perfection through filing, and provided clear priority rules based on temporal filing order. This predictability and simplicity, in principle, allowed parties to structure digital asset financing with relative confidence.

Regrettably, this regime was fundamentally misaligned with market realities, commercial practices, and the technology of digital assets. Perfection through filing—the sole method available—was particularly problematic. The slow pace and inherent time lag associated with public registration systems stood in stark contrast to the near-instantaneous execution of digital asset transfers and the frenetic pace of their trading environments. Furthermore, the pseudonymity of distributed ledger technology (DLT) networks severely impaired both the identification of appropriate filing jurisdictions and the search for existing liens. Even more telling was the emergence of an arrangement that ignored the Article 9 framework entirely. In these transactions, debtors would transfer their digital assets directly to lenders as security for loans, with the mutual understanding that the assets would be returned upon repayment. Typically consummated with minimal documentation and no public filings, these dealings reflected secured parties' preference for taking control of digital asset collateral, rather than relying

[149] U.C.C. § 9-203(b)(1)-(3)(A).
[150] U.C.C. § 9-310(a).
[151] *See* U.C.C. § 9-312(b).
[152] U.C.C. § 9-322(a)(1).
[153] Odinet, *BitProperty*, *supra* note 67.

on registries. By the early 2020s, both scholars and practitioners had come to the view that the status quo was unsustainable.[154]

2.5.2 After the 2022 UCC Amendments

By 2018, it was increasingly apparent that the UCC faced challenges in accommodating DLT and digital assets. As discussed in Chapter 1, in response to these challenges, the Uniform Law Commission (ULC) and the American Law Institute (ALI) established a joint committee to explore possible amendments to address legal uncertainties.[155] The committee consulted broadly with stakeholders, legal practitioners, and scholars and concluded that substantial revisions to the existing private law framework were required to address legal uncertainty and the disconnect with emerging commercial practices.[156]

Between 2020 and 2022, proposed revisions to the UCC underwent multiple rounds of drafting and extensive public review. This iterative and collaborative process incorporated suggestions and criticisms from a diverse coalition of industry participants, academics, lawyers, and members of the judiciary.[157]

The ALI approved the resulting 2022 Amendments in May 2022, with the ULC following suit two months later. Implementation efforts began promptly, with legislative bills introduced across multiple states. Despite encountering initial resistance, primarily stemming from misconceptions about whether the amendments paved the way for a federal central bank digital currency, these concerns have largely dissipated.[158] The 2022 Amendments have since gained significant momentum and are steadily progressing toward nationwide adoption.[159]

[154] *See* Schroeder, *supra* note 121, at 67; Ronald J. Mann, *Reliable Perfection of Security Interests in Crypto-Currency*, 21 SMU Sci. & Tech. L. Rev. 159, 172–73 (2018); Xuan-Thao Nguyen, *Lessons from Case Study of Secured Transactions with Bitcoin*, 21 SMU Sci. & Tech. L. Rev. 181, 182–83 (2018); James P. Nehf, Security Interests in Virtual Currencies (Mar. 2, 2020), https://ssrn.com/abstract=3547540; TriBar Opinion Comm., *TriBar Report on Opinions Under 2022 Amendments to the Uniform Commercial Code Regarding Emerging Technologies*, 79 Bus. Law. 407 (2024), https://www.americanbar.org/groups/business_law/resources/business-lawyer/2024-spring/tribar-report-on-opinions-under-2022-amendments/.

[155] Unif. L. Comm'n, Uniform Commercial Code and Emerging Technologies 2 (Draft for Approval, June 27, 2022), https://perma.cc/WT5D-YL2F.

[156] *See id.* at 250.

[157] *See id.* at 1–3 (noting that members of the Drafting Committee solicited advice from the Loan Syndication and Trading Association, the ABA Business Law Section, the American College of Commercial Finance Lawyers, and more).

[158] *See* Carla L. Reyes & Andrea Tosato, *Crypto's Future Is at Stake in a Dispute over Commercial Law's Definition of Money*, Barron's (Apr. 7, 2023, 4:00 AM). https://www.barrons.com/articles/crypto-commercial-laws-definition-of-money-5fbd8fe4.

[159] As of October 2025, the 2022 Amendments have been enacted in thirty-two states and introduced in six more. *See UCC, 2022 Amendments to*, Unif. L. Comm'n, https://perma.cc/S5XN-NWEH (last visited October 8, 2025).

(a) A new category: controllable electronic records

At the heart of the 2022 Amendments lies the novel Article 12. This significant expansion of the UCC establishes a bespoke private law framework for transactions involving "controllable electronic records" (CERs). CERs are a new category of personal property, distinctly grounded in American functional pragmatism and without a parallel in traditional common law taxonomies.

CERs are defined as a "record stored in an electronic medium that can be subjected to control."[160] This definition consists of three essential components, structured like a classical archway where each element serves a critical function. The first component, "record," is the foundation stone, meaning information that is both stored in a medium and "retrievable in perceivable form."[161] It establishes the most basic requirement that the information at issue must exist in a non-transient state and be understandable.

The second component, "electronic," forms the two supporting columns by encompassing any "technology having electrical, digital, magnetic, wireless, optical, electromagnetic, or similar capabilities."[162] Notably, with these two components alone, the definition of CER would be vast, encompassing virtually all digital content stored on any electronic medium, such as magnetic drives, optical discs, and flash storage.

It is the third component, "control," that completes the structure and serves as its arch.[163] It delimits this category and gives it both its distinctive shape and character. The concept of control requires that a person possesses three specific powers over the electronic record, creating a carefully calibrated test that determines which assets qualify for the special treatment afforded by Article 12.

First, a person must hold the power to "avail [themselves] of substantially all the benefit from the electronic record."[164] The concept of "benefit" is deliberately crafted to be functional and technology-agnostic, encompassing both "the rights that are afforded by the controllable electronic record and [its] uses."[165] Assessing whether someone holds this power necessitates examining the specific characteristics of the electronic record in question. For Bitcoin, the benefit consists of holding and transferring the digital asset;[166] for Ether, it would also

160 U.C.C. § 12-102(a)(1) (Am. L. Inst. & Unif. L. Comm'n 2022).
161 U.C.C. § 1-201(b)(31) (Am. L. Inst. & Unif. L. Comm'n, 2022).
162 U.C.C. § 1-201(b)(16A) (Am. L. Inst. & Unif. L. Comm'n, 2022).
163 It should be noted that the UCC uses the word "control" differently across its Articles. For example, see U.C.C. §§ 9-104 to 9-107A (Am. L. Inst. & Unif. L. Comm'n, 2022) (establishing different types of control for various collateral types) *see also* U.C.C. § 7-106 (Am. L. Inst. & Unif. L. Comm'n, 2022) (defining control of an electronic document of title).
164 U.C.C. § 12-105(a)(1)(A).
165 U.C.C. § 12-105 cmt. 3.
166 *See* Satoshi Nakamoto, *Bitcoin: A Peer-to-Peer Electronic Cash System*, Bitcoin.org https://bitcoin.org/bitcoin.pdf.

include the ability to pay the fees necessary to execute smart contracts on the Ethereum network.[167]

The second power involves the ability to "prevent others from availing themselves of substantially all the benefit from the electronic record."[168] The person must have, materially, the capability to exclude all others from using the electronic record and any of the rights it might convey. Critically, this represents a factual determination rather than an assessment of legal entitlements. A clear example is provided by an NFT on the Ethereum network: only the individual with the private key to the wallet where the NFT resides holds the power of exclusion, even if another person might legally "own" the digital asset or otherwise have a superior legal title.[169]

Importantly, this exclusivity is nuanced and sophisticated. Section 12-105(b) expressly qualifies this requirement to accommodate modern technological architectures. A power can remain "exclusive" even when system-level protocols might modify the digital asset, or when the power is shared with another person.[170] This flexible approach enables control even when a digital asset is held through multisignature arrangements, as well as in systems with programmatic limitations or governance mechanisms. The drafters recognized that rigid conceptions of exclusivity would be impractical in decentralized systems, where some degree of protocol-level control is inherent.[171]

The third power encompasses the ability to transfer both of the previous powers to another person and to ensure that the recipient can further transfer these powers to others.[172] This transferability requirement is essential to the commercial utility of controllable electronic records, as it enables the continued circulation of these assets in commerce. Specifically, a person must be able to confer upon another the capacity to enjoy substantially all benefits of the electronic record, maintain exclusivity over those benefits, and retransfer these powers to someone else.

Thus, CERs are a distinct personal property category that exemplifies the shift of American personal property law toward functional pragmatism over theoretical formalism. Taking leave from traditional classifications, Article 12 drafters consciously built CERs around the notion of control. In doing so, they emphasized a key characteristic of these novel assets: their ability to be used and enjoyed without relying on intermediaries. This functional distinction becomes

[167] For an explanation of the fees associated with the execution of smart contracts on the Ethereum network, see *Gas and Fees*, ETHEREUM.ORG, https://ethereum.org/en/developers/docs/gas/ [https://perma.cc/L7LK-GBRP] (last edited Feb. 25, 2025).

[168] U.C.C. § 12-105 (a)(1)(B)(i).

[169] Juliet M. Moringiello & Christopher K. Odinet, *Blockchain Real Estate and NFTs*, 64 WM. & MARY L. REV. 1131, 1150–62 (2023).

[170] U.C.C. § 12-105(b).

[171] *See* U.C.C. § 12-105 cmt. 5.

[172] U.C.C. 12-105(a)(1)(B)(ii).

clear when comparing Bitcoin, which users can spend directly, to other digital assets, such as Gmail accounts and Instagram photos, which can only be accessed through their respective platforms. While in practice many users opt to interact with digital assets through centralized exchanges, such as Coinbase and Binance, for convenience and security, Article 12 recognizes the underlying direct control capability that distinguishes these assets from data objects held with the likes of social media platforms.

Doctrinally, the UCC sacrifices the elegance of broad abstract categories, such as choses in action and choses in possession, in favor of a more atomized taxonomy. Yet, it gains nuance in squarely addressing the unique features of emerging digital assets. Notably, the 2022 UCC Amendments have a historical echo. In the 1950s, UCC Article 9 marked an American deviation from how other common law jurisdictions governed secured transactions by introducing an array of collateral types and adopting a functional approach. Article 12 repeats this choice, forging a new personal property category—one that is based on operational characteristics rather than doctrinal purity. This approach, as we shall see in the following subsections, enables a regime that aligns with commercial practices and market expectations.

(b) Transfer of controllable electronic records

The 2022 Amendments unquestionably accept that CERs are objects of commerce. The new provisions do not articulate a comprehensive body of rules for these transactions such as those in Article 2 for the sale of goods. Rather, they refer to other law, as the case may be, depending on the transaction in question.[173] Nevertheless, Article 12 establishes two "key tenets"[174] that apply across all voluntary transactions—whether sale, lease, security interest, gift, or "any other voluntary transaction creating an interest in property."[175]

The first tenet is that "[a] purchaser of a [CER] acquires all rights . . . the transferor had or had power to transfer."[176] This rule constitutes one of the foundational pillars of the conveyancing framework of the UCC.[177] At its core, it

[173] *See, e.g.*, U.C.C. § 12-104(d) ("Except as provided in this section, law other than this article determines whether a person acquires a right in a controllable electronic record and the right the person acquires."); U.C.C. § 12-104(f).

[174] Giuliano G. Castellano & Andrea Tosato, *Commercial Law Intersections*, 72 HASTINGS L.J. 999, 1042 (2021) (defining key tenets as "the dispositive rules and principles that articulate the legal framework necessary to realize the policy aims of a commercial law branch").

[175] U.C.C. § 1-201(b)(29) (AM. L. INST. & UNIF. L. COMM'N, 2022).

[176] U.C.C. § 12-104(d).

[177] *See, e.g.*, U.C.C. § 2-403(1) (AM. L. INST. & UNIF. L. COMM'N, 2022) (for transfers of goods); U.C.C. § 3-203(b) (AM. L. INST. & UNIF. L. COMM'N, 2022) (for negotiable instrument transfers); U.C.C. § 7-504(a) (AM. L. INST. & UNIF. L. COMM'N, 2022) (for transfers of documents of title); U.C.C. § 8-302(a) (AM. L. INST. & UNIF. L. COMM'N, 2022) (for transfers of securities). This rule is often referred to as "the security of property" principle. *See* See Thomas E. Plank, *Article 9 of the UCC: Reconciling Fundamental Property Principles and Plain Language*, 68 BUS. LAW. 439, 439–42, 442 n.6 & 449 (tracing the origins of this rule back to Roman law and its trajectory into the UCC).

embodies the idea that property owners should be free to transfer their rights to others without limitations. A direct consequence of this rule, known as the "shelter" principle, is that a transferor with clear title can pass it to a transferee, shielding them from competing claims.[178] Coextensively, transferees cannot receive rights exceeding those of their transferor—a modern incarnation of the *nemo dat* maxim.[179]

Unlike the first tenet, the second emerges from the coalescence of multiple Article 12 provisions. It introduces a "take-free" exception that significantly moderates the rigidity of the security-of-property principle outlined above.[180] The rule centers on the concept of a "qualifying purchaser" defined as a person who "obtains control of [a CER] for value, in good faith, and without notice of [conflicting claims]."[181] Qualifying purchasers acquire their rights in the CER free from third-party property claims and are shielded from any actions challenging their rights, "whether . . . framed in conversion, replevin, constructive trust, equitable lien, or other theory."[182] This take-free exception follows the familiar pattern of good faith purchaser rules that appear throughout commercial law and has the effect of rendering CERs negotiable assets, similar to checks, promissory notes, and investment securities. Consider this example: When a thief misappropriates a CER and transfers control to a person who qualifies as a qualifying purchaser, that person takes free of the original owner's claim. Even if the owner locates and identifies the qualifying purchaser, they cannot recover the CER and are left only with a damages claim against the thief—the same result as when a holder in due course acquires a stolen negotiable instrument.

Thus, the combined effect of these two tenets is to create a regime for ownership transfers of CERs that reduces title inquiry burdens, facilitates transactional certainty, and minimizes ownership disputes through its embrace of negotiability. This framework exemplifies the pragmatic orientation of American property law, particularly as embodied in the UCC—prioritizing rules that align with actual market practices rather than preserving doctrinal classifications. Indeed, this market-aligned approach directly responds to what industry stakeholders advocated for during the drafting of the 2022 Amendments.

[178] This is often referred to as the "shelter" principle. *See* U.C.C. § 12-104 cmt. 4 ("Subsection (d) sets forth the familiar 'shelter' principle, under which a purchaser of a controllable electronic record acquires whatever rights the transferor had or had power to transfer."); Menachem Mautner, *"The Eternal Triangles of the Law": Toward a Theory of Priorities in Conflicts Involving Remote Parties*, 90 Mich. L. Rev. 95, 97–99 (1991). *See generally* Steven L. Harris, *Using Fundamental Principles of Commercial Law to Decide UCC Cases*, 26 Loy. L.A. L. Rev. 637 (1993).

[179] Restatement (Fourth) of Property § 1.1 (Am. L. Inst., Tentative Draft No. 5, 2024).

[180] U.C.C. § 12-104 cmt. 7.

[181] U.C.C. § 12-102(a)(2).

[182] U.C.C. § 12-104(g).

(c) Collateralizing controllable electronic records

The 2022 Amendments also introduce a special regime for the use of CERs as collateral in secured transactions. The overarching approach is to classify these digital assets as "general intangibles" under UCC Article 9,[183] thereby subjecting them to the general framework applicable to this class of collateral, while at the same time also establishing asset-specific rules tailored to their unique characteristics. The key policy choice of the 2022 Amendments is that control of a CER is accorded similar legal significance and effects as the possession of a tangible good.

The 2022 Amendments introduce specialized rules for CERs across all three fundamental aspects of secured transactions: attachment, perfection, and priority. For attachment, the new regime provides two distinct pathways to create an enforceable security interest in a CER. The first retains the preexisting rule whereby a creditor and debtor enter into a signed security agreement containing an adequate description of the CER collateral. The second pathway represents a significant innovation: While still requiring an agreement between the parties, it eliminates the need for that agreement to be signed when the secured party has acquired control of the CER. In effect, control itself is deemed sufficient evidence of the parties' intentions regarding the specific CERs to be encumbered, providing certainty both for the immediate parties and any third parties with potential interests in the collateral.

The 2022 Amendments also establish a distinctive perfection regime for security interests in CERs. Under the new rules, perfection—the process whereby a security interest becomes effective against third parties—can be achieved through traditional methods or through a new pathway. As with all types of collateral under Article 9, secured parties retain the option to perfect by filing a financing statement in the appropriate public registry. However, the amendments create a powerful alternative: Secured parties can now perfect their interest by taking control of the CER, either directly or through another person on their behalf.

Crucially, control-based perfection has substantial advantages. Not only is it faster and more streamlined than filing, but it also eliminates the jurisdictional complexities associated with determining the correct filing location based on the debtor's physical presence—a particularly thorny issue in the context of digital assets. Moreover, secured parties taking CERs as collateral have a compelling reason to use control-based perfection: Provided they acquire control for value, in good faith, and without notice of competing claims, they can achieve qualifying purchaser status and thereby obtain their security interest free from any prior property rights in the CER that might otherwise have priority.[184]

183 *See* U.C.C. § 9-102(a)(42) (Am. L. Inst. & Unif. L. Comm'n, 2022).

184 *See* U.C.C. §§ 12-102(2), -104. It should also be noted that, for a secured party, failure to perfect by control poses a significant danger. The debtor could transfer control of the encumbered CER to a

The highly consequential nature of perfection by control becomes even more evident when analyzing the priority regime introduced by the 2022 Amendments for security interests in CERs. Under the new 9-326(A), a secured creditor who perfects by control "has priority over [] conflicting security interest[s] held by a secured party that does not have control."[185] This provision establishes a nontemporal priority rule, creating an exception to the general first-to-file-or-perfect hierarchy mandated by Article 9. As a result, if Lender A perfects a security interest in a CER by filing a financing statement, and Lender B later perfects a security interest in that same CER by obtaining control, Lender B has priority—despite Lender A's earlier perfection.

Thus, the rules introduced by the 2022 Amendments for the use of CERs as collateral exemplify the same pragmatism that characterizes the new regime for ownership transfers. They build on the adaptable architecture of Article 9 by introducing a new class of collateral and designing asset-specific rules tailored to commercial realities. Significantly, the amendments leverage the concept of "control"—the defining characteristic of CERs themselves—as the organizing principle. By elevating control to a determinative role in attachment, perfection, and priority, the amendments create a cohesive system that recognizes the distinctive features of digital assets while maintaining doctrinal consistency with the preexisting structure of Article 9.

qualifying purchaser that would then take the asset entirely free from competing claims, including any security interest despite prior perfection by filing.

185 *Id.*

3

Digital assets and tokenization

3.1 Introduction

Chapter 1 explored the legal nature of digital assets and their commercial circulation. It examined how these novel technological constructs fit within property law and the legal regime governing their transfer and use as collateral. With this foundation established, Chapter 3 now turns to one of the most fascinating and controversial applications of digital asset technology: *tokenization.*[1]

The market for digital assets extends beyond transactions driven by their intrinsic value—that is, beyond trading and securing loans based on what market participants believe these digital assets themselves are worth. A significant segment of the distributed ledger technology (DLT) ecosystem involves digital assets, the value of which stems not from their inherent characteristics but from their purported ability to represent the ownership of other assets—both tangible and intangible. Indeed, enthusiasts of this concept—commonly referred to as "tokenization"—argue that it holds the most transformative potential for society.[2]

In their view, digital assets should be deployed to serve as digital embodiments for virtually anything: real estate, paintings, watches, digital art, corporate shares, payment rights, and beyond.[3] Proponents posit that tokenization will revolutionize ownership tracking through blockchain transparency, dramatically reduce transaction costs, and democratize markets by enabling fractional ownership and instant settlement. They proffer that this increased accessibility

[1] Various portions of this chapter are drawn, in whole or in part, from Juliet M. Moringiello & Christopher K. Odinet, *The Property Law of Tokens*, 74 Fla. L. Rev. 607 (2022), and Andrea Tosato, Diane Lourdes Dick & Christopher K. Odinet, *Debt Tokens*, 173 U. Pa. L. Rev. 1103 (2025). Any reproductions are made with the express permission of the authors.

[2] World Econ. F., Digital Assets, Distributed Ledger Technology and the Future of Capital Markets (2021), https://www3.weforum.org/docs/WEF_Digital_ Assets_Distributed_ Ledger_Technology_2021.pdf; Hugo Benedetti & Gabriel Rodríguez-Garnica, *Tokenized Assets and Securities, in* The Emerald Handbook on Cryptoassets: Investment Opportunities and Challenges 107 (H. Kent Baker, Hugo Benedetti, Ehsan Nikbakht & Sean Stein Smith eds., 2023).

[3] Richard Acello, *Big Money: Nonfungible Tokens Are All the Rage Now. What Are They, and What Should Buyers Watch For?*, A.B.A. J., Oct./Nov. 2021, at 25; Joshua A.T. Fairfield, *Tokenized: The Law of Non-Fungible Tokens and Unique Digital Property*, 97 Ind. L.J. 1261 (2022); Steven L. Schwarcz, *Next-Generation Securitization: NFTS, Tokenization, and the Monetization of "Things,"* 103 B.U. L. Rev. 967 (2023).

Digital Commercial Law. Christopher K. Odinet and Andrea Tosato, Oxford University Press.
 DOI: 10.1093/9780197758656.003.0004

and efficiency will unlock unprecedented market liquidity for previously illiquid assets. Eric Posner and Glen Weyl, in their work *Radical Markets*, envision tokenization as a cornerstone of economic reorganization, proposing that it could enable continuous auctions of all assets to achieve more efficient resource allocation.[4]

Tokenization cannot be understood without a brief overview of the evolution of non-fungible tokens (NFTs).[5] Initially, NFTs were conceived as a technological proof of concept to demonstrate that unique digital tokens could be created and tracked on blockchain networks. Yet, this innovation rapidly evolved into a transformative force. The introduction of NFT standards on the Ethereum blockchain, particularly ERC-721 and ERC-1155, markedly streamlined the process of minting unique, identifiable digital assets, fostering broader adoption and innovation in the space.[6] Launched in 2017, CryptoKitties marked the first glimpse of the mass-market potential of NFTs, allowing users to collect, breed, and trade unique digital cats.[7] This seemingly whimsical application proved groundbreaking, demonstrating how blockchain technology could create verifiable digital scarcity.

The success of these early experiments sparked a broader vision: If NFTs could tokenize digital cats, why not other assets? This conceptual leap laid the groundwork for applying NFT technology to represent ownership rights in both digital and physical assets. The market's response was explosive. By August 2021, monthly NFT trading volume reached an unprecedented $2.8 billion.[8] The art world embraced the technology with particular enthusiasm, culminating in March 2021, when digital artist Beeple sold his work "Everydays: The First 5000 Days" at Christie's for $69 million—a dramatic leap from the $100 maximum he had previously commanded for prints just one year earlier.[9]

Two distinct models of NFT creation and distribution emerged.[10] The first, exemplified by major corporate issuers such as Yuga Labs (Bored Apes) and

[4] Eric A. Posner & E. Glen Weyl, Radical Markets: Uprooting Capitalism and Democracy for a Just Society 61 (2018).

[5] *See* Fairfield, *supra* note 3; Schwarcz, *supra* note 3; Brian L. Frye, A Brief History of NFTs 1–2 (Sept. 19, 2023), https://ssrn.com/abstract=4577014.

[6] William Entriken, Dieter Shirley, Jacob Evans & Nastassia Sachs, *EIP-721: Non-Fungible Token Standard*, *in* Ethereum Improvement Proposals (Jan. 24, 2018), https://eips.ethereum.org/EIPS/eip-721; *see also* Witek Radomski, Andrew Cooke, Philippe Castonguay, James Therien, Eric Binet & Ronan Sandford, *EIP-1155: Multi Token Standard*, *in* Ethereum Improvement Proposals (June 17, 2018), https://eips.ethereum.org/EIPS/eip-1155.

[7] *Technical Details*, CryptoKitties, https://www.cryptokitties.co/technical-details (last visited Apr. 16, 2015).

[8] *Dead NFTs: The Evolving Landscape of the NFT Market*, dappGambl, https://dappgambl.com/nfts/dead-nfts/ (last visited Jan. 4, 2025).

[9] *See* Jacob Kastrenakes, *Beeple Sold an NFT for $69 Million*, The Verge (Mar. 11, 2021), https://www.theverge.com/2021/3/11/22325054/beeple-christies-nft-sale-cost-everydays-69-million.

[10] Christopher K. Odinet & Andrea Tosato, *The Intersection of NFTs and Structured Finance*, 103 B.U. L. Rev. 1005, 1018 (2023).

Dapper Labs (Top Shot), as well as prominent artists such as Pak and Beeple, adopted a disintermediated approach. These issuers either used major public networks, such as Ethereum, or developed their own blockchain infrastructure, such as Dapper Labs' Flow network. They retained direct control over the minting process by hosting associated digital content on internet-connected servers and linking tokens to creative works through hyperlinks or similar mechanisms. Some issuers, like Yuga Labs, enhanced their offerings with additional rights, such as worldwide licenses to exploit the associated images.[11]

Parallel to these high-profile projects, a more accessible model emerged through platforms like OpenSea, Rarible, and Mintable, which opened the floodgates for NFT creation.[12] These platforms offered user-friendly interfaces that enabled individuals to mint NFTs through a straightforward process: create an account, connect a digital wallet, upload content to be linked or represented by the token, and select monetization options. The platforms handled the technical complexities, executing the necessary smart contracts on various blockchain networks and publicizing the resulting NFT on newly created web pages.

The NFT market's meteoric rise was followed by an equally dramatic fall. By the end of 2022, trading volumes had plummeted by over 97 percent from their peak, with many once-valuable collections becoming virtually worthless.[13] This collapse prompted increased scrutiny from multiple directions. The Securities and Exchange Commission began investigating whether certain NFT offerings constituted unregistered securities,[14] while private litigants initiated class actions against NFT issuers following catastrophic price declines.[15] However, a more fundamental critique emerged from legal scholars who raised alarming questions about the basic premise of tokenization. These academics cogently argued that NFTs almost invariably failed to confer the rights their issuers claimed they represented, exposing a yawning chasm between marketing hype and legal reality.[16]

And yet, like a phoenix rising from the ashes of the 2022 crypto winter, the NFT market resurrected in 2024. Novel implementations like Ordinals and Runes have brought NFT-like functionality to the Bitcoin network, sparking newfound

[11] *See* Frye, *supra* note 5, at 15.

[12] Odinet & Tosato, *supra* note 10, at 1018.

[13] Sidhartha Shukla, *NFT Trading Volume Down 97% From January 2022 Peak*, Bloomberg Mkts.: Cryptocurrencies (Sept. 28, 2022), https://www.bloomberg.com/news/articles/2022-09-28/nft-volumes-tumble-97-from-2022-highs-as-frenzy-fades-chart?embedded-checkout=true.

[14] See, for example, Press Release, SEC, SEC Charges LA-Based Media and Entertainment Co. Impact Theory for Unregistered Offering of NFTs (Aug. 28, 2023), https://www.sec.gov/newsroom/press-releases/2023-163.

[15] *See* Friel v. Dapper Labs, Inc., No. 21-cv-05837 (S.D.N.Y. Oct. 8, 2021).

[16] *See* Moringiello & Odinet, *supra* note 1, at 632–47; Odinet & Tosato, *supra* note 10, at 1540–45; R. Wilson Freyermuth, Christopher Odinet & Andrea Tosato, *Crypto in Real Estate Finance*, 75 Ala. L. Rev. 93 (2023); Fairfield, *supra* note 3; Edmund Schuster, *Cloud Crypto Land*, 84 Mod. L. Rev. 974 (2021).

interest and investment.[17] Simultaneously, projects to tokenize traditional assets have resurfaced with renewed impetus, with particular emphasis on real estate, securities, and receivables.[18] Nevertheless, even as the technology evolves and new use cases emerge, the fundamental private law questions that plagued earlier iterations of NFTs remain largely unexamined. Key issues include the absence of a solid legal foundation for many tokenization schemes, ambiguity regarding the property rights associated with the resulting NFTs, and uncertainty regarding the transferability and enforceability of the rights and obligations purportedly associated with them. The disconnect between the promises of tokenization on the one hand and the law on the other continues to be underestimated and understudied, even as the stakes grow higher with each new application.

3.2 Traditional tokenization in law

For all the revolutionary rhetoric surrounding digital asset tokenization, the core concept of using one thing to represent rights in another is far from novel in commercial law. Long before the digital age, legal frameworks emerged allowing inanimate objects (typically a piece of paper) to embody intangible rights, such as claims of ownership and rights to payment.[19] These storied legal devices (which we will refer to as "traditional tokenizations") include negotiable instruments, which enable payment obligations to be represented on a piece of paper and assigned through endorsement and delivery; shares, which represent ownership interests in business entities; deeds, which grant property rights in land; and bills of lading and warehouse receipts, which confer property rights in shipped and stored goods, respectively.

In all these traditional tokenization, the law has carefully crafted rules for how physical pieces of paper can represent rights or assets. Each has developed a sophisticated framework balancing the interests of multiple stakeholders—issuers, holders, and third parties—while addressing broader market dynamics. These legal regimes typically establish mandatory rules that serve crucial functions: providing certainty to parties regarding their rights and obligations,

[17] Danny Yang, *The Rise of Ordinals and NFTs on the Medium of Bitcoin*, Bitcoin Mag. (Nov. 30, 2023), https://bitcoinmagazine.com/technical/the-rise-of-ordinals-and-nfts-on-the-medium-of-bitcoin.

[18] *See, e.g.*, *Crypto Has Designs on Real Estate*, Fin. Times, https://www.ft.com/content/cf036ebf-6f4e-474f-a1ef-ca7179b712b0.

[19] Moringiello & Odinet, *supra* note 1, at 615–27; *see also* Frederick Read, *The Origin, Early History, and Later Development of Bills of Exchange and Certain Other Negotiable Instruments*, 4 Canadian Bar Rev. 440, 440 (1926); W. S. Holdsworth, *Origins and Early History of Negotiable Instruments I*, 31 Law Q. Rev. 12 (1915) [hereinafter Holdsworth, *Negotiable Instruments I*]; W. S. Holdsworth, *Origins and Early History of Negotiable Instruments II*, 31 Law Q. Rev. 173 (1915) [hereinafter Holdsworth, *Negotiable Instruments II*].

standardizing the rights these instruments convey, and providing public notice to third parties who might be affected by these tokenized rights.[20] The success of traditional tokenization thus rests not on the physical token itself, but on carefully constructed legal architectures that provide certainty, minimize information asymmetries, and align incentives among market participants.

While blockchain technology offers significant advantages over paper-based systems, including automated execution, rapid settlement, and tamper-resistant record-keeping,[21] the fundamental concept of tokenization and its legal challenges remain unchanged. Many proponents of digital tokenization, dazzled by the capabilities of distributed ledger networks, mistakenly assume that these technical advantages automatically resolve the complex private law questions that arise whenever one thing is purported to represent rights in another.[22] These questions persist regardless of whether the token is paper or digital or whether transactions occur in person or through decentralized networks.

A proper evaluation of contemporary tokenization efforts involving digital assets requires an understanding of how private law has historically addressed these fundamental challenges. To this end, we examine five traditional tokenizations that have had a profound social, legal, and economic impact: negotiable instruments, securities, deeds, bills of lading, and warehouse receipts. This analysis not only illuminates key tenets underlying all forms of tokenization but also highlights the careful legal engineering required for their effective operation.

3.2.1 Negotiable instruments as tokens

Negotiable instruments are the oldest and perhaps most pervasive form of tokenization.[23] These instruments achieve a remarkable feat: They transform an intangible payment right into a tangible object that can be physically transferred from one party to another—a transformation that fuses the right with the paper

[20] *See* Read, *supra* note 19; Holdsworth, *Negotiable Instruments I*, *supra* note 19; Holdsworth, *Negotiable Instruments II*, *supra* note 19; Martin J. Aronstein, *The Decline and Fall of the Stock Certificate in America*, 1 J. Comp. Corp. L. & Sec. Reg. 273 (1978).

[21] *Benefits of Blockchain*, IBM, https://www.ibm.com/topics/benefits-of-blockchain (last visited Jan. 4, 2025).

[22] *See Tokenization: Opening Illiquid Assets to Investors*, BNY Mellon: Insights (June 2019), https://perma.cc/2H5M-EQEN; Katy Burne, *Tokens of Appreciation?: The Benefits of Digitizing Assets Using Blockchain*, BNY Mellon: Aerial View Mag. (Feb. 2020), https://perma.cc/6N7M-BXL7; Patrick Laurent, Thibault Chollett, Michael Burke & Tobias Seers, *The Tokenization of Assets Is Disrupting the Financial Industry. Are You Ready?*, Deloitte: Inside Mag., Oct. 2018, at 62, https://perma.cc/D37Q-PT4R.

[23] A. H. Pruessner, *The Earliest Traces of Negotiable Instruments*, 44 Am. J. Semitic Languages & Literatures 88 (1928); Edward Jenks, *On the Early History of Negotiable Instruments*, 9 Law Q. Rev. 70, 73–74 (1893); Holdsworth, *Negotiable Instruments II*, *supra* note 19, at 173; Read, *supra* note 19, at 440; Amasa M. Eaton, *The Negotiable Instruments Law: Its History and Its Practical Operation*, 2 Mich. L. Rev. 260 (1903).

itself, unlike an ordinary contract, which merely documents an agreement that exists independently of the writing.[24] At their core, negotiable instruments are written documents that embody a monetary claim in such a way that the physical possession of the document itself becomes essential to exercising the underlying right (this concept is commonly referred to as the "doctrine of merger"). These instruments create self-contained, readily assignable assets in the form of marked paper.[25]

Through this legal architecture, the holder of a negotiable instrument gains direct enforcement rights against the debtor, while the debtor is assured that payment to the holder will discharge the underlying obligation. Prospective purchasers and transferees, meanwhile, can rely on possession as presumptive evidence of entitlement, enabling these instruments to circulate freely as liquid payment devices. In the United States, Article 3 of the Uniform Commercial Code (UCC) governs negotiable instruments, establishing mandatory rules for their form, transfer, and enforcement. This framework reifies payment rights in paper and allows commercial parties to create liquidity through simple methods of delivery and possession.[26]

As is the case with all tokenized property, the reification of intangible debts in the form of paper documents satisfied a concrete commercial need.[27] Indeed, the idea of using a tangible medium of little worth to represent and transfer monetary value dates to ancient times. Importantly, this representation solved a practical problem. The fundamental problem began with metallic coins: Their weight and physical presence made them dangerous and impractical to transport in large quantities. This led to the adoption of lighter alternatives, such as skins, leather, silks, and other portable goods, serving as primitive substitutes for currency. However, these textile-based payment devices introduced their own complications: Their value fluctuated arbitrarily across locations, their physical bulk still posed transportation challenges, and their availability was constrained by seasonal hunting and harvest cycles. Most problematically, textile exchange depended on intangible social constructs, rather than inherent characteristics, to confer value. These drawbacks called for transitioning to new mediums of exchange that would offer durability, portability, supply integrity, counterfeit resistance, and, most importantly, stable, standard valuations.

The search for a more reliable medium of exchange intensified in medieval Europe, particularly as cross-border trade expanded. In the fourteenth century,

[24] Grant Gilmore, *Formalism and the Law of Negotiable Instruments*, 13 Creighton L. Rev. 441, 443–44 (1979) [hereinafter Gilmore, *Formalism*].

[25] *Id.* at 449–50; *see also* Grant Gilmore, *The Commercial Doctrine of Good Faith Purchase*, 63 Yale L.J. 1057 (1954).

[26] William E. Britton, *Transfers and Negotiations Under the Negotiable Instruments Law and Article 3 of the Uniform Commercial Code*, 32 Tex. L. Rev. 153, 155 (1953).

[27] Read, *supra* note 19, at 440; Holdsworth, *Negotiable Instruments I*, *supra* note 19, at 13, 29.

merchants developed the bill of exchange (the precursor to today's check), a letter addressed from one party to another directing the addressee to pay a third person a sum of money.[28] This innovation responded not only to the general challenges of transporting value, but also to a specific legal obstacle: Many countries, including England, had begun restricting the export of their currency to combat counterfeiting.[29]

The bill of exchange proved revolutionary precisely because it solved both problems simultaneously. As a lightweight paper document, it eliminated the practical difficulties of transporting heavy coins or delicate textiles. Moreover, it circumvented currency export restrictions by allowing merchants to transfer value across borders without physically moving money: The paper instrument itself could travel while the underlying currency remained within its jurisdiction of origin.[30]

Ultimately, the Industrial Revolution served as the catalyst for developing the negotiable instrument principles that remain in effect today.[31] The money supply at the time was insufficient to allow for cash payments in the growing number of commercial transactions spawned by industrialization. As a result, commercial parties invented their own substitute for paper currency based on the bill of exchange. This money substitute was in the form of a draft (an order) in which the seller would order a buyer to pay a specified sum of money to a third person. This paper, which could pass from hand to hand to pay such debts, therefore supplemented the inadequate money supply.[32]

The large-scale problem that had to be solved to make these instruments valuable as money substitutes was *assignability*.[33] Ancient systems of law did not allow one person to assign rights against a debtor to another person. Because these creditor rights (*choses in action*) were not assignable at common law, early English negotiable instruments law developed methods of transfer to ensure that the person presenting the instrument for payment had the legal right to be paid.

To serve as a substitute for currency, the paper had to satisfy certain requirements that now form the basis of negotiable instrument law. When passed from person to person in a worldwide market, these instruments ended up in the possession of a person who had no knowledge of the transaction that created them.[34] Remote recipients of these documents needed confidence that

[28] Holdsworth, *Negotiable Instruments II*, *supra* note 19, at 173.

[29] Read, *supra* note 19, at 447.

[30] Holdsworth, *Negotiable Instruments I*, *supra* note 19, at 29.

[31] *See* Gilmore, *Formalism*, *supra* note 24, at 447.

[32] *See* Frederick H. Miller & Alvin C. Harrell, The Law of Modern Payment Systems ¶ 2.01[1] (2d ed. 2017).

[33] Alexander M. Burrill, A Treatise on the Law and Practice of Voluntary Assignments for the Benefit of Creditors § 1, at 1 (James L. Bishop & James Avery Webb eds., 6th ed. 1894); Holdsworth, *Negotiable Instruments I*, *supra* note 19, at 13.

[34] Gilmore, *Formalism*, *supra* note 24, at 448.

they would be paid. The negotiable instrument principles that endure today ensure that the ultimate holder will be paid a sum that can be ascertained from the face of the instrument.[35] By concentrating durable worth in familiar, readily verifiable formats, commercial law mobilized paper as transportable, dependable currency substitutes, thereby bridging distance and unfamiliarity for those who would seek to use the documents as mediums of exchange.

Along those lines, for paper to serve as a medium of exchange, it must be easy to determine the value of that paper. Paper currency necessitates that the paper's inherent worth be readily determinable. The paper itself would not be acceptable as payment if its value were not easily ascertainable. The paper payment devices developed over the centuries could not effectively serve as payment for goods and services without meeting what we now recognize as the requisites of negotiability.[36] To qualify as a negotiable instrument in American law today, the paper must show that the right to payment is unconditional, for a fixed amount, due on demand or at a definite time, and payable either to the bearer or to a named person.[37] By embedding stable valuations, decipherable at sight, within these everyday and easily passed pieces of paper, the law came to enable the adoption of paper currency despite its fragility relative to metal coinage.

Once these new paper substitutes for currency gained assignability, rules prioritizing competing creditors followed. The problem was this: Intangible obligations were vulnerable to double-dealing, enabling original parties to promise repayment rights to multiple parties. Negotiability law remedied this through *reification*, or, as it has come to be known, *tokenization*—the legal idea of imprinting exclusive entitlements within documents that are exchangeable as currency.[38] Whoever legally possessed these specially marked instruments (i.e., tokens) enjoyed superior claims against issuers compared to rivals without the relevant tokens evidencing debts owed specifically to them.

Finally, an important feature of negotiable instrument law is *holder-in-due-course* status. When a person takes a negotiable instrument for value, in good faith, and without notice of any forgery or claims to the instrument, that person acquires the instrument free of any defenses of the person obligated to pay the instrument.[39] For example, the person obligated on the debt evidenced by the negotiable instrument may have a defense to its payment—perhaps the goods purchased were defective. Yet a holder in due course who later acquires the right to collect under the negotiable instrument is insulated from that defense. Despite the defective goods, the debtor must still pay the holder in due course of the

[35] *See* MILLER & HARRELL, *supra* note 32, § 2.1[1].

[36] *See* James Steven Rogers, *Negotiability as a System of Title Recognition*, 48 OHIO ST. L.J. 197, 199–200 (1987).

[37] U.C.C. § 3–104 (AM. L. INST. & UNIF. L. COMM'N 2002).

[38] *See* FINANCIAL COLLATERAL: LAW AND PRACTICE 14 (Matthias Haentjens ed., 2020).

[39] U.C.C. § 3-302(a).

instrument. Therefore, it is this holder-in-due-course status that truly gives value to the token; a person can buy a payment right and know its value by looking at the token instrument, without needing to inquire into other matters. In essence, becoming a holder in due course cuts off many legal threats to the value and currency of a negotiable instrument. This facilitates smoother transactions and provides paper equivalents to cash.

3.2.2 Securities as tokens

Yet another example is the equity security—specifically the right to an ownership interest in a corporation or other business entity, such as a share of corporate stock. The concept of tokenizing corporate ownership rights through certificates or other instruments has a long history, developing in tandem with early capital markets.[40] As early as the 1100s and 1200s, Italian city-states and nearby European commercial hubs began issuing primitive equity shares—essentially tokenized rights to assets. For instance, the *Société des Moulins du Bazacle* in Toulouse, France (which operated the town mills) issued formal paper certificates granting investors ownership and decision-making power, a precursor to modern equity.[41] These documents functionally tokenized membership rights in the *Bazacle* association.

Later, in the early 1600s, the pioneering Dutch East India Company offered the first true equity securities to the public.[42] But rather than share certificates, as with the *Bazacle* association, buyers received *deeds of bargain and sale*, which were transferable receipts outlining the stake in the company being purchased.[43] While not a certificate per se, this deed was vital to facilitating early share transactions. The process typically entailed the buyer receiving the deed from the seller and then furnishing the deed to the company. Upon receipt, the company would register the transfer in the central share ledger.

By the late 1800s, the burgeoning capital markets necessitated reform in securities law to facilitate faster trading and transfers of corporate stock.[44]

[40] *See* Financial Collateral: Law and Practice, *supra* note 38, at 13.

[41] *The Fascinating 600-Year History of a French Mill, the World's Oldest Shareholding Company*, Yale Sch. of Mgmt.: Int'l Ctr. for Fin. (Aug. 19, 2014), https://som.yale.edu/news/2014/ 08/the-fascinating-600-year-history-of-french-mill-the-world-s-oldest-shareholding-company [https://perma.cc/P9JX-L82R].

[42] *See* Henry Hansmann & Mariana Pargendler, *The Evolution of Shareholder Voting Rights: Separation of Ownership and Consumption*, 123 Yale L.J. 948, 1002 (2014).

[43] Lodewijk Petram, *The Oldest Share*, The World's First Stock Exch. (Nov. 2, 2020), https://www.worldsfirststockexchange.com/2020/11/02/the-oldest-share/ [https://perma.cc /5RZ 5-G4RY]; John P. Shelton, *The First Printed Share Certificate: An Important Link in Financial History*, 39 Bus. Hist. Rev. 391, 397–99 (1965).

[44] *See* Financial Collateral: Law and Practice, *supra* note 38, at 14.

To enable seamless transactions, the legal framework evolved such that manually registering share transfers on a company's books, a tedious and time-consuming process, was no longer required.[45] Instead, true tokenization emerged whereby the paper document itself embodied the associated equity rights, much like the early Italian certificates. Now the certificate token was fully assignable and negotiable from one party to another, all without the issuer's involvement of the issuer. Put simply, the holder of the certificate alone controlled the equity rights in the corporation. This change in law and practice reflected a conceptual shift: Shareholder rights were increasingly viewed as inherent to the security token rather than rooted in underlying corporate registration records.[46] The paper token was no longer a receipt evidencing the transfer but rather was the embodiment of the right itself, and thus by merely holding the token, one held the right. Tokenization solved the problem of high-volume transfers. Tokens could pass from hand to hand, and the corporate rights followed.

Securities remained largely certificated on paper through the mid-twentieth century.[47] However, the unwieldy nature of physical certificates eventually gave rise to calls for yet another round of law reform. By the 1960s, it had become extraordinarily inefficient to continuously transport and transfer paper certificates on frenzied trading days, not to mention that this method of processing transfers was prone to recording errors. This culminated in the infamous "paperwork crisis," where trading hours were halved just to enable back offices to catch up on settling trades.[48]

The market's response was not to abandon tokenization but to transform it. In 1973, the securities industry established the Depository Trust Company (DTC), a centralized depository for immobilizing physical certificates.[49] Under this system, certificates issued by publicly traded companies were deposited with DTC and registered in the name of its nominee, Cede & Co. The physical tokens remained in the vault; what circulated instead were book entries on the records of intermediaries. Individual investors held brokerage accounts with firms such as Charles Schwab, Vanguard, and others, which in turn maintained accounts with DTC. The ultimate beneficial owner of a security thus held an interest indirectly, through a chain of account relationships running from the investor's broker up to DTC and ultimately to the issuing corporation itself.

[45] Shelton, *supra* note 43, at 392–93.

[46] *See* Robert Anderson IV, *A Property Theory of Corporate Law*, 2020 Colum. Bus. L. Rev. 1.

[47] Aronstein, *supra* note 20.

[48] *See In re* Appraisal of Dell Inc., No. 9322, 2015 WL 4313206, at *1 (Del. Ch. July 30, 2015); Wyatt Wells, *Certificates and Computers: The Remaking of Wall Street, 1967 to 1971*, 74 Bus. Hist. Rev. 193, 200–01 (2000).

[49] *See* Jeanne L. Schroeder & David G. Carlson, *Security Interests Under Article 8 of the Uniform Commercial Code*, 12 Cardozo L. Rev. 557, 561 (1990) [hereinafter Schroeder & Carlson].

The law also developed an alternative framework: uncertificated securities, in which no physical certificate exists at all, and ownership is recorded directly on the issuer's books.[50] This approach found adoption for certain categories of securities, including federal government debt and mutual fund shares. However, for publicly traded corporate stocks and bonds, the market converged on the indirect holding model rather than the uncertificated securities framework.

The indirect holding system preserved the essential function of tokenization while dispensing with the physical movement of paper. Article 8 of the Uniform Commercial Code was revised to accommodate this new reality, introducing the concept of the "security entitlement" to govern the rights of beneficial owners who hold securities through intermediaries.[51] Under this framework, an investor who holds securities through a brokerage account does not own a specific certificate or even a specific share; rather, the investor holds a security entitlement against the intermediary, which in turn holds entitlements against the next intermediary in the chain. Ownership is now denoted by ledger entries associating entitlements with holder names, and to legally acquire these tokenized rights, one must be recognized in the records of the relevant intermediary. This multilevel structure is legally memorialized in Article 8's rules on security entitlements, an area of the law to which we will return in Chapter 4.[52] Article 8's indirect holding system dominates public securities trading to this day.

Ultimately, despite shifts away from physical possession, the core concept of tokenized rights persists in modern securities law. Even as custodial models introduced degrees of separation between issuers and beneficial owners, rights remain rooted in the underlying share-tokens themselves. DTC may assume legal ownership of deposited stocks, but it still holds them on behalf of intermediaries, in effect, tokenizing claims to those pooled assets. Intermediaries, in turn, grant tiered entitlements to end investors, who possess security entitlements rather than direct titles. Despite their complexity, these financial instruments ultimately derive from actual company shares, which give their holders specific rights over the issuing company's assets. While the modern system involves multiple layers of ownership, it serves the same fundamental purpose as the early stock certificates: documenting and validating a shareholder's legal claims. In essence, it is still a token representing ownership rights. Thus, while the nature of possession has evolved from physical dominion over a paper certificate to control over book-entry positions, the idea remains the same: reifying ownership rights in a standardized, transferable form, even amid complex chains of ownership. The tokenization paradigm persists, transformed but enduring.

[50] U.C.C. § 8-102(a)(18) (Am. L. Inst. & Unif. L. Comm'n 1994).

[51] U.C.C. § 8-102(a)(17) (Am. L. Inst. & Unif. L. Comm'n 1994).

[52] *See* Charles W. Mooney, Jr., *Beyond Negotiability: A New Model for Transfer and Pledge of Interests in Securities Controlled by Intermediaries*, 12 Cardozo L. Rev. 305 (1990).

3.2.3 Real property deeds as tokens

The concept of tokenizing rights extends beyond financial instruments; a lighter form of tokenization has emerged in real estate as well.[53] Under old English common law, transferring landed interests could be accomplished orally through an elaborate ceremony known as "feoffment with livery of seisin."[54] In this ritual, the grantor of the real property right would literally hand over a clod of dirt from the land to the grantee while reciting words of conveyance to complete the legal transfer: "I enfeoff thee and thy heirs forever of black acre."[55]

However, the lack of documentation led to frequent disputes over whether ceremonies occurred or whether terms were properly conveyed. English courts at that time faced rampant deception in legal proceedings. Perjury was commonplace, as were so-called professional witnesses—individuals who loitered around courthouses, offering false testimony for hire to the highest bidder.[56] This plague of unreliable and often deliberately misleading sworn statements created immense difficulty for courts attempting to uncover the truth amid conflicting accounts of land transfers and oral agreements. To address this problem, the practice of executing confirmatory deeds as after-the-fact evidence of the feoffment began. These documents described the ceremony, parties, and estate details for posterity. Though not legally required, they provided courts with written proof to resolve competing claims over transfers.

But the growing problem of unreliable courtroom testimony soon took on larger implications. English royal revenue officers struggled to accurately track land transfers for tax purposes amid the rampant perjury undermining deed validity.[57] This administrative hurdle ultimately catalyzed legal reform in 1536 with the statute of enrolments.[58] Under the new edict, certain freehold sales were required to be consummated via written bargain-and-sale deeds, duly sealed and recorded with local land registries.[59] Thus emerged a mandate for paper documents evidencing transfers, which in turn allowed for greater oversight by the state. While limited at first only to transfers of certain kinds of interests in

[53] As we explain in this chapter, tokenization plays a role in real estate transactions. However, it does not entail imbuing the deed with bearer instrument-like qualities as is the case with negotiable instruments. This is why we refer to tokenization in this context as a lighter form. The distinction is explored more fully in Chapter 7.

[54] JAMES H. BREWSTER, THE CONVEYANCE OF ESTATES IN FEE BY DEED § 11, at 11 (1904).

[55] *Id.* § 14, at 13.

[56] G. H. L. Fridman, *The Necessity for Writing in Contracts Within the Statute of Frauds*, 35 U. TORONTO L.J. 43, 47 (1985); FRANKLIN G. SNYDER & MARK EDWIN BURGE, AMERICAN CONTRACT LAW FOR A GLOBAL AGE 259 (2017).

[57] SNYDER & BURGE, *supra* note 56.

[58] Statute of Enrolments 1536, 27 Hen. VIII c. 16 (Eng.).

[59] *Deed*, BLACK'S LAW DICTIONARY (11th ed. 2019); BREWSTER, *supra* note 54, § 12, at 12.

land, this change in the law seeded a broader shift from purely oral ceremonies toward memorialization.

The famous 1677 statute of frauds then cemented the necessity of documented instruments for most kinds of land conveyances.[60] Just as with certificated securities, the aim was to provide durable, objective proof to mitigate fraud by a physical token that in some way manifests the deal terms and party consent. These incremental steps marked an increased reliance on instruments that represented or, in some way, embodied rights (i.e., tokens) over loose agreements or unreliable witnesses when rights changed hands. The progress presaged today's vast property records apparatus serving a similar purpose.[61]

Importantly, deeds did not emerge as an absolute prerequisite to land ownership. Title could still pass through intestacy, marital property rights, or adverse possession, all absent documentation.[62] Yet voluntary transactions increasingly centered around these standardized instruments as efficient instruments for conferring rights. Deeds provided a useful way to establish the relative rights of the parties in voluntary transactions involving land. Aside from the exceptions mentioned above, a deed is necessary to convey real property interests, and it does so efficiently through notice rules. The original common law rule simply provided that one who acquired real property through a deed had a superior title to any subsequent party who also purported to acquire title to that same property via a deed.[63] Over time, this general rule was modified through the introduction of recording system statutes that incentivized grantees to make their deeds known, typically through recording them in a public registry of land transfers.[64] The deed, the token, showed not only that the transaction had actually occurred but that the delivery of the deed was the transaction itself, and deeds also served as the foundation for a property recording system that could be inspected by the public—essentially, a public repository of land tokens. Today, the holder of the token (deed) is the holder of the rights in the real property relative to others also claiming title through a deed. The token embodies rights to the land within the context of the real estate transaction and, with notice rules, helps moderate land title disputes.

[60] Statute of Frauds 1677, 29 Car. 2 c. 3 (Eng.). American courts subsequently followed English courts when construing their own statute of frauds. *See* 1 Robert T. Devlin, The Law of Real Property and Deeds 5 (3d ed. 1911).

[61] W. B. Martindale, A Treatise on the Law of Conveyancing 3 n.1 (St. Louis, Cent. L.J. Co., 2d ed. 1889).

[62] 1 Lewis N. Dembitz, A Treatise on Land Titles in the United States §§ 28, 104, 175 (St. Paul, Minn., West Publ'g Co. 1895).

[63] John H. Scheid, *Down Labyrinthine Ways: A Recording Acts Guide for First Year Law Students*, 80 U. Det. Mercy L. Rev. 91, 102–3 (2002).

[64] *See* Christopher L. Peterson, *Two Faces: Demystifying the Mortgage Electronic Registration System's Land Title Theory*, 53 Wm. & Mary L. Rev. 111, 115 (2011).

3.2.4 Bills of lading as tokens

Bills of lading offer yet another example of legal rights being tokenized into transferable documents. Bills of lading are standardized forms issued by carriers upon receiving goods for transport.[65] These documents detail the cargo, destination, terms, and delivery instructions. A "straight" bill names the specific recipient, while a "negotiable" bill directs delivery of goods to anyone holding the document. Thus, possessing a negotiable bill of lading grants authority over the referenced goods in transit. Much like early merchant certificates, the document acts as a transportable token directly controlling access to the underlying asset—in this case, freight inventory.[66] In law, bills of lading are *documents of title*,[67] able to convey and reassign constructive custody of the cargo before physical delivery.[68]

The document of title regime is codified in Article 7 of the UCC and various federal shipping laws,[69] which obligate carriers to deliver the goods only to the holder of the bill. The motivation echoes the preceding forms of tokenization mentioned on prior pages: enabling efficient transfers of rights in goods without requiring physical possession of the goods themselves, by assigning those rights to whoever legally holds the document in question. The document reliably evidences the transaction and identifies the party entitled to delivery, thereby preventing subsequent ownership disputes.

To appreciate why this legal architecture developed, consider the perennial risks involved in remote commercial trade.[70] Consider a generic goods transaction between unfamiliar parties. The buyer refuses payment until inspecting the merchandise upon arrival. Yet, the distant seller naturally hesitates to ship without payment assurances. Here enters the negotiable bill of lading, issued by a carrier to the seller when taking custody of the goods.[71] By routing this document ahead to a local agent, the seller retains constructive possession and ownership of the goods while they are en route. The local agent meets the buyer at the destination and exchanges the authorized bill (token) for payment. Only then does the buyer receive the shipment.

[65] Fred H. Miller, Sales and Leases of Goods in a Nutshell 127 (4th ed. 2003); U.C.C. § 1-201(b)(6) (Am. L. Inst. & Unif. L. Comm'n 2022).

[66] *See* Ralph H. Folsom, Michael Wallace Gordon, Michael P. Van Alstine & Michael D. Ramsey, Principles of International Business Transactions 201–3 (4th ed. 2017).

[67] *See* Lickbarrow v. Mason (1794) 101 Eng. Rep. 380 (KB). *See generally* Daniel E. Murray, *History and Development of the Bill of Lading*, 37 U. Miami L. Rev. 689 (1983).

[68] *Document of Title*, Black's Law Dictionary (11th ed. 2019); U.C.C. § 1-201(b)(6).

[69] *See* U.C.C. § 7-309(a) (Am. L. Inst. & Unif. L. Comm'n 2003); Federal Bills of Lading Act (Pomerene Act), ch. 415, 39 Stat. 538 (1916) (codified as amended at 49 U.S.C. §§ 80101–16).

[70] Miller, *supra* note 65, at 130–31.

[71] *See* Folsom, Gordon, Van Alstine & Ramsey, *supra* note 66, at 7, 9.

The foregoing example illustrates the core function of bills of lading: tokenizing transient rights in goods into a portable, transferable document.[72] The document tangibly reifies the seller's title to goods in transit, thereby forestalling handover until compensation is secured. The carrier-issued token encapsulates ongoing authority over the asset for its designated controller. Without presenting the bill, the freight remains beyond reach. And the controller can irrevocably assign rights by simply transferring possession of the bill of lading. Thus, the bill of lading is the quintessential tokenized right to remote goods: a physical manifestation of exclusive authority that enables commerce across distance and trust barriers.

3.2.5 Warehouse receipts as tokens

In keeping with documents of title, yet another modern tokenization example is the *warehouse receipt*.[73] A warehouse receipt is issued by a bailee upon receiving goods for storage.[74] Under Article 7 of the UCC, a warehouse receipt is "a document issued by a person engaged in the business of storing goods for hire."[75] The receipt not only provides evidence that specific items have been entrusted to the storage provider but also acts as a legally binding contract between the storage provider and the owner of the goods.[76] And, as a document of title, a warehouse receipt represents rights in the stored goods. In this way, the goods (which can include a wide variety of items, such as distilled spirits, industrial products, and agricultural commodities[77]) are tokenized in the form of the warehouse receipt, thereby facilitating the transfer of ownership or other property rights (such as a security interest) in the stored goods without ever having to physically move the items. To transfer the stored goods, one needs only to transfer the token (i.e., the warehouse receipt).

Warehouse receipts, like bills of lading, do not require a specific format or set of terms to be considered valid. The document qualifies as a warehouse receipt

[72] *Id.* at 203.

[73] U.C.C. § 1-201(b)(16) (Am. L. Inst. & Unif. L. Comm'n 2022); U.C.C. §§ 7-101 to 7-110 (Am. L. Inst. & Unif. L. Comm'n 2003). The literature on UCC Article 7 and documents of title in Anglo-American law is vast. *See, e.g.*, Richard A. Lord, Williston on Contracts §§ 53:55–53:79 (4th ed. 2020); Drew L. Kershen, *Comparing the United States Warehouse Act and U.C.C. Article 7*, 27 Creighton L. Rev. 735 (1994).

[74] *See generally* William D. Hawkland, Carl Bjerre, Larry T. Garvin, Alaina Gimbert, Steven L. Harris, William H. Henning, Thomas S. Hemmendinger & Sarah Jane Hughes, Hawkland's Uniform Commercial Code §§ 7-101:1-2 (West, current through 2025).

[75] U.C.C. § 1-201(b)(42) (Am. L. Inst. & Unif. L. Comm'n 2022).

[76] 4 Cal. Transactions Forms—Bus. Transactions § 28:1 (2024).

[77] 3 J. Scott Shehan & Robin Russell, Texas Practice Guide: Financial Transactions § 11:42 (Nov. 2024 update), Westlaw TXPG-FINTR § 11:42.

if it meets the definition of a document of title under the UCC and is issued by a professional storage provider.[78] Moreover, modern warehouse receipts can be either tangible or electronic.[79] This evolution in commercial law reflects the increasing digitization of business practices and documents.

Like bills of lading, warehouse receipts developed to solve specific commercial problems. The receipt allows merchants to store goods securely with a third party while retaining legally recognized proof of ownership. This, in turn, can lead to more efficient use of the goods as collateral: Rather than pledging the goods themselves, the owner can grant a security interest in the warehouse receipt. The warehouse receipt also facilitates the transfer of ownership without physically moving goods, greatly enhancing trade efficiency, especially in international trade.

3.3 The tokenization problem and numerus clausus principle

The preceding historical analysis illuminates how traditional forms of legal tokenization emerged as pragmatic solutions to persistent commercial problems. From negotiable instruments that enabled the circulation of payment rights without physical coin transfers to bills of lading that facilitated trade while goods were in transit to warehouse receipts that allowed the transfer of stored goods without physical delivery, each of these legal innovations responded to concrete business needs. These traditional tokens bridged gaps in commercial practice, reducing transaction costs, increasing deal velocity, and enabling long-distance commerce between unfamiliar parties.

What is often overlooked, however, whether obscured by the passage of time or distorted by a romanticized—yet legally and historically unfounded—vision of *lex mercatoria*, is the crucial role of property law in enabling tokenization. The popular narrative of merchants spontaneously creating private ordering arrangements that somehow transform into binding market-wide practices overlooks a fundamental point: tokenization has invariably required the creation and development of a standardized and mandatory legal framework. In centuries past, this work was performed through common law decisions, as exemplified by the English jurist Lord Mansfield's seminal contributions to shaping the regime for bills of lading.[80] In modern times, statutory interventions have increasingly served this purpose, with the Uniform Commercial Code

[78] U.C.C. § 1-201(b)(16); *see also* U.C.C. § 7-201(a) (Am. L. Inst. & Unif. L. Comm'n 2003).

[79] U.C.C. § 7-102(a)(14)–(15) (Am. L. Inst. & Unif. L. Comm'n 2022); *see also* U.C.C. § 7-106.

[80] See Lickbarrow v. Mason (1787) 2 T.R. 63, 100 Eng. Rep. 35 (KB); *see also* S. Todd Lowry, *Lord Mansfield and the Law Merchant: Law and Economics in the Eighteenth Century*, 7 J. Econ. Issues 605 (1973).

standing as the paradigmatic example in American law, providing comprehensive frameworks for negotiable instruments (Article 3), bills of lading (Article 7), warehouse receipts (Article 7), and certificated securities (Article 8).

Beyond misconceptions about the role of the law in enabling tokenization, there lies a deeper layer of complexity. These legal devices operate at what Thomas Merrill and Henry Smith describe as the "property/contract interface."[81] That is, they combine both contractual and proprietary elements, yet these components are subject to starkly different rules regarding party autonomy. The law affords parties extensive freedom to shape their respective rights and obligations in contract, while property-based dimensions are subject to strict constraints.

This dichotomy is evident when considering the UCC's regime for negotiable instruments. UCC Article 3 gives parties broad latitude to determine the underlying monetary obligation, including its amount, timing for repayment, and related terms. However, the opposite is true of a negotiable instrument's proprietary aspects, which cannot be modified by agreement. These mandatory, standardized rules govern the formal and substantive requirements for an instrument's validity, the methods for transferring the instrument, and the conditions for its negotiability.

Similarly, with bills of lading under Article 7, parties have complete flexibility regarding the commercial terms of their maritime transport arrangements. However, the validity requirements of the document itself, the rights it confers with respect to the covered goods, the manner of the document's issuance, transfer mechanisms, and the document's negotiability are all established by law and nonalterable by agreement. Put simply, when someone encounters a check or a bill of lading in commerce, they can rely on its standardized legal operation without needing to investigate the original arrangements between the parties who created it.

The tokenization landscape is defined by property law through two sets of mandatory rules. First, it limits what types of personal property can be tokenized. For instance, payment rights are embodied in negotiable instruments, bills of lading represent goods in transit, and warehouse receipts tokenize stored commodities. These categories are not left to private discretion but are instead defined by law. For instance, one can physically deposit stock certificates in a warehouse and obtain a warehouse receipt, but the receipt would represent the stored paper as goods, not the underlying equity rights in the corporation; the document of title regime does not substitute for the securities law regime. Similarly, one cannot embody a barber's promise of a future haircut in a negotiable instrument,

[81] Thomas W. Merrill & Henry E. Smith, *The Property/Contract Interface*, 101 COLUM. L. REV. 773 (2001).

because Article 3 applies only to obligations to pay money, not to obligations to perform services. These limitations reflect the law's careful control over which obligations can be transformed into transferable instruments.

Second, where tokenization is permitted, the law imposes mandatory requirements regarding both the form and substance of these instruments. A promissory note, for instance, must contain an unconditional order to pay a fixed sum of money, be signed by the drawer, and identify a specific payee.[82] Similarly, warehouse receipts must specify the location of the warehouse, describe the stored goods, and include the date of issue.[83] These formal requirements cannot be modified by private agreement—parties cannot create their own alternative versions of these instruments or alter the prescribed elements. The standardization serves to protect both the immediate parties and subsequent transferees by ensuring that each type of instrument maintains consistent, recognizable features that signal its legal character and effects.

These constraints on tokenization reflect what has been described as one of the key tenets of property: *numerus clausus*.[84] This principle establishes that parties cannot create new forms of property rights beyond the finite list of standardized categories recognized by law, thereby ensuring that property interests remain uniform and readily comprehensible. For instance, in the context of real property interests, parties must select from established categories such as fee simple, life estate, or leasehold—they cannot create novel hybrid forms at will.[85] Similarly, when it comes to personal property, the law recognizes only certain standardized interests: parties cannot invent new forms of property rights in chattels, such as a negotiable instrument that is transferable on "Wednesdays-only" or a bill of lading that is only "negotiable in bad faith."

[82] U.C.C. § 3-104(a) (Am. L. Inst. & Unif. L. Comm'n 2002).

[83] U.C.C. § 7-202(b) (Am. L. Inst. & Unif. L. Comm'n 2003).

[84] On the history of *numerus clausus*, see Bernard Rudden, *Economic Theory v. Property Law: The Numerus Clausus Problem*, *in* 3 Oxford Essays in Jurisprudence 239, 241 (John Eekelaar & John Bell eds., 1987); Nestor M. Davidson, *Standardization and Pluralism in Property Law*, 61 Vand. L. Rev. 1597, 1600 (2008) ("Versions of the numerus clausus are found in Roman law and recur throughout the history of feudal and post-feudal English common law. Likewise, some form of a standard list appears in disparate modern civil law and common law systems throughout the world."); Anna di Robilant, *Property and Democratic Deliberation: The Numerus Clausus Principle and Democratic Experimentalism in Property Law*, 62 Am. J. Comp. L. 367 (2014); Henry Hansmann & Reinier Kraakman, *Property, Contract, and Verification: The Numerus Clausus Problem and the Divisibility of Rights*, 31 J. Legal Stud. S373 (2002); Thomas W. Merrill & Henry E. Smith, *Optimal Standardization in the Law of Property: The Numerus Clausus Principle*, 110 Yale L.J. 1, 3 (2000); Meredith M. Render, *Complexity in Property*, 81 Tenn. L. Rev. 79 (2013); John Henry Merryman, *Policy, Autonomy, and the Numerus Clausus in Italian and American Property Law*, 12 Am. J. Comp. L. 224 (1963); Hanoch Dagan, Property: Values and Institutions 33–35 (2011) [hereinafter Dagan, Property].

[85] *See* Keppell v. Bailey (1834) 39 Eng. Rep. 1042, 1049 (Ch.) (stating that "incidents of a novel kind" cannot "be devised and attached to property at the fancy or caprice of any owner").

Similarly, one cannot create an equitable servitude over chattels, rather only over land.[86]

Thus, the numerus clausus principle establishes a crucial distinction between contract and property law. While contract law generally allows parties to craft any arrangement they choose (outside narrow public policy constraints[87]), property law restricts the universe of permissible legal arrangements to a closed list of standardized forms.[88]

This principle is almost universal across legal systems, though its manifestations differ slightly.[89] In civil law jurisdictions, numerus clausus is embedded in the structure of civil codes by enumerating property rights in a closed list to which courts are bound.[90] Common law jurisdictions rarely acknowledge the principle by name, yet it operates as a powerful, invisible constraint, almost an immutable characteristic, deeply entrenched in Anglo-American property law for centuries. Its operation is particularly evident in how courts treat attempted deviations from recognized property forms: They either reject them outright or recast them into one of the accepted standard forms.

In common law jurisdictions, legal scholars have advanced several compelling explanations for the persistence and desirability of the *numerus clausus* principle. Early justifications, exemplified in Holmes's *Johnson v. Whiton* opinion,[91] focused on preventing undue restraints on alienation, arguing that novel property forms could fragment rights to such an extent that future transfers would become prohibitively complex. In that case, Holmes admonished: "A man cannot create a new kind of inheritance."[92] Michael Heller later reconceptualized this concern through his *anticommons* theory, warning that excessive fragmentation could result in too many individuals holding veto rights over a resource's use or disposition.[93] In short: "[P]rivate property ownership requires unifying fragmented property rights into a usable bundle."[94]

The modern debate has produced increasingly sophisticated justifications. Merrill and Smith's influential information cost theory posits that novel

[86] 4 RESTATEMENT (FOURTH) OF PROPERTY § 4.1 cmt. g (AM. L. INST., Tentative Draft No. 3, 2022); *see also* Danielle D'Onfro, *Contract-Wrapped Property*, 137 HARV. L. REV. 1058, 1064 (2024).

[87] *See, e.g.*, Mark Koyama, *Evading the "Taint of Usury": The Usury Prohibition as a Barrier to Entry*, 47 EXPLORATIONS ECON. HIST. 420 (2010); Christine Hurt, *Regulating Public Morals and Private Markets: Online Securities Trading, Internet Gambling, and the Speculation Paradox*, 86 B.U. L. REV. 371 (2006).

[88] *See* Merrill & Smith, *supra* note 84, at 3 ("A central difference between contract and property concerns the freedom to 'customize' legally enforceable interests.").

[89] Rudden, *supra* note 84, at 241; Merrill & Smith, *supra* note 84, at 4–5.

[90] Merryman, *supra* note 84; Rudden, *supra* note 84, at 240.

[91] Johnson v. Whiton, 34 N.E. 542 (Mass. 1893).

[92] *Id.*

[93] Michael Heller, *The Tragedy of the Anticommons: Property in the Transition from Marx to Markets*, 111 HARV. L. REV. 621, 640 (1998).

[94] *Id.*

property rights impose systemic measurement costs on third parties—costs that, unlike in contract law, are externalized to all market participants who must process and respect unfamiliar rights. Henry Hansmann and Reinier Kraakman emphasize verification costs, noting that because property rights "run with assets," standardization spares third parties the burden of investigating idiosyncratic arrangements. Other scholars have offered complementary perspectives. Hanoch Dagan views *numerus clausus* as providing standardized building blocks that enable property innovation while maintaining systemic clarity.[95] Nestor Davidson highlights its role in balancing competing values like efficiency and fairness.[96] Singer explains that it allows us to align social relations with principles of democracy, individual liberty, and reciprocal dignity.[97] And Meredith Render emphasizes its function in preventing the system from becoming overwhelmed by unmanageable complexity.[98]

However, the numerus clausus principle is not without its critics. Some scholars have criticized the numerus clausus principle along socioeconomic and political dimensions. Critical legal studies scholars, for instance, have characterized the standardization of property forms as a mechanism for reinforcing hierarchical social relationships, claiming it channels parties into preset social arrangements that reflect feudal power structures.[99] Others have criticized the principle as discriminatory, arguing that it advantages sophisticated parties with access to legal counsel while disadvantaging those who lack such resources.[100] While these critiques raise important considerations, they approach the principle from a different angle than we see as its core aims: enhancing legal certainty, facilitating transactions, and reducing information costs. The standardization fostered by *numerus clausus* serves valuable functions in making property rights more accessible and predictable for market participants. However, we note that careful attention must be paid to how this standardization affects different stakeholders and its role in enhancing (rather than diminishing) equity and fairness.

Yet, for all the historical precedent and foundational property law doctrines, in today's digital asset markets, participants frequently announce tokenization schemes with little regard for the *numerus clausus* principle. We see daily proclamations about NFTs representing ownership of artwork, tokens allegedly embodying corporate equity, and digital assets purporting to confer

[95] Dagan, Property, *supra* note 84, at 33–35.

[96] Davidson, *supra* note 84, at 1601–05.

[97] Joseph William Singer, Essay, *Democratic Estates: Property Law in a Free and Democratic Society*, 94 Cornell L. Rev. 1009, 1052 (2009).

[98] Render, *supra* note 84, at 98–101.

[99] Curtis J. Berger & Joan C. Williams, Property: Land Ownership and Use 213–14 (4th ed. 1997); Susan Bright, *Of Estates and Interests: A Tale of Ownership and Property Rights*, *in* Land Law: Themes and Perspectives 529, 546 (Susan Bright & John Dewar eds., 1998).

[100] Duncan Kennedy, *Form and Substance in Private Law Adjudication*, 89 Harv. L. Rev. 1685, 1699–1700 (1976).

rights to real estate or precious metals.[101] The underlying assumption seems to be that any right or asset can be tokenized simply by declaring it so in a smart contract or terms of service. This fundamentally misunderstands the numerus clausus principle and its central teaching that property rights cannot be created by mere declaration or contractual agreement. A person claiming that an NFT represents ownership of a painting has no more legal authority to do so than someone asserting that possession of a particular pebble confers title to the Brooklyn Bridge. The technological sophistication of blockchain platforms does not override this basic principle: Without express recognition in property law, a purported tokenization remains legally ineffective regardless of how it is encoded in smart contracts.

As we explain in the chapters that follow in Part II of this book, there have been a myriad of false tokenizations proffered by digital asset companies and their proponents over the years. We set forth more fully in those chapters instances in which those promises fall short. By contrast, as we explore in section 3.4, the recently enacted Article 12 of the Uniform Commercial Code demonstrates how *genuine* tokenization emerges: through careful legal engineering that explicitly recognizes and defines new forms of digital assets within established property law frameworks.

3.4 The narrow road to digital tokenization

In Chapter 2, we introduced and explained the concept of the controllable electronic record (CER). And while the 2022 UCC amendments that created CERs certainly signify a significant step forward in the advancement of commercial law for the digital age, this new law does not, as a general matter, extend to tokenization. Indeed, Article 12 explicitly states that rights in property evidenced by a CER are governed by "law other than this article."[102] Therefore, even if a CER is purported to embody rights in a vintage car, a painting, a digital image (which, as explained in Chapter 5, is not an uncommon claim in the NFT world), or any number of other things, those other things remain subject to whatever law ordinarily applies to them. The car, painting, or digital image is not governed by the 2022 UCC Amendments regime for CERs. Instead, they are each governed by the law normally applicable to each item.

Yet, as we noted above, this lack of tokenization treatment in the 2022 amendments is a general rule—there are indeed two notable exceptions. In

[101] Moringiello & Odinet, *supra* note 1, at 607; Fairfield, *supra* note 3, at 1263; Schwarcz, *supra* note 3, at 972–73.

[102] *See* U.C.C. §§ 12-104(f) (Am. L. Inst. & Unif. L. Comm'n 1977).

other words, the 2022 Amendments *do* govern tokenization in two limited contexts: *controllable accounts* and *controllable payment intangibles.*[103] These two kinds of rights can indeed be tokenized under the UCC.[104]

The basic definition of a *controllable account* starts with that of a simple *account*: "a right to payment of a monetary obligation for property that . . . has been or is to be sold, leased, licensed, assigned, . . . or otherwise disposed or for services rendered or to be rendered."[105] The most common kind of account arises when someone sells a good or provides a service and has not yet been paid for having done so. In commercial parlance, this is often called *accounts receivable.* For instance, a homeowner might hire a plumber to fix a leaky sink and then be obligated to pay for the service within the two weeks that follow. The right to payment is the account, with the demanding party (the plumber) being the account creditor and the party obligated to make payment (the homeowner) being the account debtor.[106] A controllable account, then, is an account that is evidenced by a CER and, in respect of which, the *account debtor* agrees to pay the person in control of that CER. In other words, controllable accounts are CERs that, in law, represent a monetary obligation with payment owed to whoever is in control of the associated CER. It is a tokenized account.

In turn, a *controllable payment intangible* starts with the simple definition of a *payment intangible*: "a general intangible under which the account debtor's principal obligation is a monetary obligation."[107] A common example of a payment intangible in the commercial context involves the use of credit facilities by commercial parties.[108] For example, a merchant sells goods to a buyer who pays with a credit card issued by Bank A. Bank A's resulting right to payment from the buyer is classified as an "account" under the UCC. The merchant has a credit card processing account with Bank B. The payment travels through a payment network (such as Visa), ultimately reaching Bank B. Bank B then owes this money to the merchant, and the merchant's right to receive it from Bank B is classified as a "payment intangible."

A controllable payment intangible, therefore, is a payment intangible whereby the parties agree that the right will be evidenced by a CER and that the account debtor (i.e., Bank B in the scenario above) will only pay the person who has control of that CER.[109] Thus, in both instances, the right to payment (whether a

[103] *See* U.C.C. § 9-102(a)(27A), (27B) (Am. L. Inst. & Unif. L. Comm'n 2022).

[104] We do, however, note one other avenue, although one that is quite limited in scope: the electronic warehouse receipt. *See* Kara Bruce, Christopher K. Odinet & Andrea Tosato, *The Private Law of Stablecoins*, 54 Ariz. St. L.J. 1073, 1152–54 (2022).

[105] *See* U.C.C. § 9-102(a)(2).

[106] *See* U.C.C. § 9-102(a)(3).

[107] *See* U.C.C. § 9-102(a)(61).

[108] This example is derived from U.C.C. § 9-102, cmt. 5.d.

[109] *See* U.C.C. § 9-102(a)(27B).

payment intangible or an account) can be tokenized as a CER. And indeed, this tokenization, authorized by law, provides the transmission lines for transferring the tokenized rights. Specifically, the 2022 Amendments establish a regime for the commercial circulation of controllable accounts and controllable payment intangibles that closely mirrors that of CERs. Regarding ownership transfers (in these cases, called assignments), controllable accounts and controllable payment intangibles benefit from the same take-free rule applicable to CERs: a "qualified purchaser" acquires a controllable account or a controllable payment intangible free from any competing claims.[110]

Additionally, the 2002 Amendments allow an account debtor of a controllable account or a controllable payment intangible to agree with their original creditor not to assert claims or defenses against subsequent transferees.[111] The combined effect of these rules renders controllable accounts and controllable payment intangibles highly negotiable. Thus, qualified purchasers can acquire these assets with confidence that they are obtaining the tokenized rights to payment free from competing claims or defenses, contingent only on the creditworthiness of the account debtor.

Importantly, controllable accounts and controllable payment intangibles are paradigm shifts. Previously, the UCC only provided for tokenizing payment obligations in paper form, as we discussed at the start of this chapter—such as promissory notes, checks, and bills of exchange. Rooted in long-standing common law principles, the regime for the circulation of these instruments revolved around their tangibility and possession of the relevant writings.[112] The 2022 Amendments herald a new era of *electronic* negotiable instruments by enabling market participants to use CERs to evidence monetary obligations and bestowing on them a generous take-free rule, combined with the option for account debtors to abstain from asserting claims and defenses against transferees. This legal innovation is explicitly acknowledged by the official comments, underscoring that the lack of electronic instruments under the UCC was a significant gap bemoaned by market participants.[113]

* * *

With this foundation laid, consider how these commercial law provisions can be deployed in connection with digital asset technologies in a legally recognized way. Take the case of a controllable account: A buyer purchases goods from a seller. At the time of the sale, the parties agree that the seller's right to payment will be evidenced by a CER soon to be minted and that the buyer will pay

110 U.C.C. § 9-317(i).
111 *See* U.C.C. § 9-403(b) (Am. L. Inst. & Unif. L. Comm'n 1977).
112 *See* U.C.C. § 3-104 (Am. L. Inst. & Unif. L. Comm'n 2002).
113 *See* U.C.C. § 12-104, cmt. 10 (Am. L. Inst. & Unif. L. Comm'n 1977).

whoever controls that CER. Ideally, the seller would also obtain the buyer's agreement not to assert claims or defenses against subsequent transferees of the tokenized claim. Thereafter, the seller could mint the CER, for instance, an NFT on the Ethereum network or a similar token on another public DLT system, thereby creating a *controllable account*. At this point, the seller could monetize the receivable by assigning it to a purchaser at an agreed price. The proprietary effects of this transaction would be governed by Article 12. Accordingly, upon taking control of the NFT, the purchaser would become entitled to demand payment from the buyer. Moreover, at any time, the first purchaser could reassign the controllable account to another person who could benefit from the take-free rule under Article 12, provided that person was a qualifying purchaser.

The foregoing example illustrates how Article 12 provides a genuine path for digital tokenization. But this path is narrow. The ability to tokenize under these commercial law provisions is limited to accounts and payment intangibles; contract law cannot be used to conjure additional tokenizations without explicit legal authorization. As Parts II and III demonstrate, this has not stopped several prominent firms and proponents of digital assets from claiming that they are doing just that.

We conclude this chapter (and set the stage for what is to come) by stating this: The solution we offer here is not to abandon digital asset tokenization entirely but rather to approach it with the same legal rigor that historically governed tokenization in other contexts. This means understanding where proper frameworks exist—like controllable accounts and electronic documents of title—and working within those boundaries. It also means recognizing that technological capability alone does not create legal authority. Contrary to the views of some, code is not law.

4
Digital assets and custody

4.1 Introduction

In the preceding two chapters, we established two fundamental pillars necessary to understanding the legal framework of digital assets. Chapter 2 examined the question of whether digital assets can be owned as property and explored the legal regimes governing their commercial circulation. Our analysis revealed that while courts across common law jurisdictions have generally recognized digital assets as property, they have done so through markedly different analytical approaches. Jurisdictions outside the United States have typically employed a more formalistic methodology centered on the *Ainsworth* indicia, whereas American courts have embraced a pragmatic approach that privileges functional outcomes over theoretical classification. Moreover, we described how the United States has entirely sidestepped the doctrinal debate about whether digital assets constitute *choses in action* or a *tertium quid*. Instead, through the 2022 UCC Amendments and Article 12, American law has forged a distinctive framework that introduces "controllable electronic records" (CERs) as a novel category of personal property, adopts *control* as its organizing principle, and crafts a functional regime for the transfer and use of CERs as collateral—one that aligns with existing market practices and commercial expectations.

Chapter 3 built upon this foundation by investigating *tokenization*—the process by which digital assets, typically nonfungible tokens (NFTs), are used to represent both real-world goods and digital rights. Drawing lessons from centuries of commercial practice, we demonstrated how traditional tokenizations such as negotiable instruments, bills of lading, and warehouse receipts, emerged through careful legal engineering rather than casual, free-wheeling market practice. This historical analysis revealed a fundamental principle that remains equally vital for digital assets today: Tokenizations are viable only when explicitly recognized by positive law. Market participants cannot create property rights in digital assets through mere declaration or private agreement, as the *numerus clausus* principle limits the creation of novel property forms. The recent recognition of controllable accounts and controllable payment intangibles under UCC Article 12 exemplifies this principle—successful digital tokenization requires formal legal infrastructure, not just technological capability.

Digital Commercial Law. Christopher K. Odinet and Andrea Tosato, Oxford University Press.
 DOI: 10.1093/9780197758656.003.0005

This chapter turns to yet another essential pillar of digital commercial law: *custody*. While distributed ledger technology (DLT) enthusiasts herald disintermediation and peer-to-peer transactions as major disruptors of traditional intermediaries, reality has proven sharply different. Market participants frequently transfer their digital assets to third parties for a variety of reasons.[1] Some of these dealings are functionally similar to familiar custody arrangements, while others mirror conventional lending relationships, and still others constitute entirely novel forms of asset deployment (e.g., "staking").[2]

Further complicating matters, these relationships vary from straightforward bilateral arrangements to complex multilateral dealings with varying degrees of automation through the use of smart contracts. This landscape raises fundamental questions: What is the precise legal nature of the relationship between individuals who entrust their digital assets to others for safekeeping, trading, or various purposes (depositors), and those who accept and manage these assets (custodians)? What rights do creditors of custodians have over assets that these entities hold for depositors? When digital assets are held in joint custody by multiple parties through smart contracts, what rights and obligations do these parties have? And how should the law address automated custody arrangements where software, rather than humans, controls access to digital assets?

Answering these questions requires a return to first principles and a venture into a vast and labyrinthine province of private law, the origins of which stretch back millennia: *the law of bailment*.[3]

Dating back to medieval times, bailment has provided the conceptual framework for organizing and governing relationships that share one core element: the transfer of immediate physical control of an asset from one person to another, for an agreed-upon purpose.[4] The archetypal example is the deposit for safekeeping—as when valuables are entrusted to another with the understanding they will be returned intact upon demand. Over time, bailment has come to

[1] Clifford Chance, Custody of Cryptoassets 11 (2023), https://www.cliffordchance.com/content/dam/cliffordchance/briefings/2023/06/custody-of-cryptoassets.pdf; *see also Secure Digital Assest Custody*, Coinbase, https://www.coinbase.com/prime/custody (last visited Apr. 4, 2025).

[2] *What Is Staking?*, Coinbase, https://www.coinbase.com/learn/crypto-basics/what-is-staking (last visited Apr. 4, 2025).

[3] The Code of Hammurabi contained a basic set of rule governing deposits of goods. *See* The Code of Hammurabi §§ 112, 120–25, *translated in* Robert Francis Harper, The Code of Hammurabi, King of Babylon, About 2250 B.C., at 39, 41–43 (Robert Francis Harper trans., 2d ed. 1904); *see also* Henry de Bracton, Bracton de Legibus et Consuetudinibus Angliae 284 (Samuel E. Thorne trans., 1977) (c. 1220–40); *see* William Jones, An Essay on the Law of Bailments (London, J. Nichols 1781); Joseph Story, Commentaries on the Law of Bailments (Cambridge, Hilliard & Brown 1st ed. 1832); John D. Lawson, The Principles of the American Law of Bailments (St. Louis, F. H. Thomas 1895); James Schouler, A Treatise on the Law of Bailments, Carriers, Innkeepers, and Pledge (Boston, Little, Brown & Co., 2d ed. 1887); Armistead M. Dobie, Handbook on the Law of Bailments and Carriers (1914); William F. Elliott, A Treatise on the Law of Bailments and Carriers (1929).

[4] *See* Story, *supra* note 3, § 2.

govern an extraordinarily diverse range of transactions. These span from gratuitous storage to complex commercial warehousing, from informal loans to equipment leasing and structured finance arrangements, from simple carriage to sophisticated multimodal transport operations. This remarkable breadth signals bailment's adaptability and enduring importance in private law, even as it has prompted scholarly debate about whether bailment remains a useful and distinct legal category or whether these relationships might be better addressed through general principles of contract, tort, and property law.[5]

The twenty-first century presents bailment with perhaps its greatest paradigm shift yet: the advent of digital assets. The boundaries of this legal category were first tested by the emergence of data custody and cloud storage services.[6] These developments were a prelude to the even more intricate issues raised by custodial arrangements involving cryptocurrencies, stablecoins, NFTs, and DLT networks. The fundamental tension stems from bailment's historical and conceptual ties to tangible personal property, physical possession, and delivery—notions that map poorly onto digital assets due to their intangible nature. Yet cryptocurrencies, stablecoins, and NFTs have technological features that allow market participants to replicate the possession–ownership divide of traditional bailments through a separation between ownership and technological control. Moreover, this technological control can be shared among multiple parties and exercised either partially or entirely through smart contracts and other automated mechanisms, rather than through traditional human agency. The result is a landscape of significant uncertainty in determining the rights and obligations of parties when one person entrusts their digital assets to another.

Lest one think what is to come in these pages is a mere wandering in the scholarly woods, the analysis of the respective rights and obligations of depositors, custodians, and third parties is far from a futile academic exercise. Rather, it has profound practical implications that become painfully apparent in bankruptcy proceedings. When custodians of cryptocurrencies, stablecoins, and NFTs become insolvent, the legal characterization of their relationships with depositors determines whether digital assets under their control form part of the bankruptcy estate—available to satisfy the claims of the custodian's general creditors—or remain safe as the separate property of depositors. The stakes could not be higher: For depositors, this characterization is often the difference between recovering their digital assets in full or receiving cents on the dollar

[5] Compare Andrew Bell, *The Place of Bailment in the Modern Law of Obligations*, *in* INTERESTS IN GOODS 461–89 (Norman Palmer & Ewan McKendrick eds., 2d ed. 1998) (arguing bailment bridges contract, property and tort beyond general principles) with Gerard McMeel, *The Redundancy of Bailment*, 2003 LLOYD'S MAR. & COM. L. Q. 32 (contending that general principles pf contract, tort and property have evolved to render bailment redundant).

[6] Danielle D'Onfro, *The New Bailments*, 97 WASH. L. REV. 97 (2022).

as unsecured creditors. This issue has already proven pivotal in a wave of high-profile cryptocurrency firm failures—including Celsius, Voyager, BlockFi, Genesis, and most notably FTX—where billions of dollars in customer assets hung in the balance.[7]

This chapter proceeds in three parts. First, we examine bailment law with a particular focus on deposits of *money* and *securities*. This analysis provides essential guidance for addressing the conceptual challenges posed by custodial arrangements involving digital assets. Second, we explore how these traditional bailment frameworks strain to accommodate custodial arrangements of digital assets, particularly regarding the respective contractual rights and obligations of the parties, liability standards for custodians, and property interests in the assets in question. Finally, we analyze how the UCC Article 8 framework offers a potential solution for the custody of digital assets, albeit with limitations.

4.2 The law of bailments and deposits of money and securities

Bailment is an ancient province of private law with profound significance for trade and commerce. Originating in Roman law and developing through medieval times, this legal category has evolved continuously—particularly since the eighteenth century—to accommodate increasingly sophisticated commercial arrangements.[8] Anglo-American legal scholars have significantly advanced this field through landmark treatises, comprehensive doctrinal analyses, and careful examination of the role of bailment in commercial relationships.[9]

At its core, bailment is described by Samuel Williston as the "rightful possession of goods by one who is not the owner."[10] A more detailed definition presents it as the delivery of personal property for a specific purpose or on deposit, pursuant to an express or implied contract, with the understanding that the property will either be returned to its deliverer or dealt with according to the parties' agreement.[11] Consequently, a remarkable array of everyday and commercial transactions fall within the boundaries of bailment—from valet parking and bank deposits to warehouse storage and museum loans.

[7] See Chapter 6 in this book.

[8] *See* de Bracton, *supra* note 3.

[9] *See* Jones, *supra* note 3; Story, *supra* note 3; Schouler, *supra* note 3 (1st ed. 1880); Lawson, *supra* note 3; Theodore W. Van Zile, Elements of the Law of Bailments and Carriers (1st ed. 1902); Dobie, *supra* note 3; Elliott, *supra* note 3.

[10] *See* 19 Samuel Williston & Richard A. Lord, A Treatise on the Law of Contracts § 53:1 (4th ed. 2001) (citing cases). *See also* Lawson, *supra* note 4, at 9 (defining bailment as "the holding of possession of another's personal property in trust for some specific purpose.").

[11] *See* Williston & Lord, *supra* note 10, § 53:1.

Much like a tree, bailment law comprises a central trunk of foundational principles that apply universally, with numerous branches extending from it. Each branch represents a distinct subcategory of bailment with its own specialized rules governing the rights and obligations of bailors and bailees, as well as their respective proprietary interests. Some branches do not stretch far from the trunk, adding only a small handful of special rules beyond the core principles. Others grow far and wide, developing extensive and specialized legal regimes to address particular commercial needs.

Our analysis traces the historical development of bailment taxonomies, beginning with Bracton's early framework, proceeding through Lord Holt's seminal systematization, and culminating in the contemporary American classification scheme that prevails today. We then focus specifically on the law of custodial arrangements involving money and securities, as the legal principles governing these arrangements are especially useful to our inquiry into bailments involving digital assets.

4.2.1 Bailment taxonomies

The seminal categorization of bailment law emerged from Chief Justice Holt's opinion in the 1703 English case of *Coggs v. Bernard*.[12] Finding contemporary authority and scholarship lacking, Holt drew upon Henry de Bracton's medieval commentaries to articulate six distinct categories of bailment arrangements:[13]

(i) bare naked bailments (called *depositum*),
(ii) gratuitous loans of goods to friends (called *commodatum*),
(iii) goods lent for hire (called *locatio et conductio*),
(iv) goods given as security for a debt (*pignus*),
(v) goods given to a person, for carriage or processing, in exchange for a benefit (*locatio operis*), and
(vi) goods given to a person, for carriage or processing, without a benefit (*mandatum*).[14]

[12] *See* Coggs v. Bernard (1703) 92 Eng. Rep. 107 (KB).

[13] *Id.* at 112.

[14] *Id.* Although of less influence, the English writer Sir William Jones later suggested reducing the categories to five: (1) deposit, (2) mandate, (3) loan for use, (4) pledge, and (5) hiring, further subdividing hiring into: *locatio rei* (hiring a thing), *locatio operis faciendi* (hiring work and labor), *locatio custodiae* (hiring care and custody), and *locatio operis mercium vehendarum* (hiring the carriage of goods). *See* Jones, *supra* note 3, at 29, 69.

Holt's categorization has had an abiding influence in common law jurisdictions,[15] and courts still occasionally reference it today.[16] US Supreme Court Justice Joseph Story largely adopted this framework in his influential treatise on bailment, which shaped subsequent jurisprudence in America.[17] His classification identified five primary categories: *depositum* (gratuitous safekeeping), *mandatum* (uncompensated service involving the goods), *commodatum* (loan for use), *pignus* (pledge or pawn), and *locatio conductio* (hiring for reward).

In a sign of the attention to bailments in commercial settings, Story further subdivided *locatio conductio* into four distinct types: *locatio rei* (renting), *locatio operis faciendi* (hiring work on the goods), *locatio custodiae* (paid safekeeping), and *locatio operis mercium vehendarum* (carriage of goods).

Although praised for its comprehensiveness, the Holt/Story classification faced two main criticisms. First, it was regarded as overly complex, while failing to illuminate substantive differences among bailment types.[18] Second, its categories did not align with the practical distinctions of contemporary business life, reflecting their origins in Roman law—a system that never developed a unitary concept of bailment but instead addressed different transactions separately, with a property law framework fundamentally different from the common law.[19]

Over the course of the nineteenth century, American jurisprudence developed an alternative classification based on recompense and the required diligence of bailees.[20] This framework first divides bailments into *ordinary* and *exceptional*.

In *ordinary bailments*, the rights and liabilities of parties are determined by the benefit or compensation received and the bailee's standard of care. These ordinary bailments are further subdivided based on which party benefits. When only the bailor benefits, the bailee must exercise slight diligence and is liable for gross negligence. When only the bailee benefits, the bailee must exercise high diligence and is liable for slight negligence. Finally, when both parties benefit, the bailee must exercise ordinary diligence and is liable for ordinary negligence.

[15] Interestingly, Lord Holt was hesitant about his own framing of bailment. *See Coggs*, 92 Eng. Rep. 107, 114 (Lord Holt, C.J.). The only other major scholarly work following Holt's decision was Jones, *supra* note 3; his work, although highly praised for its elegance and style, did not have a legacy comparable to that of Holt.

[16] *See, e.g.*, Rodi Yachts, Inc. v. Nat'l Marine, Inc., 984 F.2d 880, 885 (7th Cir. 1993); Llamera v. United States, 15 Cl. Ct. 593, 598 (1988). In Louisiana, courts often classify bailments following the Holt/Bracton taxonomy. *See* Standard Motor Car Co. v. State Farm Mut. Auto. Ins. Co., 97 So. 2d 435, 437 (La. Ct. App. 1957).

[17] *See* Story, *supra* note 3, §§ 4–8 (4th ed 1846).

[18] Samuel Stoljar, *The Early History of Bailment*, 1 Am. J. Legal Hist. 5, 5 (1957).

[19] *See* Schouler, *supra* note 3 (1st ed. 1880).

[20] The first complete presentation of this classification appears in Schouler, *supra* note 3 (1st ed. 1880). Subsequently, see Lawson, *supra* note 3; William B. Hale, Hand-Book on the Law of Bailments and Carriers (St. Paul, Minn., West Publ'g 1896); Van Zile, *supra* note 9 (2d ed. 1908).

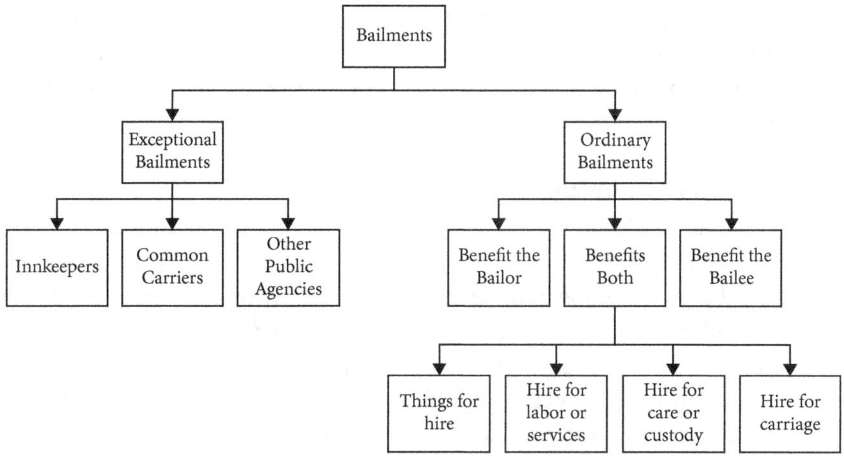

Figure 4.1 Modern bailments taxonomy and structure.

Exceptional bailments, by contrast, are nongratuitous arrangements benefiting both parties but subject to heightened duties. This category encompasses postmasters and other public agencies, innkeepers, and common carriers. As the noted American legal historian James Schouler observed, these bailees face "exceptional rules and an exceptional responsibility" not because they are fundamentally different from other bailees, but because public policy demands "unusually great" responsibility for property in their care, approaching that of insurers.[21]

This taxonomy of bailments has survived the twentieth century and remains relevant in American law, with courts and commentators consistently relying on it.[22] As we examine the novel challenges presented by custody relationships involving digital assets, the classification framework illustrated in Figure 4.1 provides powerful analytical tools for understanding these emerging arrangements.

4.2.2 Bailment key tenets

By the close of the nineteenth century, the essential elements of a bailment relationship had become solidly established within Anglo-American jurisprudence, providing a clear and enduring framework that continues to inform contemporary legal thought. In this section, we focus on five key

[21] SCHOULER, *supra* note 3 (1st ed. 1880).

[22] *See* D'Onfro, *supra* note 6, at 105; *see also* 8A AM. JUR. 2d *Bailments* § 7 (2024); WILLISTON & LORD, *supra* note 10, § 53:2.

tenets[23] that are especially significant to our inquiry into the custody of digital assets: the requirements for formation, the doctrine regarding tangible objects, the bailor's retention of title, the obligations of the parties, and the requirement of redelivery.

(a) Formation requirements

First, the creation of the traditional bailment relationship requires the concurrence of three elements.[24] The bailor must deliver possession of goods or transfer control of the object of the bailment, whether actually or constructively.[25] This principle underscores the fundamental difference between a bailment and a sale or gift, in which ownership, rather than mere possession or control, is conveyed. This distinction is also crucial for differentiating bailments from transactions where ownership is transferred, and the transferee simultaneously assumes an obligation to return equivalent goods or value to the transferor, as in a loan for consumption, financial repurchase agreements whereby securities are sold with a commitment to repurchase equivalent securities (repos), and the Roman law *mutuum*.[26] Beyond delivery, acceptance by the bailee is required, reflecting the relationship's voluntary and consensual nature—the bailee must knowingly take control of the object and its attendant responsibilities.[27] Finally, there must be an agreed upon purpose, whether explicit or implied, which defines the scope of obligations. This distinguishes bailments from leases, although it should be noted that a lease agreement may create a bailment where it gives the lessee the right to use an object without transferring ownership of the property.[28]

(b) Tangible object doctrine

Second, while the traditional domain of bailment was tangible property, commercial necessity gradually expanded its reach to embrace certain intangible assets.[29] Historically, the law of bailments was firmly rooted in the custody of tangible personal property—goods and chattels that could be physically delivered from bailor to bailee.[30] This focus on corporeal objects aligned with the historical

[23] *See* Giuliano G. Castellano & Andrea Tosato, *Commercial Law Intersections*, 72 Hastings L.J. 999, 1041 (2021) (defining key tenets as "dispositive rules and principles that articulate the legal framework necessary to realize the policy aims of" a particular area of the law).

[24] 8A Am. Jur. 2d *Bailments* § 1; Schouler, *supra* note 3, § 1.

[25] 8A Am. Jur. 2d *Bailments* §§ 40, 41; Lawson, *supra* note 3, h. II § 5; Schouler, *supra* note 3, § 2; 2 James Kent, Commentaries on American Law *559 (Boston, Little, Brown & Co., 12th ed. 1873).

[26] 8A Am. Jur. 2d *Bailments* § 16. On the Roman law *mutuum* and its distinction from bailment, see Story, *supra* note 3, at 40 (4th ed 1846); Kent, *supra* note 25, at *573–74, *589.

[27] 8A Am. Jur. 2d *Bailments* § 44; Schouler, *supra* note 3, § 19; Lawson, *supra* note 3, ch. II, § 8.

[28] 8A Am. Jur. 2d *Bailments* § 5; *see also id.* § 24.

[29] *Id.* § 3; Lawson, *supra* note 3, ch. II § 7.

[30] 8A Am. Jur. 2d *Bailments* § 3; Knapp, Stout & Co. v. McCaffrey, 52 N.E. 898 (Ill. 1899), *aff'd*, 177 U.S. 638 (1900); Schouler, *supra* note 3, § 1.

emphasis on physical possession as a prerequisite for creating the bailment relationship. However, by the early nineteenth century, the increasing complexity of commercial practices prompted legal recognition of certain intangible assets, such as stocks, bonds, and negotiable instruments, as suitable objects of bailment.[31] The enabling element was that these intangibles were embodied in physical documents, such as paper stock certificates or promissory notes, which acted as tangible representations of the incorporeal rights they represented. Although the underlying asset was intangible, such as ownership in a corporation, the right to payment, or a monetary claim, its representation in the form of a corporeal thing allowed it to be physically delivered, accepted, and redelivered, thereby fitting within the traditional framework of bailment law.[32] This principle continues to govern the bailment of intangibles today.[33]

(c) Bailor's retention of title

Third, bailment necessarily entails a separation between ownership and possession, from which flow distinctive legal consequences.[34] The bailor retains ownership throughout the bailment's duration, while the bailee holds temporary possession or control solely for the agreed purpose.[35] The bailee has such control and dominion over the property as will allow them to exclude all others from possession, including the bailor, yet remains estopped from denying the bailor's title.[36] Moreover, this separation shapes third-party claims: Bailed property in the possession of the bailee generally is not subject to attachment or levy under process against the bailee to satisfy claims of the bailee's creditors.[37] Similarly, an unauthorized transfer or encumbrance by the bailee does not divest the bailor of title to the property, and the bailor may recover the asset in question from that third party or hold that party liable for its value in cases of loss or damage.[38]

This separation between ownership and possession has long presented challenges in commercial contexts.[39] The most persistent is the ostensible ownership problem—where third parties, lacking notice of the bailor's ownership, are misled by the bailee's possession.[40] Early responses included the development of

[31] 8A Am. Jur. 2d *Bailments* § 3; Lawson, *supra* note 3, ch. II § 7; Kent, *supra* note 25, at *578.

[32] 8A Am. Jur. 2d *Bailments* § 62; Schouler, *supra* note 3, § 2; Dean Witter Reynolds Inc. v. Variable Annuity Life Ins. Co., 373 F.3d 1100 (10th Cir. 2004).

[33] 8A Am. Jur. 2d *Bailments* § 62; Powers v. Pac. Diesel Engine Co., 274 P. 512 (Cal. 1929).

[34] 8A Am. Jur. 2d *Bailments* § 51; Schouler, *supra* note 3, § 2; Kent, *supra* note 25, at *568.

[35] 8A Am. Jur. 2d *Bailments* § 51; Lawson, *supra* note 3, ch. III § 15; Kent, *supra* note 25, at 574–75.

[36] 8A Am. Jur. 2d *Bailments* § 52; *id.* § 53 (regarding estoppel); Schouler, *supra* note 3, § 22; Kent, *supra* note 25, at *585.

[37] 8A Am. Jur. 2d *Bailments* § 65; Lawson, *supra* note 3, ch. III § 17; Schouler, *supra* note 3, § 23; Kent, *supra* note 25, at *567.

[38] 8A Am. Jur. 2d *Bailments* § 58; Lawson, *supra* note 3, ch. III § 16; Kent, *supra* note 25, at *569.

[39] 8A Am. Jur. 2d *Bailments* § 58; Schouler, *supra* note 3, § 27; Lawson, *supra* note 3, ch. III § 20.

[40] *See* Douglas G. Baird & Thomas H. Jackson, *Possession and Ownership: An Examination of the Scope of Article 9*, 35 Stan. L. Rev. 175, 189–94 (1983); *contra* Charles W. Mooney, Jr., *The Mystery*

the factor's exception to the *nemo dat* rule, which allowed good faith purchasers to acquire title to goods sold by a factor even if the factor lacked explicit authority to sell.[41] However, this was a narrow exception, confined to specific commercial contexts.[42]

By the twentieth century, these challenges intensified, particularly with insolvent bailees. Creditors increasingly sought to attach property held by bailees, leading to inconsistent judicial responses.[43] This period was marked by legal uncertainty as courts struggled to balance the interests of bailors, bailees, and third parties.[44] Eventually, to bring order and legal predictability, UCC Article 9 made narrow but significant modifications to the traditional common law rules of bailment by subjecting certain leases and consignments to public filing requirements.[45] Under these provisions, bailors must file and provide public notice of their ownership interests to protect their claims against third parties dealing with the bailee.[46]

(d) Parties' obligations

Fourth, the duties of bailees vary depending on the distribution of benefits between parties and are sometimes shaped by policy considerations that lead to special liability regimes.[47] Albeit subject to exceptions, the schema can be summarized as follows: In gratuitous bailments benefiting only the bailor, the bailee owes a minimal duty of slight diligence and is liable only for gross negligence.[48] Conversely, in bailments benefiting only the bailee, such as a gratuitous loan for use (*commodatum*), the law demands exceptional diligence, making the bailee liable for even slight negligence.[49] In mutually beneficial bailments, such as paid storage or transport, the bailee must exercise ordinary diligence and is consequently liable for ordinary negligence.[50]

and Myth of "Ostensible Ownership" and Article 9 Filing: A Critique of Proposals to Extend Filing Requirements to Leases, 39 Ala. L. Rev. 683, 725–30 (1988) [hereinafter Mooney, *Mystery & Myth*].

41 See 8A Am. Jur. 2d *Bailments* § 59.

42 Originally, the exception was limited to agents entrusted with goods for sale (factors), not all bailees. *See* Pickering v. Busk (1812) 104 Eng. Rep. 758; 15 East 38 (KB); George v. Clagett (1797) 101 Eng. Rep. 1019; 7 T.R. 359, (KB); *see also* Harold C. Havighurst, Handbook of the Law of Contracts 445 (2d ed. 1971).

43 Mooney, *Mystery & Myth*, *supra* note 40, at 725–30.

44 *Id.*

45 8A Am. Jur. 2d *Bailments* § 26; Grant Gilmore, Security Interests in Personal Property § 3.6 (1965).

46 Steven L. Harris & Charles W. Mooney, Jr., Security Interests in Personal Property 295–304 (6th ed. 2016).

47 8A Am. Jur. 2d *Bailments* § 78; Schouler, *supra* note 3, § 15; Lawson, *supra* note 3, § 11.

48 Kent, *supra* note 25, at *560.

49 *Id.* at 574–75.

50 8A Am. Jur. 2d *Bailments* §§ 74–78.

These gradations of liability, firmly established by the nineteenth century, reflect a careful balancing of interests in ordinary bailments. However, this three-tiered framework of liability based on benefit proved inadequate to address certain commercial relationships where public policy demanded enhanced obligations. This, in turn, led courts to develop specialized categories of *extraordinary bailments* with heightened standards of care.[51] These heightened liability standards emerged from the unique functions and roles played by certain bailees—such as public carriers, innkeepers, and warehouse operators.[52] Such entities often occupied monopolistic or quasi-monopolistic positions, leaving bailors with few alternatives for safeguarding their property.[53]

(e) Redelivery

Fifth, upon the completion of the agreed purpose or expiration of the stipulated period, the bailee is obliged either to return the property to the bailor or to duly account for it.[54] Alternatively, the bailee may retain the property until it is reclaimed by the bailor, provided that such retention aligns with the terms of the bailment or relevant legal principles, such as the existence of a valid lien for unpaid charges. As a general rule, the redelivery obligation demands that the bailee return the exact item originally delivered, preserving its identity and condition.[55] If the purported bailee is not bound to return the same items that were delivered by the bailor but may deliver any other item or items of equal value, there is no bailment. In such cases, courts typically characterize the transaction in question as creating a debtor–creditor relationship rather than a bailment, with title to the goods passing to the purported bailee.

However, the bailment of fungible goods has long tested the boundaries of this tenet. During the course of the nineteenth century, exceptions were introduced for commodities, securities, and negotiable instruments transferable by delivery, whereby redelivery need not involve the exact same goods initially entrusted to the bailee.[56] Courts progressively recognized that when grain was stored in a communal warehouse or elevator, mixed with grain of like quality from other bailors, returning an equivalent quantity and quality of grain was sufficient to satisfy the bailee's obligation.[57] This arrangement was premised on the idea that depositors were tenants-in-common of the commingled grain, with the

[51] *Id.* § 78.
[52] *Id.*; KENT, *supra* note 25, at *593–94.
[53] 8A AM. JUR. 2d *Bailments* § 78.
[54] KENT, *supra* note 25, at *566.
[55] *Id.* at *573–74.
[56] See SCHOULER, *supra* note 3, at 64–68 (1st ed. 1880); VAN ZILE, *supra* note 9, at 125 (2d ed. 1908).
[57] Courts initially did not recognize such arrangement as bailments. *See* Wilson v. Cooper, 10 Iowa 565 (1860); Hurd v. West, 7 Cow. 752 (N.Y. Sup. Ct. 1827); Smith v. Clark, 21 Wend. 83 (N.Y. Sup. Ct. 1839); Norton v. Woodruff, 2 Comst. 153 (N.Y. 1849);. Over time, however, this position shifted. *See* Leyard v. Hibbard, 48 Mich. 421 (1882); Nelson v. Brown, 44 Iowa 455 (1876).

warehouseman maintaining an individualized bailor–bailee relationship with each depositor.[58]

Similarly, with respect to stocks and bonds, courts increasingly held that an arrangement could qualify as a bailment even if the bailee were not obligated to return the exact same certificates, provided the bailor received an equivalent number of shares of the same type and value.[59] This reflected the growing recognition that the specific identity of the certificate was becoming less important than the ability to deliver the correct number and class of shares.[60] Nevertheless, to preserve the distinction between bailment and a sale with an obligation to redeliver goods of the same kind, courts required that the bailee always maintain sufficient reserves to meet all of its redelivery obligations.[61] Any shortfall in reserves, or an option to substitute payment in place of redelivery, could result in recharacterizing the entire transaction as a sale, thereby forfeiting the protections of bailment law and, perhaps most importantly, exposing the goods to the claims of the bailee's creditors.[62]

Courts and commentators at the time argued that the legal rationale supporting these exceptions centered on practicality and commercial necessity, but they also recognized that these exceptions created challenges by blurring the line between bailments on the one hand and sales requiring return of similar goods on the other. Courts struggled to create clear rules, particularly when the bailee held fungible assets in a common pool. If the bailee was seen as having unrestricted control—such as the ability to sell goods from the common mass without maintaining sufficient reserves for redelivery—the transaction would be recharacterized as a sale, resulting in the loss of the bailment law protections outlined above.

This uncertainty surrounding the common law regime for bailment of fungible goods and securities led to yet another round of statutory interventions that resulted in today's UCC Articles 7 and 8.[63] Article 7 addressed the challenges of bailments involving fungible goods, particularly commodities stored in

[58] Central States Corp. v. Luther, 215 Fed. 2d 38 (10th Cir. 1954); Flour Mills of Am. v. Burrus Mills, 258 P.2d 341 (Kan. 1953); Zuber v. Minshall, 256 P. 806 (Kan. 1921); Moses v. Teetors, 67 P. 526 (Kan. 1902); Dawson v. United States, 203 F.2d 201 (5th Cir. 1953); Rotterman v. Gen. Mills, Inc., 61 N.W.2d 718 (Iowa 1953); Burke v. Boulder Milling & Elev. Co., 235 P. 574 (Colo. 1925).

[59] Van Zile, *supra* note 9, at 125 (2d ed. 1908); Schouler, *supra* note 3, at 45–47 (1st ed. 1880); Lawson, *supra* note 3, at 243.

[60] Early cases distinguished between specific, identifiable certificates and fungible ones, a distinction later abandoned. *See* Gorman v. Littlefield, 229 U.S. 19 (1913); Robertson v. Ramsey, 66 S.W.2d 1022 (Tenn. Ct. App. 1933); Christensen v. Pugh, 36 P.2d 100 (Utah 1934).

[61] For stocks and other financial instruments, see *Gorman*, 229 U.S. 19; *Robertson*, 66 S.W.2d 1022; *Christensen*, 36 P.2d 100.

[62] *See, e.g.*, *Burke*, 235 P. 574; *Edwards*, 137 S.W.2d 447; *Greene*, 170 S.W.2d 191; *Rotterman*, 61 N.W.2d 718.

[63] Article 7 was promulgated in 1951 and then revised in 2003 and 2022. *See* N.Y.C. Bar Ass'n Comm. on Pers. Prop. L., Report on Revised Article 7 of the Uniform Commercial Code (Feb. 2004). Article 8 was promulgated in 1951 and then revised in 1977, 1994 and 2022. *See* Charles W. Mooney, Jr., *Beyond Negotiability: A New Model for Transfer and Pledge of Interests in Securities Controlled by Intermediaries*, 12 Cardozo L. Rev. 305 (1990) [hereinafter Mooney, *Beyond Negotiability*].

common pools.[64] It established a system based on warehouse receipts, which served as documents of title representing the bailor's interest in the commingled mass, and an obligation for warehouse operators to maintain reserves sufficient to cover all outstanding receipts. This brought legal certainty, ensuring transparency, minimizing ostensible ownership issues, and protecting bailors' interests against third-party claims. Article 8, particularly after its significant revisions in 1994, brought similar clarity to the realm of financial instruments, addressing securities held in intermediated systems.[65] Together, these statutory frameworks provided a more comprehensive and coherent system that balanced the needs of commerce with the key tenets of bailment.

Having examined these key tenets of bailment law, we now turn to two specialized categories that developed distinctive legal regimes: *deposits of money* and *securities*. The unique characteristics of these assets—their fungibility, negotiability, and central role in commerce and finance—prompted courts and legislatures to craft special rules that departed significantly from traditional bailment frameworks. Understanding these historical adaptations provides valuable insights for analyzing modern custodial arrangements involving digital assets, which share some of these features.

4.2.3 Deposit of money

The key tenets of bailment we have just examined provide a framework for analyzing custodial relationships, although this body of rules should not be considered absolute. Nevertheless, the legal history of bailment reveals a recurring pattern: As commercial practices evolve, certain types of transactions strain against established doctrinal boundaries, prompting courts and legislatures to adapt the law in response. Perhaps no example better illustrates this evolutionary process than the *deposit of money*, particularly in the banking system. While money deposits initially operated within bailment's traditional confines, their unique characteristics—fungibility, economic function, and centrality to commerce—ultimately necessitated a distinct legal regime that diverged significantly from ordinary bailment principles. This historical development offers valuable insights as we consider how digital asset custody might similarly challenge conventional legal frameworks.

[64] *See generally* 6 William D. Hawkland, Alaina Gimbert, Carl Bjerre, Larry T. Garvin, Sarah Jane Hughes, Steven L. Harris, Thomas S. Hemmendinger, William D. Hawkland & William H. Henning, Hawkland's Uniform Commercial Code Series §§ 7-101:1 to 7-101:2 (Nov. 2024 update), Westlaw Hawkland §§ 7-101:1, 7-101:2.

[65] It is important to note that Article 8 provisions are not the only ones governing securities transactions; other laws, particularly federal securities regulations, also play a significant role. *See generally* Mooney, *Beyond Negotiability*, *supra* note 63.

The deposit of money, as a distinct legal concept, has ancient roots, predating even the Roman Empire. Evidence suggests that forms of banking and deposit-taking existed in Ptolemaic Egypt, where temples and royal granaries often served as repositories for valuables and facilitated transfers between accounts.[66] Similarly, the Talmud contains discussions of deposits with money changers, indicating the practice of entrusting money to specialized individuals for safe-keeping and potential investment.[67]

While these early civilizations established important precedents in money deposit practices, it was within Roman law that the deposit of money received its most exhaustive early legal treatment. In the classical period, Roman jurists treated such arrangements as they would any other loan of a fungible asset for consumption, where ownership passed to the borrower, classifying it as a *mutuum*.[68] For example, a *mutuum* transaction might involve a merchant borrowing one hundred pieces of coinage from a financier to purchase goods. Under the principles of *mutuum*, the merchant is not required to return the exact same coins received. Instead, the merchant must repay the financier with one hundred coins of equal quality within the agreed time frame, although not necessarily the original pieces.

Over time, however, the unique characteristics of money deposits, coupled with their increasing use in commerce, led to the development of an adjacent but distinct legal institution: *depositum irregulare*.[69]

Both *mutuum* and *depositum irregulare* involved the transfer of fungible assets, but the key distinction lay in the parties' intended relationship.[70] Specifically, the *depositum irregulare* offered important legal protections that set it apart from a simple loan (*mutuum*).[71] The *depositum irregulare* maintained its essential character as a deposit despite permitting the use of the deposited funds—a unique legal hybrid that combined the safekeeping purpose of *depositum* with the practical utility of *mutuum*. While the depositary could use the funds like a borrower in *mutuum*, the relationship remained fundamentally one of custody, reflecting the parties' primary intent of safekeeping rather than lending.[72]

[66] David M. Schaps, The Invention of Coinage and the Monetization of Ancient Greece 175 (2007); 1 M. Rostovtzeff, The Social and Economic History of the Hellenistic World 283–91 (1941); 2 *id.* at 1193–1202.

[67] The precise legal nature of these arrangements remains debated. *See* Babylonian Talmud, Bava Metzia 42a–43a. *See also Bailments*, *in* 2 The Jewish Encyclopedia 456 (Isidore Singer ed., 1901).

[68] *See* 2 Raymond Monier, Manuel de droit romain, Les obligations 124 (5th ed. 1954); *see also* W. W. Buckland, A Text-Book of Roman Law from Augustus to Justinian 489 (3d ed. 1963).

[69] *See* Monier, *supra* note 68, at 124 (noting that *depositum irregulare* had Hellenic roots); Max Kaser, Roman Private Law 205 (Rolf Dannenbring trans., 4th ed. 1984).

[70] Buckland, *supra* note 68, at 466–67 ("There is but a fine line between [*depositum irregulare*] and [*mutuum*], the difference being one of intent.")

[71] *See* Monier, *supra* note 68, at 124; Kaser, *supra* note 69, at 205.

[72] Kaser, *supra* note 69, at 205.

Consider the following example: Imagine that Titius deposited one thousand coins with a banker (known as an *argentarius*). Under *depositum irregulare*, Titius retained special rights that a regular borrower would not. He could demand his money back at any time, and if the banker became insolvent, Titius would have priority over the banker's ordinary creditors. In turn, the banker could use these deposited funds in its business and pay interest on them, much as is done by modern banks.

However, some key questions about these banking arrangements remain debated by scholars.[73] For instance, if Titius received interest on his deposit, would he still maintain his privileged position if the banker went bankrupt? Some ancient sources suggest Titius would lose this protection, but scholars disagree about whether this was a universal rule or how widely it was applied. Similarly, Roman law scholars continue to debate the exact nature of these banking relationships, particularly how the depositor's right to immediate withdrawal was balanced against the banker's ability to use the funds.

Yet, despite uncertainties about its historical trajectory and exact contours, the development of *depositum irregulare* and its ultimate recognition in the Roman Emperor Justinian's Digest evidences the first documented instance of a pattern that would repeat itself throughout legal history: the adaptation of general deposit and bailment principles to accommodate the unique characteristics of money, particularly in the context of banking.[74]

This pattern is lucidly visible during the late Middle Ages and Renaissance, in the Italian commercial centers.[75] As money increasingly served not just as a store of value but also as a medium of exchange and an object of investment, its deposit came to be governed by rules that departed significantly from the general principles of deposit and bailment.[76] Venetian law and practice recognized the distinction between *depositum regulare* and *depositum irregulare*, as understood by medieval jurists.[77] The former, the regular deposit, involved the consignment of valuables (including money, if in sealed bags), merchandise, or other goods for safekeeping. The custodian, whether a merchant or a moneychanger, had no right to use what remained on deposit. The items were treated as nonfungible, and custodians had to restore to the owner on demand exactly what had been entrusted to them.

[73] See BUCKLAND, *supra* note 68, at 489; MONIER, *supra* note 68, at 124.

[74] MONIER, *supra* note 68, at 124; DIG. 16.3.25.1 (Papinian, Resp. 3). For a more complete discussion, see WILLIAM GORDON, ROMAN LAW, SCOTS LAW AND LEGAL HISTORY 61–69 (2008) ("Observations on *Depositum Irregulare*").

[75] RAYMOND DE ROOVER, THE RISE AND DECLINE OF THE MEDICI BANK 1397–1494 (1963) [hereinafter DE ROOVER, THE RISE AND DECLINE]; REINHOLD C. MUELLER, THE VENETIAN MONEY MARKET: BANKS, PANICS, AND THE PUBLIC DEBT, 1200-1500, at 51–62 (1997).

[76] DE ROOVER, THE RISE AND DECLINE *supra* note 75, at 34–55 (describing the innovative practices of major Italian banking houses, including deposit operations); MUELLER, *supra* note 75, at 80–85.

[77] MUELLER, *supra* note 75, at 10.

By contrast, in irregular deposits, the depositary was permitted to employ the funds entrusted to them. This implied both the transfer of ownership from depositor to depositary and the depositor's participation in the risk of the enterprise, whether the deposit was interest-bearing or not.[78] The legal implications of this distinction were reflected in Venetian bankruptcy law: While *regular* depositors could reclaim their specific deposits in full upon the insolvency of the custodian, those who had made *irregular* deposits were treated as normal creditors, having to await their turn for repayment along with other claimants of the custodian.[79] This legal framework effectively enabled Venetian banks to operate on a fractional reserve basis, keeping only a portion of deposits available for immediate withdrawal while employing the rest in their business ventures.[80]

Similarly, Florentine banking law and practice developed the institute of *depositi a discrezione* (discretionary deposits).[81] As evidenced by the Medici Bank's practices, these were recorded separately from demand deposits in the *libro segreto* (secret book), reflecting their distinct legal character.[82] The *depositi a discrezione* served not merely as safekeeping arrangements but as investment vehicles, typically made by prominent figures who placed substantial sums with banks for extended periods.[83] Unlike regular deposits, these accounts carried interest, though this was carefully disguised as a "gift" (*discrezione*) to navigate canonical prohibitions against usury. The terminology itself reflected this delicate balance: *Discrezione* referred both to the banker's discretion in using the funds and to the discretionary nature of the return paid to depositors.[84] When financial difficulties arose, these depositors' status became particularly precarious, as illustrated by the case of the French diplomat Philippe de Commines, who lost substantial sums in disputed *discrezione* payments when the Medici Bank faced liquidity problems.[85] Like their Venetian counterparts, Florentine banks thus operated on a fractional reserve basis.

The development of distinct rules for monetary deposits continued in England, albeit along a different trajectory that centered on goldsmith-bankers. Throughout the seventeenth century, goldsmith-bankers evolved from mere custodians of precious metals into full-fledged bankers, lending out deposited funds at interest.[86] The practice gained momentum during the period of the English Civil War when merchants, concerned about security, sought safe

[78] *Id.* at 11.
[79] *Id.*
[80] *Id.* at 17.
[81] de Roover, The Rise and Decline, *supra* note 75, at 98.
[82] *Id.*
[83] *Id.*
[84] *Id.* at 101–02.
[85] *Id.* at 103–05.
[86] R. D. Richards, The Early History of Banking in England 23–24 (1929).

places for their specie and plate, thereby gradually transforming goldsmiths from simple bailees into recognized deposit keepers and lenders.[87] By the 1660s, these goldsmith-bankers were issuing promissory notes against deposits, which circulated as an early form of paper money.[88] Their practices represented a significant departure from traditional bailment principles, as they not only accepted deposits but paid interest on them and made use of such deposits for loans to customers.[89]

This evolutionary process culminated in the 1848 landmark decision of *Foley v. Hill*, where the House of Lords definitively held that the relationship between a banker and a customer concerning money deposited was that of debtor and creditor, not bailee and bailor.[90] The opinion clarified that money paid into a bank ceases to be the money of the customer and instead becomes the property of the banker, who, in turn, is then obliged to repay an equivalent sum. This meant that the banker did not act as a trustee or agent who must maintain specific coins in specie, but rather as a debtor who had contracted to repay the customer's balance on demand. The emergence of these new legal principles, distinct from the traditional rules of bailment, was built upon decades of goldsmith-banking practices that had effectively created a system of transferable credit instruments functioning as currency while simultaneously putting deposited money to productive use through lending.

The principle established in *Foley v. Hill* found fertile ground in the United States during the nineteenth century. The rapid growth of interstate trade, the proliferation of banking institutions, and the increasing sophistication of financial transactions demanded a legal framework that could accommodate both traditional custodial functions and modern banking practices. Under these pressures, American courts elaborated a sophisticated regime for money deposits that built upon, yet diverged significantly from, ordinary bailment principles.

General deposits, the most common form, created a debtor–creditor relationship wherein the bank acquired full title to the deposited funds and assumed an obligation to repay an equivalent sum on demand. Special deposits, in contrast, maintained the traditional characteristics of bailment. In other words, the bank held specific property as a custodian with no right to use it and an obligation to return the identical item. Between these categories emerged specific deposits for particular purposes, where money or negotiable instruments were deposited for collection or some other defined objective, thereby creating a hybrid relationship that could shift from agency to debtor–creditor as circumstances changed. For

[87] *Id.* at 35–36.
[88] *Id.* at 40–41.
[89] *Id.* at 29–30.
[90] Foley v. Hill (1848) 9 Eng. Rep. 1002 (HL).

example, if a customer deposited a check for $20,000 with instructions for the bank to collect the funds and use them to purchase certain debt securities when they became available, the bank would initially act as the customer's agent in collecting the check. Once collected, the funds would be held in a specific deposit until the debt securities could be purchased. If the debt securities were unavailable and the customer instructed the bank simply to credit the funds to their account, the relationship would transform into a standard debtor-creditor arrangement.

The development of these rules was neither linear nor free from contention. American courts struggled particularly with questions surrounding bank insolvency.[91] When could depositors claim their funds as special deposits rather than merely share ratably with the bank's general creditors? What rights did depositors have when banks accepted deposits while knowingly insolvent? Courts reached divergent conclusions, sometimes treating public deposits differently from private ones, while at other times focusing on whether the funds could be specifically traced.

The doctrinal confusion and inconsistent outcomes surrounding bank insolvency, particularly the treatment of different types of deposits, persisted well into the twentieth century.[92] However, a combination of legislative reforms and regulatory oversight gradually brought greater stability and predictability to the field. The establishment of the Federal Reserve System in 1913 marked a pivotal step toward centralizing banking regulation and providing a lender of last resort to mitigate the risk of bank runs.[93] Even more transformative was the creation of the Federal Deposit Insurance Corporation (FDIC) in 1933, and later the National Credit Union Administration (NCUA) in 1970, which fundamentally altered the landscape by providing federal insurance for deposits held in banks and credit unions, respectively, up to specified limits.[94] This federal guarantee significantly reduced the risk to depositors, effectively eliminating the need to distinguish between different types of deposits for most practical purposes and largely resolving the contentious issue of depositor priority in insolvency.[95]

[91] *See, e.g.*, St. Louis & S.F. Ry. Co. v. Johnston, 133 U.S. 566 (1890); Quin v. Earle, 95 F. 728 (E.D. Pa. 1899).

[92] *See* Joseph H. Sommer, *Special Deposits*, 76 Bus. Law. 841, 848 (2021); *see also* Recent Case, *Trusts-Bank Deposit for Specific Purposes*, 16 Harv. L. Rev. 228 (1903).

[93] *See generally* Federal Reserve Act of 1913, ch. 6, 38 Stat. 251 (codified as amended at 12 U.S.C. §§ 221 et seq.).

[94] *See generally* Banking Act of 1933, ch. 89, § 8, 48 Stat. 162, 168 (codified as amended at 12 U.S.C. §§ 1811 et seq.) (establishing the FDIC); Federal Credit Union Act of 1970, Pub. L. No. 91-468, 84 Stat. 994) (codified as amended at 12 U.S.C. § 1782) (establishing the NCUA); *see also* Milton Friedman & Anna J. Schwartz, A Monetary History of the United States, 1867-1960, at 434–41 (1963).

[95] Carter H. Golembe, *Origins of Deposit Insurance in the Middle West, 1834-1866*, 51 Ind. Mag. Hist. 113 (1955); Charles W. Calomiris & Eugene N. White, *The Origins of Federal Deposit Insurance*, *in* The Regulated Economy: A Historical Approach to Political Economy 145 (Claudia Goldin & Gary D. Libecap eds., 1994).

The adoption of the Uniform Commercial Code in the 1950s, particularly Article 4 on Bank Deposits and Collections, further consolidated this evolution by providing a comprehensive legal framework governing the mechanical aspects of the bank–customer relationship. The statute covered a range of issues from the process of deposit and collection to the allocation of risks and responsibilities.[96] While specialized rules continue to exist for certain types of deposits or specific circumstances, the combination of federal deposit insurance, systematic regulation, and uniform commercial laws has largely overcome the historical uncertainties and inconsistencies that once plagued this area of law.

4.2.4 Deposit of securities

Another bailment relationship that has evolved significantly from traditional principles and developed its own specialized legal framework is the deposit of securities. While the core concept of custody remains, the nature of securities, their crucial role in financial markets, and the complex web of intermediaries involved in their holding and transfer have necessitated a departure from the traditional bailor–bailee relationship.[97] It is important to note at the outset that approaches to regulating intermediated securities holdings vary considerably across jurisdictions, with significant differences across the European Union, Great Britain, and the United States.[98] The discussion that follows focuses primarily on the American legal framework.

As discussed earlier in this chapter, securities posed significant challenges to the traditional bailment framework as early as the nineteenth century. The fungibility of these assets and their use as investments strained against the general requirement that bailees return the same items they received. American courts adapted by recognizing that an arrangement could qualify as a bailment even if the bailee were not obligated to return the exact same securities, provided that the bailor received assets of the same type and value.[99] However, to maintain the distinction between such bailments and sales with an obligation to redeliver goods of the same kind, the common law required bailees to maintain sufficient reserves to meet all their redelivery obligations. While this solution enabled securities-related commercial practices to continue, it was far from perfect. It

[96] James J. White & Robert S. Summers, Uniform Commercial Code § 20-1 (6th ed. 2010).

[97] Guy Morton, *Historical Introduction: The Growth of Intermediation and Development of Legal Analysis of Intermediated Securities*, *in* Intermediation and Beyond 23 (Louise Gullifer & Jennifer Payne eds., 2019); Joanna Benjamin, Interests in Securities: A Proprietary Law Analysis of the International Securities Markets (2000).

[98] Eva Micheler, Property in Securities: A Comparative Study (2007); Roy Goode, Hideki Kanda & Karl Kreuzer, Hague Securities Convention: Explanatory Report (2005).

[99] *See* Van Zile, *supra* note 9, at 9–10.

created challenges in determining and verifying adequate reserves, exacerbated ostensible ownership problems, and generated significant uncertainty in bailee insolvency scenarios where bailors and the bailee's creditors might clash over the deposited assets.[100]

These limitations of the common law framework for securities bailments became even more problematic in the latter half of the twentieth century, as financial markets underwent a transformative shift toward indirect holding systems.[101] By the 1970s, the sheer volume of securities transactions had rendered the physical delivery of certificates impractical, leading to what became known as the "paperwork crisis" on Wall Street.[102] This crisis spurred the development of centralized securities depositories like the Depository Trust Company (DTC) and accelerated the transition to a system where most securities were immobilized with these depositories and beneficial ownership interests were transferred through book entries on the records of securities intermediaries.[103]

This paradigm shift demanded a new legal framework. Initial reform attempts, such as the 1978 revisions to UCC Article 8, focused on the concept of uncertificated securities. Yet, this legal device ultimately proved inadequate to address the complexities of the rapidly evolving indirect holding system.[104] A more comprehensive solution emerged through the 1994 revision of Article 8, which was adopted by all US states and has since been amended, most recently in 2022.[105]

This landmark revision represented a fundamental reconceptualization, creating a coherent legal architecture specifically designed for modern transactions in intermediated securities. Moving decisively away from traditional common law notions, Article 8 introduced an entirely new set of legal categories and relationships.[106] At the heart of this innovative schema lie four interconnected concepts: *securities intermediary*, *financial asset*, *securities account*, and *securities entitlement*.

Securities intermediary encompasses any "person . . . that in the ordinary course of its business maintains securities accounts for others and is acting in that capacity."[107] This definition is thus anchored in function rather than

[100] See Jeanne L. Schroeder, *Is Article 8 Finally Ready This Time? The Radical Reform of Secured Lending on Wall Street*, 1994 Colum. Bus. L. Rev. 291, 328–31.

[101] *Id.* at 322.

[102] James Steven Rogers, *Policy Perspectives on Revised U.C.C. Article 8*, 43 UCLA L. Rev. 1431, 1442 (1996).

[103] Schroeder, *supra* note 100, at 324–25.

[104] For a comprehensive assessment, see *id.*

[105] The 1994 revisions were subsequently amended in 2022, but these changes have not altered the fundamental indirect holding system framework.

[106] As discussed in Chapter 1 in this book, this represents another instance where the UCC has introduced novel legal categories, largely superseding traditional common law frameworks in response to commercial practices.

[107] U.C.C. § 8-102(a)(14) (Am. L. Inst. & Unif. L. Comm'n 2001).

form—focusing on the activity of maintaining securities accounts rather than limiting its scope to traditional financial institutions like banks, brokers, and clearing corporations.

Similarly, the definition of *financial asset* is broader than one might instinctively presume. The term comprises three subcategories: "(i) a security; (ii) an obligation . . . , participation, or other interest in a person or in property or an enterprise of a person, which is dealt in or traded on financial markets;" and "(iii) any property that is held by a securities intermediary for another person in a securities account if the securities intermediary has expressly agreed with the other person that the property is to be treated as a financial asset."[108] Notably, this definition is only relevant for the UCC and, as such, can differ markedly from the definition of financial asset as that term is used in financial regulation.

Consider a simple, mainstream example to put these concepts into context. Take Fidelity Investments, a well-known brokerage firm, and shares of stock in Apple Inc. Fidelity Investments maintains securities accounts for its clients as a central part of its business. These accounts allow Fidelity's clients to buy, sell, and hold various financial assets, including shares of corporate stock. Thus, Fidelity is a classic example of a *securities intermediary* under Article 8. Shares of stock in Apple Inc. held in such an account would qualify as financial assets for two reasons: first, they fall squarely within the definition of a security[109] (the first category); and, second, they also represent an "interest in a person" (i.e., Apple Inc.) that is "dealt in or traded on financial markets" (the second category).

Article 8 vests persons holding financial assets in securities accounts with a package of rights and property interests, collectively termed a *security entitlement*. From a functional perspective, they can be summarized as follows: First, financial assets held by a securities intermediary for an entitlement holder are not subject to the claims of the intermediary's creditors.[110] Second, a securities intermediary must always hold sufficient assets to cover all claims of its entitlement holders.[111] Third, a securities intermediary must turn over all payments or distributions received with respect to a financial asset to its corresponding entitlement holder.[112] Fourth, a securities intermediary must only exercise any rights and privileges of ownership stemming from a financial asset pursuant to the directions of its corresponding entitlement holder.[113] Fifth, a securities intermediary must dispose of the financial assets at the discretion of the corresponding entitlement holder.[114]

[108] U.C.C. § 8-102(a)(9) (Am. L. Inst. & Unif. L. Comm'n 2001).
[109] U.C.C. § 8-102(a)(15) (Am. L. Inst. & Unif. L. Comm'n 2001).
[110] *See* U.C.C. § 8-503 (Am. L. Inst. & Unif. L. Comm'n 2001).
[111] *See* U.C.C. § 8-504 (Am. L. Inst. & Unif. L. Comm'n 2001).
[112] *See* U.C.C. § 8-505 (Am. L. Inst. & Unif. L. Comm'n 2001).
[113] *See* U.C.C. § 8-506 (Am. L. Inst. & Unif. L. Comm'n 2001).
[114] *See* U.C.C. § 8-507 (Am. L. Inst. & Unif. L. Comm'n 2001).

Thus, under Article 8, a person who holds financial assets with a securities intermediary does not have a claim "to a specific identifiable thing," rather, they have a unique set of rights and interests exercisable against the securities intermediary and third parties.[115] In the words of Professor James Steven Rogers, "the fundamental principles of the indirect holding system rules are that an entitlement holder's own intermediary has the obligation to see to it that the entitlement holder receives all of the economic and corporate rights that comprise the security, and therefore, that an entitlement holder can look only to that intermediary for performance of the obligations."[116]

Having established these foundational categories, Article 8 then proceeds to provide a comprehensive framework governing both the transfer and use of securities entitlements as collateral. The substance of these rules echoes our earlier discussions of CERs in Chapter 2 and negotiable instruments in Chapter 3, prioritizing negotiability and bolstering the commercial circulation of securities. As a starting point, it provides that a person acquires a security entitlement when a securities intermediary credits a financial asset to the person's securities account or receives and accepts a financial asset for credit to that account.[117] To facilitate the commercial circulation of financial assets held through intermediaries, Article 8 also establishes strong protection for good faith purchasers of security entitlements. Specifically, an action based on an adverse claim to a financial asset "may not be asserted against a person who purchases a security entitlement . . . for value and without notice of the adverse claim."[118]

The significance of this good faith/bona fide purchaser protection—much like analogous rules governing negotiable instruments, documents of title, and CERs—lies in its crucial role in eliminating the need for exhaustive due diligence into title chains, enhancing transactional certainty, and facilitating high-volume trading, thereby supporting market liquidity. Consider a scenario where Investor holds one hundred shares of Apple Inc. stock in their Fidelity Investments brokerage account. Hacker, without Investor's knowledge or consent, gains access to the account and fraudulently transfers the shares to their own account, subsequently selling them to Buyer. Buyer, unaware of the fraudulent transfer and acting in good faith, purchases the shares at market price. Upon discovering the theft, Investor might seek to reclaim the shares from Buyer. However, under the Article 8 bona fide purchaser rule, if Buyer gave value and had no notice of Investor's adverse claim (as we deem to be the case under these facts), Investor cannot successfully recover the shares. This outcome,

[115] James S. Rogers, *Policy Perspectives on Revised U.C.C. Article 8*, 43 UCLA L. Rev. 1431, 1457 (1996).

[116] *Id.*

[117] *See* U.C.C. § 8-501(b) (Am. L. Inst. & Unif. L. Comm'n 2001).

[118] *See* U.C.C. § 8-502 (Am. L. Inst. & Unif. L. Comm'n 2001).

while potentially harsh for Investor, prioritizes the smooth functioning of the securities market by allowing participants to transact with confidence, secure in the knowledge that their ownership rights (when acquired in good faith) will be protected.

Article 8, in conjunction with Article 9, further provides a specialized framework for using security entitlements as collateral. Central to this framework is the concept of "control"—though readers should note that Article 8's "control" is entirely distinct from "control" for CERs defined in Article 12 and examined in Chapter 2. As explained in the UCC official commentary, under Article 8 "control" means that a secured party has taken the necessary steps in accordance with the manner in which the securities are held to place itself in a position where it can have the securities sold without further action by the debtor.[119] With regard to security entitlements, a secured party can obtain such control by having the debtor transfer the collateral into an account in its own name or by obtaining an agreement under which the debtor's securities intermediary agrees to act on the secured party's instructions without further consent from the debtor.[120] Article 9 complements this framework by bringing all financial assets under the umbrella of *investment property*.[121] While security interests in these assets can be created by agreement,[122] the crucial feature is their perfection: Secured parties can perfect either through filing or control, with control-perfected interests taking priority regardless of timing.[123]

4.3 The challenges posed by custody of digital assets

Having surveyed the historical evolution and present form of bailment law, including the specialized regimes for the deposit of money and securities, we are now equipped to confront the central question of this chapter: What is the private law regime for digital asset custody?

As shown in Part I, bailment is a tree composed of multiple legal branches. It encompasses numerous categories, each with its own nuanced rules shaped by factors ranging from remuneration entitlements to corresponding standards for liability. Against this background, we must now determine whether custodial arrangements for digital assets can be accommodated. Should they be governed by traditional bailment principles, do they require specialized treatment similar

[119] U.C.C. 8-106 cmt. 1 (Am. L. Inst. & Unif. L. Comm'n 2001).

[120] *See* U.C.C. § 8-106(d) (Am. L. Inst. & Unif. L. Comm'n 2001).

[121] U.C.C. § 9-102(a)(49) (Am. L. Inst. & Unif. L. Comm'n 2010).

[122] *See* U.C.C. § 9-203 (Am. L. Inst. & Unif. L. Comm'n 2010).

[123] *See* U.C.C. §§ 9-310(a), 9-312(a), 9-314(a), 9-328(1) (Am. L. Inst. & Unif. L. Comm'n 2010).

to what has been developed for money and securities, or do these dealings demand a new framework entirely?

Our analysis proceeds in two stages. First, we examine whether and under what conditions digital asset custody can satisfy bailment's foundational requirements. Second, for those arrangements that do qualify as bailments, we address specific challenges, particularly regarding the obligation to redeliver the bailed assets.

4.3.1 Can digital assets be bailed?

The threshold question that must be addressed is whether custodial arrangements for digital assets can qualify as bailments. As discussed above, the formation of a bailment relationship has three constitutive elements: delivery of possession or control of an asset from the bailor to the bailee, acceptance of that asset by the bailee, and an agreed-upon purpose for the arrangement. While the latter two requirements are unaffected by the intangible nature of digital assets, delivery is more problematic.

As we discussed earlier in this chapter, the delivery requirement has historically involved a transfer of possession or physical control, actions inherently dependent on the tangibility of the asset. Even when courts gradually expanded bailment principles to encompass certain types of intangible property, such as stocks and negotiable instruments, the delivery requirement was satisfied through the physical transfer of paper documents in which these rights were embodied. The legal innovation lay not in dispensing with the delivery requirement. Rather, the law came to recognize that the paper certificates themselves could serve as the objects of bailment by tokenizing the underlying intangible rights at the heart of the transaction.

The critical question, therefore, is whether the delivery requirement can be satisfied for digital assets, which exist not as physical objects but as data entries recorded in a distributed ledger. We submit that the answer is *yes*—indeed, they can.

As discussed in Chapter 2, digital assets possess unique features that distinguish them from other forms of intangible property. Specifically, the technology underpinning these novel assets makes it possible for a single person, at any given time, to enjoy their benefits fully in a manner that excludes all others. Because of this feature, digital assets can be characterized as rivalrous. They are unlike pure intangibles, such as patentable inventions, trademarkable symbols, or authorial works, which can be used concurrently by an unlimited number of individuals without diminishing their availability. This capacity for exclusive enjoyment, rooted in the technology itself, provides a pathway for satisfying the delivery requirement in the context of a bailment.

We suggest drawing upon the framework developed by UCC Article 12, specifically the concepts of *controllable electronic records* and *control*. We offer here that the common law should recognize that, for CERs, a transfer of control from the prospective bailor to the prospective bailee satisfies the traditional delivery requirement for the formation of a bailment. Our proposal rests on the view that control, as conceptualized in Article 12, is a functional analogue to possession under American common law.[124] Both concepts consist of a positive element—the ability to enjoy the benefits of the asset—and a negative element—the ability to exclude others from doing so. Moreover, neither control nor possession requires a subjective intent (*animus*); rather, they are construed as an objective state of fact.

Our analysis leads to an ancillary, but important, principle: The transfer of control should be absolute for a valid bailment of digital assets to arise. Just as traditional bailment law rejects arrangements that involve joint possession between bailor and bailee, we submit that no bailment can exist where control of a digital asset is shared between the prospective bailor and bailee. This proposition can be inferred from the key tenets of bailment law. The entire framework of rights and obligations that characterizes the bailor–bailee relationship, including the bailee's duty of care and the bailor's right of redelivery, is premised on the bailor's divestment of direct power over the asset. Shared control, like shared possession, would fundamentally undermine this structure, thereby making it impossible to clearly delineate the parties' respective rights and responsibilities.

Therefore, we posit that custodial arrangements for digital assets should be classified according to whether they satisfy the three requirements we have identified: exclusive transfer of control, acceptance by the recipient, and an agreed purpose that contemplates the return of the specific assets. Only arrangements meeting all these criteria should be recognized as bailments. In these relationships, the transferor would retain ownership of the digital assets and could recover them in the event of the custodian's insolvency. As we detail in Chapter 6, the recent wave of bankruptcies among cryptocurrency platforms has highlighted the crucial importance of this property-based protection.

Conversely, custodial arrangements that fail to meet the bailment requirements should be classified as loans or other debtor–creditor relationships. This includes arrangements where, for example, control remains shared, or the transferee may commingle and use the assets, or the agreement contemplates return of equivalent assets at the transferee's discretion. In such cases, the transferor would only have a personal claim against the transferee and would be an unsecured creditor in insolvency proceedings absent a perfected security interest.

[124] U.C.C. § 12-105 cmt. 9.

For example, if Alice were to transfer her Bitcoin to a cold storage service that undertook to hold those tokens without using them and to return the identical assets upon request, this would be a bailment. Should the service file for bankruptcy, Alice could recover her specific Bitcoin rather than standing in line with other creditors. By contrast, if Bob were to deposit Ether with a platform that pools customer assets for lending and investment activities, promising to return the same amount of Ether plus interest, this would be a debtor–creditor relationship. Were this platform to become insolvent, Bob would be treated as an unsecured creditor.

4.3.2 Solving the redelivery problem

Having suggested that custodial arrangements involving digital assets can, under certain conditions, qualify as bailments, we now turn to the application of this framework. As a general principle, we submit that such transactions should be governed by the key tenets of bailment law outlined above. Most importantly, the bailor would retain ownership of the digital assets throughout the period of custody. Further, the standard of care required of a custodian would vary based on the presence and nature of remuneration. In gratuitous arrangements, the custodian must exercise only slight diligence. Where the custodian alone benefits, they must demonstrate exceptional diligence. And in mutual benefit arrangements—likely the most common in commercial settings—the custodian bears a duty of ordinary diligence to safeguard the digital assets.

However, one tenet of traditional bailment law does not apply seamlessly in the digital asset context: the *redelivery obligation*. A bailee is generally required, upon termination of the bailment, to return the *exact* asset that was originally delivered by the bailor, along with any fruits or profits derived from it during the bailment's term. This duty can engender acute complexities depending on the nature of the digital assets in bailment and the agreement between the parties.

For custodial arrangements involving uniquely identifiable digital assets, such as NFTs, the redelivery obligation poses no special difficulty. Indeed, the unique characteristics of each NFT make exact redelivery not only feasible but natural—a bailor entrusting a specific NFT would expect, and likely require, return of that precise token.

The analysis is similarly uncomplicated for custodial relationships centered on fungible digital assets, provided the parties agree to maintain them separate from other similar tokens. Modern DLT inherently facilitates such arrangements with unprecedented transparency and efficiency. A custodian can create a dedicated wallet specifically for the bailed assets, maintaining them in isolation throughout the bailment period. The distributed ledger provides a verifiable record of this segregation, allowing the bailor to verify continuously that the specific assets remain untouched. When the bailment concludes, the custodian can return the same tokens that were initially delivered. This technological infrastructure makes the traditional redelivery obligation remarkably simple to execute and verify—far more so than with traditional, tangible assets.

By contrast, significant legal complexities arise in custodial arrangements where fungible digital assets, such as Bitcoin or Ether, are commingled in omnibus accounts holding assets from multiple parties. This scenario is common in practice, particularly where the agreed purpose between the parties extends beyond mere safekeeping to include trading, staking, or other transactions. This is, in fact, the predominant arrangement among major platforms such as Binance, Coinbase, and Kraken, and was the operational model of now-bankrupt entities like BlockFi, Voyager, Celsius, and FTX.

In such arrangements, the custodian cannot comply with the strict redelivery obligation as traditionally understood. The combination of fungibility and commingling renders it impossible for the custodian to return the *exact* units of the digital asset that were initially deposited. This situation gives rise to a critical question: Can these relationships be classified as bailments, with the custodian acting as a true bailee, or must they be treated as loans, creating a debtor–creditor relationship? Indeed, as described above, the stakes surrounding this determination are high. The parallels to historical developments in the law of money, commodity, and securities deposits are striking—a point to which we shall return.

One approach to address this conundrum could be to draw an analogy with money deposits. This comparison would find support in the design and intended purpose of certain digital assets that were originally conceived as distributed digital cash—hence the common expression "cryptocurrencies." Moreover, Bitcoin has achieved the status of legal tender in several jurisdictions and is increasingly accepted as a method of payment in commercial transactions. Similarly, stablecoins—another widely adopted type of digital asset—were explicitly conceived and are usually deployed as payment instruments, typically functioning as digital equivalents to traditional currency. Following this reasoning to its logical conclusion, custodial arrangements involving such assets and their commingling into a common pool should be characterized as creating debtor–creditor relationships rather than bailments. This solution would echo the principle established in *Foley v. Hill* whereby money deposited with a bank becomes the property of the bank. In turn, the bank assumes a mere obligation to repay an equivalent sum.

However, the apparent similarities between money and digital assets, and, thus, the force of this analogy, weaken under closer scrutiny. Despite the original and oft-proclaimed ambition of Bitcoin and other digital assets to function as currency, empirical evidence suggests that market participants predominantly treat them as investment vehicles or stores of value rather than media of exchange.[125] This pattern of usage aligns these assets more closely with securities or commodities than with money. Notably, stablecoins present a possible exception to this critique, as their primary function and actual usage patterns more closely mirror those of traditional fiat currency. However, relying on an analogy applicable only to a small subset of digital assets is insufficient for developing a comprehensive framework to address the wider digital asset custody landscape.

An alternative avenue could be to draw an analogy with the common law treatment of bailments of fungible goods, such as grain and other dry commodities, in the nineteenth and early twentieth centuries. This approach would find its premise in understanding digital assets, such as Bitcoin or Ether, as fungible commodities, a characterization that would align with how market participants predominantly trade these assets. Under this analysis, custodial arrangements involving commingled digital assets could qualify as bailments, provided the custodian maintained sufficient reserves of the same type and quality to satisfy all depositors' claims. This approach would recognize the depositors as tenants-in-common of the commingled mass, with the custodian owing a duty to each depositor to redeliver their proportional share upon demand. Just as nineteenth-century grain elevators could commingle deposits while maintaining their status as bailees by preserving adequate stocks for redemption, digital asset custodians could theoretically preserve bailment relationships by maintaining reserves equal to their total customer deposits.

However, this analogy suffers from the same weaknesses that plagued the doctrine in its historical application to commodities. Determining and verifying the adequacy of reserves held by the custodian poses significant practical challenges, particularly given the opacity of many digital asset trading platforms and the lack of standardized accounting practices. Moreover, the historical record is replete with instances of disputes and litigation arising from insufficient reserves, commingling, and fraud in the context of commodity bailments. All of this suggests that such an approach may simply replicate, rather than resolve, the complexities inherent in such arrangements. It should also not be forgotten that one of the drivers for the adoption of UCC Article 7 was precisely to address these issues.

A third possible approach would be to develop a bespoke regime, carving out of traditional bailment law the arrangements in question, through either

[125] European Parliament, *Virtual Money: How Much do Cryptocurrencies Alter the Fundamental Functions of Money?* (PE 642.360, July 2020), https://www.europarl.europa.eu/cmsdata/207652/12.%20PE%20642.360%20LSE%20final%20publication-original.pdf.

common law evolution or statutory intervention. Although we can learn from existing legal frameworks for custody, they don't fit well in this context. Digital assets defy established taxonomies, combining characteristics of investment instruments, commodities, and currency in unprecedented ways. Moreover, the automated and distributed nature of the technological infrastructure underlying digital asset custody presents idiosyncrasies that existing legal frameworks were not designed to accommodate.

Drawing inspiration from the framework governing indirect securities holdings under UCC Article 8, this new regime would need to establish core definitional categories, possibly comprising digital asset, digital asset custodian, digital asset entrustor, digital asset account, and digital asset custody agreement. This taxonomical foundation would then serve as a basis for a comprehensive framework of mutual rights and obligations for custodians and entrustors, addressing key matters such as the custodian's duty of care, authorized asset usage, transparency obligations, and record-keeping standards.

Crucially, this body of rules would need to establish the precise nature of entrustors' proprietary interests when their digital assets are held in an omnibus account by custodians. Similar to the *security entitlement* concept under Article 8, the regime could recognize a similar form of intangible property right specifically designed for digital assets. This would provide entrustors with a clear and enforceable interest in the commingled mass, protecting them from the claims of the custodian's general creditors. Furthermore, the framework would need to address the consequences of a shortfall in the custodian's reserves, potentially through mechanisms such as mandatory insurance, reserve requirements, or a priority scheme for distributing available assets in insolvency.

Notably, this third approach appears to be gaining some traction in the United States and internationally. The UNIDROIT Principles on Digital Assets and Private Law advocate for a distinct set of rules governing the custody of digital assets held through intermediaries, recognizing the limitations of applying traditional legal frameworks.[126] California has taken a concrete step in this direction with its Digital Financial Assets Law, which specifically addresses the custodial obligations of certain digital asset businesses licensed as money transmitters under its laws.[127] Similarly, the Uniform Law Commission, first through the Uniform Regulation of Virtual-Currency Businesses Act (URVCBA) and, subsequently, through the Virtual Currency Customer Protection Act, has proposed

[126] *See* Int'l Inst. for the Unification of Priv. L. (UNIDROIT), UNIDROIT Principles on Digital Assets and Private Law 68–94 (2023), https://www.unidroit.org/wp-content/uploads/2024/01/Principles-on-Digital-Assets-and-Private-Law-linked-1.pdf.

[127] S.B. 401, 2023–2024 Leg., Reg. Sess. (Cal. 2023), https://leginfo.legislature.ca.gov/faces/billNavClient.xhtml?bill_id=202320240SB401; *see id.* § 3503.

a distinct framework for regulating the custody of digital assets, drawing on concepts from both bailment and securities law.[128]

Thus, even accepting the proposition advanced in above—specifically, that custodial arrangements for digital assets can be bailments—we are still far from finding a panacea. Relationships between entrustors and custodians involving NFTs and segregated holdings of digital assets can be accommodated by the bailment paradigm, though only with minor adjustments and careful transactional structuring. By contrast, the prevalent industry practice of commingling fungible digital assets in omnibus accounts stumbles when confronted by bailment law's traditional redelivery obligation. Although historical treatments of money and commodities offer potential analytical frameworks, a comprehensive and fully satisfactory solution remains to be developed.

4.4 Digital assets custody through UCC Article 8

The preceding sections have shown that the private law analysis of digital asset custody is rife with theoretical and practical complexities. We have grappled with the threshold question of whether these arrangements can be classified as bailments and submitted that there are strong arguments in favor. Nevertheless, even assuming the applicability of bailment law, we have observed that significant uncertainties persist, particularly regarding custodial arrangements of fungible digital assets held in omnibus accounts.

Unsurprisingly, the legal framework governing these relationships is presently in flux and shrouded in doubt. Currently, the characterization of digital asset custody arrangements, including the respective rights and obligations of the parties and, most crucially, whether entrustors retain property interests in their assets, appears to hinge on a case-by-case analysis of representations, contractual provisions, and evolving market practices. This fragmented approach inevitably produces disparate outcomes for arrangements that market participants likely view as functionally equivalent. The insolvencies of major cryptocurrency platforms like Voyager, Celsius, BlockFi, and FTX, which we examine later in Chapter 6, have cast these legal fault lines into stark relief.

Yet amid this legal turbulence, we identify a potential safe harbor. While not perfectly tailored to the technological characteristics of digital assets, we submit that the UCC Article 8 framework offers a pathway to structure custodial arrangements of digital assets with enhanced legal certainty. This approach,

[128] *See Regulation of Virtual-Currency Businesses Act*, Unif. L. Comm'n (2017), https://www.uniformlaws.org/committees/community-home?CommunityKey=e104aaa8-c10f-45a7-a34a-0423c2106778; *New Study and Drafting Committees*, Unif. L. Comm'n (July 26, 2023), https://www.uniformlaws.org/discussion/new-study-and-drafting-committees.

though imperfect, provides market participants with established mechanisms to achieve their commercial objectives while maintaining clear property rights.

4.4.1 UCC Article 8 and digital assets

As described earlier in this chapter, UCC Article 8 establishes a comprehensive framework for intermediated securities holdings. At its core, the framework creates a unique set of legal relationships centered around four key concepts: financial assets, securities intermediaries, securities accounts, and security entitlements. Under this framework, entitlement holders are granted a package of rights against their intermediary, including the right to receive distributions, to have the intermediary comply with their directions, and most critically, to have their assets protected from the intermediary's creditors. Article 8 also provides robust protection for good faith purchasers of security entitlements and establishes a clear regime for using these entitlements as collateral, with control-based perfection receiving priority over other security interests.

The Article 8 framework, while designed for traditional financial instruments, possesses remarkable flexibility. Under UCC § 8-102(a)(9)(iii), the definition of *financial asset* extends to "any property that is held by a securities intermediary for another person in a securities account if the securities intermediary has expressly agreed with the other person that the property is to be treated as a financial asset."[129] This expansive provision creates an opt-in mechanism whereby virtually any property can be brought within the Article 8 framework through explicit agreement between a securities intermediary and its customer. Digital assets, despite their novel technological characteristics, can readily fit within this adaptable definition. The definitions of *securities intermediary* and *securities account* are similarly flexible, focusing on function rather than form, thereby allowing digital asset custodians to position themselves within this established legal architecture.

The updated comments to UCC Article 8, following the 2022 Amendments, explicitly endorse this application to digital assets. Most directly, the comments clarify that "if the parties agree to treat a digital asset as a financial asset under Article 8 and the digital asset is in fact held in a securities account for an entitlement holder, the rules applicable to controllable electronic records under Article 12 would not apply to the entitlement holder's security entitlement related to the financial asset."[130] This establishes a clear hierarchy between legal regimes

[129] U.C.C. § 8-102(a)(9)(iii) (Am. L. Inst. & Unif. L. Comm'n 2001).
[130] U.C.C. § 8-102 cmt. 9.

and confirms that parties can opt into the Article 8 framework for digital assets. The drafters further expanded the scope of entities that can qualify as securities intermediaries, with Comment 14 to Section 8-102 explicitly stating that "a cryptocurrency exchange that holds only cryptocurrencies (and not securities) for customers might be a securities intermediary."[131] This recognition critically extends the Article 8 framework to entities operating exclusively in the digital asset space.

If digital assets are brought within the Article 8 framework, entitlement holders benefit from a robust set of protections under Part 5 (§§ 8-501 to 8-511).[132] As Comment 9 explicitly recognizes, "many of the duties set forth in Part 5 will often be relevant to a digital asset such as a 'controllable electronic record' . . . treated as a financial asset credited to a securities account."[133] These duties include the securities intermediary's obligation to maintain sufficient quantities of the financial asset to satisfy all entitlement holders' claims,[134] to obtain and pass along payments and distributions,[135] to exercise rights as directed by the entitlement holder,[136] to comply with the entitlement holder's entitlement orders,[137] and to change the entitlement holder's position to another form of holding as directed.[138] Perhaps most critically, Article 8 provides that financial assets held by a securities intermediary are not property of the intermediary and are not subject to claims of the intermediary's general creditors.[139] This property-based protection creates a form of asset partitioning that insulates the entitlement holder's interests from the intermediary's insolvency risk—addressing precisely the concern that has plagued digital asset custody arrangements.

To illustrate how this framework might operate in practice, consider a hypothetical cryptocurrency platform, CryptoExchange, that offers trading and custody services for digital assets. Like many large cryptocurrency platforms, CryptoExchange operates a custodial system in which customers deposit their digital assets to the platform's blockchain addresses, with their individual holdings tracked through the platform's internal database rather than through separate on-chain wallets for each customer. When Alice deposits ten Bitcoin with CryptoExchange, her digital assets become part of a larger pool held in the platform's consolidated wallets. As we observed earlier in this chapter, such commingling arrangements often fail to satisfy the requirements for a valid

[131] U.C.C. § 8-102 cmt. 14.
[132] U.C.C. §§ 8-501 to -511.
[133] U.C.C. § 8-102, cmt. 9.
[134] U.C.C. § 8-504.
[135] U.C.C. § 8-505.
[136] U.C.C. § 8-506.
[137] U.C.C. § 8-507.
[138] U.C.C. § 8-508.
[139] U.C.C. § 8-503.

bailment, potentially leaving Alice in the precarious position of a mere unsecured creditor rather than a property owner. While some customers may knowingly accept this insolvency risk in exchange for the platform's convenience and features, others may be unaware of these legal implications or may be uncomfortable with them. Similarly, CryptoExchange itself may find this legal uncertainty problematic for business development, as it creates barriers to attracting risk-averse customers and institutional investors who require clearly defined property rights.

By choosing to opt into the Article 8 framework, CryptoExchange could overcome these uncertainties with minimal operational changes. The process would involve three key steps. First, CryptoExchange would need to ensure it qualifies as a "securities intermediary" by maintaining securities accounts for others in the ordinary course of its business—a condition it would likely satisfy once it designates customer accounts as securities accounts. Second, it would need to revise its user agreement to explicitly designate customer digital assets as "financial assets" under Article 8 and to specify that these assets are credited to customer securities accounts. Third, CryptoExchange would need to comply with the substantive obligations of Article 8, including maintaining sufficient assets to satisfy all customer entitlements. Once implemented, Alice would hold a security entitlement to her ten Bitcoin, granting her property-based protection that would insulate her interest from CryptoExchange's bankruptcy estate and general creditors. This legal structure would allow CryptoExchange to maintain its operationally efficient omnibus custody model while at the same time providing customers with the certainty of clearly defined property rights.

4.4.2 The limits of UCC Article 8 for digital assets

As described in the preceding section, UCC Article 8 presents an alluring avenue for the custody of digital assets. This established and well-understood body of rules is sufficiently flexible to accommodate all types of digital assets, whether fungible (such as cryptocurrencies and stablecoins) or nonfungible (such as NFTs), and offers much-needed legal certainty. Importantly, Article 8 can cater to arrangements whereby platforms maintain client assets in omnibus accounts to facilitate trading and transaction netting, which has become the predominant market practice. Perhaps most critically, Article 8 offers entrustors of digital assets a regime in which they maintain a property interest in their deposited digital assets even when they are commingled in a fungible bulk. This, in turn, provides crucial protection in the event of custodian insolvency.

Nevertheless, before we close this chapter, we must acknowledge that Article 8 suffers from three inherent limitations that warrant careful consideration.

The first limitation stems from the voluntary opt-in nature of the Article 8 regime. Absent regulatory mandates,[140] some market participants will embrace this framework while others will not, creating a splintered legal landscape that undermines certainty and consistency. Indeed, this fragmentation is readily apparent in the digital asset ecosystem at the time of this writing. While some leading platforms, such as Coinbase,[141] have explicitly incorporated Article 8 into their terms of service, the majority of platforms operating in the United States do not.[142] The bankruptcy proceedings of Celsius, Voyager, and FTX—all major platforms that had not opted into Article 8—offered a stark reminder of the consequences of this inconsistency. These cases spawned protracted litigation aimed at determining the respective rights and obligations of the insolvent platforms, their clients, and creditors. In those lawsuits, the central question was whether customers who had entrusted their digital assets to these platforms retained ownership interests or merely held unsecured claims.

It is difficult to establish exactly why many platforms choose not to opt into the Article 8 framework. Some may simply be unaware of this possibility or else lack the legal sophistication to implement it. Other platforms might balk at the substantive obligations that Article 8 imposes on custodians, particularly the requirement to maintain sufficient quantities of financial assets to satisfy all entitlement holders' claims.[143] Others still may be wary of a framework historically associated with securities, given the industry's well-documented aversion to this classification for digital assets. Still others might reject formalized legal frameworks altogether, embracing instead the cypherpunk and crypto-anarchist ethos that originally animated blockchain networks, cryptocurrencies, and decentralized autonomous organizations.[144] Whatever the specific reasons in individual cases, the opt-in nature of Article 8 significantly limits its effectiveness as a comprehensive solution for the custodial issues examined in this chapter.

The second limitation of Article 8 when applied to digital assets arises from its original design. Although it provides a flexible and self-sufficient private law framework, this branch of the UCC was specifically engineered for the indirect

[140] California's Digital Financial Assets Law requires licensees offering custodial services to hold digital assets sufficient to satisfy aggregate client entitlements at any time, and shields such assets from the licensee's creditors. *See* CAL. FIN. CODE § 3503(a)(1) (2024). Licensees may comply by contractually treating digital assets as Article 8 financial assets. *See* CAL. FIN. CODE § 3503(c).

[141] *[User Agreement] 2.7.2 Application of the Uniform Commercial Code*, COINBASE USER AGREEMENTS, https://www.coinbase.com/legal/user_agreement/united_states (last updated June 13, 2025).

[142] See *Terms of Service*, KRAKEN, https://www.kraken.com/legal (last visited Apr. 13, 2025); *see also Custody Agreement*, GEMINI TR. CO., LLC, https://www.gemini.com/legal/custody-agreement (last visited Apr. 13, 2025).

[143] U.C.C. § 8-504.

[144] Kara Bruce, Christopher Odinet & Andrea Tosato, *Bankrupt Crypto Organizations*, N.C. L. REV. (forthcoming 2026), https://papers.ssrn.com/sol3/papers.cfm?abstract_id=5115277.

holding of securities. In doing so, it presupposes distinct structural and regulatory elements that, although readily found in the securities markets, are largely absent from the digital assets landscape.

To make this point more concrete, consider the structure of the securities trading market. Article 8 depends upon an established market infrastructure for securities trading. Its rules regarding transfers, corporate actions, and intermediary communication rely upon traditional securities systems. However, essential operational components, including clearing and settlement processes, proxy services, and dedicated communication channels among intermediaries and issuers, have no fully developed equivalents in the world of digital assets.

The effectiveness of Article 8 also derives in meaningful part from the fact that it interfaces with a comprehensive regulatory regime. Here again, we can look to the securities market. Securities intermediaries, for example, are subject to capital requirements, asset segregation and safekeeping rules, reporting obligations, and robust customer protection measures, such as Securities Investor Protection Corporation (SIPC) insurance. Securities intermediaries are also held to clear standards of conduct and operate under rigorous supervisory oversight. In contrast, intermediaries handling digital assets do not operate in a comprehensive and well-defined regulatory environment, thereby significantly limiting the protective mechanisms offered by Article 8.

The third and final limitation of Article 8 is that it does not address certain technological events and governance structures that are inherent to digital assets but have no parallels in the context of securities. A so-called hard fork,[145] for instance, splits a distributed network into two, raising questions about whether and how custodians should credit both resulting assets to client accounts. Article 8 offers no guidance on managing such events, leaving affected parties without clear duties or standards. Similarly, "airdrops" and "staking" introduce complexities regarding allocation and client entitlement that are not explicitly addressed by Article 8.

Equally challenging is the governance of many digital assets, which often relies on mechanisms whereby holders vote by carrying out specific operations, such as using cryptographic signatures. While Article 8 facilitates proxy voting for traditional securities, it is ill-equipped to handle those idiosyncratic processes and events. It neither defines custodians' obligations to enable client participation in such processes nor clarifies their responsibilities to inform clients about governance proposals or execute their preferences. These gaps in the Article 8 framework engender operational uncertainties that would need to be addressed through either custom contractual provisions or future regulatory guidance.

[145] See *What Is a Fork?*, COINBASE, https://www.coinbase.com/en-es/learn/crypto-basics/what-is-a-fork (last visited Apr. 13, 2025).

Thus, despite the significant advantages of UCC Article 8 for digital asset custody, its effectiveness is constrained. We think that these shortcomings, however, do not detract from the fact that Article 8 can serve as a viable legal framework for the custody of digital assets. Rather, these limitations merely underscore the need for tailored regulatory frameworks specifically designed for digital assets. Such an undertaking is beyond the scope of this book and mainly concerns the domain of public and regulatory law. Nevertheless, although our focus here is on private law dimensions, we acknowledge that as the digital asset ecosystem continues to evolve, addressing these gaps will be essential to provide the legal certainty and customer protection that market participants require.

PART II

5

NFTs and creative works

5.1 Introduction

Part I of this book established the first principles of digital commercial law. We analyzed the property status and commercial circulation rules governing digital assets, the concept of tokenization and its operation within established property law frameworks, and the theoretical challenges presented by the custody of these novel electronic records. Across these foundational chapters, we argued that private law has been dangerously disregarded in the digital asset landscape and, relatedly, denounced the flexibility fallacy.

In Part II, we apply these first principles in real, specific cases. First, this chapter analyzes *non-fungible tokens* (NFTs) that purport to embody creative works. Then, Chapter 6 interrogates the nascent practice of issuing *debt tokens* that purport to represent bankruptcy claims. By situating these case studies within the doctrinal framework elaborated on in Part I, we illustrate that digital assets create new objects of intangible personal property only within the mandatory confines established by law—including those codified in UCC Article 12. We further demonstrate in Part II that any attempted reification of rights through tokens must conform with the fundamental tenets of property law, including the *numerus clausus* principle. Neglect of these constraints, as we show in these two chapters, results in legally ineffective arrangements that collapse under their own structural flaws. In so doing, they frustrate participants' expectations and expose them to uncompensated risks, regardless of the technology or the boldness of its proponents' claims.

As noted in our discussion of tokenization in Chapter 3, NFTs constitute one of the key elements of the current digital asset landscape.[1] Our first case study in this chapter examines how NFTs have been used to purportedly embody creative works, an application that has generated significant legal confusion and

[1] Various portions of this chapter are drawn, in whole or in part, from Juliet M. Moringiello & Christopher K. Odinet, Response, *The Property Law of Tokens*, 74 Fla. L. Rev. 607 (2022) [hereinafter Moringiello & Odinet, *Tokens*]; Christopher K. Odinet & Andrea Tosato, Response, *The Intersection of NFTs and Structured Finance*, 103 B.U. L. Rev. 1005, 1005 (2023); and Juliet M. Moringiello & Christopher K. Odinet, *Non-Fungible Tokens in Commercial Transactions*, *in* The Cambridge Handbook of Emerging Issues at the Intersection of Commercial Law and Technology 3 (Nancy Kim & Stacy-Ann Elvy eds., 2025). Any reproductions are made with the express permission of the authors.

Digital Commercial Law. Christopher K. Odinet and Andrea Tosato, Oxford University Press.
 DOI: 10.1093/9780197758656.003.0007

market volatility.[2] We begin by charting the remarkable trajectory of NFTs, from niche technical experiments, through a period of intense speculative fervor, a subsequent sharp decline, and an ongoing resurgence. This historical exposition helps us frame the relevant technical, social, and economic dimensions that shape the legal issues under consideration in this specific context.

NFTs were initially conceived as a technological proof of concept to demonstrate the capacity of blockchain networks to create, maintain, and transfer uniquely identifiable data objects.[3] Yet, this innovation rapidly evolved into a transformative framework for digital scarcity.[4] The introduction of NFT standards on the Ethereum blockchain, particularly ERC-721 and ERC-1155, markedly streamlined the process of minting these digital assets, fostering broad adoption across various domains.[5]

In 2017, CryptoKitties marked the first glimpse of the mass-market potential of NFTs. Dapper Labs deployed a smart contract, *KittyCore*, on the Ethereum network that contained the information for thousands of digital "cats" (each with a 256-bit "genetic code," a birth timestamp, parent identifiers, and breeding status).[6] Simultaneously, they minted NFTs that each pointed to one of the cats in KittyCore. A separate web application retrieved the on-chain information and rendered cartoon cats with distinctive appearances based on their genetic code. Furthermore, NFT holders could utilize a function within KittyCore to "breed" new cats by combining the genetic codes of two existing cats, thereby producing a new cat with a distinct genetic code. CryptoKitties became a cultural and commercial phenomenon, generating thousands of transactions with rare cats selling for hundreds of thousands of dollars.

This early success in using NFTs to create and trade unique digital assets led to the insight that this technology could be used in connection with a diverse array of tangible and intangible property.[7] The market's response was

[2] *See* Joshua A. T. Fairfield, *Digital Property Cycles*, 80 Wash. & Lee L. Rev. 1115, 1116 (2023) [hereinafter Fairfield, *Property Cycles*].

[3] *See* Moringiello & Odinet, *Tokens*, *supra* note 1; *see also* Joshua A. T. Fairfield, *Bitproperty*, 88 S. Cal. L. Rev. 805, 825–28 (2015) [hereinafter Fairfield, *Bitproperty*].

[4] Brian L. Frye, Luxury Tokens 5 (Aug. 16, 2023) (unpublished manuscript), https://papers.ssrn.com/sol3/papers.cfm?abstract_id=4541913.

[5] William Entriken, Dieter Shirley, Jacob Evans & Nastassia Sachs, *EIP-721: Non-Fungible Token Standard*, Ethereum Improvement Proposals (Jan. 24, 2018), https://eips.ethereum.org/EIPS/eip-721; *see also* Witek Radomski, Andrew Cooke, Philippe Castonguay, James Therien, Eric Binet & Ronan Sandford, *EIP-1155: Multi Token Standard*, Ethereum Improvement Proposals (June 17, 2018), https://eips.ethereum.org/EIPS/eip-1155.

[6] Kraken Learn Team, *What Are CryptoKitties?*, Kraken (Apr. 12, 2024), https://www.kraken.com/learn/what-are-cryptokitties-nft; Elisa Campaci, *The Story of the CryptoKitties, the NFTs That Wrote Blockchain History*, Young Platform (Dec. 2, 2022), https://youngplatform.com/en/blog/news/cryptokitties-guide-history-nft-flow-blockchain/.

[7] Irina Heaver, *What Crypto Investors Need to Know About Tokenizing Real World Assets*, Forbes (Mar. 14, 2024), https://www.forbes.com/sites/irinaheaver/2024/03/14/what-crypto-investors-need-to-know-about-tokenizing-real-world-assets/?sh=3628d6945a96; Jesse Lund, Shanker Ramamurthy

explosive.[8] In February 2021, an NFT linked to the GIF of an animated cat with a pop-tart body flying through the sky (known as "Nyan Cat") sold for approximately $580,000.[9] The following month, digital artist Beeple auctioned an NFT representing his work "Everydays: The First 5000 Days" at Christie's for $69 million.[10] By August 2021, monthly NFT trading volume reached a staggering $2.8 billion,[11] with individual tokens like Bored Ape #8817 fetching $3.4 million in October of that year.[12] In each case, albeit with technical implementation differences, the basic architecture remained consistent: The NFT itself contained minimal data but functioned as a blockchain-authenticated pointer to imagery stored off-chain.

This meteoric rise was followed by an equally dramatic fall. In 2022, the NFT market cratered due to macroeconomic headwinds, including rising inflation and subsequent interest rate hikes, rampant speculation, widespread scams, and diminishing novelty. Trading volumes plummeted by over 97 percent from their peak, with many once-valuable collections becoming virtually worthless.[13] Emblematically, Jack Dorsey's first tweet NFT, which had sold for $2.9 million in 2021, received a top bid of just $280 when relisted in April 2022.[14]

This collapse prompted increased scrutiny from multiple directions. The Securities and Exchange Commission began investigating whether certain NFT sales constituted unregistered securities offerings,[15] while private

& Bridget van Kralingen, IBM Inst. for Bus. Value, Moving to a Token-Driven Economy: Enabling the Digitization of Real-World Assets (2018), https://www.ibm.com/downloads/documents/us-en/10a99803fcafdd29.

[8] *See generally* Moringiello & Odinet, *Tokens*, *supra* note 1, at 609 n.4.

[9] Erin Griffith, *Why an Animated Flying Cat with a Pop-Tart Body Sold for Almost $600,000*, N.Y. Times (June 23, 2023), https://www.nytimes.com/2021/02/22/business/nft-nba-top-shot-crypto.html.

[10] Josie Thaddeus-Johns, *What Are NFTs, Anyway? One Just Sold for $69 Million*, N.Y. Times (Oct. 4, 2021), https://www.nytimes.com/2021/03/11/arts/design/what-is-an-nft.html.

[11] *Dead NFTs: A Comprehensive Guide to the World of Dead NFTs*, dappGambl, https://dappgambl.com/nfts/dead-nfts/ (last visited Aug. 4, 2025).

[12] Rajpalsinh, *BAYC #8817 Makes New Record with $3.4M Sale on Sotheby's Metaverse*, Crypto Times (Oct. 26, 2021, 10:28 PM), https://www.cryptotimes.io/bayc-8817-makes-new-record-with-3-4m-sale-on-sothebys-metaverse/.

[13] Sidhartha Shukla, *NFT Trading Volumes Collapse 97% From January Peak*, Bloomberg (Sept. 28, 2022), https://www.bloomberg.com/news/articles/2022-09-28/nft-volumes-tumble-97-from-2022-highs-as-frenzy-fades-chart?embedded-checkout=true.

[14] Oluwapelumi Adejumo, *NFT of Jack Dorsey's First Tweet, Originally Purchased for $2.9M, Is Worth Less Than $4 in Today's Market*, CryptoSlate (July 20, 2023), https://cryptoslate.com/the-nft-of-jack-dorseys-first-tweet-originally-purchased-for-2-9m-is-worth-less-than-4-in-todays-market/.

[15] *See, e.g.*, Press Release, U.S. Secs. & Exch. Comm'n, No. 2023-163, SEC Charges LA-Based Media and Entertainment Co. Impact Theory for Unregistered Offering of NFTs (Aug. 28, 2023), https://www.sec.gov/newsroom/press-releases/2023-163. *See also* Brian L. Frye, The Securities Art LLC Non-Fungible Token Bond (Oct. 28, 2021) (unpublished manuscript), https://papers.ssrn.com/sol3/papers. cfm?abstract_id=3943776.

litigants initiated class actions against NFT issuers following catastrophic price declines.[16] Concurrently, legal scholars began documenting a yawning chasm between marketing hype and legal reality. Their analyses showed that while buyers believed they were securing ownership rights in digitally scarce artistic works, they typically acquired little more than the NFT itself, with any claim to the purportedly tethered asset left vague or illusory.[17]

And yet, like a phoenix rising from the ashes of the 2022 meltdown, the NFT market resurrected in 2024–2025. New momentum has stemmed from the Ordinals protocol, which enables the creation of NFT tokens on the Bitcoin network.[18] Established consumer brands, including Adidas and Nike, have introduced NFT-gated merchandise and experiential rewards.[19] Even luxury fashion houses, such as Gucci, Louis Vuitton, and Prada, have started experimenting with this technology, pairing NFTs with exclusive access to physical goods and events.[20] More recently, Courtyard.io has found success selling NFTs tied to vaulted Pokémon and sports cards, with its revenues soaring from $9 million in December 2024 to $48 million in March 2025.[21] In parallel, NFT financing has expanded steadily, with the dominant peer-to-peer platform, Blend, reaching trading volumes in excess of $400 million in early 2025.[22] This renewed vibrancy, however, has not been accompanied by greater attention to the private law framework governing NFTs, which remains severely understudied.

Self-proclaimed experts and industry proponents make sweeping assertions that NFTs can convey ownership,[23] embody "intellectual property,"[24] and enable

[16] *See* Friel v Dapper Labs, Inc., No 21-cv-05837 (S.D.N.Y. 2021).

[17] *See* Moringiello & Odinet, *Tokens*, *supra* note 1, at 632–47; Odinet & Tosato, *supra* note 1, at 1021–22; R. Wilson Freyermuth, Christopher Odinet & Andrea Tosato, *Crypto in Real Estate Finance*, 75 ALA. L. REV. 93 (2023); Joshua A. T. Fairfield, *Tokenized: The Law of Non-Fungible Tokens and Unique Digital Property*, 97 IND. L.J. 1261 (2022); Edmund Schuster, *Cloud Crypto Land*, 84 MOD. L. REV. 974 (2021).

[18] Ordinals allow for the inscription of data directly onto individual *satoshis* (the smallest unit of Bitcoin), enabling NFT-like functionality. Cam Thompson, *In NFT Sales, Bitcoin Jumps to No. 2 Spot in a Matter of Months*, COINDESK (May 22, 2023), https://www.coindesk.com/web3/2023/05/22/in-nft-sales-bitcoin-jumps-to-no-2-spot-in-a-matter-of-months.

[19] Rosie Perper, *Nike's OF1 NFT Sale Surpasses $1M Despite Delays, Tech Issues*, COINDESK (June 8, 2023), https://www.coindesk.com/web3/2023/05/25/nike-of1-nft-sale-surpasses-1m-despite-delays-tech-issues; *Top NFT Trends in 2025–From Tokenization to Utility*, COINSCLONE (Mar. 18, 2025), https://www.coinsclone.com/top-nft-trends/.

[20] Stephanie Hirschmiller, *Unpacking the Web3 Strategy Behind Louis Vuitton's €39k Digital Treasure Trunk NFTs*, FORBES (June 8, 2023), https://www.forbes.com/sites/stephaniehirschmiller/2023/06/07/unpacking-the-strategy-behind-louis-vuittons-39k-digital-treasure-trunk-nfts.

[21] Olga Kharif, *Pokémon and Sports Cards Breathe Life into NFT Marketplace*, BLOOMBERG (Apr. 29, 2025), https://www.bloomberg.com/news/newsletters/2025-04-29/pokemon-and-sports-cards-breathe-life-into-nft-marketplace.

[22] Hadiqa Crypto Master, *Blur Dominates NFT Market in January 2025 with Record-Breaking Volume*, BINANCE SQUARE (Feb. 3, 2025), https://www.binance.com/en/square/post/19809629692369.

[23] *See* Johnny Harris, *NFTs, Explained*, at 0:57 (YouTube, Apr. 27, 2021), https://www.youtube.com/watch?v=Oz9zw7-_vhM.

[24] Rhett Mankind, *What Is an NFT? (Crypto Beginners)*, at 1:30 (YouTube, Oct. 13, 2020), https://www.youtube.com/watch?v=a8ww4aNlPQU.

"rights and legal responsibilities [to be] embedded directly onto the token" alongside "an immutable record of ownership."[25] Commentators explain that "NFTs are designed to give you something that can't be copied: ownership of the work (though the artist can still retain the copyright and reproduction rights, just like with physical artwork). To put it in terms of physical art collecting: anyone can buy a Monet print. But only one person can own the original."[26] The widely used ChatGPT notes that "NFTs, or non-fungible tokens, are unique digital tokens stored on a blockchain that represent ownership or proof of authenticity of a specific digital or physical asset."[27] Even some lawyers have claimed that "nonfungible tokens can be used to represent ownership of all sorts of original digital items."[28] These bold claims demand critical examination.

Building upon our previous analysis of tokenization in Chapter 3, this chapter focuses on NFT transactions and their often-touted ability to embody and transfer rights (proprietary or otherwise). We first examine the two predominant models through which NFTs are created and offered to the public: the standardized approach used by platforms like OpenSea and Mintable, and the bespoke approach adopted by major issuers like Yuga Labs, Dapper Labs, and several prominent artists. Next, we analyze the terms of service governing these offerings, revealing the profound disconnect between marketing claims and legal reality.[29] This chapter concludes by demonstrating that while profound misunderstandings of private law plague current NFT markets, legitimate commercial applications for NFTs can be achieved through structures that embrace rather than evade existing legal frameworks.

5.2 NFT creation and distribution models

There are currently two dominant models for the creation and distribution of NFTs.[30] The first involves individuals, typically with limited technical expertise,

[25] Patrick Laurent, Thibault Chollett, Michael Burke & Tobias Seers, *The Tokenization of Assets Is Disrupting the Financial Industry. Are You Ready?*, Deloitte: Inside Mag., Oct. 2018, at 62, 63, https://perma.cc/D37Q-PT4R; *see also* Marko-WhiteBoard Finance, *What Are NFTs and How Do They Work?*, at 2:53 (YouTube, Mar. 6, 2021), https://www.youtube.com/watch?v=LU5Mv4TQEE8.

[26] Mitchell Clark, *NFTs, Explained*, The Verge (June 6, 2022), https://www.theverge.com/22310188/nft-explainer-what-is-blockchain-crypto-art-faq.

[27] OpenAI, *NFT Explainer*, ChatGPT (queried on Jun. 3, 2024), https://chatgpt.com/c/683f0e3c-ddb8-8003-b67e-2c5aba89c558 (responding to prompt "What are NFTs and what do they have to do with property rights and ownership?").

[28] Richard Acello, *Big Money: Nonfungible Tokens Are All the Rage Now. What Are They, and What Should Buyers Watch For?*, A.B.A. J., Oct./Nov. 2021, at 25.

[29] *See* Fairfield, *supra* note 17, at 1268; *see also* Joshua A. T. Fairfield, *Making Virtual Things*, 64 Wm. & Mary L. Rev. 1057, 1062–63 (2023).

[30] For source material, see Odinet & Tosato, *supra* note 1, at 1005.

relying on minting platforms that offer infrastructure and relatively modularized services to create and sell NFTs (the *standardized* model). The second features issuers deploying tailored smart contracts to mint and distribute their NFTs, controlling almost every aspect of the process directly (the *bespoke* model). In our view, this landscape is bimodal rather than strictly binary. Most projects cluster around these two distinct approaches: either embracing platform services or executing independently. In between, there are hybrid implementations that, for example, deploy custom smart contracts while using established marketplaces for secondary trading or that use platform infrastructure with enhanced customization options. Nevertheless, examining these two models separately provides a useful framework for our subsequent analysis, which focuses on private law rights and obligations.

5.2.1 The standardized model

The *standardized* model is prevalent in high-volume, low-value NFT issuances. Through an online "studio" or "launchpad," such as those operated by prominent platforms like OpenSea, Rarible, Binance, SuperRare, Foundation, Mintable, or Zora, individuals can create and sell NFTs using prebuilt tools and standardized protocols.[31] Although these entities often present themselves as mere facilitators of peer-to-peer transactions, they effectively control critical aspects of the minting, listing, and selling of NFTs. This multistep process can roughly be summarized as follows. At the outset, an individual creates an account with a minting platform and links it to their crypto wallet, through which they will send and receive funds in connection with the minting and selling of their NFT.[32] Relying on the platform's interface, the individual then uploads a digital image, text, or music, which will be linked to their soon-to-be-minted NFT.[33] This file is typically uploaded to a cloud storage provider, such as Amazon, Microsoft, or Google, although some platforms offer decentralized solutions, such as the InterPlanetary File System (IPFS).[34] Thereafter, the individual selects the

[31] *Top NFT Minting Platforms in 2023*, COINBOUND, https://coinbound.io/top-nft-minting-platforms/ (last visited Jan. 12, 2022).

[32] Moringiello & Odinet, *Tokens*, *supra* note 1, at 628–29.

[33] Clark, *supra* note 26.

[34] Some platforms, such as Zora, store NFT metadata using IPFS, a set of open protocols designed for transferring data on the web. *Coins Metadata*, ZORA DOCS, https://docs.zora.co/coins/contracts/metadata (last visited June 8, 2025). IPFS enables content-addressed, verifiable, and peer-to-peer data storage and delivery, allowing files to be located based on their cryptographic hash rather than specific servers. *See What Is IPFS?*, IPFS DOCS, https://docs.ipfs.tech/concepts/what-is-ipfs/#defining-ipfs (last visited June 8, 2025),. IPFS defines protocols for addressing, routing, and transferring data, but it is not a storage network itself. *Id.* Rather, files uploaded to IPFS are temporarily cached. *See IPFS: Why Does Pinning Matter Anyways?*, FILEBASE BLOG (Sep. 22, 2022), https://filebase.com/

manner in which they want to monetize their NFT; typically, this will be through a sale either at a predetermined price or at auction.[35]

At this stage, the platform mints the NFT and generates a public webpage, featuring the uploaded image, text, or music, along with ancillary metadata. Alternatively, to reduce upfront costs, the platform only creates the web page, delaying the minting of the token until a buyer has committed to purchasing it (often referred to as "lazy-minting").[36] This web page is typically hosted by a centralized web-services provider and remains under the control of the minting platform. The NFT is created either through a newly deployed smart contract or, more commonly, by reusing an existing one that is coded by the minting platform and executed on a distributed ledger technology (DLT) network, such as Ethereum, Polygon, or Solana.[37] Once all these operations have been carried out, the NFT is offered to the public. Generally, both the minting platform and the token creator strive to attract prospective purchasers through social media and other channels. Once a person agrees to acquire the NFT, the minting platform facilitates both the transfer of the token and the payment processing,[38] deducting its service fee before releasing the balance to the creator.[39] This standardized intermediation typically extends beyond the initial sale, as these platforms serve as the primary venues for secondary market transactions, capturing fees on each subsequent transfer while maintaining significant control over the display and accessibility of content associated with the NFT.

5.2.2 The bespoke model

The second model for NFT creation and distribution is more *bespoke*. This approach has been employed in some of the most economically successful projects by prominent issuers, including Yuga Labs[40] and Dapper Labs,[41] as well as

blog/ipfs-why-does-pinning-matter-anyways. These files are only permanent if they are "pinned" in the node's permanent storage. *Id.* Unpinned files are subject to deletion by automatic garbage collection. *Id.* While pinning can preserve a file, many services pin to only one node, creating a single point of failure. *Id.* If that node goes offline, the pinned files may become inaccessible. *Id.* Some providers, like Filebase, mitigate this risk by pinning across multiple nodes, creating redundancy and increasing accessibility. *Id.*

[35] Moringiello & Odinet, *Tokens*, *supra* note 1, at 628–29.

[36] *See Lazy Minting on Rarible*, RARIBLE, https://help.rarible.com/hc/en-us/articles/10837015465101-Lazy-Minting-on-Rarible (last visited Aug. 5, 2025).

[37] Moringiello & Odinet, *Tokens*, *supra* note 1, at 628–29.

[38] *See generally NFT Marketplace Revenue Model–Fees, Royalties & Beyond!*, COINSCLONE, https://www.coinsclone.com/nft-marketplace-revenue-model/ (last visited Aug. 5, 2025).

[39] Moringiello & Odinet, *Tokens*, *supra* note 1, at 629–30.

[40] YUGA LABS, https://www.yuga.com (last visited Feb. 6, 2023).

[41] DAPPER LABS, https://www.dapperlabs.com (last visited Feb. 6, 2023).

famous artists, such as Pak[42] and Beeple.[43] Unlike minting platforms that rely on standardized tools, creators using this model deploy custom smart contracts to generate their unique digital assets. This technical independence enables them to implement enhanced functionalities, unique utility features, and sophisticated control mechanisms that differentiate their offerings in the marketplace.[44] Additionally, creators can program customized revenue streams through mechanisms that would be unavailable or limited on minting platforms, giving them greater long-term economic control over their NFTs.

The process can be summarized as follows. A person generates or acquires one or more creative works in the form of digital images, videos, or music. Relying either on a major public DLT network (e.g., Ethereum) or one under their control (e.g., Dapper Labs' Flow Blockchain), the issuer mints one or more NFTs and then links them with their creative works. This technological operation typically involves storing relevant images, videos, or music on servers connected to the internet and then connecting each token to a specific creative work through a hyperlink or a functionally similar pointer mechanism.[45]

Thereafter, the NFTs are offered to the general public either directly by the issuers or through specialized agents, including storied auction houses such as Christie's and Sotheby's.[46] These transactions typically command substantially higher valuations compared to the sales of NFTs created through minting platforms, with buyers drawn by the combination of exclusivity, creator renown, and prospective utility benefits.[47] Moreover, issuers using the bespoke model often offer ancillary goods or services alongside their NFTs and, in some cases, intellectual property licenses that permit commercial exploitation of the associated digital artwork.[48] However, it should be noted that artists such as Beeple

[42] *Merge by Pak*, Nifty Gateway Studio, https://www.niftygateway.com/collections/pakmerge (last visited Feb. 6, 2023).

[43] Beeple, https://www.beeple-crap.com (last visited Feb. 6, 2023).

[44] John Vester, *An Introduction to the Flow Blockchain*, Better Programming (Sept. 19, 2022), https://medium.com/better-programming/an-introduction-to-the-flow-blockchain-60ccc7a35598.

[45] Fairfield, *supra* note 17, at 1296.

[46] Digital Art, Southeby's, https://www.sothebys.com/en/departments/digital-art (last visited Aug. 5, 2025); *Next Wave*, Christie's, https://nft.christies.com (last visited Aug. 5, 2025).

[47] *See, e.g.*, Jacqui Palumbo, *First NFT Artwork at Auction Sells for Staggering $69 Million*, CNN Style (Mar. 12, 2021), https://www.cnn.com/style/article/beeple-first-nft-artwork-at-auction-sale-result/index.html.

[48] For example, Bored Ape Yacht Club NFTs function as access credentials to exclusive community spaces and events. *See* Myriam Brouard, *Setting Sail in a Tokenized World: An Exploration of the Bored Ape Yacht Club and the Co-Created Consumer Experience*, 41 Int'l J. Res. Mktg., article no. 100471, Mar. 24, 2024, https://www.sciencedirect.com/science/article/pii/S0167811624000193. Additionally, Yuga Labs grants each purchaser "an unlimited, worldwide license to use, copy, and display the purchased Art for the purpose of creating derivative works based upon the Art." *Licenses*, Bored Ape Yacht Club, https://www.boredapeyachtclub.com/licenses/bayc (last visited Jun. 3, 2025) [hereinafter *BAYC Licenses*]. This licensing arrangement has enabled holders to develop

have been successful in auctioning NFTs that are only loosely linked to their artworks, without granting purchasers any license, let alone assigning the underlying copyright.[49]

Having described the technical architecture and market dynamics of both standardized and bespoke NFT issuance models, we now turn to a comprehensive private law analysis of these transactions.

5.3 The private law of standardized model NFT transactions

In the pages that follow, we examine the standardized NFT issuance model through contract law and property law lenses. Drawing on prior work,[50] we chronicle an NFT-minting exercise conducted on June 15, 2021, illustrating the key mechanics common to most platforms that facilitate the creation and distribution of these digital assets. This is followed by an analysis of a dataset of terms of service from various minting platforms, compiled between May and August 2021, to examine what creators and holders of these tokens actually agree contractually, as opposed to the promises about NFTs that circulate in popular press and trade publications.

5.3.1 Overview

The first step in our chronicled exercise involved choosing a reference asset to link to the NFT we intended to mint.[51] Since digital art has emerged as a popular category for this purpose, we chose an electronic rendering of a physical oil painting by the artist Dub Lee, titled "The Clearest Light is the Most Blinding," which depicts a Charolais cow.[52] We then selected Mintable as our platform company of choice, as it operates a widely used launchpad that allows an individual to create a free account and mint an NFT in connection with digital art, at no cost. After creating an account, we began the process by clicking "Start Minting Now" and then "Create a New Item." Before going any further, Mintable

commercial merchandise, derivative artworks, and even physical business establishments featuring their specific Ape characters. *See id.*

[49] Taylor Locke, *Millionaire Artist Beeple: This Is the Very Important Thing 'I Think People Don't Understand' About Buying NFTs*, CNBC (Mar. 29, 2021), https://www.cnbc.com/2021/03/26/digital-artist-beeple-common-misunderstanding-about-nfts.html.

[50] *See generally* Moringiello & Odinet, *Tokens*, *supra* note 1.

[51] *See id.* at 628–29.

[52] *Id.* at 628.

requires users to link a crypto wallet to their platform account. For this purpose, we created such a wallet through Coinbase, the largest exchange and custodial wallet provider in North America.[53] This wallet connection was required because purchasers pay for Mintable NFTs using Ethereum's native token Ether, which Coinbase supports for trading.

Having linked our Coinbase wallet and Mintable account, we then uploaded the digital painting, its name, and a brief description. During this process, we also selected the "Transfer Copyright when purchased?" checkbox, which Mintable explained would grant purchasers "the rights to use the file commercially." Finally, we were prompted to select a modality of sale: fixed price, auction, or auction with a "Buy Now" option. We chose the auction format and set the minimum bid at $400.[54]

This process created an NFT that Mintable displayed as connected to the digital painting. As shown in Figure 5.1, the platform generated a publicly searchable listing page showing the artwork with its name and description, along with various item metadata that we reproduce.

To properly analyze Mintable's terms of use, we must first understand what users expect from NFT transactions on the platform. We inferred these expectations from the information Mintable itself provided during the minting process and on its website. The most prominent information appeared next to the "Start Minting Now" button on the platform's website. It stated that one could "turn any creation into an item on the blockchain" or "trade digital items on Mintable to easily earn crypto."[55] This seemed to suggest that through Mintable's platform, one could turn any kind of creation (e.g., a digital painting) into an item (an NFT) that would purportedly be recorded on the blockchain. Relatedly, one could then exchange the NFT item for cryptocurrency (which could in turn be converted into fiat money). Also, when creating the NFT, a user was first asked to indicate "[w]hat kind of item [they] are . . . making[.]"[56] The choices were art, music, videos, collectibles, sports, and utility. There was no way to add another category. It was also not clear whether users were being told that they were making the actual reference asset or that they were creating the NFT, although the categories suggested the former. Overall, the user was never directly told what this transaction would accomplish. Users expecting the platform to provide clearer explanations than those available from social media influencers and news stories would find no such guidance during the minting process.

However, there was a blog post on Mintable's site titled "A Guide to Selling NFTs (ERC-721s) Using Mintable."[57] A portion of this post contained the

[53] *Id.* at 629.
[54] *Id.*
[55] *See id.* at 630.
[56] *Id.* at 631.
[57] *See id.*

<table>
<tr><th colspan="2">Item Metadata</th></tr>
<tr><th>Contract Address</th><th>Token Metadata</th></tr>
<tr><td>0x8c5aCF6dBD24c66e6FD44d4A4C3d7a2
D955AA ad2</td><td rowspan="9">{
"symbol": "Mintable Gasless store",
"image": "https://d1iczm3wxxz9zd.cloudfront.net/
613b908d
0000000000/86193240282618763854367501608353605
31676033165
"animation_url": "",
"royalty_amount": 500,
"copyright_transfer": true,
"address":
"0x8c5aCF6dBD24c66e6FD44d4A4C3d7a2D955AAad2",
"tokenId":
"86193240282618763854367501608353605316760331
"resellable": true,
"original_creator":
"0xBe8Fa52a0A28AFE9507186A817813eDC1
"edition_number": 1,
"description": "<p>A beautiful bovine in the summer sun
"auctionLength": 43200,
"title": "The Clearest Light is the Most Blinding",
"url":
"https://metadata.mintable.app/mintable_gasless/86193
240

"file_key": "",
"apiURL": "mintable_gasless/",
"subtitle": "bovine from South Texas",
"name": "The Clearest Light is the Most Blinding",
"auctionType": "Auction",
"category": "Art",
"edition_total": 1,
"gasless": true
}</td></tr>
<tr><th>Token ID</th></tr>
<tr><td>86193240282618763854367501
608353605316760331651808345700
084608326762837402898</td></tr>
<tr><th>Token Name</th></tr>
<tr><td>The Clearest Light is the Most Blinding</td></tr>
<tr><th>Original Image</th></tr>
<tr><td>https://d1iczm3wxxz9zd.cloudfront.net/6
13b908d-19ad-41b1-8bfa0e016820739c/
0000000000000000/861932402
8261887638543675016083536053
1676033165180834570008460832676
2837402898/ITEM_PREVIEW1.png</td></tr>
<tr><th>Original Creator</th></tr>
<tr><td>0xBe8Fa52a0A28AFE9507186A817813eD
C14
54E004</td></tr>
</table>

Figure 5.1 Item metadata associated with the NFT "The Clearest Light is the Most Blinding," showing the contract address, token ID, original creator, and token metadata fields recorded on the Mintable marketplace.

header: "So How Can You Use These Tokens in the Real World?" The most noteworthy assertions for purposes of this discussion were that a Mintable token could be used for the following:

- Establishing ownership of an item external to the token;
- Establishing who is allowed access to content or locations;
- Linking the token owner to a web URL, a photo, video, or other web-based asset;
- Establishing ownership of something in the [token's] metadata;
- Tokenizing content; and
- Tokenizing anything that could have value.

Note that, collecitlvely, the assertions in the list above suggest a broad ability to tokenize virtually anything, though often in terms that strain comprehension.

The most explicit instance of this was the first assertion, which purported to give the holder of the token actual ownership rights in a linked asset. The third assertion mentioned linking the NFT owner to another thing, thereby creating a rights-based connection (i.e., tokenization) between the NFT and another digital asset. The fourth assertion again mentioned ownership, although puzzlingly this time in a meta component of the token itself. The fifth and sixth assertions each gesture at creating a thing that represents rights in something else (content or "anything that can have value").[58]

In sum, all this information would ostensibly inform the user of the nature of the transaction and the rights being created or acquired. The token would convey property rights (and in some cases, ownership explicitly) in something, with that something often being another asset altogether. With this in mind, we turn to the terms of service used by Mintable and several other minting platforms.

5.3.2 Exploring terms of service

As with so many aspects of the digital asset economy, the terms of service agreements are paramount. And indeed, the creation and transfer of NFTs are governed by such terms of service proffered by the platforms. Drawing again from prior work, we reviewed several terms of service documents that prospective NFT creators must accept to mint and transfer their tokens.[59] We focused on seven platforms that appeared on various "Top NFT platform" lists.[60] In reviewing these terms, our primary goal was to ascertain the property rights purportedly created in the NFT and the relationship between ownership of the NFT on the one hand and rights in the linked asset on the other. The vast majority of the public does not read these contracts (or any fine print in contracts of adhesion, for that matter), but they often inform how courts adjudicate related contract claims.[61]

We also compared the terms of service of each platform with the statements made on their websites and in marketing materials about their services. For example, Foundation claimed to bring "digital creators, crypto natives, and collectors together to move culture forward."[62] The MakersPlace website

[58] *Id.*

[59] These platform companies are Foundation, KnownOrigin, Makersplace, Mintable, OpenSea, Rarible, and SuperRare. *See* Moringiello & Odinet, *Tokens*, *supra* note 1.

[60] *See id.* at 632 & n.160.

[61] Yannis Bakos, Florencia Marotta-Wurgler & David R. Trossen, *Does Anyone Read the Fine Print? Consumer Attention to Standard-Form Contracts*, 43 J. Legal Stud. 1, 2 (2014); Colin P. Marks, *Online and "As Is,"* 45 Pepp. L. Rev. 1, 3, 6–7 (2018).

[62] *See* Moringiello & Odinet, *Tokens*, *supra* note 1, at 632 (citing Foundation's terms of service).

offered artists the opportunity to "protect . . . their unique digital creations" and "[e]stablish a permanent proof of ownership" for their digital creations.[63] SuperRare also focused on uniqueness, touting its site as "a marketplace to collect and trade unique, single-edition digital artworks."[64] Mintable advertised on its website that its users could "[t]urn any creation into a blockchain item."[65]

Finally, it is important to note that this study of the terms of service is a snapshot in time. The discussion in the pages that follow considers the terms of service as they existed at the time they were studied, between May and August 2021. As is often the case across the digital asset ecosystem, firms periodically change their terms of service, without giving formal notice to their NFT holders. Indeed, the terms of service for these various platforms explicitly stated that changes were permissible without any kind of affirmative notice or only minimal notice.[66] Nevertheless, our analysis remains highly relevant because the core substance and structure of these contractual terms have remained largely consistent across platforms, with the core legal issues we identify persisting in contemporary NFT marketplace agreements.

(a) Ownership and control of the NFT

All major NFT minting platforms studied presented themselves as mere technical facilitators in their terms of service. Foundation established the baseline approach, characterizing itself as solely a "non-custodial service provider."[67] SuperRare adopted more expansive language, explicitly stating that it did "not take 'custody, possession or control' of any SuperRare token."[68] OpenSea provided the most comprehensive disclaimer, asserting that it was "not party to any agreement between any users" and declaring that the platform had no "custody or control over the digital tokens, blockchains, or third parties you engage with."[69]

These uniform disclaimers, which remain substantially unchanged across the industry, created the impression that minting users had complete dominion over every facet of their digital creations, with platforms serving as passive infrastructure with no rights or power over the NFTs. Closer scrutiny, however, revealed a more nuanced reality. While the terms of service recognized that ownership

[63] *Id.* (citing MakersPlace's terms of service).
[64] *Id.* at 632–33 (citing SuperRare's terms of service).
[65] *Id.* at 633.
[66] *Id.*
[67] *See id.* at 633–34.
[68] *Id.*
[69] *Id.*; *see also Terms of Service*, OpenSea § 1, https://opensea.io/tos (last updated June 18, 2025). Notably, as of June 2025, OpenSea's terms of service continue to use this expansive to disclaimer almost verbatim. *See id.*

and control in the NFTs rested with their creators through their holding of the public/private key pairings respectively, platforms retained substantial influence over the commercial circulation of these digital assets.

First, users agreed to display, list, and trade their tokens on the minting platforms in question, creating a practical dependency. Without platform mediation, NFT holders had limited practical ability to demonstrate ownership or facilitate transfers, despite owning and controlling the underlying tokens. Second, creators who minted NFTs through these platforms, linking them to digital art, music, or other artworks, agreed to arrangements whereby platforms controlled where or how that content was stored. As shown in our experience with Mintable, users contractually accepted that the platforms were in charge of hosting arrangements, content delivery mechanisms, and ongoing accessibility. If these agreements ceased or platforms changed their infrastructure, users would retain ownership and control of their tokens, yet the embedded links would lead to nonexistent content, effectively rendering the NFTs as pointers to digital voids or the familiar and dreaded "404 error."

Third, users also accepted the content removal policies of many of these platforms under their terms of service. For example, Mintable reserved "the right to remove any content that violates the law or the terms of use" while simultaneously describing itself as merely a "passive conduit for your online distribution and publication of your User Content."[70] Similarly, OpenSea warned users that violations of its terms of service could result in removal of "users' assets from its site," including content violating intellectual property laws or containing abusive material.[71]

Thus, when considering ownership of NFTs created through the standardized model, a fundamental tension emerged. On one hand, users held both legal title and control over their digital assets. On the other hand, platforms maintained substantial operational influence by controlling the practical utility of these assets through their power over accessibility, display, and transfer. As the next subpart shows, however, even more problematic than this operational contradiction was the legal nature of the link between NFTs and the associated creative works themselves.

(b) The property link between the token and the underlying asset

The most important and most confusing aspect of the terms of service studied related to the property rights that NFT ownership conveyed in the asset to which it is purportedly linked, such as a digital image or music. Several platforms made

[70] *See* Moringiello & Odinet, *Tokens*, *supra* note 1, at 634.
[71] *Id.*

grand statements about the similarities between owning NFTs and owning real-world art. KnownOrigin asserted that "[o]wning a Token is just like owning a physical artwork."[72] The SuperRare Terms of Service made the same claim, describing ownership of a SuperRare Item (SuperRare's term for an NFT) as "similar to owning a piece of physical art."[73]

Sites used terms such as "represent" to describe the relationship between the NFT and the digital art underlying the token. Some said that the token represented title to the underlying work. For example, under the KnownOrigin terms of service, users could allegedly create "limited-edition digital items" that included original artwork.[74] The terms defined the creative work as "Content" and the linked NFT as the "Token."[75] The terms said that the Token represented the title of "that item," although it was unclear what *that item* was.[76]

Other sites focused on something akin to provenance, stating that the NFT provided a chain of ownership to the underlying artwork.[77] SuperRare's terms said that NFTs "are forever tracked and stored on the Ethereum blockchain, providing the Collector of a SuperRare Item with a permanent record of authenticity and ownership."[78] Mintable said that its token could be used for "[e]stablishing ownership" of external items.[79]

In contrast to these promises, none of the terms of service substantiated, let alone established, a private law link between ownership of a token and rights in the underlying creative work. In fact, they all denied that the owner of an NFT had any rights in the underlying asset. The SuperRare Terms of Service contained a simple statement of the relationship between ownership of a token and rights in the underlying work, stating that a buyer obtains ownership of "a cryptographic token representing the Artist's creative Work as a piece of property" but obtains no ownership of the "creative Work itself."[80]

The Foundation terms were a particularly striking example. Under this agreement, the "Creator" of the NFT retained all rights in the associated artwork.[81] The buyer of the token only obtained the right to display the artwork, much like the purchaser of a physical artwork owns the object and may freely display it, but does not hold the underlying.

72 *Id.* at 634–35.
73 *Id.* at 635.
74 *See id.*
75 *Id.*
76 *Id.*
77 *See id.* at 635 n.185.
78 *See id.* at 635.
79 *See id.* at 635 n.187.
80 *See id.* at 635 & n.188.
81 *Id.* at 635–36.

Beyond that, the Foundation terms of service described the property rights of NFT owners in a confusing manner. First, the terms conflated the underlying artwork and the NFT by defining the entire package as the "digital artwork."[82] The document then stated that collectors received a "cryptographic token representing the Creator's Digital Artwork as a piece of property, but do[] not own the Digital Artwork itself."[83] In the next paragraph, the terms granted collectors "a limited, worldwide, non-assignable and non-transferable . . . [,] non-sublicensable, royalty-free license to display the Digital Artwork *legally owned* and properly obtained by the Collector."[84] While collectors had the right to sell their Digital Artwork, they could not make commercial use of it. The terms also imposed a number of restrictions on the use of the Digital Artwork, prohibiting its use in advertising, movies, and video games and prohibiting any attempt to tokenize the same digital artwork.[85]

Similarly, the KnownOrigin terms of service stated that ownership of an NFT did not convey intellectual property rights in the associated creative work.[86] The terms clearly gave buyers ownership of the tokens, but reserved all rights in the content (defined as "original visual artwork, animations, audio and photographs") to the creator.[87] In its "Intellectual Property" section, the KnownOrigin terms elaborated on this division, specifying that token buyers obtained title to the NFT and the right to display and resell it, but could neither prevent creators from using the Content for future commercial work nor use it commercially themselves.[88]

MakersPlace's terms of service also addressed property rights haphazardly, failing to clearly delineate the position of different platform users. For example, the "Ownership" paragraph opened with an expansive claim:

> Unless otherwise indicated in writing by us, content and other materials contained therein, including . . . all designs, text, graphics, pictures, information, data, software, sound files, other files and the selection and arrangement thereof (collectively, "Content"), the Site, and any Crypto Assets are the proprietary property of MakersPlace or our affiliates, licensors or users, as applicable.[89]

[82] *Id.* at 636 n.192.
[83] *Id.* at 636 n.193.
[84] *Id.* at 636 n.194.
[85] *Id.* at 636 n.196.
[86] *Id.* at 636 n.197.
[87] *See id.* at 636 n.198 ("[T]he Content which forms part of the Token is owned solely by the Artist.").
[88] *See id.* at 636.
[89] *Id.* at 636–37.

Despite this overbroad language, certain property concepts emerged clearly from the terms. First, MakersPlace claimed no property rights in any user's crypto assets.[90] Second, buyers of crypto assets did not obtain any copyright in the underlying work and were prohibited from using it for commercial purposes.[91]

The Mintable terms of use did not say much about property rights. These terms defined the NFTs as "User Content,"[92] and stated that users of the site retained all ownership rights in their User Content, acknowledging rights in the token but not in the underlying asset. However, a particularly perplexing provision required User Content owners to grant to each user of the site a "worldwide, non-exclusive, royalty-free license to access [the] User Content" through Mintable, along with expansive rights to "use, reproduce, distribute, prepare derivative works of, display and perform" such User Content.[93]

Rarible's Terms and Conditions covered both the creation and the trade of NFTs, as well as the distribution of the platform's native coin (RARI tokens).[94] However, these terms differed from other platforms by adopting a highly technical approach to defining NFTs. The terms defined "Collectible" as the "association on Ethereum of an NFT with a Uniform Resource Identifier ('URI') identifying an appropriately configured JSON file" and specified the technical standards such files must satisfy.[95] Under this framework, the "Collectible ID" referred to the JSON file itself, which described the Collectible, including the URI identifying the image file and any associated metadata.[96] While technically precise, this approach focused on blockchain mechanics rather than legal implications.

Despite this technical framing, Rarible's legal treatment of property rights aligned with all other platforms studied. Absent an agreement between the creator and purchaser, the latter obtained no license to, ownership of, or any right or entitlement to the Collectible Metadata or the associated intellectual property. The only ownership rights granted to the buyer were in the NFT itself.[97]

5.4 The private law of bespoke model NFT transactions

Having completed our analysis of the standardized model, we now analyze the bespoke issuance of NFTs through a contract and property law lens. Projects

[90] *Id.* at 637.
[91] *Id.*
[92] *Id.* at 637 n.204.
[93] *Id.* at 637 n.206
[94] *See id.* at 637–38 & n.207.
[95] *Id.* at 638 & n.209.
[96] *Id.* at 638 & n.211.
[97] *Id.* at 638 & n.212.

adopting this approach again exhibit a profound disconnect between marketing rhetoric and the actual substance of their terms of service. Moreover, unlike standardized intermediated platforms, these projects often establish convoluted intellectual property licensing frameworks that further obscure the legal reality. To illustrate these problems, we examine the terms of service for NBA Top Shot (Top Shot) and Bored Ape Yacht Club (BAYC), two of the most prominent examples of bespoke NFT issuance.

5.4.1 Overview

Launched by Dapper Labs in 2020, Top Shot allows users to purchase, collect, and trade NFTs, known as *Moments*, which are linked to officially licensed NBA video highlights. Moments have generated hundreds of millions of dollars in sales, with individual NFTs selling for as much as $387,000.[98] Top Shot perfectly exemplifies the bespoke model, with the issuer fully controlling the creation, initial sale, custody, and, until recently, secondary trading of the digital assets.

Dapper Labs built Top Shot on its proprietary DLT network, Flow.[99] Unlike projects launched on existing, permissionless blockchains like Ethereum, Dapper Labs largely controls the infrastructure and governance of Flow.[100] To interact with Top Shot, users must create a Dapper Wallet, which is integrated into the Top Shot platform. This wallet simplifies the user experience but places custody and transaction finality in Dapper Labs' hands.[101] This architecture diverges sharply from NFT offerings under the standardized model, in which users connect their noncustodial wallets to their minting platform of choice.

Top Shot customers acquire Moments in randomized "packs" that mimic the mechanics of physical trading cards. Subsequent trading occurs primarily on the Top Shot Marketplace, which is integrated into the Flow network. Dapper Labs automatically withholds a 5 percent fee on these transactions, capturing

[98] Chris Bumbaca, *LeBron James NBA Top Shot Moment of Dunk Honoring Kobe Bryant Auctions for $387,600*, USA TODAY (April 16, 2021), https://www.usatoday.com/story/sports/nba/lakers/2021/04/16/lebron-james-nba-top-shot-moment-auction/7251326002/.

[99] *See Core Protocol*, FLOW, https://flow.com/core-protocol (last visited Aug. 7, 2025).

[100] Flow employs a multirole proof-of-stake architecture derived from the HotStuff consensus protocol; validator nodes perform distinct Collection, Consensus, Execution, and Verification functions to increase throughput. Although third-party staking is possible, Dapper Labs retains significant influence over network governance and validator admission, underscoring the permissioned character of the system. *See* Tanay Ved, *An Overview of the Flow Blockchain*, COIN METRICS' STATE OF THE NETWORK (Oct. 15, 2024), https://coinmetrics.substack.com/p/state-of-the-networks-issue-281.

[101] *See Dapper Interface Terms of Use*, DAPPER, https://eth.meetdapper.com/terms (last updated Jan. 14, 2020).

additional revenues from trading activity.[102] Since February 2025, users have been able to bridge Moments to an EVM-compatible Flow address and list them on OpenSea, though liquidity remains concentrated on the Flow network.[103]

Similarly, Yuga Labs launched BAYC in 2021 as a collection of ten thousand NFTs each linked to the digital image of a unique cartoon ape.[104] These digital assets have commanded extraordinary prices, with some selling for millions of dollars, and have become status symbols embraced by celebrities, including Eminem, Snoop Dogg, and Stephen Curry.[105] BAYC further illustrates the bespoke model for NFT issuances.

Yuga Labs launched BAYC on the Ethereum blockchain by deploying its own bespoke ERC-721 smart contract to mint the NFTs.[106] In parallel, the ape images were stored on the IPFS, with each NFT containing a metadata link to its corresponding image.[107] During the primary sale, purchasers interacted directly with the Yuga Labs smart contract, sending 0.08 ETH and receiving an NFT linked to a randomly generated ape image, with the token then transferred to their personal Ethereum wallet.[108] Ever since, secondary trading has occurred through marketplace platforms such as OpenSea and Blur, with transactions ultimately recorded on the Ethereum blockchain.

Differing from Dapper Labs' chosen architecture for Top Shot, Yuga Labs' technical implementation creates distinct limitations on its control over BAYC NFTs. The core functions of the original smart contract are immutable,

[102] *Buying, Listing, and Delisting Moments*, NBA TOP SHOT: SUPPORT, https://support. nbatopshot. com/hc/en-us/articles/7548081741587-Buying-Listing-and-Delisting-Moments (last visited Aug. 7, 2025).

[103] *How to List Your NBA Top Shot Moments on OpenSea*, NBA TOP SHOT: SUPPORT, https://support.nbatopshot.com/hc/en-us/articles/38916417025939-How-to-List-Your-NBA-Top-Shot-Moments-on-OpenSea (last visited Aug. 7, 2025).

[104] NFTing, *The History of BAYC: A Billion-Dollar Ecosystem of Cartoon Apes*, MEDIUM: NFTING BLOG (Aug. 23, 2022), https://nfting.medium.com/the-history-of-bayc-a-billion-dollar-ecosystem-of-cartoon-apes-fcc67e032408. On BAYC, see generally J. Scott Colesanti, *Caging the Bored Ape: How the FTC's Expanded Anti-Monopoly Authority Can Tame "NFTS" for Web 3.0*, 15 WM. & MARY BUS. L. REV. 117 (2024).

[105] As of 2024, Eminem, Snoop Dog, Steph Curry, and several other celebrities owned a BAYC NFT. *See* Oliver North, *10 Top Famous Celebrities Who Aped into the Bored Ape Yacht Club NFTs*, NFTEVENING (May 16, 2025), https://nftevening.com/10-top-famous-celebrities-who-aped-into-the-bored-ape-yacht-club-nfts/; Shanti Escalante-DeMattei, *Eminem and Snoop Dogg Performed as Their Bored Ape Yacht Club Avatars at the VMAs*, ARTNEWS (Aug. 29, 2022, 2:30 PM), https://www.artnews.com/art-news/news/eminem-snoop-dogg-bored-ape-yacht-club-vmas-1234637677/ [https://perma.cc/3NSG-X7S5].

[106] YBM, *Bored Ape Yacht Club: Mechanics + Smart Contract Analysis*, MEDIUM (June 3, 2022), https://medium.com/coinmonks/bored-ape-yacht-club-mechanics-smart-contract-breakdown-6345bffd75ec.

[107] Each token's baseURI points to a directory of JSON metadata pinned to IPFS, and each metadata file in turn references a PNG image likewise hosted on IPFS. *See id.*

[108] BAYC NFTs were minted for 0.08 ETH each, selling out within twelve hours. *See A Complete Guide to Bored Ape Yacht Club in 2024*, NFT PLAZAS (Nov. 16, 2024), https://nftplazas.com/bored-ape-yacht-club-guide-2024/.

preventing the creation of additional NFTs beyond the original ten thousand, any interference with their existence, or any disruption of past and future transfers. Nevertheless, Yuga Labs retains the power to redirect each NFT to a new location, potentially affecting the image linked to each token.[109] Notably, the 2.5 percent creator fee widely associated with BAYC is not hard-coded in either the smart contract or the NFTs. Rather, it relies on voluntary marketplace compliance. Yuga Labs has no technical mechanism to enforce this fee, a limitation that became particularly evident when several major marketplaces, including OpenSea, chose to make such payments optional.[110] Similarly, there is no enforcement mechanism if users transfer their NFTs peer to peer without involving a trading platform.[111]

5.4.2 Exploring terms of service

We now turn to the private law analysis of the terms of service of Top Shot and BAYC. As we noted earlier in this chapter, our analysis is a snapshot in time, based on the terms of service as they existed in mid-2025. Although we acknowledge that such agreements evolve rapidly in the digital asset ecosystem, we believe that our examination provides illuminating insights into how bespoke model projects conceive property rights and structure their intellectual property licensing frameworks.

(a) Ownership and control of the NFT

Both Top Shot and BAYC make broad (arguably eccentric) claims about the ownership and control of their NFTs in their terms of service. This contrasts sharply with the more cautious disclaimers of minting platforms and possibly stems from the extensive control they maintain over the entire life cycle of their digital assets. Crucially, several clauses in their agreements betray a misguided understanding of both the interplay between law and technology and the interface between property and contract law.

[109] The BAYC smart contract includes a setBaseURI function that allows Yuga Labs to change the base location where NFT metadata is stored, effectively controlling what content each NFT displays. Bored Ape Yacht Club Smart Contract, Ethereum Address 0xBC4CA0EdA7647A8aB7C2061c2E118A18a936f13D, ETHERSCAN, https://etherscan.io/address/0xbc4ca0eda7647a8ab7c2061c2e118a18a936f13d#writeContract(last visited Aug. 7, 2025).

[110] Jacob Kastrenakes, *Bored Ape Yacht Club Creator to Block OpenSea in Fight Over Payments*, THE VERGE (Aug. 18, 2023) https://www.theverge.com/2023/8/18/23837677/bayc-opensea-drops-support-creator-royalty-fees.

[111] *The Complete Guide To NFT Royalties–What You Should Know*, WAGMI.TIPS, https://wagmi.tips/guides/nft-royalties/ (last visited Aug. 7, 2025).

Yuga Labs' terms of service for BAYC are relatively brief. They include an "Ownership" section that reads as follows: "Each Bored Ape is an NFT on the Ethereum blockchain. . . . Ownership of the NFT is mediated entirely by the Smart Contract and the Ethereum Network: at no point may we seize, freeze, or otherwise modify the ownership of any Bored Ape."[112]

The statement that ownership of the NFTs is "mediated entirely" by the smart contract and the Ethereum network is puzzling. Yuga Labs appears to suggest that ownership of its NFTs is established and transferred based on the data entries of its smart contract in the Ethereum ledger. This proposition is categorically at odds with property law. Whether ownership exists and how and when it is transferred are matters determined by law, not by computer code or entries in a ledger. For example, if an NFT owner dies, ownership would transfer to their heirs according to applicable inheritance law, regardless of whether this transfer is recorded on the blockchain. Similarly, if a court orders the transfer of an NFT as part of a judgment, that transfer is legally effective regardless of blockchain state.

The final statement, "at no point may we seize, freeze, or otherwise modify the ownership of any Bored Ape," further highlights this legal mirage, where technical features are mischaracterized as property law precepts. As noted above, it is true that the BAYC smart contract is coded in such a way that Yuga Labs does not retain the power to seize, freeze, or otherwise modify the NFTs. However, this is a software design issue, completely distinct from ownership and control. Once a person becomes the lawful owner of an NFT under applicable property law, any unauthorized technological interference by Yuga Labs would give rise to tortious and potentially criminal liability.

The NBA Top Shot terms of service contain more extensive provisions regarding ownership than BAYC, yet they reveal equally profound conceptual flaws in their treatment of property rights.[113] The Top Shot terms state that "[b]ecause each Moment is an NFT on the Flow Network, when you purchase a Moment in accordance with these Terms (and not through any of the Category B Prohibited Activities) you own the underlying NFT completely. This means that you have the right to swap your Moment, sell it, burn it, exchange it, upgrade it or give it away to the extent that such uses are made available in the App. Ownership of the Moment is mediated entirely by the Flow Network."[114]

[112] *BAYC Licenses*, *supra* note 48.

[113] *Terms of Use*, NBA Top Shot, https://nbatopshot.com/terms [https://perma.cc/LGH5-7MGC] (last visited Jun. 3, 2025) (last updated May 6, 2025) [hereinafter *NBA Top Shot Terms of Use*].

[114] *Id.* § 4(i).

While Dapper Labs acknowledges that purchasers of Moments own the NFT itself, their terms perpetuate the same misconceptions found in BAYC's agreement. They reprise the flawed notion that ownership of NFTs is "mediated" by a DLT network, coupled with the misguided idea that an owner's legal powers are determined by the technological capabilities of the network and the App. Both propositions misconstrue the source of property rights, which arise from law, not software.

Even more striking is Dapper Labs' attempt to condition recognition of NFT ownership upon compliance with their contractual terms. In bold, all caps, Dapper Labs warns, "YOUR OWNERSHIP OF MOMENTS WILL ONLY BE RECOGNIZED BY US IF YOU HAVE PURCHASED OR OTHERWISE RIGHTFULLY ACQUIRED SUCH MOMENTS FROM A LEGITIMATE SOURCE AND NOT THROUGH ANY OF THE CATEGORY B PROHIBITED ACTIVITIES (AS DEFINED BELOW)."[115] This statement is followed by a delimitation of the legitimate routes to acquire NFTs, either by buying packs directly from Dapper or purchasing a Moment in the in-app Marketplace,[116] while explicitly prohibiting purchases "through one or more transactions conducted on auction sites that we have not approved in writing."[117] This distinction is then buttressed by a clause in which Dapper Labs reserves the right to "seize, freeze, or otherwise modify the ownership of any Moment" obtained contrary to those rules.

These terms fundamentally mischaracterize the nature of property rights. Dapper Labs proposes that it can unilaterally decide whose "ownership" it chooses to recognize. This implies that ownership is a subjective concept, a revocable privilege, malleable through contract terms and conditional determinations. This is unequivocally wrong and serves as a quintessential example of the *flexibility fallacy*. Ownership is a property right, effective *erga omnes* (meaning, against all others), and not contingent on anyone's approval. The law establishes its substance, scope, and breadth; how it can be acquired and transferred; and how it ceases to be. Such private discretion is legally immaterial and inconsequential.

It is particularly problematic that Dapper Labs claims not to recognize ownership acquired through transactions involving unapproved auction sites. This is untenable. To put it plainly, Dapper Labs could refuse to provide services to someone who purchased a Moment through an auction site. It could sue for breach of contract and terminate its agreement with a person who lists a Moment at auction. However, it cannot, as a matter of property law, annul or refuse to

[115] *Id.* § 4.
[116] *See id.* § 2(iv).
[117] *Id.* § 5(i)(b)(7).

recognize ownership of a Moment purchased at auction. Moreover, the threat to "seize, freeze, or otherwise modify the ownership" of Moments purchased through unapproved channels is a vacuous contractual overreach that attempts to fashion platform policy into property law. Once a valid transfer of ownership occurs under applicable law, Dapper Labs has no authority to invalidate it.

(b) The property link between the NFT and the underlying asset

Beyond ownership and control, the BAYC and NBA Top Shot terms of service articulate inadequately (if not ambiguously) the property law relationship between NFTs and the digital art to which they are linked.

Under the "Ownership" heading, the BAYC terms of service read: "When you purchase an NFT, you own the underlying Bored Ape, the Art, completely."[118] This assertion suggests that acquiring the NFT automatically transfers ownership of the associated digital artwork. However, the terms provide no legal framework explaining how the NFT could embody ownership rights in the Bored Ape image. As we explained in Chapter 3, tokenizations require express recognition in law, which is absent in this case. The BAYC terms thus attempt to create a form of property transfer that existing law simply does not recognize.

One possible interpretation that might align with property law principles is that Yuga Labs simultaneously sells two distinct assets in its initial offerings: the NFT itself and the digital image file. However, this construction would create devilish complications. Since the two assets are separate, subsequent transactions involving only the NFT would not transfer ownership of the digital file (assuming it can be owned at all), which would remain with the initial purchaser unless separately agreed. In other words, the NFT and the associated image file could be owned by different parties, creating a logically untenable scenario where neither party could effectively exploit what they believed they had purchased. One would own a token pointing to artwork they cannot use, while the other would hold digital art with no connection to the NFT marketplace that gives it value.

The only viable interpretation, therefore, is that despite the assertion in the terms of service that purchasers own the underlying artwork, buyers acquire property rights exclusively in the NFT itself. This reading finds strong support in Yuga Labs' elaborate licensing provisions governing the use of the associated images, which would be superfluous if NFT purchasers actually owned the artwork outright.

The licensing framework itself, however, is rife with uncertainty. Consistent with the minimalistic approach throughout the terms, Section 3 provides a

[118] *BAYC Licenses*, *supra* note 48.

"worldwide, royalty-free license to use, copy, and display the purchased Art" for personal, noncommercial use.[119] Section 4 extends this to "an unlimited, worldwide license" for commercial purposes, including creating derivative works and merchandise.[120]

These licensing provisions, however, suffer from significant indeterminacy. They do not specify which intellectual property is being licensed. We presume it to be the copyright in the Ape images; however, in the 2023 trademark infringement case against Ryder Ripps, Yuga Labs conspicuously avoided asserting copyright claims despite apparent infringement opportunities.[121] Moreover, the terms are silent regarding whether the licenses are exclusive or nonexclusive. Given the strict formal requirements for exclusive copyright licenses in most jurisdictions, these licenses are almost certainly nonexclusive. In the United States, for example, such copyright licenses must be in writing and signed by the copyright owner, with clear specification of terms, duration, and scope.[122] Similar requirements exist in other major jurisdictions, often with additional registration formalities. The BAYC terms fail to satisfy these requirements, leading to the conclusion that NFT holders receive merely nonexclusive rights.

However, this non-exclusive nature has significant implications. Yuga Labs retains the ability to grant identical licenses to multiple parties beyond NFT owners, and it could itself commercially exploit any of the Ape images despite having granted licenses to token holders. We also note that the description of the license as "worldwide" spawns another issue. While such ambiguity might be tolerable in jurisdictions with flexible copyright frameworks, such as the United Kingdom and the United States, it creates serious enforceability concerns in countries with more prescriptive regimes. French intellectual property law, for instance, requires each transferred right to be separately enumerated with precise definitions of scope, purpose, and duration.[123] Similarly, Chinese copyright law demands specific content in license agreements, including exact rights parameters and explicit compensation terms. These jurisdictional variations cast doubt on the global validity of BAYC's licensing scheme.[124]

The most troubling aspect is the vagueness regarding the granting of the license and its expiration. BAYC's terms of service fail to specify a mechanism to

[119] *Id.* §§ 3, 4.

[120] *Id.*

[121] In *Yuga Labs v. Ryder Ripps*, No. 2:22-cv-04355-JFW-PVC (C.D. Cal. 2023), Yuga Labs sued for trademark infringement over an allegedly identical NFT collection but notably omitted copyright claims despite apparent visual copying. This omission likely signals either uncertainty about their copyright ownership or fear of exposing vulnerabilities in their ownership claims.

[122] *See* 17 U.S.C. § 204(a).

[123] Code de la propriété intellectuelle [C. prop. intell.] art. L131-3 (Fr.).

[124] Copyright Law of the People's Republic of China art. 24 (promulgated by the Standing Comm. Nat'l People's Cong., Sept. 7, 1990, amended Nov. 11, 2020, effective June 1, 2021) (China).

identify the licensee, the timing of the grant, or the conditions for maintaining the license, merely stating that the license is "subject to continued compliance with these terms."[125] Admittedly, one could interpret the terms of service to mean that Yuga Labs undertakes to grant a license to every new owner of a BAYC NFTs. What is less clear, however, is whether the license is terminated. Does the license cease if a person loses control of the NFT? Or, when a person ceases to be the owner of the NFT?

This ambiguity engenders troubling scenarios in practice. Consider the case of actor Seth Green, who in 2022 had his Bored Ape #8398 stolen in a phishing attack. Green had been developing an animated show featuring this character, but the theft raised questions about whether he still maintained the commercial license to use the image.[126] While being hacked would likely not constitute a "failure to comply with these terms," the incident highlights the precarious connection between NFT ownership and license rights. Moreover, had the thief sold the NFT to a qualified purchaser under UCC Article 12 (concepts we explained more fully in Chapter 2), would Green's commercial ventures become infringing? The terms provide no clear answer to this critical question.

The NBA Top Shot terms of service articulate the link between Moments and the associated video highlights with more clarity.[127] Unlike Yuga Labs, Dapper Labs unequivocally frames the relationship as a limited license arrangement. Their terms explicitly state that Moment owners receive "a worldwide, non-exclusive, non-transferable, royalty-free license" to use the associated NBA highlights.[128] There is no explicit or implied representation that ownership of the content itself or the associated copyright is being transferred.

This license is narrowly crafted with specific permitted uses: personal enjoyment, display on verified marketplaces that authenticate ownership, and inclusion in third-party applications with cryptographic verification requirements.[129] The terms also methodically enumerate prohibited activities, including modifying the content, using it for advertising, incorporating it in commercial merchandise, or attempting to acquire separate intellectual property rights in the material.[130]

Unlike Yuga Labs' terms, Top Shot's license is unambiguous in its nonexclusive nature. However, the same implications we observed in connection with BAYC apply here as well: Dapper Labs retains the ability to grant multiple licenses for

[125] *BAYC Licenses*, *supra* note 48, §§ 3, 4.

[126] David Thomas & Andrew Rossow, *Seth Green Buys Back Stolen BAYC for $260K, Will Resume TV Show*, BeIn Crypto (June 12, 2022), https://beincrypto.com/seth-green-pays-260k-ransom-to-recover-bored-ape/.

[127] *NBA Top Shot Terms of Use*, *supra* note 113.

[128] *Id.* § 4(v).

[129] *Id.* § 4.

[130] *Id.* § 5(i).

the same content to different parties or to exploit the NBA highlights directly. The clarity in Top Shot's terms does not change this fundamental limitation but instead makes it even more transparent.

Moreover, Dapper Labs' terms openly address third-party intellectual property, particularly NBA and player content. They explicitly state that Moment owners have no rights to this third-party intellectual property, except as incorporated in the licensed content.[131] Additionally, Top Shot warns that depending on the nature of the license granted from the NBA to Dapper Labs, additional restrictions might be imposed on owners of Moments regarding their use of the associated video clips.

This provision illuminates a critical issue: If the NBA, for any reason, terminates its license agreement with Dapper Labs, Moment owners could lose access to the content linked to their NFTs entirely. This is not deceptive; rather, it is the inevitable consequence of copyright law's hierarchical licensing structure, with the NBA as rights holder, Dapper Labs as licensee, and Moment owners as sublicensees. This reality starkly illustrates that there is neither a property law nor a copyright law connection between the NFT and its associated content. While the Moment may be technologically tamper-resistant and traceable, the right to access and use the NBA highlight exists in a separate legal realm, flowing through copyright law and contractual tributaries that can run dry regardless of what blockchain ledgers proclaim to be the immutable truth.

The conditions under which the license ends are also explicitly addressed in Top Shot's terms: "The license . . . applies only to the extent that you continue to Own the applicable Purchased Moment. If at any time you sell, swap, donate, give away, transfer, or otherwise dispose of your Purchased Moment for any reason, the license . . . will immediately expire."[132] Unlike Yuga Labs' vague provisions, the granting and termination of the license are intrinsically tied to the ownership of the Moment.

However, as with BAYC, Dapper Labs' terms also leave unresolved the status of licenses when a Moment is either stolen through hacking or acquired through transactions tainted by fraud or misrepresentation. In principle, a Moment owner who has been victimized should retain their license rights, creating the same potential conflicts we observed in the Seth Green case when stolen NFTs reach subsequent Article 12 qualified purchasers. While Dapper Labs' control over the Flow network and integrated marketplace infrastructure provides some advantages in addressing unauthorized transfers, this protection is not absolute. Moments transferred through fraudulent transactions might circulate for significant periods before Dapper Labs becomes aware,

[131] *Id.* § 4.
[132] *Id.* § 4(viii).

creating genuine questions about license rights when these NFTs reach qualified purchasers.

5.5 Beyond the illusion: reconciling NFTs with private law

So far in this chapter, we have revealed that the use of NFTs to represent works of art is marked by fundamental misunderstandings of private law. Standardized minting platforms advertise that users can easily tokenize any asset yet systematically disclaim any accountability for outcomes. Bespoke issuers claim to create novel forms of digital property but deliver at most NFT ownership coupled with a bevy of problematic intellectual property licenses.

Yet our critique, while necessary, represents only half of the analytical equation. The existence of these flaws in current NFT offerings does not negate the fact that there is strong interest and demand for unique digital assets, nor does it preclude achieving legitimate business objectives through properly structured legal arrangements.[133] In the final part of this chapter, we not only distill the core private law deficiencies that plague contemporary NFT markets, but we also demonstrate how underlying commercial needs can be met through mechanisms that embrace, rather than evade, established principles of private law.

5.5.1 Core private law deficiencies in contemporary NFT markets

As a preliminary observation, we note that there is a troubling chasm between rhetoric and law in the NFT space.[134] NFT market participants routinely claim the effortless tokenization of any asset and that authentic ownership chains can easily be established through their platforms. However, these representations are largely irreconcilable with legal substance. In some cases, what is being promised simply cannot be accomplished within the constraints of private law. In others, the contractual reality reflected in the terms of service systematically contradicts the marketed vision. This is especially apparent with the standardized minting platforms whose terms of service explicitly disclaim responsibility for verifying that creators possess the rights they purport to transfer, as well as reject the

[133] *See* Guy A. Rub, *Owning Nothingness: Between the Legal and the Social Norms of the Art World*, 2019 BYU L. Rev. 1147; *see also* Amy Adler, *Why Art Does Not Need Copyright*, 86 Geo. Wash. L. Rev. 313 (2018); Amy Adler, *Artificial Authenticity*, 98 NYU L. Rev. 706 (2023).

[134] *See* Brian L. Frye, NFTs & the Death of Art 8 (Apr. 19, 2021), https://papers.ssrn.com/sol3/papers.cfm?abstract_id=3829399 (unpublished manuscript) (observing rightly that "[a]n NFT is a token for nothing but itself."); *see also* Brian L. Frye, The Uncanny Token (Apr. 10, 2023) (unpublished manuscript), https://ssrn.com/abstract=4413881.

notion that purchasers will receive any meaningful legal entitlements beyond bare ownership of the NFT itself.

Yet these promotional misrepresentations pale beside the underlying doctrinal flaws. Both types of NFT issuers—standardized and bespoke—fundamentally misapprehend key tenets of property law.[135] Their terms of service treat concepts such as *ownership*, *transfer*, *control*, and even *possession* of NFTs as matters wholly determined by contract. As we explained in Chapter 2, whether and how digital assets can be owned, possessed, or controlled, as well as the manner in which ownership transfers, are questions of property law, which is governed by state common law and now also UCC Article 12. This fundamental error reaches its apex in provisions that claim NFT ownership is "mediated entirely" by DLT networks, with some bespoke issuers asserting that they will recognize ownership transfers only when conducted through their prescribed channels. These contractual provisions are legally meaningless in property law. While minting platforms and NFT issuers may indeed establish contractual obligations requiring parties to use specific transfer methods or technologies, such agreements have no bearing on property law and its effects *erga omnes*. When an NFT owner transfers, donates, bequeaths, or pledges their digital asset as collateral under UCC Article 9, property law—not terms of service—determines the legal effectiveness of the transactions vis-à-vis third parties. While it may be true that contractual violations may trigger breach of contract claims, such disputes cannot invalidate property transfers validly created under applicable law.

Equally problematic is that market participants in this space either remain oblivious to or openly flout the *numerus clausus* principle. Several minting platforms purport that any asset can be tokenized. While their terms of service disclaim responsibility for achieving these promised outcomes, they nonetheless create the impression that tokenization is possible whenever creators possess the necessary underlying rights. Among bespoke NFT issuers, we observed how BAYC's terms ambiguously purport to create an entirely novel form of property, whereby ownership of their NFTs confers rights in the associated digital art "in its entirety." However, as explored in Chapter 3, property law strictly controls both what can be tokenized and how tokenization must occur through a limited menu of standardized forms.[136] In reality, these contrived arrangements vest owners with nothing more than the NFT itself. Property law simply does not provide recognition for the novel rights structures BAYC purports to create.

To illustrate this principle, consider a person who mints an NFT purporting to represent ownership of a painting, sells the NFT to one buyer while retaining

[135] *See* Fairfield, *Property Cycles*, *supra* note 2, at 1119 (discussing a broader pattern of unclear digital asset rights).

[136] *See generally* Joshua A. T. Fairfield, *Virtual Property*, 85 B.U. L. Rev. 1047, 1065–67 (2005).

the physical artwork, then sells and delivers the actual painting to a second buyer. Under established property law and UCC Article 2, the second buyer prevails.[137] NFTs confer no title to the painting because the law does not recognize them as instruments of title for tangible goods. The first buyer has merely a breach of contract claim against the seller, not a property interest enforceable against the second buyer—let alone one that is good against the world. Market participants would be well advised to remember Justice Holmes's admonishment in *Johnson v. Whiton*: "A man cannot create a new kind of inheritance."[138]

The flexibility fallacy is nowhere more apparent than in the intersection between NFTs and intellectual property rights. This confusion may stem from the complexity of copyright, a branch of the law that remains understudied and frequently misunderstood.[139] It may also stem from what Fairfield describes as decades-long "overreaching intellectual property rights [that have crowded] out and undermine[d] personal property interests online" thereby creating an environment where "intellectual property interests . . . completely overshadow[] the personal property interest in digital assets."[140]

Consider how Mintable provides a simple checkbox labeled "Transfer Copyright when purchased?" during the minting process, suggesting that this intellectual property right can be transferred through this trivial interface action. This approach directly contradicts US copyright law, which requires that transfers be memorialized in "an instrument of conveyance, or a note or memorandum of the transfer, []in writing and signed by the owner of the rights conveyed."[141] Lest one think this requirement is unique to America, virtually all copyright systems worldwide impose similar formalities for transferring rights.[142] More fundamentally, the process creates the misleading impression that copyright can be tokenized within an NFT. Copyright owners cannot mint

[137] *See* Lanfear v. Sumner, 17 Mass. 110, 113 (1821); *see also* Slaton v. Davis, 246 P. 863, 864 (Okla. 1926) (articulating the rule).

[138] Johnson v. Whiton, 34 N.E. 542 (Mass. 1893) (citing Co. Litt. 27).

[139] *See* Jessica Litman, Digital Copyright 145 (2001) (describing the Digital Millennium Copyright Act as "long, internally inconsistent, difficult even for copyright experts to parse and harder still to explain"); *see also* Peter K. Yu, *Digital Copyright and Confuzzling Rhetoric*, 13 Vand. J. Ent. & Tech. L. 881, 883–87 (2011) (describing the complexity of copyright law). For a noted exception that features an analysis of copyright in the NFT context, see Brian L. Frye, *Are CryptoPunks Copyrightable?*, 2022 Pepp. L. Rev. 105; *see also* Brian L. Frye, *Tokenized Brands*, 9 St. Thomas J. Complex Litig. 31, 32 (2023) ("When lawyers and law professors look at NFTs, they tend to see a copyright market. I think they're mistaken."). For a discussion of the complexities generated by the intersection of copyright and advanced/emerging technologies, see James Grimmelmann, *There's No Such Thing as a Computer-Authored Work*, 39 Colum. J.L. & Arts 403 (2016); Mark A. Lemley, *IP in a World Without Scarcity*, 90 N.Y.U. L. Rev. 460 (2015).

[140] Fairfield, *Property Cycles*, *supra* note 2, at 1119, 1124.

[141] 17 U.S.C. § 204(a).

[142] See Andres Guadamuz & Andrew Rens, *Comparative Analysis of Copyright Assignment and Licence Formalities for Open Source Contributor Agreements*, 10 SCRIPTed 207(2012), https://script-ed.org/wp-content/uploads/2013/08/rens.pdf.

tokens and unilaterally declare them to function as bearer instruments for the transfer of this intellectual property right. Copyright law recognizes no such bearer instruments anywhere in the world. No individual or corporate entity can alter this reality. Rights holders may promise to assign their copyright to NFT purchasers, but this creates merely a contractual obligation to do so. Even in these cases, however, there is no merger between the token and the copyright in question; the two assets remain separate, with the purchaser acquiring two distinct assets: ownership of the NFT and the copyright.

Finally, the licensing agreements used in NFT transactions have similar problems. Again, signaling a complete disregard for private law, many standardized minting platforms and bespoke issuers grant licenses that are indeterminate in scope, incomplete in their terms, and potentially invalid under the mandatory requirements of multiple jurisdictions. Yet even looking beyond these technical defects, a more fundamental misconception emerges: the mirage that NFTs can somehow be deployed to tokenize copyright licenses themselves. Generally, copyright law does not recognize bearer instruments for licenses in any jurisdiction.[143] No amount of technological sophistication or contractual creativity can alter this fundamental limitation. It is telling that, when examined closely, the terms of service of a few bespoke issuers appear tacitly to acknowledge this constraint, revealing that they are merely assuming contractual undertakings to grant licenses to NFT owners. These arrangements typically include weighty caveats and revocation provisions, and they terminate automatically when the NFT is transferred. Crucially, these contract clauses provide no assurance that new licenses will be granted to subsequent purchasers, no guarantee against future termination of licensing, and no protection against unilateral changes to licensing terms or fees. Indeed, this structure undermines any pretense of tokenized intellectual property licensing: the license and the digital asset are entirely distinct, and no contractual arrangement can merge the two.

5.5.2 Designing NFT structures that work

To be clear: we are not out to completely demolish the NFT market in this chapter—NFTs have their virtues. Indeed, the preceding critique should not obscure the fact that NFTs possess genuine commercial potential. Despite the hype and speculative mania, the widespread enthusiasm for these digital assets

[143] *See generally* World Intellectual Prop. Org., WIPO Guide on the Licensing of Copyright and Related Rights 8–10, 14 (2004).

reflects concrete market demand.[144] We think that this appetite is unsurprising. NFTs inspire numerous use cases given their tamper-resistance, trackability, intermediary-free transferability, and resistance to physical deterioration. Moreover, as Brian Frye has observed, NFTs may represent an entirely new economic paradigm—one focused on social status or "clout" rather than traditional property rights.[145] The crucial point we make here, however, is that such applications must all operate within the boundaries of private law.

As we explained in Chapter 3, using NFTs to tokenize rights in other assets is unquestionably possible within the boundaries established by property law. Under the UCC, these digital assets can function as electronic warehouse receipts and bills of lading under Article 7, embodying ownership of goods stored in warehouses or transported by carriers. The UCC also allows digital assets to function as electronic chattel paper under Article 9, representing payment obligations secured by specific goods. And last, the UCC blesses the use of digital assets in the form of controllable accounts and payment intangibles under Article 12, tokenizing various payment rights. While these examples reflect US law, several other jurisdictions offer similar statutory frameworks that, like their American counterparts, are carefully limited in both scope and substance. Moreover, it appears that, as of this writing, legally recognized tokenizations are on the rise, with ongoing discussions focusing particularly on redemption rights linked to stablecoins and various types of securities.[146]

Beyond employing NFTs to embody property rights in other assets, we posit that there are numerous additional applications that are entirely consistent with private law frameworks. Some have already gained a foothold in the market, while others are still largely experimental. These use cases embrace, rather than circumvent, private law principles while delivering meaningful value to market participants. Below we present three types of use cases.

The most straightforward application is the commercial deployment of NFTs as pure collectibles, which are entirely divorced from any other asset. Like trading cards or concert memorabilia, these digital assets derive value from their provenance, scarcity, and collector appeal rather than from purported rights in other property. Consider NFTs issued by prominent musicians or digital collectibles

[144] *See* Brian L. Frye, *How to Sell NFTs Without Really Trying*, 13 Harv. J. Sports & Ent. L. 113, 135 (2022).

[145] Brian L. Frye, *After Copyright: Pwning NFTs in a Clout Economy*, 45 Colum. J.L. & Arts 341, 342–43 (2022); *see also* Brian L. Frye, *The Art of the Token*, 5 Stan. J. Blockchain L. & Pol'y 238, 239 (2022).

[146] *See generally* Amanda Blanco, *What Could the Rise of Stablecoins, Tokenization Mean for the Broader Financial System?*, Fed. Res. Bank of Boston (May 19, 2025), https://www.bostonfed.org/news-and-events/news/2025/05/stablecoins-tokenization-conference-2025-boston-new-york-fed.aspx?utm_source=chatgpt.com.

released by professional sports teams. While these tokens might include hyperlinks to images or metadata, they do not purport to tokenize copyrighted material, trademarks, or any other protected material. Purchasers acquire them precisely because they are unique, tamper-resistant digital collectibles, the value of which stems from their inherent scarcity and the creator's reputation.[147] From a private law perspective, the legal framework governing such NFTs is unambiguous: ownership and transfer fall squarely within common law property principles and the UCC Article 12 provisions for controllable electronic records.

A more sophisticated application involves coupling NFT ownership with contractual undertakings to provide specific services or rights of access. Paradigmatic examples include concert tickets, event passes, or club memberships created as NFTs. In these cases, the issuer contractually offers admission that is conditional upon presentation of the token at entry. This structure offers genuine commercial utility while still respecting established legal boundaries. The commercial proposition is compelling: NFTs provide superior functionality compared to traditional tickets or membership cards because they are durable, tamper-resistant, and trackable and can serve as lasting digital mementos with value beyond merely providing access.

The private law mechanics merit careful consideration. Crucially, there is no tokenization here. The contractual rights and the NFT remain entirely distinct assets under law, though they are commercially intertwined. Two structural approaches are possible.

In the simpler iteration, a nonassignable contract exists between the NFT issuer and the original purchaser, with the token functioning as a digital access key that must be presented to gain entry. This essentially creates a named ticket or membership. If the original purchaser later sells the NFT to another person—which they may freely do under property law and UCC Article 12—a structural mismatch ensues. The original purchaser retains the contractual right to admission but can no longer exercise it because the venue conditions entry on presentation of the token. Correspondingly, the buyer of the NFT holds the digital key but has no contractual entitlement to admission: they are not party to the original contract, and the NFT is not a bearer instrument that confers rights on its holder.

Alternatively, the arrangement can permit the original contracting party to assign its access rights. Again, the contractual rights and NFT remain legally distinct assets with no tokenization occurring. Secondary market purchasers must acquire *both* the contractual right of access and the NFT that operationalizes that access, since presenting the token is necessary to attend the event or enter

[147] *See generally* Peter J. Karol, *Permissive Certificates: Collectors of Art as Collectors of Permissions*, 94 Wash. L. Rev. 1175 (2019).

the club. Contractual rights transfer pursuant to the body of rules and principles governing assignments of *choses* in action, while NFT ownership transfers according to common law and UCC Article 12.

Perhaps the most commercially promising application involves NFTs as digital certificates of authenticity accompanying physical luxury goods. Sellers of high-end watches, jewelry, handbags, wines, and spirits could provide NFTs alongside their products.[148] This use serves functions similar to traditional "boxes and papers" but with superior characteristics. Indeed, some purveyors of luxury goods ranging from Scotch whiskey to high-end watches are already experimenting with exactly this kind of NFT use.[149]

Crucially, the NFT does not tokenize ownership rights in the linked asset: The digital certificate and the luxury good remain entirely distinct assets under law, connected only through commercial association. This separation has important implications. The owner of the goods and the NFT can lawfully dispose of them independently. However, for luxury items with respect to which authenticity commands premium pricing, secondary market buyers would typically require both the physical good and its accompanying NFT to verify provenance and to maintain resale value.

NFTs offer substantial advantages over traditional authentication methods. Unlike paper certificates, digital tokens cannot be damaged, they require no physical storage space, and they can link to extensive information that evolves over time. More importantly, because these digital assets are unique and trackable from the moment of their creation, they cannot be convincingly counterfeited (a perennial challenge in luxury goods markets).

Moreover, this application offers substantial secondary market advantages for luxury goods houses. By controlling either the smart contracts governing the NFTs in question or by establishing proprietary DLT networks, these companies gain unprecedented visibility into secondary market transactions. This architecture also enables high-end brands to implement transfer fees on each NFT transaction, creating ongoing revenue streams from resale activity. Even more significantly, they can exercise varying degrees of control over secondary transactions, from imposing approval requirements to enforcing transfer restrictions. Such capabilities represent a fundamental shift in luxury brand relationships with secondary markets, transforming what has traditionally been an opaque, unmonitored sphere into a transparent, revenue-generating ecosystem.

[148] *See* Frye, *supra* note 4, at 8.

[149] Beth Squires, *Glenlivet Releases 50 Year Olds Via NFTs*, The Whiskey Wash (Feb. 19, 2024), https://thewhiskeywash.com/new-release-ml/glenlivet-releases-50-year-olds-via-nfts/; Rob Corder, *Panerai Issues Blockchain-Based Passports for Every New Watch*, WatchPro (Oct. 3, 2023), https://www.watchpro.com/panerai-issues-blockchain-based-passports-for-every-new-watch/.

6
Debt tokens and bankruptcy

6.1 Introduction

In the wake of high-profile collapses of FTX, Voyager, and Celsius, the worlds of digital assets and bankruptcy law have collided in unprecedented ways. As the preceding chapters have shown, this intersection has exposed significant gaps in our understanding of how traditional legal frameworks apply to these novel intangibles. Yet amid what many dubbed the crypto winter, an unexpected innovation emerged: *debt tokens*.[1]

Debt tokens represent a fascinating attempt to bridge the gap between the world of distributed ledger technology (DLT) and the centuries-old practice of bankruptcy claims trading. At their core, these tokens aim to transform certain kinds of bankruptcy claims—traditionally illiquid and subject to a cumbersome circulation regime—into easily tradable digital tokens on a blockchain network. Proponents argued that this innovation could democratize access to claims trading, increase liquidity for creditors, and bring unprecedented transparency to what has historically been an opaque market.

As we continue our exploration of digital commercial law, this chapter delves deep into the world of debt tokens, exploring their potential to reshape the landscape of bankruptcy proceedings and creditor rights. We begin by examining the context that gave rise to this innovation, including the wave of crypto bankruptcies that occurred in the years preceding the writing of this book, as well as the long-standing practice of claims trading. We then turn our attention to real-world attempts to create and market debt tokens, examining the offerings of the now-defunct crypto company OPNX.

As with other examples in Part II of this book, our analysis reveals a stark disconnect between the grand promises made by debt token promoters and the reality of private law. Indeed, this is yet another instance of a flawed tokenization. Where Chapter 5 highlighted how NFT issuances have failed to tokenize property and intellectual property (IP) rights, here we examine similar failures regarding attempts to reify bankruptcy claims into token form. As we shall see in

[1] Various portions of this chapter are drawn, in whole or in part, from Andrea Tosato, Diane Lourdes Dick & Christopher K. Odinet, *Debt Tokens*, 173 U. Pa. L. Rev. 1103 (2025). Any reproductions are made with the express permission of the authors.

Digital Commercial Law. Christopher K. Odinet and Andrea Tosato, Oxford University Press.
 DOI: 10.1093/9780197758656.003.0008

the pages that follow, many of these schemes fall far short of their stated goals, providing holders of the digital assets in question with little more than a contractual claim against the debt token issuer, rather than a true interest in the underlying bankruptcy claim.

Beyond this critique, our analysis also offers a constructive vision. In the final part of this chapter, we posit that while implementations by firms like OPNX were misguided, the concept of debt tokens is not inherently unworkable. Drawing on the newly enacted 2022 Amendments to the Uniform Commercial Code (UCC), particularly the introduction of controllable accounts (a concept that we first described in Chapter 2), we explain how private law can properly support the tokenization of bankruptcy claims, creating tokens that actually embody the rights they purport to represent.

6.2 Crypto bankruptcies and the rise of debt tokens

On the morning of Saturday, November 12, 2022, customers of the global crypto giant FTX woke up to find that, despite feverish overnight tweets by then-CEO and wunderkind Sam Bankman-Fried stating that everything was "fine,"[2] their user accounts were frozen.[3] Customers were locked out, unable to access their crypto investments or withdraw their money.

Unbeknownst to its customers, investors, and celebrity endorsers, FTX had filed for bankruptcy in Delaware, no longer able to conceal the gaping $7 billion chasm between its liabilities and assets.[4] The ensuing bankruptcy case opened a Pandora's box of legal challenges, leaving the bankruptcy court, major stakeholders, and law enforcement agencies to grapple with myriad contentious issues. FTX customers were told they no longer owned the digital assets in their accounts and instead held only a bankruptcy claim of indeterminate value.

Unwilling or unable to wait, many anxious and frustrated customers attempted to sell their claims in a desperate attempt to recoup some of their losses. Lying in wait and ready to pounce was a ravenous pack of distressed debt investors eager to profit from FTX's collapse.[5] By December

[2] Allison Morrow, *Here's What Happened Today in Sam Bankman-Fried's Trial*, CNN Bus. (Oct. 30, 2023), https://www.cnn.com/business/live-news/sbf-crypto-fraud-trial-10-30/h_e43a35d03c2550ce9bf1872980e825dd.

[3] Max Zahn, *A Timeline of Cryptocurrency Exchange FTX's Historic Collapse*, ABC News (Mar. 28, 2024), https://abcnews.go.com/Business/timeline-cryptocurrency-exchange-ftxs-historic-collapse/story?id=93337035.

[4] *See* Chapter 11 Voluntary Petition for Non-Individual, *In re* FTX Trading Ltd., No. 22- 11068 (Bankr. D. Del. Nov. 11, 2022).

[5] *See About X-Claim*, X-Claim, https://www.x-claim.com/about (last visited Oct. 15, 2023).

2023, commentators noted that "the market for FTX claims [had] exploded."[6]

As FTX claims trading intensified, it sparked a transformation in what is known in the scholarly literature as the "bankruptcy exchange."[7] First, online platforms emerged dedicated to trading these claims. Next came the crypto entrepreneurs; they proposed blending blockchain technology with bankruptcy claims trading to create novel digital assets: *debt tokens.*

Before delving into these debt tokens and their legal implications, we must first build a foundation of understanding through an exploration of two areas: (1) bankruptcy claims trading and (2) the three high-profile bankruptcies of once-prominent crypto platforms Voyager, Celsius, and, most notoriously, FTX.

6.2.1 Bankruptcy claims trading

Bankruptcy claims trading has a long history. Over the past three centuries, it has evolved from a niche practice into a large, established market.[8] This evolution has captured the attention of historians, while the merits and consequences of claims trading have been the subject of intense debate among practitioners and academics.[9]

Today, the market for bankruptcy claims is broad, international, and liquid.[10] It encompasses a range of distressed assets and is populated by sophisticated, well-resourced participants. As of this writing, estimates peg the annual volume at $50–$300 billion, although it is hard to arrive at a precise figure due to the private nature of many of these dealings, and fluctuations in activity driven by the economic cycle.[11] Almost all large corporate bankruptcies involve some trading of claims against the insolvent entity, although levels vary significantly across cases. Empirical evidence shows that, in most instances, trading consolidates claims into the hands of distressed debt investors who have

[6] David Yaffe-Bellany & Matthew Goldstein, *The Hot New Market in Crypto? Trading FTX's Carcass*, N.Y. Times (Dec. 20, 2023), https://www.nytimes.com/2023/12/20/technology/crypto-trading-ftx-bankruptcy.html.

[7] *See* Douglas G. Baird, *The Bankruptcy Exchange*, 4 Brook. J. Corp. Fin. & Com. L. 23, 23 (2009) (using the expression "bankruptcy exchange" to describe the bankruptcy claims market).

[8] *See generally* Tosato, Dick & Odinet, *supra* note 1, at 1111–12 n.36.

[9] *Id.*

[10] *See generally* Karol K. Denniston, Distressed Debt Trading: Understanding International and Domestic Secondary Markets (2000).

[11] *See* Jared A. Ellias, *Bankruptcy Claims Trading*, 15 J. Empirical Legal Stud. 772, 772–73 & n.2 (2018); Adam J. Levitin, *Bankruptcy Markets: Making Sense of Claims Trading*, 4 Brook. J. Corp. Fin. & Com. L. 67, 76 (2009) [hereinafter Levitin, *Bankruptcy Markets*]; Adam J. Levitin, Jr., *Finding Nemo: Rediscovering the Virtues of Negotiability in the Wake of* Enron, 2007 Colum. Bus. L. Rev. 83, 86.

become pivotal players in bankruptcy cases, influencing both liquidations and reorganizations.[12]

The legal architecture governing bankruptcy claims trading has evolved significantly alongside the market itself. It has adapted to both the changing commercial landscape and broader societal shifts in how bankruptcy is perceived. In particular, there is now recognition that insolvencies are ordinary events within capitalist economies and that there is a growing willingness among investors to allocate capital toward distressed assets. Today, two streams form the applicable legal framework: federal bankruptcy law and the private law rules governing the *commercial circulation* of each type of claim.[13]

Under federal law, the Bankruptcy Code of 1978 takes a *laissez-faire* approach to trading bankruptcy claims.[14] This statute defines "creditor" as a person with a claim against the debtor that arises at or before the order for relief, and a "claim" as any right to payment regardless of its status.[15] Neither definition distinguishes between an original claim holder and subsequent acquirers. This is reinforced by Section 501 under which all "creditors," whether they are the original obligee or a secondary purchaser, may file a "proof of claim" once insolvency proceedings have commenced.[16]

Federal Rule of Bankruptcy Procedure 3001(e) is the sole provision lightly regulating the bankruptcy exchange. Rule 3001(e)(1) provides that "[i]f a claim has been transferred . . . before proof of the claim has been filed, the proof of claim may be filed only by the transferee." If a claim is traded *after* the proof of claim is filed, Rule 3001(e)(2) requires transferees to file evidence of the transfer, effectively making the transaction visible to the debtor and giving public notice.[17] Yet, even this limited filing requirement has significant restrictions. It does not apply to the trading of claims "based on a publicly traded note, bond or debenture"—effectively leaving all corporate bonds outside its scope. Moreover, it does not impose a specific time frame for the filing and does not apply when only the beneficial interest in the claim is transferred, as opposed to the claim itself.

While federal bankruptcy law provides a relatively unconstrained environment for trading bankruptcy claims, it is crucial to recognize that the legal

[12] Levitin, *Bankruptcy Markets*, *supra* note 11; *see also* Ellias, *supra* note 11; Victoria Ivashina, Benjamin Iverson & David C. Smith, *The Ownership and Trading of Debt Claims in Chapter 11 Restructurings*, 119 J. FIN. ECON. 316 (2016).

[13] We use "commercial circulation" to indicate both the transfer of ownership and use as collateral.

[14] Notably, the Bankruptcy Code of 1978 omitted the provisions of §§ 212 and 249 of the Bankruptcy Act of 1898 (codified at 11 U.S.C. §§ 612, 649 (1976)), as well as Rules 10-211 (FED. R. BANKR. P. 10-211 (1973) (repealed 1978)) and 10-215(c)(4) (FED. R. BANKR. P. 10-215(c)(4) (repealed 1983). *See* Allan L. Gropper, *Comments on the Articles of Professors Baird and Janger*, 4 BROOK. J. CORP. FIN. & COM. L. 59 (2009).

[15] 11 U.S.C. §§ 101(10) & 101(5).

[16] 11 U.S.C. § 501(a).

[17] 11 Fed. R. Bankr. P. 3001(e)(2).

framework governing these transactions also includes the rules applicable to the commercial circulation of these assets. In corporate insolvencies, bankruptcy claims can be divided into three primary groups: corporate bonds, bank debts, and trade debts.[18] The transfer of ownership and use as collateral of each are subject to a specific private law regime with significant implications.

Corporate bonds are debt securities issued to raise capital. Harkening back to our earlier discussion in Chapter 3, their commercial circulation falls under the purview of UCC Article 8, wherein they are classified as *financial assets*.[19] As we described in that earlier chapter on custody, Article 8 seeks to facilitate a financial asset's assignment and use as collateral, offering robust protections to good faith "purchasers" and, thus, cloaking these assets in the mantle of negotiability.[20]

Bank debt refers to loans extended by financial institutions to a corporation. Looking back to our discussions in Chapter 2, the commercial circulation of these assets is governed by UCC Article 9 as a *payment intangible*.[21] This statute provides that the transfer and use as collateral of these payment rights requires a signed agreement between the parties that adequately describes the debt in question.[22] Differing from corporate bonds, bank debts are not highly negotiable; rather, they are subject to a strict *nemo dat* rule with minimal protections for good faith purchasers.[23] This implies that investors interested in this type of bankruptcy claim must exercise caution and carry out due diligence, as they acquire the debt with all its existing conditions and potential encumbrances.

Trade debts are obligations owed to suppliers and customers for goods and services provided. Their commercial circulation is also governed by UCC Article 9 as *accounts*.[24] Under these rules, the transfer and use as collateral of these assets require a written and signed agreement between the parties, and third-party effectiveness of these transactions is conditional upon filing a financing statement in the applicable public registry at the location of the debtor.[25] Moreover, priority is established on a strict first-to-file basis.[26] This means that if the holder of a bankruptcy trade debt in the form of an account has previously granted a security interest over all their present and future assets, any subsequent disposition

[18] The picture is different for personal insolvencies. *See* Levitin, *Bankruptcy Markets*, *supra* note 11, at 81–92.
[19] U.C.C. § 8-102(a)(9) (Am. L. Inst. & Unif. L. Comm'n 2001).
[20] U.C.C. § 8-303.
[21] U.C.C. § 9-102(a)(61) (Am. L. Inst. & Unif. L. Comm'n 2010). This discussion does not encompass transactions involving the negotiation of negotiable promissory notes under Article 3 of the UCC.
[22] U.C.C. § 1-201(b)(35) (Am. L. Inst. & Unif. L. Comm'n 2022); U.C.C. §§ 9-102(a)(28), 9-102(a)(73).
[23] Tosato, Dick & Odinet, *supra* note 1, at 1116 & n.71.
[24] U.C.C. § 9-102(a)(1).
[25] U.C.C. §§ 9-203, -310.
[26] U.C.C. § 9-322.

of that account results in its purchaser acquiring an interest subordinate to that of the secured creditor.

The legal distinctions between the rules governing the commercial circulation of each of these types of bankruptcy claims significantly affect their trading activity. Due to being highly negotiable, corporate bonds tend to be traded more actively and at high velocity.[27] Typically, bank debt is either syndicated, participated, or both, and trades in tranches, primarily among large financial institutions and hedge funds.[28] Trade debts are, in relative terms, the least actively traded bankruptcy claims, as they are subject to more burdensome regimes for their commercial circulation and are typically lower in value.[29] Table 6.1 depicts claim types and key characteristics.

6.2.2 A tale of three crypto bankruptcies

Having surveyed the landscape of bankruptcy claims trading, we now turn our attention to the tumultuous world of crypto bankruptcies. Here we spotlight three major cases: Voyager, Celsius, and FTX. We describe the complexities inherent in the failures of these firms and identify how they engendered the necessary conditions for the emergence of debt tokens.

The cryptocurrency platform Voyager Digital Holdings, Inc., ("Voyager") filed for Chapter 11 bankruptcy in July 2022.[30] Allegedly, events were precipitated by a " 'run on the bank' due to the downturn in the cryptocurrency industry generally," as well as a default on a $650 million loan to the cryptocurrency hedge fund Three Arrows Capital.[31] At the time of the filing, Voyager had approximately 3.5 million customers and held on its books over $5.9 billion of crypto assets.

The company entered bankruptcy with its own stalking horse proposal: a stand-alone restructuring plan that contemplated restoring account access and

[27] *See generally* Ellias, *supra* note 11, at 778–82 (finding that Chapter 11 corporate bonds are among the most heavily traded bonds in the corporate bond market). By contrast, Victoria Ivashina, Benjamin Iverson, and David C. Smith report significantly lower trading activity for trade debts. *See* Ivashina, Iverson & Smith, *supra* note 12, at 318–19. This difference in liquidity supports our proposition that the negotiability of corporate bonds under UCC Article 8 facilitates secondary market trading, as compared to trade debts, which are generally classified as "accounts" under UCC Article 9 and are nonnegotiable.

[28] *See* Levitin, *Bankruptcy Markets*, *supra* note 11, at 87–88.

[29] *See* Ivashina, Iverson & Smith, *supra* note 12.

[30] *See, e.g.*, Chapter 11 Voluntary Petition for Non-Individual, *In re* Voyager Digit. Holdings, Inc., No. 22-10943 (Bankr. S.D.N.Y. July 5, 2022).

[31] Declaration of Stephen Ehrlich, Chief Executive Officer of the Debtors, in Support of Chapter 11 Petitions and First Day Motions at 1, 4, 9, 13, *In re* Voyager Digit. Holdings, Inc., No. 22-10943 (Bankr. S.D.N.Y. July 6, 2022).

Table 6.1 Bankruptcy claim types, legal regimes, and trading activity

Type of bankruptcy claim	Rule 3001(e) applicability	Commercial circulation regime	Trading Activity
Corporate bonds	Not applicable (excludes claims based on publicly traded notes, bonds, or debentures)[a]	Governed by UCC Article 8[b]; provides strong protection for good faith purchasers, making these assets highly negotiable.[c]	Very high
Bank debt	Applicable (requires filing of transfer evidence post-proof of claim)[d]	Governed by UCC Article 9 as "payment intangibles"[e]; assignment and use as collateral require a signed agreement for transfer, subject to strict *nemo dat* rule[f]	Intermediate
Trade debts	Applicable (requires filing of transfer evidence post-proof of claim)	Governed by UCC Article 9 as "accounts"[g]; assignment and use as collateral require a written agreement and filing for third-party effectiveness	Low

[a]*See* Victoria Ivashina, Benjamin Iverson & David C. Smith, *The Ownership and Trading of Debt Claims in Chapter 11 Restructurings*, 119 J. Fin. Econ. 316, 318 (2016) ("Rule 3001(e) reporting requirements explicitly exclude transfers in ownership of publicly traded debt securities (notes and bonds).").

[b]*See* U.C.C. § 8-101 (Am. L. Inst. & Unif. L. Comm'n 2001) ("This Article may be cited as Uniform Commercial Code—Investment Securities."). UCC § 8-102(a)(15).

[c]*See* U.C.C. §§ 8-303(a)–303(b).

[d]While trading in bank debts, in principle, is covered by Rule 3001(e), such transaction are often unreported. *See* Adam J. Levitin, *Bankruptcy Markets: Making Sense of Claims Trading*, 4 Brook. J. Corp. Fin. & Com. L. 67, 77–78 (2009).

[e]*See* U.C.C. § 9-102(a)(61) (Am. L. Inst. & Unif. L. Comm'n 2010).

[f]*See* U.C.C. § 9-203.

[g]*See* U.C.C. § 9-102(2).

distributing to each account holder a mix of cryptocurrencies, common equity shares in the reorganized company, Voyager's own "liquidity token" (VGX), and the right to share in any recovery from Three Arrows Capital.[32] A press release issued in the earliest days of the case explained that the plan would allow customers to "elect the proportion of common equity and crypto they will

[32] A liquidity token is a type of digital asset created by cryptocurrency platforms to facilitate and incentivize trading activities within their ecosystems. Since 2017, Voyager had issued and administered its own liquidity token, Voyager Token (VGX).

receive, subject to certain maximum thresholds."[33] Concurrently, the company solicited competing proposals from financiers and acquirers.

Early in the Chapter 11 proceedings, Voyager agreed to a $1.42 billion sale to the cryptocurrency platform FTX, yet this deal evaporated[34] when the latter also became insolvent.[35] Voyager then negotiated a $1.02 billion sale to the crypto exchange Binance.US.[36] These deals were presumably based on the view that Voyager owned valuable intangible assets, such as customer information, intellectual property, other rights and various causes of action.

Under the proposed sale to Binance.US, Voyager customers would have received a mix of cryptocurrency and cash, with Voyager actively trading crypto assets, including VGX, to help balance and settle accounts. However, the US Securities and Exchange Commission (SEC) objected to this plan, asserting that it might violate US securities laws as an "unregistered offer, sale, or delivery after sale" of securities.[37] The regulatory risk was significant because the plan contemplated that Voyager would "execute trades of various types of cryptocurrency to ensure that the proper types of coins are available for distribution to each customer."[38] The SEC placed the burden of persuasion squarely on Voyager, asserting that "it is the Debtor's burden to present credible evidence that the provisions of the Plan are feasible and not in violation of applicable law."[39]

In March 2023, when the court challenged the SEC to provide a definitive legal position on whether the proposed plan complied with US securities laws, the SEC equivocated.[40] First, the agency declined to take a position, then suggested that the VGX token might be a security, while emphasizing that such

[33] Press Release, Voyager Digit. Ltd., Voyager Digital Commences Financial Restructuring Process to Maximize Value for All Stakeholders (July 6, 2022), https://www.prnewswire.com/news-releases/voyager-digital-commences-financial-restructuring-process-to-maximize-value-for-all-stakeholders-301581177.html.

[34] Stipulation and Agreed Order, *In re* Voyager Digit. Holdings, Inc., No. 22-10943 (Bankr. S.D.N.Y. Dec. 9, 2022).

[35] On the FTX failure, see Tosato, Dick & Odinet, *supra* note 1.

[36] Press Release, Voyager Digit. Ltd., Voyager Announces Agreement for Binance.US to Acquire Its Assets (Dec. 19, 2022), https://www.prnewswire.com/news-releases/voyager-announces-agreement-for-binanceus-to-acquire-its-assets-301706065.html.

[37] Objection of the US Securities and Exchange Commission to Final Approval of the Adequacy of the Debtors' Disclosure Statement and Confirmation of the Chapter 11 Plan at 3, *In re* Voyager Digit. Holdings, Inc., No. 22-10943 (Bankr. S.D.N.Y. Feb. 22, 2023) [hereinafter Objection].

[38] Tosato, Dick & Odinet, *supra* note 1, at 1124 & n.124.

[39] Objection, *supra* note 37, at 4 (citing *In re* Gramercy Twins Assocs., 187 B.R. 112, 126 (Bankr. S.D.N.Y. 1995)); *see also* 11 U.S.C. § 1129.

[40] *See* Jack Schickler, *Voyager Bankruptcy Judge Says He Is 'Absolutely Shocked' by SEC Objection to Binance.US Deal*, CoinDesk (Mar. 2, 2023, 11:16 AM), https://www.coindesk.com/policy/2023/03/02/voyager-bankruptcy-judge-says-he-is-absolutely-shocked-by-sec-objection-to-binance-us-deal [https://perma.cc/LEC5-SRE5].

staff opinions could not bind the agency.[41] Voyager responded by seeking to amend its plan to exempt distributions from securities registration requirements and shield parties from liability,[42] prompting SEC objections against what it deemed an attempt to enjoin "its police and regulatory powers."[43]

Unmoved, the court confirmed Voyager's plan.[44] Commentators surmised that the judge had been frustrated by the SEC's vague, eleventh-hour objections, which threatened a restructuring plan supported by approximately 97 percent of account holders.[45] In the wake of the plan confirmation, VGX's trading price soared, yet celebrations would be short-lived.[46] In April 2023, Binance.US terminated the asset purchase agreement, citing an "unpredictable operating environment" caused by a "hostile and uncertain regulatory climate."[47]

Celsius Network LLC was a cryptocurrency bank, lender, bitcoin miner, and retail investment platform with 1.7 million customers and deposits worth approximately $8 billion.[48] It also sought bankruptcy protection in July 2022.[49] Its Chapter 11 filing came approximately one month after the company froze withdrawals and transfers from customer accounts due to extreme market conditions.[50]

[41] Supplemental Declaration of Mark A. Renzi in Support of Confirmation of the Third Amended Joint Plan of Voyager Digital Holdings, Inc. and Its Debtor Affiliates Pursuant to Chapter 11 of the Bankruptcy Code at 2, *In re* Voyager Digit. Holdings, Inc., No. 22-10943 (Bankr. S.D.N.Y. Mar. 5, 2023) [hereinafter Supplemental Declaration of Mark A. Renzi].

[42] Specifically, the debtor asserted the protections offered by 11 U.S.C. § 1145. *See* Supplemental Declaration of Mark A. Renzi, *supra* note 41, at 3.

[43] Supplemental Objection of the U.S. Securities and Exchange Commission to Final Approval of the Adequacy of the Debtors' Disclosure Statement and Confirmation of the Chapter 11 Plan at 1, *In re* Voyager Digit. Holdings, Inc., No. 22-10943 (Bankr. S.D.N.Y. Mar. 6, 2023).

[44] *See* Corrected and Amended Order (I) Approving the Second Amended Disclosure Statement and (II) Confirming the Third Amended Joint Plan of Voyager Digital Holdings, Inc. and Its Debtor Affiliates Pursuant to Chapter 11 of the Bankruptcy Code at 6, 24-25, *In re* Voyager Digit. Holdings, Inc., No. 22-10943 (Bankr. S.D.N.Y. Mar. 10, 2023).

[45] Declaration of Leticia Sanchez Regarding the Solicitation and Tabulation of Votes on the Third Amended Joint Plan of Voyager Digital Holdings, Inc. and Its Debtor Affiliates Pursuant to Chapter 11 of the Bankruptcy Code at 13 n.10, *In re* Voyager Digit. Holdings, Inc., No. 22-10943 (Bankr. S.D.N.Y. Feb. 28, 2023).

[46] *See* Michael Bodley, *Voyager's VGX Token Soars as Bankruptcy Judge Signs Off on Binance.US Plan*, BLOCKWORKS (Mar. 7, 2023, 5:42 PM), https://blockworks.co/news/judge-approves-voyager-binance-plan [https://perma.cc/Y62U-GRUT].

[47] Caitlin Ostroff, *Binance.US Terminates Deal to Buy Voyager Assets*, WALL ST. J. (Apr. 25, 2023, 1:43 PM), https://www.wsj.com/livecoverage/stock-market-today-dow-jones-04-25-2023/card/binance-us-terminates-deal-to-buy-voyager-assets-JsMijeVAzLdwhw5CcH42 [https://perma.cc/BW3P-U7MW].

[48] Jim Probasco, *The Celsius Withdrawal Pause Rattles Crypto World*, INVESTOPEDIA (June 13, 2022), https://web.archive.org/web/20221004055324/https://www.investopedia.com/crypto-lender-celsius-pauses-withdrawals-5409545.

[49] Chapter 11 Voluntary Petition for Non-Individual, *In re* Celsius Network LLC, No. 22-10964 (Bankr. S.D.N.Y. Jul. 13, 2022).

[50] *See, e.g.*, Tom Wilson, Hannah Lang & Elizabeth Howcroft, *Crypto Contagion Fears Spread After Celsius Network Freezes Withdrawals*, REUTERS (June 14, 2022), https://www.reuters.com/technology/crypto-firm-celsius-pauses-all-transfers-withdrawals-between-accounts-2022-06-13.

For the present inquiry into debt tokens, the Celsius bankruptcy is noteworthy for Bankruptcy Judge Glenn's precedent-setting January 2023 decision. In that decision, Judge Glenn held that the debtor (rather than its customers) owned most of the cryptocurrency held pursuant to its "Earn" program.[51] This meant that customers neither owned the assets themselves nor held anything more than general unsecured claims to recover the value of the assets they deposited into interest-earning accounts on the Celsius platform.

In a moment of private law reckoning, this decision sent shockwaves through the industry. It denied customers the protections that they believed they were entitled to in the event of a cryptocurrency platform bankruptcy.[52] The decision highlighted that, in the absence of the special rules and protections afforded to traditional banking and brokerage accounts, customers of cryptocurrency platforms are merely unsecured creditors should the platform become insolvent. In some cases, this allocation of risk reflects a deliberate business model. In others, it is the result of ignorance or oversight, as these crypto platforms could have legally structured themselves so that account holders would hold a property interest safe from creditors' claims. Indeed, as we discussed in Chapter 4, Celsius could have used Article 8 to hold customers' assets in custody in a way that would have protected them from the firm's creditors.

Finally, we come to the FTX bankruptcy. Founded in 2019 by Sam Bankman-Fried, this platform quickly rose to prominence in the world of digital assets.[53] Its activities covered the whole gamut of crypto finance, encompassing a major exchange, derivatives and options trading, and an NFT marketplace.[54] It operated in multiple jurisdictions and had a significant US presence. At its height, FTX had over one million users worldwide and a valuation of over $32 billion.

FTX's growth was propelled by multiple factors: a close relationship with Alameda Research, a trading firm indirectly controlled by Bankman-Fried, investments from renowned venture capital firms, and an aggressive marketing campaign[55] that included naming rights to a Miami stadium and celebrity endorsements from the likes of Matt Damon, Reese Witherspoon, and Kim Kardashian.[56] The company and its founder were notably active in philanthropic

[51] Memorandum Opinion and Order Regarding Ownership of Earn Account Assets, *In re* Celsius Network LLC, No. 22-10964 (Bankr. S.D.N.Y. Jan. 4, 2023).

[52] *See, e.g.*, Ronit J. Berkovich, Jessica Liou & John Marinelli, *Winter Wears On: Celsius Court Rules That Certain Customer Deposits are Property of the Bankruptcy Estate*, WEIL RESTRUCTURING BLOG (Jan. 6, 2023), https://restructuring.weil.com/cryptocurrency-issues/winter-wears-on-celsius-court-rules-that-certain-customer-deposits-are-property-of-the-bankruptcy-estate.

[53] *See generally* MICHAEL LEWIS, GOING INFINITE (2023); ZEKE FAUX, NUMBER GO UP (2023).

[54] *In re* FTX Trading Ltd., No. 22-11068 (Bankr. D. Del. Nov. 17, 2022), https://pacer-documents.s3.amazonaws.com/33/188450/042020648197.pdf.

[55] FAUX, *supra* note 53.

[56] Lora Kelly, *Which Celebrities Are Facing Backlash for Crypto Promotion?*, N.Y. TIMES (Mar. 23, 2023), https://www.nytimes.com/2023/03/23/style/crypto-sec-lindsay-lohan-jake-paul.html.

initiatives and US politics, making substantial donations to political candidates and engaging with regulators.[57]

The collapse of FTX began on November 2, 2022, when a CoinDesk article alleged that the company was using customer funds to cover the losses of Alameda.[58] This sparked a wave of customer panic that accelerated on November 6 when Changpeng Zhao, the CEO of rival exchange Binance, tweeted that his firm would sell all its FTX holdings.[59] As withdrawals mounted, FTX approached Binance for a buyout, but the deal collapsed on November 9.[60] Sam Bankman-Fried resigned two days later, with FTX facing an expanding black hole on its balance sheet. That same day, the company filed for bankruptcy protection in Delaware and entered into similar proceedings in the Bahamas a day later.[61]

Shielded by Chapter 11 bankruptcy protection, FTX underwent a series of hearings and motions to consolidate corporate assets, establish creditor committees, and appoint new leadership.[62] The new management's mandate involved stabilizing operations, cooperating with investigators, and maximizing creditor recovery.[63] Throughout the proceedings, judges, examiners, and international law enforcement worked to unravel FTX's intricate web of over 130 corporate entities.[64] Their investigations centered on allegations of misused customer funds, market manipulation, and political donation irregularities.[65]

The FTX bankruptcy proceedings have been extremely complex, giving rise to an array of novel legal issues that will require extensive scholarly analysis in the years to come.[66] For present purposes, however, we want to concentrate our attention exclusively on the bankruptcy claims trading aspect. First, from the early days of the FTX insolvency proceeding, it became readily apparent that

[57] *See generally* Faux, *supra* note 53.

[58] *See* Ian Allison, *Divisions in Sam Bankman-Fried's Crypto Empire Blur on His Trading Titan Alameda's Balance Sheet*, CoinDesk (Nov. 2, 2022) https://www.coindesk.com/business/2022/ 11/02/divisions-in-sam-bankman-frieds-crypto-empire-blur-on-his-trading-titan-alamedas-balance-sheet/.

[59] Steven Zeitchik, *This Enigmatic Billionaire Just Took Down a Crypto Rock Star*, Wash. Post (Nov. 9, 2023), https://www.washingtonpost.com/business/2022/11/08/binance-ftx-crypto-zhao/.

[60] MacKenzie Sigalos, *Binance Backs out of FTX Rescue, Leaving the Crypto Exchange on the Brink of Collapse*, CNBC (Nov. 10, 2022), https://www.cnbc.com/2022/11/09/binance-backs-out-of-ftx-rescue-leaving-the-crypto-exchange-on-the-brink-of-collapse.html.

[61] *See* Zahn, *supra* note 3.

[62] *Id.*

[63] In January 2023, liquidation proceedings separately began for FTX's Bahamas-based subsidiary FTX Digital Markets. *See* Dietrich Knauth, *FTX Resolves Dispute with Bahamian Liquidators*, Reuters (Dec. 19, 2023), https://www.reuters.com/technology/ftx-digital-markets-reaches-settlement-with-debtors-2023-12-19/.

[64] Scott Nover, Amanda Shendruck & Nate DiCamillo, *The Scrollable, Annotated, Incredibly Complex Org Chart of FTX and Sam Bankman-Fried's Fallen Empire*, Quartz (Nov. 17, 2022), https:/qz.com/ftx-bankruptcy-filing-reveals-a-remarkably-convoluted-c-1849797496.

[65] *See generally* Matthew Goldstein & David Yaffe-Bellany, *FTX Inquiry Expands as Prosecutors Reach Out to Former Executives*, N.Y. Times (Feb. 4, 2023), https://www.nytimes.com/2023/02/04/business/ftx-sbf-inquiry-executives.html.

[66] For an overview, see Tosato, Dick & Odinet, *supra* note 1.

a considerable number of individual investors and customers held unsecured claims against FTX. Notably, the Delaware bankruptcy court developed a special proof-of-claim process for "customer claims," defined to mean those claims "arising out of or related to (a) any cash, cryptocurrency, digital assets or other assets held by such person or entity in an account on any FTX Exchange as of the Petition Date . . . or (b) any other investment or trading activities on any FTX Exchange."[67] The special process gave customers a more generous filing date and facilitated the submission of sensitive personal and financial information through a customer claims portal rather than via publicly available filings.[68]

Second, as we noted at the beginning of this chapter, individual creditors have been eager to dispose of their FTX bankruptcy claims. In the days immediately following the collapse, there were reports of claims of individual depositors being actively traded between five and eight cents on the dollar.[69] One month after FTX filed for bankruptcy, approximately $92 million in individual customer claims were already listed on the claims trading platform X-Claim.[70] Concurrently, other creditors were selling their claims via another online firm, Claims Market, for eight to twelve cents on the dollar.[71] This bankruptcy trading activity has not abated. Court records show that distressed debt specialist hedge funds—including Farallon Capital, Silver Point Capital, Hudson Bay, Contrarian Capital Management, and Canyon Partners—steadily acquired claims during the first twelve months of the case. More recently, one of FTX's original fundraisers started an online claims trading platform for FTX customers and also began buying claims for himself.[72] This frenzied trading activity reflects creditors' eagerness to salvage value and speculators' desire to profit from the exchange's remains.

6.2.3 The forging of debt tokens

Collectively, the bankruptcies of Voyager, Celsius, and FTX created a unique set of conditions that catalyzed the emergence of debt tokens.[73] First, a large number

[67] Order (I)(A) Establishing Deadlines for Filing Customer Proofs of Claim, (B) Approving Procedures for Submitting Proofs of Claim and (C) Approving the Form and Manner of Notice Thereof and (II) Granting Related Relief at 2, *In re* FTX Trading LTD., No. 22-11068 (Bankr. D. Del. June 28, 2023).

[68] *Id.* at 5; *see also* Kara J. Bruce, *Crypto Failure in the Shadows*, 69 VILL. L. REV. 691 (2024).

[69] Joe Weisenthal, *People Are Already Buying Depositor Claims on FTX*, BLOOMBERG (Nov. 17, 2022), https://www.bloomberg.com/news/articles/2022-11-17/people-are-already-buying-depositor-claims-on-ftx; Yaffe-Bellany & Goldstein, *supra* note 6.

[70] *See* X-CLAIM, https://www.x-claim.com (last visited Dec. 20, 2023).

[71] Sarah Jansen, *This Firm Offers 8 To 12 Cents On A Dollar Of FTX User Deposit Claims*, NEWSBTC, https://www.newsbtc.com/news/this-firm-offers-8-to-12-cents-on-a-dollar-of-ftx-user-deposit-claims (last visited July 7, 2025).

[72] Yaffe-Bellany & Goldstein, *supra* note 6.

[73] *See* Tosato, Dick & Odinet, *supra* note 1, at 1130.

of individual customers of crypto platforms suddenly found themselves locked out of their accounts and unable to access their valuable digital assets. Shortly thereafter, they were informed that they had become creditors in bankruptcy proceedings.

Second, these bankruptcies proved to be especially contentious and tortuous. They were rife with substantive and procedural legal issues, attracted considerable public and regulatory scrutiny, and involved illiquid and highly volatile digital assets.

Third, a large number of these creditors wanted to liquidate their bankruptcy claims without waiting for the legal proceedings to play out and were keen to use electronic platforms and blockchain technology to do so.

Against this backdrop, entrepreneurs familiar with DLT networks sought to engage with this cohort of distressed creditors by offering them a blockchain-based solution. During the early stages of the Celsius bankruptcy, rumors circulated that the platform was exploring a so-called "tokenized recovery," pursuant to which Celsius customers would receive distributions in the form of a newly created debt token.[74] According to these reports, "[t]okens would essentially represent a ratio of what customers are owed and what the firm has left on its balance sheet."[75] However, these rumors never turned into a concrete offering.

Then, in early 2023, a decentralized autonomous organization known as DebtDAO issued a crypto token called FUD.[76] This token purportedly represented a bond or debt instrument linked to obligations owed by the now-bankrupt company FTX to its "highest quality creditors," amounting to tens of millions of dollars.[77] The promise behind the FUD token was that its holders would have a right to receive a portion of the payout that FTX would eventually distribute to its creditors. Notably, on February 17, 2023, FTX issued a warning, stating that it had not issued any debt tokens and that any such offering was unauthorized.[78] The value of FUD tokens subsequently collapsed, inflicting heavy losses on early investors.

In April 2023, a fledgling platform known as OPNX (short for Open Exchange) launched its debt token offering.[79] Notably, OPNX was formed under

[74] *See, e.g.*, Paige Tortorelli, *Celsius Has a Hail Mary Bankruptcy Plan: Turn Its Debt into a New Cryptocurrency*, CNBC (Sept. 23, 2022), https://www.cnbc.com/2022/09/23/celsius-has-a-hail-mary-bankruptcy-plan-turn-its-debt-into-a-new-cryptocurrency-.html.

[75] Jamie Redman, *Celsius Floats Possibility of Debt Token to Repay Creditors; Secures Court Approval to Process Customer Withdrawals*, Bitcoin (Jan. 25, 2023), https://news.bitcoin.com/celsius-floats-possibility-of-debt-token-to-repay-creditors-secures-court-approval-to-process-customer-withdrawals.

[76] *See* Tosato, Dick & Odinet, *supra* note 1, at 1131.

[77] *See id.*

[78] *See* FTX (@FTX_Official), Twitter (Feb. 17, 2023, 9:30 AM), https://twitter.com/FTX_Official/status/1626605058698752001?s=20.

[79] *See* Tosato, Dick & Odinet, *supra* note 1, at 1131.

the laws of the Republic of Seychelles, and was established by the founders of the now-bankrupt crypto hedge fund Three Arrows Capital, and the cofounders of the bankrupt Hong Kong-based crypto exchange Liquidity Technologies, Ltd. (more commonly known as CoinFLEX).[80]

OPNX announced that "in the wake of [crypto] insolvencies" where "user accounts were frozen/inaccessible, with claims payouts likely to take many years," it had come up with a solution: the creation of "a public marketplace for claims onboarding and trading on order books."[81] Through their platform, crypto bankruptcy claim holders could "immediately unleash their locked claims directly into crypto or use them as margin capital."[82] The platform proudly declared that it was "building an open, transparent and accessible financial world."[83]

OPNX stated that it aimed to meet the needs of "over 20 [million] users who currently have $20 billion of claims trapped in bankruptcy proceedings."[84] Its platform was designed to "allow individuals with no other solution to easily register their claims, then sell them directly into crypto on orderbooks at fair prices, or use their claim as portfolio margin."[85] OPNX explained that it accomplished the so-called tokenization of bankruptcy claims through "a membership model based on staking bankruptcy claims to derive benefits such as zero-fee trading."[86] With plans to eventually tokenize the claims of all active crypto bankruptcy cases, the company launched its first bankruptcy tokenization product for Celsius customers in late May 2023.

In press coverage, OPNX cited liquidity as the key benefit for Celsius customers: "The product provides an alternative to the lengthy bankruptcy administration process, which can take many years to resolve."[87] As to what prompted the company to choose Celsius as the first set of bankruptcy claims to tokenize, the company cited the availability of Celsius user data: "Celsius has a completely unredacted database, so it's very easy to mine that information, parse it in the way you need and make sense of it to work towards a seamless

[80] *See* OPNX, http://web.archive.org/web/20230601175731/https://opnx.com/ (last visited Jan. 27, 2025); Tosato, Dick & Odinet, *supra* note 1, at 1135.

[81] *Our Story: We Are Building an Open, Transparent and Accessible Financial World,* OPNX, http://web.archive.org/web/20240206014201/https://opnx.com/en/about-us (last visited Jan. 26, 2025) [hereinafter OPNX, *Our Story*].

[82] *Id.*

[83] *Id.*

[84] *See* OPNX, *supra* note 80.

[85] *Id.*

[86] Samuel Wan, *OPNX Opening Its Bankruptcy Claims Product for Celsius Users Soon,* CryptoSlate (May 24, 2023), https://cryptoslate.com/opnx-opening-its-bankruptcy-claims-product-for-celsius-users-soon.

[87] Samuel Wan, *OPNX Explains Why Celsius Was Prioritized over FTX, Others for Bankruptcy Tokenization,* CryptoSlate (July 11, 2023), https://cryptoslate.com/opnx-explains-why-celsius-was-prioritized-over-ftx-others-for-bankruptcy-tokenization.

validation."[88] In essence, the accessibility of the company's database helped create an opportunity for major financial market innovation.

These examples illustrate what became an intense, industry-wide impulse to tokenize bankruptcy claims following the Celsius, Voyager, and FTX collapses. Amid this rush to create blockchain-based solutions for distressed creditors, OPNX emerged as the most developed effort. In the following section, we examine this platform's offering in detail, not merely as a historical curiosity, but as a revealing case study that exemplifies themes central to this book.

6.3 A study of debt tokens in bankruptcy: the case of OPNX

In this section, we offer a detailed case study of OPNX's debt token offerings. Our focus on this particular platform is both deliberate and strategic. Among the various attempts to tokenize bankruptcy claims, OPNX stands out for two key reasons. First, it arguably represented the most developed and structured debt token initiative of its time[89] (i.e., not merely a conceptual proposal, but a functioning platform that conducted actual transactions with bankruptcy claim holders). Second, unlike many of its contemporaries, OPNX made its terms of service and related documentation publicly available, providing crucial information that permits rigorous analysis of its underlying scheme and transaction mechanisms.[90]

Two important caveats frame our research. This analysis represents a historical snapshot, focusing on OPNX's legal documents as they existed in early August 2023. Like many other crypto ventures, OPNX periodically revised its terms of service; however, the chosen period captures the platform at its operational peak and offers a coherent corpus of documents for doctrinal assessment. Moreover, in February 2024, OPNX abruptly announced the discontinuation of all services, instructing users to withdraw their assets within a few days.[91] Nevertheless, we believe that this case study remains highly relevant as it provides a striking example of how private law principles are routinely disregarded in the digital assets landscape. The OPNX case vividly illustrates the *flexibility fallacy* and the

[88] *Id.*

[89] Patricia Zamwana, *FUD (FTX User Debt), a Strange Token . . .*, COINPRI (Feb. 9, 2023), https://coinpri.com/news/cryptocurrency/fud-ftx-user-debt-a-strange-token.

[90] In early April, OPNX posted a series of offering documents to the online portal GitHub. *See OPNX-Github/OPNX-Policies*, GITHUB, https://github.com/opnx-github/opnx-policies [https://perma.cc/2QAH-3GKS] (last visited Jan. 27, 2025).

[91] Tom Mitchell Hill, Three *Arrows Capital Co-founders' OPNX Exchange Is Shutting Down*, COINTELEGRAPH (Feb. 1, 2024), https://cointelegraph.com/news/three-arrows-capital-opnx-exchange-shutting-down-february. We note that OPNX's shutdown occurred shortly after we posted our working paper analyzing its debt token offering in January 2024, subsequently published as Tosato, Dick & Odinet, *supra* note 1.

related tokenization illusion, namely, the belief that code can manufacture new property forms *ex nihilo*.

Finally, before we go into detail, we note a striking paradox. On its *Our Story* webpage, OPNX lamented that, in the recent past, the crypto industry had operated as a "black box of obscured risk, leverage, and non-custody."[92] Founders and their now-defunct companies had "bet big and rel[ied] too much on trust," leading to catastrophic losses and "hard lessons."[93] In our view, however, the worst scams and failures in the crypto industry were caused by a glaring lack of transparency, coupled with a complete disregard for private law. The irony, as we detail more fully below, is that OPNX recreated these very design errors in its debt token offering.

6.3.1 Issuer, offering materials, and token design

In its offering materials, OPNX made a number of claims about the notion of tokenization, its potential uses and implications, and how tokens might be used to represent bankruptcy claims. This information was primarily contained in a portion of the OPNX website titled "Learn: Crypto and Claims 101," which provided access to a series of modules and white papers covering topics from the basics of the FTX bankruptcy to information for Celsius creditors and the tokenization of claims.[94]

In its marketing materials, OPNX portrayed tokenization as a "game-changing technology" that "provides a secure and transparent way to track ownership and transactions."[95] The company described this process as one that "has many advantages over traditional methods of ownership" in that it offers superior "fungibility, transparency, and liquidity."[96]

Regarding bankruptcy claims specifically, OPNX described a pooling mechanism whereby these receivables would be aggregated and fractionalized.[97] This, OPNX suggested, would allow for more efficient trading on order books while reducing transaction costs through economies of scale. Moreover, the company stated that creditors who used the platform to trade their bankruptcy claims would enjoy "[m]inimized counterparty risk and fraudulent transactions,"

[92] OPNX, *Our Story*, *supra* note 81.

[93] *Id.*

[94] *Learn About OPNX Crypto*, OPNX, https://web.archive.org/web/20231209160829/https://opnx.com/en/learn [https://perma.cc/X5NC-LX49] (last visited Jan. 28, 2025).

[95] *Tokenizing Bankruptcy Claims: A Revolutionary Approach to Maximizing Claim Utility*, OPNX, http://web.archive.org/web/20231203032307/https://opnx.com/en/learn/tokenizing-bankruptcy-claims (last visited Jan. 28, 2025).

[96] *Id.*

[97] *Id.*

"[t]ransparent market-based pricing," "[f]air price discovery," "[l]ow trading costs," and "[a]dded utility by using claims as collateral to trade crypto futures."[98] For investors seeking to purchase these claims, OPNX promised "[p]ooled liquidity and buying claims in size, ability to easily resell claims, lower trading costs," and the ability to use the claims for crypto futures trading collateral.[99]

Crucially, OPNX conspicuously advertised on its website that its account holders could buy claims from the FTX and Celsius bankruptcies, while concurrently advertising to bankruptcy creditors that they could access "immediate liquidity" by converting their claims "into reOX tokens or oUSD."[100] The company underscored that holders of these tokens could then use them as collateral to engage in various crypto derivative trades through the OPNX platform.

Central to OPNX's value proposition were two distinct token types, reOX and oUSD, which it detailed in a separate white paper. These digital assets were described as "collateral choices" and "distinct avenues to unlock value from claims."[101]

First, as to the reOX tokens (known more technically as *Reborn OX tokens*), OPNX described them as "unlocked" OX tokens—a digital asset that served dual functions as a liquidity and governance token within the OPNX ecosystem.[102] They were presented as unlocked in the sense that they could be liquidated with OPNX once "the preference risk for a claim is settled."[103] However, we found this description to be ambiguous, if not altogether misleading. The white paper did not specify what settling "the preference risk for a claim" entailed, or the timing of such an event. In bankruptcy jargon, the term "preference risk" typically refers to the possibility that payments made by the debtor to creditors within the statutory look-back period before the bankruptcy filing may be avoided by the trustee. In this scenario, however, the bankruptcy would already have been initiated, and the tokens would already have been issued in connection with filed proofs of claim.[104]

[98] OPNX, *Our Story*, *supra* note 81; *How to Transform Your Bankruptcy Claim into a Valuable Asset*, OPNX, https://web.archive.org/web/20231130104336/https://opnx.com/ en/learn/how-to-transform-your-bankruptcy-claim-into-a-valuable-asset [https://perma.cc/ BPX5-C69F] (last visited Jan. 26, 2025).

[99] *See id.*

[100] *Unlocking Liquidity for FTX Claimants*, OPNX (July 14, 2023), https://web.archive.org/web/ 20240202220918/https://news.opnx.com/25196-unlocking-liquidity-for-ftx-claimants; *Meet the OPNX App*, OPNX (June 9, 2023), https://web.archive.org/. web/20240202220543/https://news. opnx.com/22344-meet-the-opnx-app.

[101] *Claims as Collateral: reOX vs. oUSD*, OPNX, https://web.archive.org/web/20240203075045/ https://support.opnx.com/en/articles/8182068-claims-as-collateral-reox-vs-ousd(last visited Jan. 28, 2025).

[102] *Introducing $OX Token: Stake to Trade for Free*, OPNX, https://web.archive.org/web/2023120 9152304/https://opnx.com/en/learn/ox-token-opnx [https://perma.cc/4N5Y-66TP] (last visited Jan. 28, 2025); *see also* Oliver Knight, *Bankruptcy Claims Exchange OPNX Issues New Governance Token, FLEX Rises 16%*, CoinDesk (June 2, 2023), https://www.coindesk.com/business/2023/06/ 01/bankruptcy-claims-exchange-opnx-issues-new-governance-token-flex-rises-16/.

[103] Tosato, Dick & Odinet, *supra* note 1, at 1137 n.225; *Claims as Collateral: reOX vs. oUSD*, *supra* note 101.

[104] *See* 11 U.S.C. § 547.

OPNX priced a reOX token's value at the "current value of the claim according to [over-the-counter] price live-feeds sourced from Claims Market."[105] Additionally, OPNX provided a bonus system whereby a claim holder could choose to multiply their reOX, with the multiplier decreasing linearly over time, starting at the point of claim conversion.[106] Availing oneself of the multiplier during the first month earned a 100 percent bonus, which decreased to 0 percent after one year. According to OPNX, one who took advantage of the bonus would end up having more reOX tokens (and subsequently more OX tokens once the preference risk was settled—whatever that might have meant). Interestingly, OPNX presented the reOX token as ideal for claim holders who wanted "immediate liquidity" and "an opportunity to leverage their claims" but who had a certain risk tolerance for fluctuations in the value of OX tokens.[107]

Alternatively, an OPNX user could choose an oUSD token.[108] As with reOX, OPNX determined the amount of oUSDs a person could receive in return for their bankruptcy claim. However, this token, OPNX asserted, served as a more stable choice because the oUSD token was purportedly held "relative[ly]" stable against the US dollar, unlike the OX token whose price fluctuated based on supply and demand. Specifically, OPNX offered that the holder of an oUSD could have it "swapped or redeemed for USDT, a stablecoin that is pegged 1:1 with the U.S. dollar."[109] This essentially positioned oUSD as a type of stablecoin.[110] OPNX lauded the token as being particularly suitable for futures traders and those "who prefer near-stable value and the ability to fully mobilize their claims."[111]

To initiate what OPNX termed the tokenization process, an FTX creditor was instructed to create accounts with both OPNX and the FTX Customer Claims Portal,[112] the latter of which was a system for submitting a proof of claim in FTX's Chapter 11 proceeding.[113] Notably, OPNX did not allow individuals in the United States to create OPNX accounts,[114] even though, as of 2023, US customers of FTX accounted for approximately 1.2 million claim holders.[115]

[105] Tosato, Dick & Odinet, *supra* note 1, at 1138 n.228.
[106] *Id.* at 1138–39 & n.230.
[107] *Id.* at 1138 n.231.
[108] *Id.* at 1139.
[109] *Id.* at 1139 n.234.
[110] Kara Bruce, Christopher K. Odinet & Andrea Tosato, *The Private Law of Stablecoins*, 54 Ariz. St. L.J. 1073 (2022).
[111] Tosato, Dick & Odinet, *supra* note 1, at 1139 n.235.
[112] *Welcome to the FTX Customer Claims Portal*, FTX, https://claims.ftx.com/welcome [https://perma.cc/D48U-6XPZ] (last visited Jan. 28, 2025).
[113] *Unlocking Liquidity for FTX Claimants*, *supra* note 100.
[114] *See OPNX Affiliate Program Services Agreement*, GitHub (Apr. 3, 2023), https://github.com/opnx-github/opnx-policies/blob/main/Affiliate%20Terms.md [https://perma.cc/QP2B-PLTD].
[115] André Beganski, *Three Arrows Founders Roll Out Bankruptcy Claims Exchange—but US Residents Are Barred*, Decrypt (Feb. 9, 2023), https://decrypt.co/120982/three-arrows-bankruptcy-claims-exchange-us-barred.

After accounts were created, the user, according to OPNX, could "easily verify and trade their claims thanks to our swift onboarding process."[116] The process for Celsius-related bankruptcy claims was roughly the same.[117]

Once a claim had been verified by the OPNX system and a "transfer agreement" was signed, users could convert their claim into either reOX or oUSD tokens, as noted above.[118] A "business tokenization solution provider" called Heimdall[119] partnered with OPNX to provide what appeared to be the back-end technology for this process. Tellingly, the OPNX blog describing this procedure noted that the transfer agreement "initiate[s] the claim transfer process."[120]

OPNX further explained that Heimdall would aggregate claims into dedicated trusts, purportedly reducing risk for individual creditors.[121] Then, once the claims were held in these "dedicated trusts," tokens are issued against the vehicle, which are liquid and made tradeable on OPNX. OPNX offered that "[t]his process extracts the legal headache around managing the claim as the holder transfers their legal ownership of the underlying claim to the trust, whilst maintaining the economic rights attached to the token."[122]

6.3.2 Illusory tokenization

We now turn to a critical examination of its foundational claims. At the core of OPNX's offering lay a profound misunderstanding of what tokenization legally entails. As we discussed in Chapter 3, this misapprehension is not unique to OPNX but is symptomatic of a broader trend within certain segments of the digital assets industry. Crypto enthusiasts often invoke and, knowingly or unknowingly, misrepresent the words of Professor Lawrence Lessig: "code is law."[123] They contend that when a "smart contract" performs a transaction between two parties, it is the code of this program alone that dictates the terms of their engagement.[124] In their eyes, black-letter law is irrelevant in the realm of these digitally coded arrangements.

[116] *Unlocking Liquidity for FTX Claimants*, *supra* note 100.

[117] *See Bankruptcy Update: What Celsius Creditors Need to Know*, OPNX, https://web.archive.org/web/20240226163045/https://opnx.com/en/learn/bankruptcy-update-what-celsius-creditors-need-to-know (last visited Jan. 28, 2025).

[118] Tosato, Dick & Odinet, *supra* note 1, at 1140 n.243.

[119] At the time of the study, the link on OPNX's blog to Heimdall only linked to the company's Twitter account. *Id.* at 1140 n.244.

[120] *Id.* at 1140 n.245.

[121] *Id.* at 1140 n.246.

[122] *Id.* at 1140 n.248.

[123] Lawrence Lessig, Code and Other Laws of Cyberspace (1999).

[124] *See* Tosato, Dick & Odinet, *supra* note 1, at 1140 n.250.

In our examination of the materials described above, we observed a discernible "code is law" ethos. However, just as crypto-related transactions have never truly existed outside legal frameworks, OPNX's platform was no exception. Below, we highlight how the legal agreements and related front-facing materials for these debt tokens disregarded essential principles of private law, thereby generating significant legal risks and uncertainties for all involved parties. These shortcomings were, in some instances, so pronounced that they fundamentally undermined, or even contradicted, the very objective of tokenizing bankruptcy claims that OPNX purported to achieve.

Our analysis begins with a critical observation drawn from these various documents, modules, and white papers: A number of OPNX's claims about tokenizing debts are at least misleading, and at worst, fundamentally inaccurate. In its module titled *Tokenizing Bankruptcy Claims: A Revolutionary Approach to Maximizing Claim Utility,* OPNX suggested that through its platform one could "[turn] an asset . . . into a digital certificate stored on a piece of immutable blockchain data" and thereby "[convert] financial instruments . . . into digital tokens that have a financial value."[125] The company further asserted these tokens could potentially even "present a fraction of an asset's value."[126]

Yet, OPNX's assertions regarding its platform's power to "turn" bankruptcy claims into new digital assets reveal a fundamental misapprehension of the private law rules that determine how rights in one asset can be legally represented by another. As we explored extensively in Chapter 3, the concept of tokenization, or reification, is not a novel creation of the digital age; rather, it possesses a rich history within property and commercial law. Traditional legal frameworks have long enabled certain inanimate objects, typically paper, to represent payment obligations in the form of negotiable instruments, ownership in a firm via securities, or rights in goods through documents of title, such as bills of lading and warehouse receipts.

Crucially, these established forms of tokenization, while originating in market practices and commercial innovations, ultimately gained legal recognition not through unilateral declarations or private contracts but through judicial decisions and legislative enactments. They are rooted in specific, often statutory, legal regimes that govern their substance and form, providing certainty and standardizing the property rights conferred. This necessity for express legal recognition stems from the *numerus clausus* principle, a bedrock of property law. This tenet establishes that parties cannot create new forms of property rights beyond the finite list of standardized categories recognized by

[125] *Tokenizing Bankruptcy Claims: A Revolutionary Approach to Maximizing Claim Utility, supra* note 95.
[126] *Id.*

law, thereby ensuring that property interests remain uniform and readily comprehensible. Without the standardization this principle imposes, property rights would become fragmented and opaque, imposing prohibitive costs on market participants forced to navigate an increasingly labyrinthine landscape of bespoke arrangements.

The critical flaw in OPNX's approach lies precisely in its assumption that tokenization can be achieved simply through assertions in its terms of service or through the technical execution of a smart contract. A purported tokenization that falls outside the finite forms of property sanctioned by law remains legally ineffective: a sophisticated illusion rather than a legally binding reality. The law, not technological ingenuity or contractual creativity, determines which property forms receive legal recognition and protection.

6.3.3 Structural weaknesses, operational deficiencies, and misleading disclosures

Having laid bare the fundamental defects in OPNX's tokenization narrative, we now undertake a detailed private law analysis of the structure of its debt-token offering. This examination uncovers a litany of structural weaknesses, operational deficiencies, and misleading disclosures. The picture that emerges is one of a platform whose operations diverged sharply from its professed aims, exposing its users to considerable risks for potentially meager rewards.

First, concerning the legal nature of the transaction, despite OPNX's rhetoric about empowering creditors through tokenization, the platform's mechanics suggested a more conventional and far less favorable reality. Indeed, OPNX's own materials contradicted the tokenization narrative set out in the early parts of its *Tokenizing Bankruptcy Claims* module. Later in that same module, OPNX stated that bankruptcy "claims are pooled and made tradeable on order books."[127] This, coupled with the reference in OPNX's step-by-step setup guide to signing a "transfer agreement,"[128] strongly suggests that a creditor actually ceased to be the obligee under the bankruptcy claim. Instead, through a legal transfer, OPNX or an affiliated entity likely became the new obligee of the bankrupt debtor. In effect, the bankruptcy claims were being assigned to an OPNX-related entity in exchange for its proprietary reOX or oUSD tokens, rather than creditors retaining ownership of their claims and merely using OPNX to create a digital representation thereof.

[127] *Id.*

[128] OPNX, Claims Factsheet (n.d.) (on file with author) ("Digitally sign your transfer agreement to initiate your claim transfer.").

Second, the nature of the claim pooling carried out by OPNX and its relationship to creditors reveal a troubling lack of transparency. In its blog entry titled *Tokenizing Bankruptcy Claims: A Revolutionary Approach to Maximizing Claim Utility*, OPNX stated that "Heimdall collates claims into dedicated trusts, which derisks standalone creditors."[129] In its FAQ section, OPNX claimed that bankruptcy claims are kept safe because they "are transferred and kept in a separate trust, reducing the risk for individual creditors."[130] Yet, it remained entirely unclear in whose favor the trust(s) existed. Was there one "separate trust" or were there multiple "dedicated trusts?" One might have assumed that the trusts were in favor of the individual creditors who then held either oUSD or reOX tokens, but the OPNX terms of service suggested otherwise.

Crucially, token holders did not appear to have any direct agreements with Heimdall (OPNX's service provider) and certainly not with any unnamed trusts. This essential information might have been contained in the referenced transfer agreement, but that agreement was not publicly available for review alongside other documents on OPNX's website or through GitHub.[131] Moreover, OPNX's terms of service explicitly limited the scope of the agreement, stating: "This Agreement is between you and us. No person shall have any rights under or connection with this Agreement under the Contracts (Rights of Third Parties) Act 1999."[132] Additionally, the agreement asserted that "[t]he parties are the sole parties to this Agreement which is personal to them and acknowledge that they do not hold the benefit of any provisions on behalf of third parties."[133] The only two parties identified in the introductory paragraph of the agreement were OPNX (by its legal name, Open Technology Markets, Ltd.) and the user.[134] Therefore, it would appear that there could be no third-party beneficiary rights at play and, as such, no enforceable rights for token holders in any trust agreement between OPNX or Heimdall and a trustee.

Even with respect to the trusts themselves, the kind of trust and the identity of the trustee (Heimdall or another party?) were not revealed in these materials. If the trust held the claims for the benefit of OPNX, which then credited each of the users with an interest in the claims on its own books and records, then it may very well be that all the users had was an unsecured claim against OPNX in

[129] *Tokenizing Bankruptcy Claims: A Revolutionary Approach to Maximizing Claim Utility*, *supra* note 95.

[130] *FAQ*, OPNX, https://web.archive.org/web/20231130100401/https://support.opnx.com/en/articles/7966466-faq [https://perma.cc/F28P-5TH7] (last visited Jan. 28, 2025).

[131] *See OPNX-Github/OPNX-Policies*, *supra* note 90 (showing publicly available policy documents, which did not appear to include individual transfer agreements).

[132] Tosato, Dick & Odinet, *supra* note 1, at 1144 n.283 (citing *Terms and Conditions*, OPNX, § 22.2).

[133] *Id.* (citing *Terms and Conditions*, OPNX, § 22.4).

[134] *Id.* (citing *Terms and Conditions*, OPNX, § 1.1).

connection with OPNX's proprietary rights to the bankruptcy claims held in the trust. This concern was amplified by OPNX's broad statement in its terms and conditions that users consent to OPNX being able to commingle any "deposited and traded Cryptocurrency" with "those of other Customers of OPNX in OPNX's Client Account."[135] The defined term "cryptocurrency" meant "any digital asset . . . which we support on the Platform,"[136] which assumedly included the bankruptcy tokens (either oUSD or reOX) created by the company for claim holders. The term "Client Account," although indicated as a defined term, was not actually defined in the Terms and Conditions Agreement.[137]

If indeed the trust was in favor of OPNX, then claimants could only rely on their contractual agreement with OPNX when it came to receiving the benefits of their claims. This is because the claims were now owned by OPNX, and the former claimants were mere OPNX customers. Here again, the Terms and Conditions Agreement was instructive. The company stated in its Risk Disclosure Warning Statement (an addendum to its Terms and Conditions): "We provide no warranty as to the suitability of the Digital Assets traded on OPNX and assume no fiduciary *or any other duty to you in connection with your use of our platform for any purpose whatsoever*."[138]

Even though it seems quite clear that OPNX was indeed acting as an intermediary, or at least its service provider Heimdall was doing so, the Risk Disclosure Warning Statement indicated that "OPNX is not your broker, intermediary, agent, or advisor and has no fiduciary relationship or obligation to you in connection with any trades or other decisions or activities affected by you using the services on our platform."[139]

All of this is a far cry from claimants actually tokenizing their claims in a way that would grant them direct, legally cognizable rights in the underlying assets. As noted previously, OPNX stated that "[t]his process extracts the legal headache around managing the claim as the holder transfers their legal ownership of the underlying claim to the trust, whilst maintaining the economic rights attached to the token."[140] But in fact, how these rights were maintained in favor of the claimant was left quite unclear. Overall, we found the entire trust structure and the role of Heimdall to be worryingly opaque.

Third, the debt tokens issued by OPNX did not appear to be as liquid or stable as promotional materials suggested. The reOX token, for instance, faced

[135] *Id.* (citing *Terms and Conditions*, OPNX, § 4.10).
[136] *Id.*
[137] The term is only used once in section 4.10. *See id.*
[138] *OPNX Risk Disclosure Warning Statement*, GitHub (June 8, 2023), https://github.com/opnx-github/opnx-policies/blob/main/Risk%20Disclosure%20Warning%20Statement.md [https://perma.cc/E3YR-LLSN] (emphasis added).
[139] *Id.*
[140] Tosato, Dick & Odinet, *supra* note 1, at 1146 n.291.

significant liquidity challenges. While OPNX suggested it was ideal for those seeking "immediate liquidity," this claim was dubious. The OX (and reOX for that matter) tokens had only limited liquidity: They could only be sold if there was a ready buyer on OPNX's own platform. Moreover, the supply of OX tokens was entirely controlled by OPNX, thereby placing the market value firmly in the hands of the platform. Taking advantage of the bonus system to multiply one's reOX was entirely contingent on a gamble regarding the eventual scarcity and trading value of the OX token.

The oUSD token, promoted as a stable alternative, presented its own set of problems. This token was ostensibly a stablecoin representing a 1:1 relationship between a single oUSD coin and a single US dollar (reduced by OPNX's predetermined discount rate for certain claims). OPNX stated, however, that it would allow users to redeem their oUSD, but not for US dollars.[141] Rather, the swap would be one oUSD for one USDT—another stablecoin offered by a different crypto company.[142] But this was not even absolute. In its so-called litepaper on oUSD, OPNX stated that "oUSD is not guaranteed to be redeemable for 1 USDT at all times."[143] Instead, OPNX alluded to the fact that it might not actually have enough USDT on hand to meet redemption demand, depending on the level of demand at any given time, and therefore redemptions would only resume "when the redemption quota of USDT becomes available once again."[144] While a person might believe that they had turned their claim in the FTX bankruptcy into a token redeemable in USDT, in reality, they simply held a claim against a pool of bankruptcy claims, held by a third-party service provider of OPNX, with no guarantee of redemption at any given moment.

Moreover, even if OPNX did have enough USDT to make good on the redemption, the user would still not have fiat currency but merely another stablecoin. As we have discussed in other work, whether Tether, the issuer of USDT, actually has enough fiat currency to fulfill redemption demands by holders of its stablecoins is itself a questionable matter.[145] Indeed, in February 2021, Tether entered into a settlement with the Attorney General of New York on account of having made misrepresentations about the reserve assets it actually held to make good on USDT redemption promises.[146] The state attorney general noted that "Tether's claims that its virtual currency was fully backed by U.S. dollars at all

[141] *Id.* at 1146 n.294.

[142] *Id.* at 1146 n.295.

[143] OPNX, oUSD Litepaper—Credit Currency of OPNX (n.d.) (on file with author).

[144] Tosato, Dick & Odinet, *supra* note 1, at 1146 n.297.

[145] *See* Bruce, Odinet & Tosato, *supra* note 110.

[146] Press Release, Letitia James, N.Y. State Att'y Gen., Attorney General James Ends Virtual Currency Trading Platform Bitfinex's Illegal Activities in New York (Feb. 23, 2021), https://ag.ny.gov/press-release/2021/attorney-general-james-ends-virtual-currency-trading-platform-bitfinexs-illegal.

times was a lie."[147] Thus, the promised stability and liquidity of oUSD were contingent on multiple layers of counterparty risk and market uncertainties.

Last, compounding these operational issues was a pattern of deficient and confusing disclosure in OPNX's core legal documents. For all the focus on the ability to use the OPNX platform to tokenize and then trade bankruptcy claims as tokens, the main legal agreements—specifically the Terms and Conditions and the Risk Disclosure Warning Statement—contained remarkably little about bankruptcy claim-related tokens. Indeed, only two clauses addressed the issue in some way or another, and both were contained in the Risk Disclosure Warning Statement.

That document first mentioned the concept of "justice tokens." These were considered to be a type of complex product (not defined) where "the underlying claims in filed lawsuits or arbitration matters are tokenized without our determination of the merits, substance, validity, viability, value or collectability of judgments or awards of such filed claims."[148] On the one hand, these could have constituted some of the bankruptcy claims to the extent that they related to lawsuits that were already filed against the debtor at the time the bankruptcy commenced. But for claims that had not yet resulted in filed lawsuits and were still eligible for the filing of a proof of claim, these would not be so-called justice tokens. It was not clear what the substantive legal relationship between the justice token and the claim actually was, insofar as privity between the plaintiff, defendant, and OPNX (or any of its service providers) was concerned. Even more confusing, a separate white paper on OPNX's website described justice tokens as something quite different.[149] Justice tokens were explained as "independent meme tokens with no intrinsic value, no backing and no expectation of return."[150] Additionally, the lawsuits that were seemingly related to the tokens (though, confusingly, not backed by them) would all relate to defamation claims—with a "focus on OPNX-specific defamation, then expand to non-OPNX cases."[151]

The Risk Disclosure Statement mentioned bankruptcy tokens a second time in connection with the CoinFLEX bankruptcy. The document discussed the rvUSD token, which arose out of a reorganization order from the courts of the Republic of the Seychelles.[152] According to this order, the rvUSD tokens—titled

[147] Ryan Brown, *Cryptocurrency Firms Tether and Bitfinex Agree to Pay $18.5 Million Fine to End New York Probe*, CNBC (Feb. 23, 2021), https://www.cnbc.com/2021/02/23/tether-bitfinex-reach-settlement-with-new-york-attorney-general.html.

[148] *OPNX Risk Disclosure Warning Statement*, *supra* note 138. This provision also indicates that "[i]n addition to risks inherent in complex product [sic], justice tokens include additional highly significant inherent risks." *Id.*

[149] OPNX, Justice Token White Paper (n.d.) (on file with author).

[150] *Id.*

[151] *Id.*

[152] *OPNX Risk Disclosure Warning Statement*, *supra* note 138.

recovery tokens—represented a pro rata claim for the assets of a special purpose vehicle (SPV).[153] This SPV had been assigned, under the supervision of the Seychelles court, an $84 million lawsuit claim against a certain individual named Roger Ver. Ver was a CoinFLEX customer whose failure to meet margin call requirements caused "a hole in the balance sheet" of CoinFLEX that ultimately led to its bankruptcy.[154] The idea behind the token was that "rvUSD holders will be able to redeem their tokens on the Platform upon successful recovery of liquid assets from Roger Ver."[155] Essentially, this meant that once the litigation against Roger Ver resulted in sufficient assets, the claimants would be able to exchange their tokens for those recovered amounts (presumably in fiat currency). OPNX's Risk Disclosure Statement cautioned that "[t]rading in tokenised debt instruments, such as rvUSD, carries inherent risks" and proceeded to list a series of prototypical risk factors, ranging from legal risk to liquidity risk to counterparty risk, as reasons that "[p]otential investors should [be careful]."[156] The warnings seemed particularly tailored to the CoinFLEX token because it mentioned the fact that the issuer was engaged in ongoing litigation where the debt was in dispute and therefore created "risks [that] are heightened."[157] None of this, however, pertained to the ability to tokenize the FTX and Celsius claims using the OPNX platform. If anything, these references only caused additional confusion, further obscuring the true nature and risks of OPNX's primary debt token offerings.

Thus, OPNX's purported tokenization was, in reality, a straightforward assignment of bankruptcy claims, stripping creditors of direct ownership. This transfer occurred within an alarmingly opaque legal structure where the rights of token holders were ill-defined and likely unenforceable. Furthermore, the promised benefits of enhanced liquidity and stable value for the reOX and oUSD tokens proved largely nonexistent, undermined by OPNX's control over supply and highly dubious redemption mechanisms. These substantial operational and structural failings were also compounded by confusing, irrelevant, or simply inadequate disclosures within the platform's core legal documentation, leaving users to navigate a high-risk environment with little clear guidance. Ultimately, the OPNX case serves as a stark reminder that regardless of sophisticated technology or compelling promotional narratives, the substance of commercial relationships lies in the synallagmatic rights and obligations of the parties involved, alongside the established property interests recognized and enforceable under private law.

[153] Tosato, Dick & Odinet, *supra* note 1, at 1149 (citing Order at 3, *In re* Liquidity Technologies LTD (Seychelles Sup. Ct. Mar. 6, 2023)).

[154] *Id.*

[155] *Id.*

[156] *OPNX Risk Disclosure Warning Statement*, *supra* note 138.

[157] *Id.*

6.4 Achieving true tokenization of bankruptcy claims

The preceding analysis of OPNX highlighted the grave deficiencies inherent in its debt token offering. Creditors who exchanged their bankruptcy claims for reOX or oUSD tokens were left in an extremely precarious position; they received assets of uncertain value and liquidity, backed merely by a contractual claim against OPNX, which would have invariably left them as unsecured creditors in the event of its insolvency.

Critically, beyond these serious issues, OPNX's approach, and that of similar crypto entrepreneurs in this space, suffered from an even more fundamental flaw: they were not *actually* tokenizing bankruptcy claims. Despite their press releases, promotional materials, and other representations, the tokens they issued did not, *in law*, represent a genuine ownership interest in the claims of creditors from firms like FTX, Voyager, or Celsius.

But this does not mean that the tokenization of bankruptcy claims is an outright legal impossibility. In the analysis that follows, we return to our discussion in Part I of this book to explain the private law pathway for creating digital assets that in law represent rights to payment, specifically through the 2022 UCC Amendments. Our analysis has a dual purpose. First, we elucidate how these recent statutory developments enable the valid creation of digital assets that embody bankruptcy claims and vest in their holders the right to receive distributions from the estate. This explanation serves as a concrete illustration that true reifications of such claims, pursuant to the numerus clausus principle, follow a narrow route, strictly demarcated by established property rules, and cannot be achieved through mere technological assertion or contractual declaration alone. Second, we aim to provide a corrective to the grandiose narratives often surrounding tokenization and DLT. While pronouncements that these technologies will wholly revolutionize finance or democratize society are markedly overstated, we believe they can nonetheless introduce tangible benefits; these benefits, however, are typically more nuanced and limited than is often portrayed.

6.4.1 Tokenizing bankruptcy trade debts under the UCC

In Chapter 2, we discussed the 2022 Amendments to the Uniform Commercial Code (the 2022 Amendments). We explained that the new Article 12 introduces a novel category of personal property, controllable electronic records (CERs), and establishes a private law framework for the commercial circulation of these assets. At the heart of this regime lies the concept of "control," a state of fact conditional upon a person holding three distinct powers: first, the power to derive substantially all the benefit from the electronic record; second, the exclusive power to prevent others from deriving such benefit; and third, the power to transfer both previous powers to another person, so that the recipient can further transfer all these powers to others.[158]

Our discussion in Chapter 3 examined in detail the impact of the 2022 Amendments on tokenizations. We cautioned that, as a general rule, Article 12 does not extend to tokenization in the broad sense; that is, a CER purporting to embody rights in an unrelated asset (such as a vintage car or a digital image) does not bring that underlying asset under the purview of Article 12. Instead, the linked asset remains subject to its ordinarily applicable property law regime. However, we also highlighted two crucial exceptions where the 2022 Amendments *do* govern tokenizations: *controllable accounts* and *controllable payment intangibles*. For our present inquiry into the tokenization of bankruptcy claims, controllable accounts are particularly salient.

To understand the notion of *controllable account*, one must look first to the definition of an *account*: "a right to payment of a monetary obligation for property that . . . has been or is to be sold, leased, licensed, assigned, . . . or otherwise disposed or for services rendered or to be rendered."[159] A controllable account, then, is an account that is evidenced by a CER, whereby the *account debtor* agrees to pay the person in control of that CER. In other words, controllable accounts are CERs that, *in law*, represent a monetary obligation with payment owed to whoever has control of the associated CER.

The 2022 Amendments establish a commercial circulation regime for controllable accounts that closely parallels that of CERs. It includes the same critical "take-free" rule,[160] under which a "qualifying purchaser"[161] acquires the controllable account free from competing property claims. Furthermore, the 2022 Amendments allow an account debtor to agree with the original creditor not to assert claims or defenses against subsequent transferees; such an agreement enhances the liquidity and marketability of the account by providing greater certainty to potential buyers, as they are insulated from the risk of the account debtor refusing payment due to unrelated claims.[162] The cumulative effect of these provisions is to create digital assets that are functionally equivalent to negotiable instruments.[163]

With this foundation now laid, we can explain how controllable accounts can be used to tokenize bankruptcy claims. For descriptive clarity, we will consider

[158] U.C.C. § 12-105 (Am. L. Inst. & Unif. L. Comm'n 2022).
[159] *See* U.C.C. § 9-102(a)(2) (Am. L. Inst. & Unif. L. Comm'n 2010).
[160] *See* U.C.C. § 12-104(e), (g).
[161] *See* U.C.C. § 12-102(a)(2).
[162] *See* U.C.C. §§ 12-104(e), 12-104(g).
[163] This is expressly acknowledged in comment 10 under section 12-104.

the possible approaches along a spectrum of intermediation, from models with minimal third-party involvement to those that are extensively intermediated. Although the potential configurations are countless, an examination of representative points along this spectrum illuminates the diverse methods by which these tokenizations could be achieved.

At the most disintermediated end of the spectrum, the tokenization could be structured in a fully peer-to-peer manner. The process could unfold as follows. A bankruptcy creditor would enter into an agreement with the bankruptcy trustee whereby the parties would agree that the creditor's claim would be evidenced by a CER soon to be minted and that the trustee would eventually pay the liquidated claim to whoever controlled that CER. Ideally, the creditor would also obtain the bankruptcy trustee's agreement not to assert claims or defenses against subsequent transferees of the tokenized claim. Thereafter, the creditor could mint the CER, such as an NFT on the Ethereum network, thereby creating a controllable account. At this point, the creditor could monetize their claim by assigning it to a purchaser at an agreed price. The proprietary effects of this transaction would be governed by Article 12. Accordingly, upon taking control of the NFT, the purchaser would become entitled to demand payment from the bankruptcy trustee. Moreover, at any time, the first purchaser could reassign the controllable account to another person who could benefit from the take-free rule under Article 12, provided they were a qualifying purchaser.

Moving along our intermediation spectrum, the tokenization process could involve a third-party company that facilitates both the creation of the controllable account and its subsequent monetization. For example, such a company could assist creditors by providing technological support to forge a digital asset that is a CER under Article 12, potentially recommending an appropriate token standard and DLT network. This company could also offer digital wallet services to hold the tokenized bankruptcy claim in custody after issuance. When the creditor seeks to monetize the asset, the company could manage the transfer of control to purchasers, either directly transferring control of the CER or acknowledging custodial control for the benefit of purchasers. Moreover, in the event that the claim is eventually paid out, the company could streamline the payment process by interfacing between purchasers of the controllable account and the bankruptcy trustee.

Further toward greater intermediation, it is possible to envision a scenario in which an entity could play an even greater role in each facet of the tokenization process. For example, a company could establish its own network specifically designed to enable creditors to tokenize their bankruptcy claims and provide a suite of ancillary services. It could act as the creditors' agent in negotiations with the bankruptcy trustee to convert their claims into controllable accounts and oversee the technical aspects of minting appropriate CERs. Furthermore, the company could assist in the monetization of the tokenized bankruptcy claims by helping creditors identify potential buyers, facilitating these transactions, overseeing the transfer of control of the CERs to purchasers, and even holding these assets on their behalf. Additionally, it could coordinate with the bankruptcy trustee to manage the distribution of payments. While reintroducing significant intermediation, this model could potentially enhance efficiency.

Finally, at the most intermediated end of the spectrum, one can imagine the indirect tokenization of bankruptcy claims. For example, a sponsor could establish an SPV to acquire either bankruptcy claims from creditors of a particular debtor in bankruptcy or claims from multiple bankruptcies to diversify risk. Thereafter, the SPV could mint controllable accounts backed by the pool of acquired assets by utilizing proprietary technology infrastructure or leveraging a public DLT network. Each controllable account would entitle the person who controls it to a pro rata share of distributions from the commingled claims pool. Finally, the SPV could offer the controllable account for sale on cryptocurrency exchanges or over-the-counter markets. This approach would allow for collective tokenization without each creditor individually tokenizing their claim. While entailing a high degree of intermediation, such a structure could improve liquidity and price discovery through aggregated trading. Notably, it would obviate the need for direct agreements between individual creditors (or the SPV) and the bankruptcy trustee regarding the creation of the controllable accounts and payment of the claims.

Thus, the legal framework created by the 2022 Amendments delineates a precise legal avenue for the tokenization of bankruptcy claims. It offers enormous latitude regarding the transactional structures and technological solutions. On the transactional side, the number and types of intermediaries, their relationships with creditors and bankruptcy trustees, and the pooling and segmentation of claims are all sources of diversity. On the technology front, there are multifarious options concerning token standards, digital wallets, public versus private networks, direct and indirect control transfers, and interoperability. Yet this operational flexibility pivots on a mandatory fulcrum, with respect to which latitude yields to legal necessity: bankruptcy claims must be tokenized as controllable accounts. This adherence to the specific property form established by Article 12, in line with the numerus clausus principle discussed in Chapter 2, does not unduly restrict market participants' ability to innovate in their business models or differentiate their offerings. Rather, it provides an unshakable bedrock of legal certainty for all parties, clearly defining what is being bought and sold and how it is transferred. Ultimately, this foundation in established private law ensures that token holders possess legally recognized and enforceable entitlements to any forthcoming bankruptcy distributions—a stark contrast to the ambiguities encountered in less rigorously structured endeavors.

6.4.2 The impact of debt tokens

The preceding section explained a viable legal pathway for tokenizing bankruptcy claims through the device of controllable accounts, as articulated by the 2022 Amendments. Now, we turn our attention to the potential ramifications should debt tokens gain widespread adoption. This analysis aims to illuminate the tangible, albeit nuanced, impact that this novelty might have on commercial law and bankruptcy. Moreover, we seek to offer a counterpoint to the hyperbolic narratives prevalent in the digital assets sphere, including those advanced by failed ventures like OPNX, which vastly overstated the potential of debt tokens to democratize the bankruptcy exchange and usher in a financial inclusion revolution. Our purpose is to delineate what the actual evolution might entail, thereby providing both a clear explanation of these potential changes and a sober corrective to such grandiose pronouncements.

A preliminary caveat is in order. Predicting the future is notoriously difficult, particularly when the underlying legal framework remains in its nascent stages. The 2022 Amendments are still being adopted across the fifty states, and market participants are only beginning to grapple with their implications. Against this backdrop of uncertainty, we cautiously forecast three key developments that we hope will prompt ex post empirical analyses.

First, the tokenization of trade debts, such as those held by FTX, Celsius, and Voyager account holders, will lead to a significant legal paradigm shift. Historically, the commercial circulation of these claims has operated within the confines of UCC Article 9's framework for accounts, which demands written agreements between parties, public registry filings for third-party effectiveness, and adherence to strict temporal priority rules. While this regime has provided legal certainty, it imposes substantial due diligence burdens and administrative costs that impede the liquidity of these payment rights. Consider the practical obstacles: Each prospective purchaser must draft written agreements, conduct registry searches to identify existing encumbrances, and navigate complex priority determinations, processes that significantly slow circulation and deter potential buyers.

The 2022 Amendments offer an alternative path. Provided they satisfy the requirements, holders of bankruptcy trade debts can imbue their rights to payment into a CER, opting out of the aforementioned regime for mere *accounts* and into that for *controllable accounts*. In so doing, their bankruptcy claim becomes a highly negotiable digital asset, transferable with speed and near-immediate finality, even across jurisdictions and between pseudonymous parties.

However, we believe that this novelty will involve a learning curve for all market participants. The introduction of any new commercial law framework invariably requires adaptation, and the 2022 Amendments present particularly complex challenges. Article 12 introduces novel legal categories and concepts, such as CERs and the associated principle of "control." While these are not entirely divorced from existing legal notions,[164] they have idiosyncratic features stemming from the intangible and disintermediated nature of the digital assets to which they apply. Focusing specifically on the intersection of controllable accounts and bankruptcy trade debts, several elements will likely require substantial time and practice before complete mastery by the commercial bench and bar: scope of application issues (determining whether a particular trade debt qualifies as an Article 9 account), the necessity for agreements between creditors and account debtors to create controllable accounts, and the notification procedures required for transferees to collect on monetary obligations.

The second development we forecast is the potential for improved markets in bankruptcy trade debts. Current empirical evidence suggests that these claims are among the least actively traded, possibly due to the procedural requirements and title inquiry burdens imposed by the Article 9 regime for accounts.[165] Tokenization via controllable accounts could significantly reshape this landscape. The negotiability bestowed upon these electronic records by Article 12 could foster markets characterized by greater liquidity, reduced transaction costs, improved price discovery, and narrower bid-ask spreads. These dynamics could be further amplified by the enhanced transparency and data availability inherent in digital assets traded on electronic networks. Moreover, by simplifying both the legal and technological aspects, tokenization could stimulate broader participation on both sides of the bankruptcy trade debts market, particularly if entrepreneurs develop dedicated platforms to facilitate these transactions.

Yet we also envision significant risks that demand careful consideration. The speculative frenzies surrounding cryptocurrencies and NFTs serve as cautionary reminders of potential market irrationality. Tokenization of bankruptcy trade debts might inspire unfounded exuberance, leading market participants to mistakenly conflate legal and technological improvements with inherent upgrades to claim quality and expected returns. While highly negotiable digital assets can bolster market liquidity, they cannot, in themselves, improve the fundamental recovery prospects from bankruptcy proceedings. Without proper safeguards, unsophisticated investors might view tokenized claims as superior investments, rather than recognizing tokenization as merely improved trading infrastructure. Furthermore, the digital nature of these assets exacerbates the ever-present risk

[164] For instance, "control" shares many conceptual similarities with "possession." *See* commentary to U.C.C. § 12-105.

[165] *See* U.C.C. § 9-109(a)(3) (Am. L. Inst. & Unif. L. Comm'n 2010); *see also* Massimo Capretta, David Ciancuillo & Richard Ziegler, *6 Things Every Accounts Receivable Buyer Should Know*, Law360 (June 16, 2017), https://www.law360.com/articles/935602.

of fraud, including the hacking of digital wallets or malfeasance by platforms, necessitating vigilant oversight by regulators.

Third, the advent of tokenized bankruptcy trade debts is likely to impact both intercreditor and creditor–debtor dynamics within the bankruptcy process itself. Currently, holders of trade debts often face significant hurdles to effective collective action, including organizational costs and difficulties in coordinating strategy, which can limit their influence in proceedings. Tokenization, particularly if facilitated by specialized intermediaries, could transform this environment by providing digital infrastructure for claimants to coordinate, share information, and even pool resources to retain experienced counsel. Such organized and cohesive action could significantly enhance the voice of dispersed trade creditors, potentially leading to more diverse perspectives being incorporated into the bankruptcy system.

Furthermore, controllable accounts and tokenization might affect the composition of the constituency that holds trade debts in bankruptcy. While a long-standing debate exists regarding whether claims trading impedes reorganizations, current empirical studies on the existing, albeit limited, commercial circulation of trade debts suggest it often leads to creditor concentration, yielding higher recoveries for this class, without negatively impacting proceedings. The conundrum posed by the 2022 Amendments is whether the new rules will alter the *status quo*. Will tokenized trade debts create a more volatile and fragmented creditor base due to speculative investment or further bolster beneficial aggregation? On balance, we cautiously hypothesize that tokenization will more likely act as a conduit toward greater concentration of trade debts in fewer, specialized hands. The inherent complexities of valuing distressed assets and navigating bankruptcy will likely ensure that sophisticated funds remain primary acquirers, even if tokenization expands the buyer pool. This trend, possibly reinforced by original creditors leveraging tokenization for collective action, could ultimately benefit bankruptcy outcomes and social welfare, though rigorous empirical scrutiny will be essential.

PART III

7
Tokenizing real estate

7.1 Introduction

In Chapters 5 and 6 (Part II), we examined the use of non-fungible tokens (NFTs) to represent creative works and the tokenization of bankruptcy claims. These case studies, while insightful, each centered on discrete breakdowns in the understanding of private law. In this chapter and the following (collectively, Part III of this book), we turn to transactions of greater complexity in which such missteps arise at several junctures. Within these arrangements, multiple layers of conceptual shortcomings compound one another. The resulting structures not only fail to deliver their promised benefits but, more critically, expose participants to significant (and we think often unanticipated) risks, as well as outcomes contrary to their expectations. Our investigation brings into even sharper relief the extent to which the digital asset landscape is beset by the flexibility fallacy and a dangerous neglect of private law.

We begin with the ambitious application of distributed ledger technology (DLT) to real estate markets. Some have hailed this endeavor as the revolutionary integration of cutting-edge innovations with one of society's oldest and most fundamental asset classes: land.[1] Fueling this fire are crypto entrepreneurs, boldly proclaiming that blockchain-based solutions can streamline and enhance every aspect of these transactions. Ranging from marketing to title transfers to financing, they argue that decentralized ledgers and tokenization will increase transparency, reduce costs, and open up real estate investing to a broader pool of participants.

At first glance, the promised efficiencies are tantalizing. Purchasing a home or a piece of commercial real estate is notoriously laden with complexities, reams of paperwork, and many costly intermediaries. If DLT could truly cut through the red tape while preserving the integrity of each stage of the transactional process, all parties would benefit.

[1] Various portions of this chapter are drawn, in whole or in part, from R. Wilson Freyermuth, Christopher K. Odinet & Andrea Tosato, *Crypto in Real Estate Finance*, 75 ALA. L. REV. 93 (2023); Christopher K. Odinet & Andrea Tosato, *Tokenized Real Estate: The Law and Tech of Digital Deeds*, OHIO ST. L.J. ONLINE (2026); and Juliet M. Moringiello & Christopher K. Odinet, *Blockchain Real Estate and NFTs*, 64 WM. & MARY L. REV. 1131 (2023). Any reproductions are made with the express permission of the authors.

Digital Commercial Law. Christopher K. Odinet and Andrea Tosato, Oxford University Press.
 DOI: 10.1093/9780197758656.003.0010

This chapter examines the two primary models through which digital assets have been implemented, or their use attempted, to embody real estate ownership rights.

The first involves *direct* ownership of real estate interests through digital assets.[2] Under this approach, ownership rights in real property are supposedly tokenized, with the digital asset serving as the embodiment of the real property interest itself. The proclaimed objective is to leverage DLT to simplify real estate transactions and even facilitate fractional ownership, thereby increasing market liquidity and accessibility.

The second model employs a somewhat more traditional approach using digital assets to establish *indirect* ownership of real estate. In this structure, tokens are minted to represent ownership interests in a corporate entity that, in turn, holds title to real property. This method ostensibly seeks to create a beneficial interest in the underlying property through the corporate vehicle, making it conceptually similar to traditional real estate investment trusts (REITs) but implemented through DLT.

But as we explain below, these two novel transactional structures suffer from fundamental flaws. Invariably, they either misunderstand or underestimate the private law framework that governs real property. This body of rules and principles, developed over centuries, is characterized by a complex web of rights, duties, powers, liabilities, privileges, and so-called no-rights—often thought of as a bundle of sticks—all underpinned by mandatory contractual forms and public notice mechanisms. The purported DLT solutions typically ignore this mandatory legal architecture or attempt to reshape it to accommodate incompatible digital scenarios and structures. What emerges are not merely illusory tokenizations and terms of service that flagrantly disregard the *numerus clausus* principle but also a constellation of interrelated private law issues that negatively affect buyers, sellers, and financiers.

7.2 Digital assets as direct ownership of real property

We start with the first model, which is built on the idea of using a digital asset as a conduit for directly owning an interest in real property. This is, at its core, an issue of tokenization. The fundamental question is whether a digital asset can embody ownership rights in real property, thereby entitling the token holder to the corresponding real property rights. As we explained in Chapter 3,

[2] *See* John D'Angelo, Jeffrey J. Smith, Tim Coy & Parul Bhargava, *Digital Dividends: How Tokenized Real Estate Could Revolutionize Asset Management*, Deloitte Ctr. for Fin. Servs. (Apr. 24, 2025), https://www2.deloitte.com/us/en/insights/industry/financial-services/financial-services-industry-predictions/2025/tokenized-real-estate.html.

tokenization cannot be conjured out of thin air by contract. Rather, the law must sanction it. There are two sources of law that could potentially serve as the foundation for it in this context: commercial law and property law. As we will explain, the first does not provide the necessary support for what many crypto proponents claim, and the second can only do so under highly contingent and uncertain circumstances that, ultimately, only add more transaction costs and procedural steps to the real estate transaction.

7.2.1 The legal framework

When it comes to commercial law—and the Uniform Commercial Code (UCC), specifically—the tokenization of real estate using digital assets is not possible. As we explained in Chapters 2 and 3, Article 12 provides for only two types of tokenization through a controllable electronic record (CER): *controllable accounts* and *controllable payment intangibles*. Entitlements in and to real property are excluded, and this exclusion is unsurprising given that such interests fall entirely outside the scope of the UCC. Indeed, the Prefatory Note to Article 12 expressly states that, in general, "law other than Article 12 would govern what steps must be taken or conditions must be satisfied for a person to acquire an interest in a controllable electronic record and the rights, if any, that the person acquires in other property . . . as a result of acquiring an interest in the record."[3]

In looking to such "other law," we naturally turn to property law. Yet, this domain presents only the most narrow and fraught path for such tokenization. To understand why, one must first understand the fundamental concept of *title* in American private law. As Rufford Patton and Joyce Palomar's seminal treatise on land titles defines it: "title means the right to or ownership of property."[4] Heather Way describes title as "a legal construct that defines" the rights held by someone in a particular asset.[5]

When it comes to real estate transactions, voluntary, *inter vivos* transfers of title are effectuated through the instrument known as a deed of conveyance—"[a] written instrument by which land is conveyed."[6] Importantly, every American jurisdiction has enacted a statute of frauds that requires each conveyance of an interest in land (with some exceptions, like short-term leases) to be in writing.[7]

[3] U.C.C. art. 12 prefatory note 4.b (Am. L. Inst. & Unif. L. Comm'n 1977).

[4] 1 Joyce Palomar, Patton and Palomar on Land Titles § 1, at 2 (3d ed. 2002) [hereinafter Patton & Palomar].

[5] Heather K. Way, *Informal Homeownership in the United States and the Law*, 29 St. Louis U. Pub. L. Rev. 113, 192 (2009).

[6] *Deed*, Black's Law Dictionary (12th ed. 2024).

[7] Dale A. Whitman, Ann M. Burkhart, R. Wilson Freyermuth & Troy A. Rule, The Law of Property 701–02 (4th ed. 2019).

Under traditional statute of frauds requirements, a digital asset alone cannot possibly serve as a vehicle for embodying or conveying title to real property, as a digital asset is a form of electronic record while a deed traditionally required a physical written document.[8]

7.2.2 The law of electronic transactions and digital deeds

Yet, this is not the end of the story. At the turn of the twenty-first century, there was growing recognition that an increasingly large number of transactions, both commercial and consumer in nature, were becoming electronic. To facilitate this transition, Congress passed the Electronic Signatures in Global and National Commerce Act in 2000, commonly known as "E-Sign."[9] This legislation marked a significant shift in legal thinking about transactions. At its core, the statute provided that no signature or contract could be denied legal effect simply because it existed in electronic form.[10] This effectively overrode state laws that might otherwise have hampered electronic commerce, such as statutes of frauds that required certain kinds of contracts to be *physically* in writing.

In parallel with this federal law, the ULC introduced the Uniform Electronic Transactions Act (UETA). This legislation provided states with a blueprint for embracing electronic transactions by offering comprehensive guidelines for recognizing electronic records, signatures, and related matters.[11] UETA explicitly provided that electronic records could satisfy any legal requirements for written documents, and electronic signatures could fulfill any statutory signature requirements. Additionally, going further than E-Sign, UETA changed the role of notaries in real estate transactions by permitting them to perform their duties electronically, thereby eliminating the need for physical stamps or seals.

These legislative reforms effectively removed the barrier of physical form, permitting electronic records to satisfy traditional writing requirements. This development theoretically opens the possibility for digital assets, including NFTs and similar tokens, to serve as deeds. Such an interpretation is reinforced by the 2022 UCC Amendments, which, as explained in Chapter 2, recognize many of these digital assets as controllable electronic records (CERs) and, therefore, as "electronic records." However, establishing that a digital asset can

[8] For a discussion of whether computer code could be sufficient to satisfy the statute of frauds, see Justin D. Lischak Earley, *Bear With Me: The Bearer-Asset Dangers of Tokenizing Real Estate*, Prac. Real Est. L., Jan. 2024, at 25, 29 n.35.

[9] Electronic Signatures in Global and National Commerce Act, Pub. L. No. 106-229, 114 Stat. 464 (2000) (codified at 15 U.S.C. §§ 7001–31).

[10] Electronic Signatures in Global and National Commerce Act § 101(a), 114 Stat. at 465 (codified at 15 U.S.C. § 7001(a)).

[11] Unif. Elec. Transactions Act (Unif. L. Comm'n 1999).

fulfill the format of a deed is distinct from ensuring it meets the substantive legal requirements necessary to convey real property rights—a crucial distinction we explore in the pages that follow.

7.2.3 Technical requirements for digital deeds

The mere possibility of using an electronic record as a deed does not mean that a CER automatically embodies the rights in real estate. Most statutes of frauds for the conveyance of real estate require, at a minimum, that the deed describe the property to be conveyed, contain the signature of the grantor, and that the identity of the grantee be ascertainable from the instrument.[12] The property description can readily be provided in the metadata of the CER, and it will most likely remain static from transfer to transfer. However, the identities of the parties and the signature of the grantor may present complications, since these elements will change with each transaction. As to the grantor, "The deed must name the grantor in the granting clause"[13] and, as to the grantee, "[a] deed which does not name or in some manner designate a grantee is inoperative to convey the legal title."[14]

One could envision a CER that, in its metadata, identifies the grantor and grantee, along with the proper legal description of the property being conveyed. The grantor would then transfer control of the CER to the grantee, thereby ostensibly delivering the CER deed and causing title to the property to pass just as with the delivery of a paper deed.[15] The "signature of the party to be bound"[16] requirement would arguably be met by the grantor using their private key to "sign" the authorization to transfer the digital asset.[17] This should likely suffice since UETA defines an "electronic signature" as any "*electronic* sound, symbol, or *process* attached to or logically associated with a record and executed or adopted by a person with the intent to sign the record."[18]

But, having so accomplished this task, the mere transfer of the NFT to a subsequent purchaser would not make this transferee the owner of the real estate. This is because the parties listed in the NFT's metadata would still be the original grantor and grantee. To effectuate a new transfer using that same CER as

[12] 1 Patton & Palomar, *supra* note 4, § 334.

[13] 5A Tex. Jur. Pl. & Pr. Forms § 93:2, Westlaw TX-PP § 93:2.

[14] *See* Roeser & Pendleton v. Stanolind Oil & Gas Co., 138 S.W.2d 250, 252 (Tex. Civ. App. 1940) (writ ref'd).

[15] 18 Mo. Prac., Real Estate Law—Transact. & Disputes § 3:16 (3d ed., July 2024 update), Westlaw 18 MOPRAC § 3:16.

[16] 1 Patton & Palomar, *supra* note 4, § 334.

[17] *See* Christopher K. Odinet & Andrea Tosato, Essay, *Floating Liens over Crypto-in-Commerce*, 99 Ind. L.J. 367, 387 (2023).

[18] Uniform Elec. Transactions Act § 2(8) (Unif. L. Comm'n 1999) (emphasis added).

a new deed, one would need to alter this metadata to reflect the new grantor and their electronic signature—all modifications that might or might not be possible depending on the design of the digital assets in question. We make these observations not to suggest that using digital assets as deeds in this fashion is impossible but rather to explain how current title transfer rules (specifically, deed requirements) do not allow for the CER to operate as a "bearer instrument"[19] whereby mere control automatically confers ownership of the underlying real estate.

7.2.4 The evolution of title assurance

But where current law appears to narrowly allow for the use of a CER as an instrument of conveyance (i.e., a deed), the law of title assurance throws up yet more roadblocks. Title assurance laws blend common law doctrines and statutory regimes that impart legal recognition of title and make such information readily available for public inspection.[20] This system ensures that title is relatively certain and establishes priority among competing interests in the same property. Without accompanying title assurance, a deed-based title can be rendered worthless.[21]

Historically, the English law method for conveying interests in land lacked formal recording because such transfers were infrequent.[22] Moreover, as the populace was largely illiterate, written records would have been of little utility. Instead, parties conducted a solemn ceremony known as *enfeoffment*, involving the symbolic transfer of a twig, dirt, or similar token, accompanied by the grantor's spoken declaration of intent to transfer, witnessed by multiple observers.[23] Thereafter, any subsequent attempts by the grantor to transfer the same property to someone else would be ineffective, since the rule was that the first transfer prevailed over any subsequent ones (or, said another way, the *nemo dat* rule prevents the grantor from making a subsequent transfer of the same land because the grantor no longer has any interest to convey).[24]

[19] *See* Deutsche Bank Nat'l Tr. Co. v. Campbell, 2018 IL App. (1st) 170817-U, ¶ 19; *see also* Earley, *supra* note 8.

[20] Gerald Korngold, *Resolving the Intergenerational Conflicts of Real Property Law: Preserving Free Markets and Personal Autonomy for Future Generations*, 56 Am. U. L. Rev. 1525, 1564 (2007).

[21] *See* Moringiello & Odinet, *supra* note 1, at 1140.

[22] 14 Powell on Real Property § 82.01 (Michael Allan Wolf ed., 2023) [hereinafter Powell]; *see also* Claire Priest, Credit Nation: Property Laws and Legal Institutions in Early America 166–68 (2021).

[23] Sheldon F. Kurtz, Herbert Hovenkamp, Carol Brown & Christopher K. Odinet, Cases and Materials on American Property Law (7th ed. 2019).

[24] Powell, *supra* note 22, § 82.01.

However, as commercial real estate transactions became more frequent, mortgage finance markets developed, and with the rise of the merchant class, the law began to move away from the twig-and-turf ceremony.[25] In 1535, the English Parliament passed the Statute of Uses, allowing conveyances without enfeoffment. Moreover, the Statute of Enrolments—enacted concurrently with the Statute of Uses partly to counter secret transfers and tax avoidance—mandated public filings to evidence the conveyance of certain estates in land.[26] Finally, with the passage of the Statute of Frauds in 1677,[27] a written document became required in order to effectuate a transfer of title to real property.[28]

In America, several colonies began experimenting with written records of land ownership in the 1600s.[29] In what some historians consider the fountainhead of modern recording acts, the General Court of Massachusetts Bay enacted an ordinance in October 1640 to prevent fraudulent conveyances. In the interest of creating a system such that "every man may know what estate or interest other men may have in any houses, lands, or other hereditaments they are to deal in,"[30] the new law required certain transfers of interests in real property to be recorded in the records of the court. These instruments required acknowledgment by some kind of public officer and, once recorded, created an order of priority of rights in the same property among multiple grantees. By the American Revolution, all the English colonies had some form of recording system for conveying rights in realty.[31]

As the United States expanded westward, the influence of these colonial recording acts grew.[32] This evolution eventually produced the three primary recording systems in use today: race, race-notice, and notice.[33] In notice and race-notice jurisdictions, the *nemo dat* rule is subject to a key exception: A subsequent bona fide purchaser who acquires an interest for value and without notice of a prior interest will prevail (provided, in a race-notice jurisdiction, they also record first). In the race system, the prevailing party is the first to record their instrument and pay value.

Regardless of the system, the underlying principles of title assurance remain consistent. As the famous Peruvian economist Hernando de Soto described, land recording systems make property "standardized . . . accountable . . . [and]

[25] *Id.*
[26] 27 Hen. 8, cc. 10 & 16 (1538).
[27] 29 Charles 2, c. 3, § 1 (1677).
[28] *See* Lord Wright, Legal Essays and Addresses 225 (1939).
[29] *See* Powell, *supra* note 22, § 82.01.
[30] 1 Records of the Governor and Company of the Massachusetts Bay in New England 306 (Nathaniel B. Shurtleff ed., Boston: William White 1853).
[31] 1 Patton & Palomar, *supra* note 4, § 4.
[32] Powell, *supra* note 22, § 82.01.
[33] Kurtz, Hovenkamp, Brown & Odinet, *supra* note 23, § 15.3.1, at 1370–71.

functional."[34] They are, in short, a "public memory system" that takes the form of "rule-bound, and publicly accessible registries."[35]

Yet, the aim of the recording acts is not only to "favor the creation of clear and reliable property interests, while disfavoring ambiguous or contested ownership interests" but also to "facilitate[] the creation of secure title interests by insuring a property owner from third party claims to the property."[36] While recording is not necessary for the transaction to be effective between the parties, it "is essential . . . to provide an official record of the state of the title" as well as "to protect the buyer against any competing claims that may be created by the grantor in others."[37] The act of recording, combined with the public nature of the registry itself, puts "buyers on notice of prior claims or limits on land use rights."[38]

Beyond buyers, the recording system serves multiple constituencies, including borrowers, lenders, those with leasehold interests, title insurance firms, government entities, judgment creditors, those entitled to statutory liens, and many others.[39] For example, before leasing property or lending against real estate, one would want to know the state of the title. Who actually owns the property? What other interests exist, whether owner-granted (easements, covenants, leaseholds) or law-imposed (judgment or statutory liens)?

7.2.5 Electronic recording challenges

Circling back, the crucial role of the public records in title assurance systems exposes a fundamental vulnerability for the real estate direct tokenization model. One may indeed acquire an interest in real property through a digital asset that functions as a deed. However, without the ability to record it, the title is not assured under the recording acts. This means that the same person who conveyed the NFT deed to the grantee may subsequently convey that same property again through a written deed to another grantee, and, in accordance with the rules of the relevant recording act, the second grantee may very well prevail. Avoiding this outcome requires, essentially, a method to record the digital asset.

[34] Hernando de Soto, Remarks at the Opening Ceremony at the Int'l Bar Ass'n Annual Conference (Oct. 12, 2008), *in Law Connects*, INT'L B. NEWS, Dec. 2008, at 14, 18, Westlaw 62 No. 6 INTLBN 14.

[35] Hernando de Soto, *The Destruction of Economic Facts*, BLOOMBERG BUSINESS (Apr. 28, 2011), https://web.archive.org/web/20150726092825/http://www.bloomberg.com/bw/magazine/content/11_19/b4227060634112.htm.

[36] Way, *supra* note 5, at 121.

[37] JOSEPH WILLIAM SINGER, PROPERTY § 11.4.5 (4th ed. 2014).

[38] *Id.*

[39] Donald J. Kochan, *Certainty of Title: Perspectives After the Mortgage Foreclosure Crisis on the Essential Role of Effective Recording Systems*, 66 ARK. L. REV. 267, 275–76 (2013).

To be sure, there have been efforts to establish an electronic land recording system. The push for such reform gained momentum after the promulgation of UETA and E-Sign and was further highlighted by the havoc of the 2008 mortgage crisis. Moreover, several scholars denounced the indexing challenges inherent in systems relying on human document handlers to maintain searchable records for property title research.[40]

As a result, electronic recording has made some progress. Thirty-nine US jurisdictions have enacted the Uniform Real Property Electronic Recording Act, promulgated by the ULC in 2004.[41] The Act deems any legal requirement for original, paper, or manually signed documents to be satisfied by electronic documents.[42] It also establishes in enacting states an Electronic Recording Commission to set statewide electronic recording standards, while giving local offices the authority to automate recording procedures.[43]

Yet, the adoption of the Act in a jurisdiction does not mean that every recording office—which exists and operates on a county-by-county basis—has implemented the technology for electronic deed recording. As of February 2023, roughly 30 percent of the approximately thirty-six hundred recording jurisdictions in the United States still lacked e-recording capabilities.[44] Even within the 70 percent of jurisdictions where e-recording is permissible, significant practical barriers prevent the recording of a digital asset like an NFT. The standard e-recording system, as the American Land Title Association explains, processes a scanned digital image of a deed transmitted through a secure portal.[45] The county recorder receives the image, stamps it, and returns a confirmation. To record a digital asset deed, one would have to transmit its metadata in a format compatible with the county's portal. This process would create two ledgers for a single conveyance: the distributed ledger, where the NFT resides for technological purposes, and the county land records, where a representation of its metadata is stored for title assurance. The result would be the need to conduct double title searches.

[40] *See* Tanya Marsh, *Foreclosures and the Failure of the American Land Title Recording System*, 111 Colum. L. Rev. Sidebar 19 (2011); *see also* Dale A. Whitman, *Are We There Yet? The Case for a Uniform Electronic Recording Act*, 24 W. New Eng. L. Rev. 245, 246–50 (2002).

[41] *See Project Page for Uniform Real Property Electronic Recording Act*, Unif. L. Comm'n, https://www.uniformlaws.org/committees/community-home?communitykey=643c99ad-6abf-4046-9da4-0a6367da00cc (last visited Aug. 2, 2025).

[42] Unif. Real Prop. Elec. Recording Act § 3 (Unif. L. Comm'n 2004).

[43] Unif. L. Comm'n, The Uniform Real Property Electronic Recording Act: A Summary (n.d.), https://perma.cc/5Q75-7HBF.

[44] *See PRIA Technology*, PRIA, https://pria.us/resources/pria-technology/ (last visited Aug. 2, 2025).

[45] *The Basics of E-Recording*, Am. Land Title Ass'n: ALTA Blog (June 25, 2019), https://blog.alta.org/2019/06/the-basics-of-e-recording.html.

7.3 Digital assets as indirect ownership of real property

We now turn to the second model introduced at the outset of this chapter: the use of digital assets to establish *indirect* ownership of real property. This indirect ownership structure represents a more conservative approach to real estate tokenization, one that at least attempts to bridge traditional corporate structures with blockchain technology. To better understand this model, this chapter first describes a prototypical residential real estate transaction and then explains how this crypto-based counterpart differs.

7.3.1 The real estate transaction on traditional rails

We begin with a brief description of how residential real estate transfers unfold in the absence of blockchain technology. A buyer and a seller are brought together by a broker or agent who helps the former find a property that suits their needs, and the latter to market their property to potential purchasers. The transaction commences when both parties agree to the terms of a purchase agreement.[46] In this contract, the parties specify the property to be transferred and the price to be paid; they may also include sundry other conditions, such as merchantability of title, physical inspections, and financing.

Contract execution initiates a period during which buyers undertake various due diligence tasks. They ensure that the property is in an acceptable physical condition through inspections that may include extensive structural assessments. Buyers also conduct searches to investigate whether the seller has merchantable title to the property free from unacceptable encumbrances. Simultaneously, they typically also work with a lender to obtain a mortgage loan to enable them to pay the purchase price.

Around the closing table, the parties exchange documents and funds to complete the property transfer agreed to in the purchase agreement. The conductor of the closing ensures the execution, delivery, and recording of essential documents, specifically the deed and mortgage instruments, in the county land records. Last, a title policy is issued in the names of both the new owner and the mortgagee.

All these activities involve time, energy, multiple parties, and expenses. Parties pay fees, typically at the closing, for the services provided by closing attorneys, lenders, title insurers, real estate agents, special inspectors, appraisers, and surveyors. Estimates suggest that these costs range from 2 percent to 7 percent of

[46] Kurtz, Hovenkamp, Brown & Odinet, *supra* note 23, at 1237.

the sale price.[47] Thus, the purchase of a home for $250,000 would incur an additional transaction cost ranging between $5,000 and $17,500.[48]

7.3.2 The real estate transaction on DLT rails

With that foundation laid, we turn to crypto's promise. Advocates for the use of digital asset technology in real estate transactions seek to reinvent the buying and selling of property. The core element remains unchanged: The right to possess real property is transferred in return for money.[49] But the methods for (1) conducting and (2) financing these conveyances are entirely novel.

(a) Real property ownership transfers via DLT

Although still in their infancy and still rapidly evolving, we studied the transactional structure used by the crypto real estate firm Propy to identify the key steps in crypto real estate transactions. According to Propy's CEO, the goal is to "automate the entire real-estate purchasing process."[50] Propy has already sold a $917,000 home in Daly City, California, in 2019[51] and a ten-acre tract of land in Kern County, California, in 2018.[52] In February 2022, Propy also facilitated the sale of an NFT linked to a house in Gulfport, Mississippi,[53] in April 2022, a condo in Tampa, Florida,[54] in June 2022, a townhouse in Orlando, Florida,[55] and in January 2025, a condominium in Honolulu, Hawaii.[56]

First, a company active in the blockchain space (the "sponsor") creates a business entity, such as an LLC. Simultaneously, the sponsor uses Ethereum or another major DLT network (Algorand, Solana, Stellar, TRON, or Avalanche) to "mint" an NFT. Crucially, the governing documents of this business entity must

[47] Emily Starbuck Gerson, *How Much Does It Cost to Buy a House?*, CREDIT KARMA (Jan. 19, 2023), https://www.creditkarma.com/home-loans/i/cost-to-buy-house [https://perma. cc/F669-CXXW].

[48] Tara Mastroeni, *How Much Does It Cost to Buy a Home?*, CREDIBLE (Feb. 16, 2023), https://perma.cc/4RYH-HGGU; *see also* Gerson, *supra* note 47.

[49] Moringiello & Odinet, *supra* note 1.

[50] *See* Freyermuth, Odinet & Tosato, *supra* note 1, at 101, n.60.

[51] *Propy Executes Its Second Blockchain-Recorded Property Deal in California*, CYRPTONINJAS (Feb. 8, 2019), https://www.cryptoninjas.net/2019/02/08/propy-executes-its-second-blockchain-recorded-property-deal-in-california/ [https://perma.cc/94P7-UWQX].

[52] *See* Freyermuth, Odinet & Tosato, *supra* note 1, at 101, n.62.

[53] *See id.* at 102, n.63.

[54] *See id.* at 102, n.64.

[55] *Propy Plans Sale of New NFT Property in Orlando, Florida*, RISMEDIA (June 30, 2022), https://www.rismedia.com/2022/06/30/propy-sells-new-nft-property-orlando-florida/.

[56] *Propy Announces Unprecedented, Instant Onchain Loan for Tokenized Real Estate Sale in Hawaii*, PR NEWSWIRE (Jan. 24, 2025), https://www.prnewswire.com/news-releases/propy-announces-unprecedented-instant-onchain-loan-for-tokenized-real-estate-sale-in-hawaii-302359210.html.

specify that this NFT embodies an equity interest in the entity. The NFT thus functions as a digital share certificate.[57]

Second, the sponsor ensures that title to a piece of real property is transferred to the business entity. This asset may be owned by either a prospective seller or the sponsor itself. Thereafter, the traditional deed of this transfer is recorded in the appropriate land records.

Third, the property is marketed to potential buyers through an online platform. The sponsor emphasizes that this real estate asset can be purchased simply, quickly, and cheaply by taking advantage of blockchain technology and an NFT transfer.

Propy claims that it takes parties about twenty-two minutes to execute the necessary electronic paperwork, with smart contracts automatically handling the processing of the buyer's payment to the seller and the transfer of the NFT.[58] Crucially, title to the real property does not change hands—it remains with the holding company. The purchaser acquires the holding company and, in turn, beneficial ownership in the real property. In this schema, the NFT is handed over by the sponsor to the purchaser because it embodies the ownership interest in the holding company. Figure 7.1 provides a depiction of the transaction.

The efficiency gains of this model would purportedly extend beyond the initial transaction. Once the entity-NFT structure is established, Propy envisions that subsequent property transfers could occur simply by transferring the digital asset in question, without the need for additional steps. New buyers would acquire ownership of the property indirectly by purchasing the NFT representing the entity that holds the property.

(b) Financing real estate transactions via DLT

Beyond the title transfer mechanics, this NFT-centric structure has profound implications for the financing of real estate transactions. As explained above, in the prototypical real estate transaction, the buyer (mortgagor) grants a mortgage over the acquired property to a lender (mortgagee), which provides financing for part of the purchase price. The law recognizes the mortgagee as a secured creditor, with rights to seize and sell the property if the buyer fails to repay the outstanding loan.

In the crypto real estate transaction, it is unlikely that a mortgage over the acquired real property would be created. This is because the buyer would need financing to buy the ownership interest in the holding company embodied by the NFT, not the real property itself. This arrangement shifts the governing

[57] We do not, in this project, attempt to undertake the necessary analysis to determine whether such a business entity tokenization is possible under the relevant company laws.

[58] *See* Freyermuth, Odinet & Tosato, *supra* note 1, at 100.

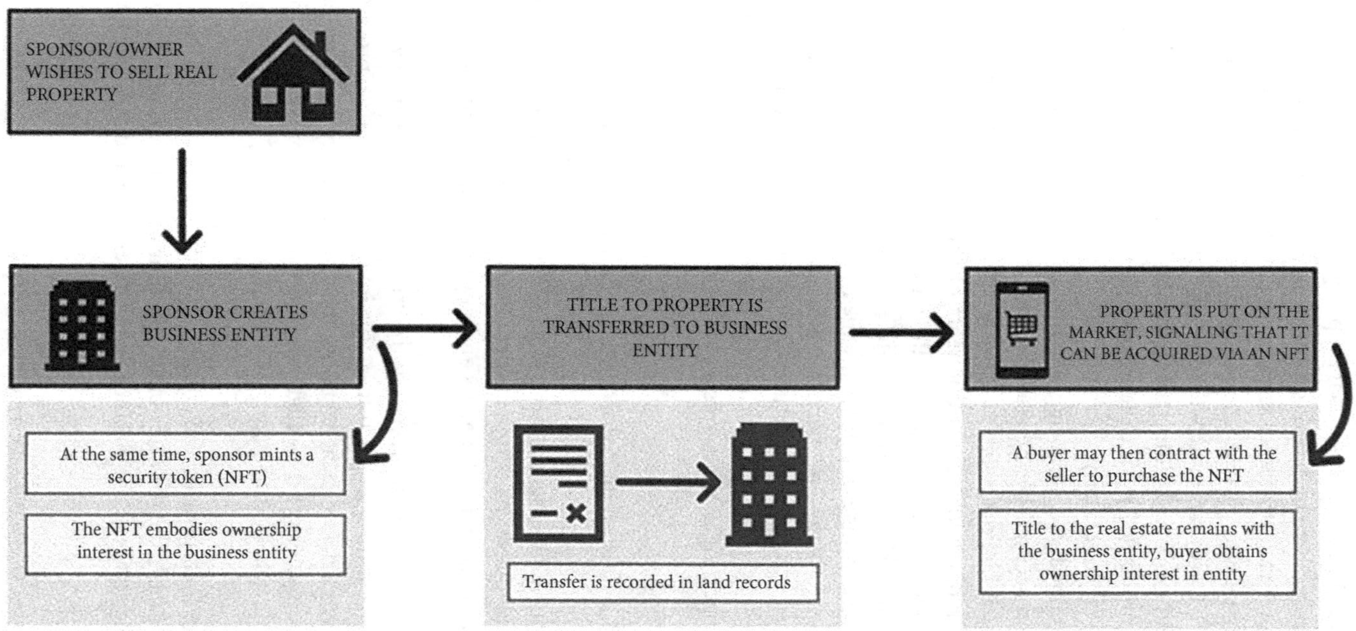

Figure 7.1 Real property transfer using an NFT.

legal framework entirely from real property law to Article 9 of the UCC, which governs security interests in personal property.[59]

If the borrower were to default on the loan, then the creditor would enforce its security interest in the NFT (i.e., the membership interest in the holding company) pursuant to the regime established by Article 9.[60] This process would transfer the NFT to the secured party or a third-party purchaser at a sale, thereby conveying control of the holding company and beneficial ownership of the underlying real property. In principle, mortgage law, including its limitations and safeguards, would be entirely bypassed.

To an untrained eye, choosing whether to fund a real estate transaction through a loan secured by the real property itself or an NFT embodying the equity interest in the real estate holding company might appear to be purely a matter of technology. Indeed, proponents of this novel transaction structure suggest that there are no substantive differences,[61] emphasizing the simplicity, intuitiveness, speed, economy, and efficiency of NFTs and blockchain, while criticizing the byzantine complexity, expense, and slowness of the old ways. But, as we explain below, this narrative is deeply flawed from a private law perspective. The two financing structures under consideration bear profound legal differences, with significant implications for lenders and, more importantly, potentially unsuspecting home buyers.

7.3.3 Differing enforcement regimes: mortgage law

Having described how crypto attempts to reinvent the housing finance transaction, the natural question is to what extent, if at all, does this new structure affect the rights and obligations of lenders and buyers, compared to the prototypical mortgage?

The answer concerns enforcement; the crux of the change involves the rights of creditors. The crypto-centric transaction invites the creditor to proceed under the enforcement rules of Article 9 rather than real property mortgage law, even though the true object of the collateralization is possession and control of real property.

(a) Mortgage foreclosures and equity

When a mortgage loan goes into default, the mortgagee may accelerate the debt's maturity, making the entire balance immediately due and payable. Under the

[59] *See* Freyermuth, Odinet & Tosato, *supra* note 1, at 103 n.72.
[60] *See* U.C.C. § 9-610 (Am. L. Inst. & Unif. L. Comm'n 2022).
[61] *See* Freyermuth, Odinet & Tosato, *supra* note 1, at 104 n.78.

weight of authority, the mortgagee may then choose, either concurrently or consecutively, to sue for judgment on the debt and to foreclose on the real estate. While, on rare occasions, a mortgagee may decide to proceed against the mortgagor for an *in personam* judgment on the debt and forgo the mortgage security, the mortgagee typically chooses, and in some states is required by law, to foreclose first.

Historically, enforcement of a common law mortgage could be especially harsh on the mortgagor, as its operation effected a forfeiture of their interest in the encumbered property. If the mortgagor failed to repay on the specified day for payment (called "Law Day"), they would lose their interest in the collateral, regardless of the amount of the outstanding indebtedness and the value of the encumbered property. This harshness inevitably yielded to the moderating influence of equity, which intervened to aid the defaulting mortgagor who could establish traditional equitable grounds for relief such as fraud, accident, misrepresentation, or duress.[62] By the seventeenth century, the granting of such relief became sufficiently routine that a mortgagor was able to redeem the land by tendering the principal and interest within a reasonable time after Law Day, without having to establish specific equitable grounds for relief.[63] This right became known as the mortgagor's equity of redemption and was recognized as an equitable estate in land.[64]

Once equity established this right, it was necessary to establish a time limit so that a mortgagee would not have to wait indefinitely to see whether the mortgagor would redeem. Equity began to fix an outside date by which redemption would have to be carried out; if not, the right of redemption would terminate (or literally be "foreclosed").[65] Originally, this foreclosure was *strict*, meaning that if the redemption were not carried out by the foreclosure date, the mortgagee would retain title to the property free and clear. However, as English mortgage law was transplanted to the United States, strict foreclosure was widely regarded as unduly harsh. Though it provided the clarity needed to cut off the otherwise indefinite nature of the equity of redemption, it did so at considerable risk of the mortgagee's unjust enrichment, especially in circumstances where the value of the mortgaged land exceeded the unpaid debt. Thus, most American jurisdictions adopted a requirement (continued today) that foreclosure occur by public auction sale.[66] In this form of foreclosure, the property is auctioned to the highest bidder, with the proceeds paid to the mortgagee as necessary to

[62] George Edward Osborne, Handbook on the Law of Mortgages § 6, 12–14 (2d ed. 1970).

[63] William F. Walsh, A Treatise on Mortgages § 3, 6–13 (1934).

[64] 1 Grant S. Nelson, Dale A. Whitman, Ann M. Burkhart & R. Wilson Freyermuth, Real Estate Finance Law § 1:3, 8–9 (6th ed. 2014) [hereinafter 1 Nelson et al., Real Estate Finance Law].

[65] *Id.* § 1:3, at 8–9.

[66] *Id.* § 1:4.

discharge the secured debt. If the winning bid exceeds the balance of the mortgage debt (i.e., the sale produces a "surplus") and there are no junior liens on the property, this surplus is paid to the borrower and represents a return of the borrower's "equity" in the property.

(b) Judicial v nonjudicial mortgage foreclosure

Traditionally, American mortgage foreclosure was *judicially* supervised.[67] The mortgagee filed an equity bill to foreclose the mortgage; the borrower could file an answer, as in any civil lawsuit. If factual allegations in the complaint were contested, the court would conduct a hearing and resolve the dispute. If the court found a proper legal basis for foreclosure, it would order a judicial sale, typically a public auction conducted by the sheriff as a court officer. The sheriff would distribute the proceeds, disbursing them to the foreclosing mortgagee up to the amount of the delinquent debt, then allocating any surplus first to junior lienors in descending priority order, and finally to the borrower. If the sale yielded insufficient proceeds to cover the debt, the mortgagee could obtain a personal judgment for the deficiency against the mortgagor unless the parties had agreed otherwise (such as in a nonrecourse loan) or if prohibited by the applicable law.[68] Although this judicial process is costly and time-consuming,[69] it continues to be available in all American states.[70] In a little under half of the states, it is the required (and thus the exclusive) method of foreclosure; in others, it is the customary method.

In a slight majority of states, legislatures have enacted *nonjudicial* foreclosure statutes largely supplanting judicial foreclosure, at least in most transactions where the mortgage or deed of trust explicitly contains a "power of sale" authorizing the mortgagee or trustee to sell the mortgaged property following default. While processes vary among states that allow it, typically, the foreclosing mortgagee must give a notice of default to the mortgagor and junior interest holders in the property.[71] If the default continues uncured after a grace period (typically thirty days to six months), the mortgagee or trustee may schedule a public auction with required notice to the mortgagor and junior interest holders.[72] The mortgagee must also publish an auction notice in newspapers as

[67] Freyermuth, Odinet & Tosato, *supra* note 1, at 107 n.100.

[68] *See* Ann M. Burkhart, R. Wilson Freyermuth, Christopher K. Odinet, Grant S. Nelson & Dale A. Whitman, Real Estate Transfer, Finance, and Development: Cases and Materials 3–24 (10th ed. 2021) [hereinafter Burkhart et al., Real Estate Transfer].

[69] *See generally* Fed. Hous. Fin. Agency, An Overview of the Home Foreclosure Process (2012), https://www.fhfaoig.gov/Content/Files/SAR%20Home%20Foreclosure%20Process.pdf [https://perma.cc/2KDU-TSBS] [hereinafter Fed. Hous. Fin. Agency, An Overview].

[70] Burkhart, Freyermuth, Odinet, Nelson & Whitman, Real Estate Transfer, *supra* note 68.

[71] *See* Freyermuth, Odinet & Tosato, *supra* note 1, at 108, nn.109, 111.

[72] *See* Fed. Hous. Fin. Agency, An Overview, *supra* note 69, at 13.

dictated by statute. Absent cure or redemption, the auction proceeds are distributed as in judicial foreclosure but without court supervision.[73]

Both foreclosure modes are expensive and time-consuming.[74] Loan servicers typically handle the process, incurring costs ultimately borne by creditors (though mortgagors are often contractually obligated for these expenses). Costs include legal counsel (judicial foreclosure) or trustee/auctioneer fees (nonjudicial), title examinations to identify junior lienholders and current ownership, and notice publication. Both processes take at least several months, with judicial foreclosures potentially taking much longer due to court congestion, as during the post-2007 mortgage crisis,[75] and borrower defenses. A study by the Federal Housing Finance Agency (FHFA) in 2013 showed foreclosure times ranging from 240 days (Alabama and Missouri) to 850 days (New York), with a 438-day national average.[76]

(c) Post-foreclosure rights

Furthermore, in approximately one-half of the states, not even the completion of a foreclosure fully extinguishes the mortgagor's interest in the land. In addition to the equity right of redemption discussed above, these states grant mortgagors a *statutory right of redemption* that enables them (and, in some states, junior lienholders whose interests were otherwise extinguished by the sale) to redeem the property after the foreclosure sale for a limited period of time. The parameters of this right (where it exists) vary widely from state to state. In most states, the redemption price is not based on the unpaid balance of the debt (which established the "price" for the mortgagor to exercise its equity of redemption prior to foreclosure). Instead, the statutory redemption price is typically an amount equal to the high bid at the foreclosure sale plus interest at the date of redemption. The time for statutory redemption may be as short as a few months or as long as twenty-four months. In some states, the duration of the redemption period varies depending on the nature of the mortgaged property itself; in others, the right of statutory redemption does not apply if the parties have waived it. A few states exclude such statutory redemptions following nonjudicial foreclosure.[77] In most states allowing statutory redemption, the mortgagor

[73] *See, e.g.*, Ariz. Rev. Stat. Ann. § 33-812(A) (2014).

[74] *See* Grant S. Nelson & Dale A. Whitman, *Reforming Foreclosure: The Uniform Nonjudicial Foreclosure Act*, 53 Duke L.J. 1399, 1417–25 & nn.91–107 (2004).

[75] *See* Martha Graybow, *Credit Crisis Spurs More Bank Lawsuits in Courts*, Reuters (Aug. 6, 2008, 12:06 PM), https://www.reuters.com/article/us-bank-litigation/credit-crisis-spurs-more-bank-lawsuits-in-courts-idUKN0630980620080806 [https://perma.cc/ZBA5-T9ES].

[76] Fed. Hous. Fin. Agency, State-Level Guarantee Fee Analysis 20 tbl.2 (2013), https://perma.cc/FD7Z-QYY6 [hereinafter Fed. Hous. Fin. Agency, Fee Analysis].

[77] *See* Freyermuth, Odinet & Tosato, *supra* note 1, n.130.

remains entitled to possession of the land during the entire statutory redemption period.

These statutes serve two primary purposes. First, they pressure foreclosing mortgagees to bid fair market value (up to the debt amount) by setting redemption price at sale price rather than full debt. Second, they provide hard-pressed mortgagors additional possession time and a final redemption opportunity, while potentially delaying mortgagee acquisition of marketable title.[78]

7.3.4 Differing enforcement regimes: commercial law

The Article 9 enforcement framework for security interests differs markedly from that described above for mortgages. Under this statute, upon default, secured creditors are afforded broad discretion and can generally liquidate the collateral expeditiously. Debtors retain limited options to delay or halt this process and only maintain a residual interest in the collateral. This marked divergence from the mortgage foreclosure regime is due to the nature and purpose of Article 9. This statute is designed to facilitate the use of personal property, both tangible and intangible, as collateral to finance operational and capital expenditures for businesses and, to a lesser degree, individuals' personal consumption. In these transactions, upon debtor default, a swift liquidation of the collateral is necessary to incentivize lenders to provide financing and enable them to mitigate eventual losses. Notably, the economic and individual interests at stake are fundamentally different from those present in the financing of real estate, particularly when it is a home.

(a) Enforcement standards

Although Article 9 allows for both judicial and nonjudicial enforcement of security interests, creditors typically prefer the nonjudicial option,[79] as it allows them to control the process, rather than being subordinate to a court officer. Unlike with the law of mortgages, Article 9 provides secured parties with a range of possibilities for disposing of the collateral, including selling, leasing, and licensing the assets in question.[80] Crucially, the mandatory enforcement standard is that *every aspect* of the chosen disposition must be conducted in a *commercially reasonable* manner.[81]

[78] 1 Nelson, Whitman, Burkhart & Freyermuth, Real Estate Finance Law, *supra* note 64, § 8:4.

[79] Lynn LoPucki, Elizabeth Warren & Robert Lawless, Secured Transactions: A Systems Approach 79–80 (9th ed. 2019).

[80] *See* Freyermuth, Odinet & Tosato, *supra* note 1, at 121.

[81] U.C.C. § 9-610(b) (Am. L. Inst. & Unif. L. Comm'n 2022).

For our analysis, we focus on the regime applicable to sales of collateral. This is based on the assumption that, in crypto real estate transactions, the secured lender will sell the NFT upon the debtor's default (effectively transferring control over the entity holding the real property).

Article 9 grants secured parties the choice of proceeding through either a public or a private sale. Though not defined in the statutory text, a public sale is generally considered to be one in which the price is generated from a "meaningful opportunity for competitive bidding."[82] This has broadly been understood to mean that there has been sufficient public advertising and that the sale was accessible to any interested person.

Conversely, a private sale is one that is not public. In other words, one that is not publicly advertised and that is not accessible without an invitation to participate. A common example involves liquidation sales of automobiles: secured parties often conduct auctions limited to car dealers, which courts have recognized as valid private sales under Article 9.[83]

(b) Creditor discretion

Whether to use a public or a private sale is not entirely in the creditor's discretion. This decision must itself be commercially reasonable. For example, if a creditor believes that the collateral will sell for a higher price at a private sale but conducts a public sale that results in lower bidding, this will be a violation of enforcement standards required by Article 9,[84] and may give rise to liabilities.[85] Creditors must choose the method that is most likely to "result in higher realization on collateral for the benefit of all concerned."[86] Car sales to auto dealers typically generate higher bids than public auctions, as dealers specialize in acquiring and selling vehicles. Similarly, private hotel equity sales to hotel companies often outperform public auctions.[87] In general, the more idiosyncratic the collateral, the more secured creditors will need to tailor private sales to ensure commercial reasonableness by targeting specialized buyers, providing adequate notice periods, and selecting appropriate venues.

A major limitation in choosing to go the private-sale route is that it eliminates the ability of the creditor to make a bid for the collateral. At a public sale, the creditor itself can attempt to purchase the collateral. But at a private sale, the creditor is only allowed to do so if the thing is "customarily sold on a recognized

[82] U.C.C. § 9-610 cmt. 7.
[83] *See* Freyermuth, Odinet & Tosato, *supra* note 1, at 121 nn.195–96.
[84] *See, e.g.*, United States v. Willis, 593 F.2d 247, 259 (6th Cir. 1979).
[85] U.C.C. § 9-625.
[86] U.C.C. § 9-610 cmt. 2.
[87] D2 Mark LLC v. OREI VI Invs. LLC, No. 652259/2020, 2020 WL 3432950, at *2 (N.Y. Sup. Ct. June 23, 2020).

market or the subject of widely distributed standard price quotations."[88] Such property is of quite a limited nature. It generally is restricted to items like stocks or commodities, both of which are sold on a recognized market.[89]

In 2010, additional guidance was provided to address online auctions as a method to liquidate collateral, under Article 9. Comment 2 to Section 9-610 now expressly provides that online auctions can constitute valid public or private sales if commercially reasonable.[90] Parties may also agree in advance that online auctions are commercially reasonable, provided the agreement is not "manifestly unreasonable" (e.g., using an inappropriate auction format for the collateral type).[91] Though there have been limited cases on these issues, courts have generally approved online auctions when they effectively reach potential buyers, as in *Moore v. Wells Fargo Construction* (approving online excavator auction)[92] and *U.S. Bank Equipment Finance v. Windy City Drilling* (finding eBay auction of drilling equipment commercially reasonable because it "reaches more potential customers . . . than in-person or other online sites").[93]

The Article 9 temporal framework for the enforcement of security interests further illuminates the sharp contrast with mortgage foreclosure. Article 9 requires only ten days' notice to debtors and interested parties before the sale can take place.[94] Taking into account any extra time needed to advertise the sale in the proper venues and to conduct a search for any interest holders, the overall number of days from default to sale can be as quick as about a month—a stark contrast to the multimonth mortgage foreclosure timelines discussed earlier.[95]

7.4 The private law conundrums of crypto real estate financing

A lender financing a crypto real estate transaction by taking security in the NFT representing ownership of the property-holding entity would presumably have the following expectations upon borrower default. They would anticipate seizing and selling the NFT through Article 9 procedures, delivering clear title to the purchaser free from subordinate interests, and enabling that purchaser to obtain possession of the underlying real estate through standard judicial remedies. If the crypto lender held senior priority, both the lender and the purchaser

[88] U.C.C. § 9-610(c)(2).
[89] U.C.C. § 9-610 cmt. 9.
[90] U.C.C. § 9-610(c)(2). *See generally* Stephen S. Gilstrap, Comment, *Refreshing the Page on Online Collateral Auctions*, 120 Yale L.J. 679 (2010).
[91] U.C.C. § 9-603(a).
[92] 903 N.E.2d 525, 533 (Ind. Ct. App. 2009).
[93] No. 19-CV-2291, 2021 U.S. Dist. LEXIS 120397, at *10 (C.D. Ill. Apr. 26, 2021).
[94] U.C.C. §§ 9-611(c)(3)(B), 9-611(c)(3)(C).
[95] *See* Freyermuth, Odinet & Tosato, *supra* note 1, at 123 n.214.

would expect priority over conflicting interests in the real property in question. The purchaser should receive the same clear title protection available in traditional real estate transactions, without the need to contest competing property claims. However, as we demonstrate below, these expectations are fundamentally misplaced.

7.4.1 The two-systems problem

Property law and commercial law have historically struggled with the so-called *two-systems problem*. Under property law, fixtures, crops, timber, and minerals are traditionally treated as part of the land to which they are connected, at least to the extent that a deed to a parcel of land presumptively delivers title to such items (which it does, except in those cases where the deed expressly or impliedly reserved those items to the grantor or a prior conveyance legally severed those interests).[96] Concurrently, commercial law, including the UCC, recognizes agreements assigning such assets separately, either outright or as security for a debt, by viewing them as only temporarily attached to the land.

This gives rise to a two-systems problem: Two creditors can hold conflicting interests in the same item, one deriving its interest from *property law* and the other from a transaction governed by *commercial law*. In such a situation, a primacy rule is necessary to determine which system prevails. As a general rule, the UCC defers to real property law through its scope provisions, which generally exclude real estate interests and real estate transactions from its coverage.[97]

In an ideal world, a crypto financier controlling an NFT that tokenizes the equity in a land-owning entity would enjoy priority over subsequent creditors without also having to take a mortgage on the land. Certainly, as explained earlier in this chapter, such an outcome could reduce the transaction costs associated with the negotiation, execution, and recording of a mortgage. But this outcome is a mirage.

More directly, under private law, tokenizing legal control over the ownership entity is not certain to preclude a variety of conflicting interests from attaching to the land under real property law. To illustrate this point, we explore several potential conflicts between the crypto financier's security interest in the NFT-embodied equity interest on the one hand and other creditors who could obtain security rights in the underlying real property on the other. Our analysis starkly reveals that these competing claims create a web of legal vulnerabilities that can subordinate or even extinguish the crypto financier's expected priority, thereby

96 *Id.* at 126 n.230.
97 *Id.* at 127 n.233.

fundamentally undermining the security that such financing arrangements purport to provide.

(a) Conflict #1: crypto financier vs. IRS

We first consider the most ubiquitous of creditors, the Internal Revenue Service (IRS). Suppose that Wilson purchases an NFT pursuant to which he can exercise control over CryptoHome1 LLC, which holds title to a home that Wilson will occupy as his personal residence. Crypto Lending, which finances the purchase, takes an Article 9 security interest in the NFT and properly perfects it. Thereafter, Wilson fails to pay his personal income taxes, giving rise to a lien on all of Wilson's "property" and "rights to property" under the Internal Revenue Code. At that point, the IRS issues a notice of tax lien and begins the process of attempting to enforce that tax lien against the home through a sale.[98] One can anticipate Crypto Lending's argument:

> The IRS does not have a lien against the home. CryptoHome1 LLC owns the home, not Wilson. The IRS can only assert a lien against Wilson's ownership rights in the LLC, but those rights are already subject to our perfected, first priority lien.[99]

Unfortunately for Crypto Lending, the ship containing this argument sailed with the Supreme Court's 2002 decision in *United States v. Craft*. In *Craft*, the IRS asserted a federal tax lien against the proceeds of the sale of the marital home of Don and Sandra Craft on account of Don's individual federal tax liabilities.[100] The Crafts had owned the home (located in Michigan) as "tenants by the entirety."[101] Under Michigan law, as a tenant by the entirety, Don had no individual interest in the home capable of being attached by an individual creditor of Don—as distinct from a joint creditor of both spouses.[102] The Crafts thus argued that the IRS, as an individual creditor of Don, stood in the same position as any other creditor and could not lien the home for a tax debt for which both spouses were not jointly liable. Prior to *Craft*, federal courts had consistently ruled that in states such as Michigan, a federal tax lien could not attach to entireties property to satisfy an individual spouse's tax liability.[103] These rulings reflected the underlying view that a federal tax lien could attach only to "property" as defined by state law—and that in Michigan and other states where entireties property is

[98] *See, e.g.*, 26 U.S.C. §§ 6321, 6335.

[99] 1 Nelson, Whitman, Burkhart & Freyermuth, Real Estate Finance Law, *supra* note 64, § 9:9.

[100] United States v. Craft, 535 U.S. 274, 276 (2002).

[101] *See* Walters v. Leech, 761 N.W.2d 143, 146–47 (Mich. Ct. App. 2008).

[102] *See* Mich. Comp. Laws Ann. § 600.2807(1) (West 2010).

[103] Freyermuth, Odinet & Tosato, *supra* note 1, at 129 n.243.

owned by the marital unit, neither spouse had any individual "property" right in entireties property during marriage.

In *Craft*, however, the Court rejected these prior decisions, noting that while state law may control "which sticks are in a person's bundle," whether those state-law-defined sticks qualify as "property" or "rights to property" for purposes of the federal tax lien statute is a question of federal law.[104] Turning to the nature of Don Craft's rights regarding the home, the Court noted his "sticks" included:

> [T]he right to use the property, the right to exclude third parties from it, the right to a share of income produced from it, the right of survivorship, the right to become a tenant in common with equal shares upon divorce, the right to sell the property with the respondent's consent and to receive half the proceeds from such a sale, the right to place an encumbrance on the property with the respondent's consent, and the right to block respondent from selling or encumbering the property unilaterally.[105]

The Court characterized these rights as "property" or "rights to property" belonging to Don Craft for purposes of the federal tax lien statute, reasoning that a contrary result would facilitate abuse of the federal tax system. As a result, the Court held that the IRS's tax lien attached to one-half of the sale proceeds of the Craft home. If the Crafts had attempted to convey the home to a third party without the IRS having agreed to release its lien, the third party would have taken the home subject to the IRS's lien claim encumbering a one-half interest in the real estate.

In our CryptoHome1 example, of course, Wilson is not an entireties tenant. Nevertheless, in most significant respects, his relationship to the LLC is analytically comparable to Don Craft's relationship to the marital unit that "owned" the Craft home under Michigan law. Wilson's position as the sole member of the LLC provides him with equivalent (if indirect) rights to possess and manage the home. Unless the LLC agreement provides otherwise, he will have the right to use of the home, the right to exclude others, the right to collect rents generated by the home, and the right to encumber the home by directing the LLC to grant a mortgage loan. He would even have a right of survivorship of a sort; if the LLC failed to remain in good standing and was dissolved under applicable law, ownership of the home would vest in Wilson as the LLC's sole member.[106] In *Craft*, the IRS was allowed to pierce the veil that state law otherwise provided to the

[104] *Craft*, 535 U.S. at 278–79

[105] *Id.* at 282.

[106] *See, e.g.*, MICH. COMP. LAWS §§ 450.4808(1)(b), 450.4808(1)(c) (2018).

entireties tenancy, thereby making the Craft home lienable (at least in part) for Don Craft's individual tax liability. In the Wilson/CryptoHome1 transaction, would the IRS likewise be allowed to pierce the veil that the organic LLC statute would otherwise provide?

Presumptively, the law would respect the distinction between an LLC and its sole member. Under state law, this means that the assets of CryptoHome1 (i.e., the home) would not be subject to the claims of Wilson's individual creditors (absent a contrary agreement) and that the assets of Wilson would not be subject to the claims of CryptoHome1's creditors (again, absent a contrary agreement).[107] But the protection offered by this formal separation is not absolute. Where a legally distinct entity functions as a mere "alter ego" of an individual, a court may permit the assets of the entity to be used to satisfy the debts of the individual under the doctrine of "reverse veil-piercing."[108]

Of course, the mere fact that Wilson is the sole member of the LLC is not a sufficient reason to disrespect the formal distinction between himself and the LLC. If Wilson acquired the home in the LLC for investment or business purposes (e.g., if he were renting the home to tenants rather than occupying it as his personal residence), there is substantial reason to respect the distinction and not consolidate the personal assets and liabilities of Wilson with those of the LLC. Under such circumstances, it would be improper for a court to allow an individual creditor of Wilson (such as the IRS) to reach the assets of the LLC (the home).

But if Wilson is the sole member, the LLC exists solely to hold title to the home, and Wilson occupies the home as his personal residence, the IRS seems certain to argue—successfully—that the LLC is merely the alter ego of Wilson. Under IRS rules,

> alter ego situations typically involve one or more of the following: . . . (c) The taxpayer is a shareholder, director, or officer of the corporation, or otherwise exerts substantial control over the corporation. . . . (f) A failure to disregard the corporate fiction presents an element of injustice or "fundamental unfairness."[109]

These two factors have special salience as applied to Wilson and CryptoHome1 LLC. Not only would Wilson control the LLC as its sole member, but the IRS's creditor remedy against Wilson's rights in the LLC would be entirely inadequate to protect the government's interest in tax collection. Under organic LLC

[107] *See, e.g.*, MICH. COMP. LAWS § 450.4501(4).
[108] Freyermuth, Odinet & Tosato, *supra* note 1, at 131 n.255.
[109] I.R.M. 5.17.2.5.7.1(4) (Mar. 19, 2018).

laws, if the debtor is a member of an LLC, a judgment creditor cannot lien the debtor's control rights but may only obtain a charging order against member distributions.[110] Wilson would remain the sole member of the LLC, with all of the rights to manage and control the LLC, including the right to decide whether and when any distributions would ever be made. Because these two factors, when combined, would entirely frustrate the government's substantial interest in tax collection (as recognized in *Craft*), there seems little doubt that a court would treat CryptoHome1 LLC as Wilson's alter ego for purposes of the federal tax lien statute. Further, even if a state's LLC statute accords single-member LLCs the same protection from veil-piercing as is customarily ascribed to multiple-member LLCs, this protection would not apply against the IRS, which takes the position (again, bolstered in *Craft*) that federal common law, rather than state law, governs alter-ego analysis for purposes of federal tax lien disputes.[111]

If the IRS can lien the home to facilitate collection of Wilson's tax liability, it can conduct a sale of the home to satisfy that lien, and the sale will pass title to the home—potentially cutting off the LLC's title to the home and vesting fee simple title to the purchaser, notwithstanding Crypto Lending's control of the NFT. The only way that Crypto Lending could structure its financing transaction to be *certain* of preventing this outcome is by also taking and recording a direct lien on the land itself—in other words, to have the LLC grant a mortgage on the home and to record that mortgage prior to Wilson's taxes becoming delinquent.[112] This, of course, would defeat a significant objective of the tokenized financing—to avoid the transaction costs associated with the taking, recording, and enforcement of a mortgage. And indeed, from the crypto financer's perspective, it would increase the overall costs of the transaction.

(b) Conflict #2: Crypto financier vs. the judgment creditor

The prior discussion regarding the IRS also has salience with respect to nongovernmental creditors who might reduce otherwise unsecured claims to a judgment (whether those claims arise in tort or contract). Suppose that Alice, a tort or contract creditor with an unsecured claim against Josephine, reduces that claim to a judgment and then asks the court to allow the enforcement of the judgment against the home. If the court respects the corporate veil between Josephine and CryptoHome1 LLC, Alice's judgment will not constitute a lien against the home. Alice can obtain a charging order against distributions made to members of the LLC, but Alice (as a judgment creditor) could not "step into Josephine's shoes" as a member of the LLC. Josephine would remain a member of the LLC with

[110] *See, e.g.*, CAL. CORP. CODE §§ 17704.07, 17705.02–17705.03 (West 2014).

[111] I.R.M. 5.17.2.5.7.1(3) (Mar. 19, 2018).

[112] *See* Freyermuth, Odinet & Tosato, *supra* note 1, at 129 n.248, 132 n.260.

all of the same rights to manage and control its actions. By contrast, if the court engages in reverse veil-piercing, Alice's judgment will constitute a lien against the home under real estate law, and Alice (like the IRS as described above) could force a sale of the home to satisfy the judgment.

In several cases involving nontokenized transactions, courts have manifested a willingness to consider reverse veil-piercing when the circumstances potentially justified such an equitable intervention. For example, in *Curci Investments, LLC v. Baldwin*,[113] James Baldwin formed JPBI, a Delaware LLC, for the purpose of holding and investing the cash balances of Baldwin (who had a 99 percent interest in JPBI) and his wife (who held a 1 percent interest). After forming JPBI, Baldwin borrowed $5.5 million on an unsecured promissory note. The loan eventually went into default, and in 2012, Curci Investments, LLC (Curci), which held the note, obtained a judgment in the amount of $7.2 million (including unpaid interest and attorney fees) and a charging order against JPBI. However, though Baldwin had caused JPBI to distribute over $178 million to himself and his wife between 2006 and 2012, no such distributions were made after 2012, so Curci received no money as a result of the charging order. In 2015, Curci moved to add JPBI as a judgment debtor, basing its motion on the reverse veil-piercing doctrine. The trial court denied the motion, ruling that reverse veil-piercing was unavailable in California.[114] The California Court of Appeal reversed, concluding that third-party reverse veil-piercing of an LLC was possible and remanding the case for a factual hearing, noting that the circumstances merited consideration of veil-piercing:

> With Baldwin's possession of near complete interest in JPBI, and his roles as CEO and managing member, Baldwin effectively has complete control over what JPBI does and does not do, including whether it makes any disbursements to its members (he & his wife). Since the time judgment was entered in Curci's favor, Baldwin has used that power to extend the payback date on loans made to ultimately benefit his grandchildren . . . and to cease [having JPBI] making distributions to . . . himself and his wife.[115]

More recently, in *Blizzard Energy, Inc. v. Schaefers*,[116] the California Court of Appeal for the Second District reaffirmed that the organic LLC statute does not preclude a judgment creditor of an LLC member from adding the LLC as a judgment debtor on an alter-ego theory where the circumstances justify reverse veil-piercing. Further, the drafters of the Revised Uniform Limited

[113] 221 Cal. Rptr. 3d 847 (Ct. App. 2017).
[114] Freyermuth, Odinet & Tosato, *supra* note 1, at 134 n.269.
[115] *Id.* at 134 n.270.
[116] 286 Cal. Rptr. 3d 658 (Ct. App. 2021).

Liability Company Act (RULLCA) made clear that the Act—and in particular, its provision limiting a general creditor of a member to a charging order—was not intended to prevent a court from allowing a third-party creditor to reverse veil-pierce an LLC to reach the LLC's assets on an alter-ego theory where the circumstances justify that result.[117] Thus, absent an explicit statutory provision barring a court from reverse veil-piercing, the remedy appears available (at least conceptually) in states with organic LLC statutes based on the RULLCA.

The foregoing is not to suggest that courts can or should pierce the veil in any transaction in which control of an LLC that owns real estate is tokenized. In many cases, there will be compelling reasons to respect the legal separation of the LLC and its member(s). As noted previously, if Josephine acquires the token for CryptoHome1 LLC and proceeds to use the home as a rental property, the transaction structure facilitates Josephine's ability to separate legal affairs relating to the home from her other personal assets and liabilities. Reverse veil-piercing in that circumstance would be entirely inappropriate absent failure to maintain the requisite LLC formalities. If the LLC has one hundred members who have essentially pooled their capital and appointed an agent to manage the economic use of the home as a rental, courts should likewise respect the veil (again assuming requisite LLC formalities are maintained). But if Josephine is the sole member of the LLC, the LLC exists solely to hold title to the home (i.e., it is a single-asset entity), and Josephine occupies the home as her personal residence, a successful alter-ego argument by Alice as an individual creditor of Josephine is possible, and Crypto Bank disregards that possibility at its own risk.[118] If Alice can lien the home, she can conduct a sale of the home to satisfy that lien, cutting off the LLC's title to the home and vesting fee simple title to the purchaser, notwithstanding Crypto Bank's control of the NFT. Again, the only way Crypto Bank can eliminate this risk altogether is to collateralize not just the token but the land itself by having the LLC grant a mortgage on the home and recording that mortgage (thereby establishing priority over future judgment-lien creditors).[119]

7.4.2 Equitable doctrines problems

As explained in the prior subpart, the two-systems problem practically compels the crypto financer into taking and recording a mortgage on the land rather than relying solely on a security interest in the token that embodies control of the ownership entity. This necessity raises two critical questions. First, if the crypto

[117] Freyermuth, Odinet & Tosato, *supra* note 1, at 134 n.272, 135 n.273.
[118] *Id.* at 135 n.274.
[119] We do not analyze it here, but the Crypto Financier would also lose in a priority dispute with a mechanics' lien holder. For discussion of this conflict, see *id.* at 136–38.

financer has taken a mortgage, does the crypto financer's taking of a security interest in the token serve any purpose different from the mortgage? Stated differently, does a security interest in the token create an equitable mortgage on the land? Second, under what circumstances, if any, does the security interest in the token (or the enforcement of that security interest) constitute an invalid clog on the mortgagor's equity of redemption? Our exploration of these issues demonstrates that private law principles will likely lead courts to treat crypto-collateralized transactions as substantively equivalent to traditional residential mortgages, thereby negating the purported advantages of the blockchain-based structure.

(a) The clogging rule

Equity courts created the equity of redemption in violation of the explicit, formal intention of the parties to early mortgage contracts. In essence, equity courts allowed a mortgagor to redeem real property by performing the secured obligation even though absolute legal title to that property had ostensibly vested in the mortgagee.[120] When a borrower/owner grants an interest in real property to secure payment of a debt, the lender cannot extinguish the owner's title without going through the foreclosure process dictated by the law of the state where the property is located.[121] As explained above, that process requires (with rare exceptions) a public auction sale of the land. Until that process is completed, the owner retains its equitable interest in the land (its "equity of redemption").

As soon as equity courts established the equity of redemption, creditors began devising strategies to circumvent it. In response, equity courts developed a doctrine prohibiting agreements that "clogged" the mortgagor's equity of redemption.[122] As the *Restatement (Third) of Property: Mortgages* recognizes, until a mortgage is foreclosed, the mortgagor has the right to redeem the land from the mortgage and "[a]ny agreement in or created contemporaneously with a mortgage that impairs the mortgagor's right [of redemption] is ineffective."[123]

Under this doctrine, courts have treated as invalid certain transfers of the mortgaged property or agreements to transfer the mortgaged property in circumstances where they served no purpose other than to circumvent the foreclosure process and the mortgagor's redemption right.[124] For example, courts have used the "clogging rule" to invalidate the following creditor devices:

[120] *See* Christopher K. Odinet, *Modernizing Mortgage Law*, 100 N.C. L. Rev. 89, 155 (2021).

[121] *See* 3 Leonard A. Jones, A Treatise on the Law of Mortgages of Real Property §§ 2010–2198, at 7 (8th ed. 1928).

[122] *See id.* at 155–56.

[123] Restatement (Third) of Prop.: Mortgs. § 3.1(b) (Am. L. Inst. 1997).

[124] Bruce Wyman, *The Clog on the Equity of Redemption*, 21 Harv. L. Rev. 459, 462 (1908).

Waiver of the right of redemption in the mortgage documents. Courts have invalidated agreements in the loan documents whereby the borrower waived or agreed not to assert the right of redemption.[125]

Contractual time limits on the right of redemption. Courts have also invalidated agreements in the loan documents that placed time limits on the borrower's ability to redeem after default, such as a provision that "[m]ortgagor agrees that the right to redeem [the property] shall terminate four months after [m]ortgagee declares a default under this mortgage."[126]

The contemporaneous deed or the "deed in escrow." Suppose that Bank loans $200,000 to Josephine, the owner of Blueacre, with Josephine granting a mortgage on Blueacre to secure repayment of the debt. As part of their agreement, Josephine also contemporaneously delivers to Bank a deed purporting to transfer title to Blueacre to Bank, with the understanding that Bank will either (a) return the deed to Josephine if she timely repays the debt, or (b) record the deed if Josephine defaults. The unanimous weight of authority treats such a deed as void as an invalid clog on the equity of redemption. Likewise, courts have held the contemporaneous deed as equally invalid where it is instead delivered to an escrow agent to hold on behalf of the mortgagee.[127]

The contemporaneous option. Suppose that Bank loans $200,000 to Josephine, the owner of Blueacre, with Josephine granting a mortgage on Blueacre to secure repayment of the debt. As part of their agreement, Josephine also delivers a written agreement (either in the mortgage itself or in a separate agreement) granting Bank an option to purchase the mortgaged property that is exercisable by Bank upon default by Josephine. The significant weight of authority treats a contemporaneous option as an invalid clog on the equity of redemption.[128] Such a result is plainly justified if the option can be exercised only in the event of default and for an amount equal to or below the balance of the debt.[129] Such an agreement could be explained only on the ground that it would permit the mortgagee to acquire a possessory right after default but without the obligation to foreclose the mortgage.[130]

(b) The equitable mortgage

In the preceding examples, the parties openly execute a mortgage but then enter into a contemporaneous agreement designed to obviate the need for the

[125] Freyermuth, Odinet & Tosato, *supra* note 1, at 140 n.294.
[126] *Id.* at 140 n.295.
[127] *Id.* at 140 n.296, 141 n.297.
[128] *See id.* at 141 n.298.
[129] Restatement (Third) of Prop.: Mortgs. § 3.1(c).
[130] Freyermuth, Odinet & Tosato, *supra* note 1, at 141 n.300.

mortgagee to foreclose following the borrower's default. Sometimes, creditors go to even greater lengths to use legal forms to hide the true nature of the transaction, i.e., the fact that they are using title to real property to secure a debt.[131] For example, suppose that Josephine owes Creditor $50,000 that is due and payable immediately. Creditor agrees not to institute a collection lawsuit and to give Josephine another nine months to pay the debt if Josephine will immediately execute and deliver to Creditor a deed purporting to convey fee simple absolute title to Blueacre (a parcel of unencumbered land worth $100,000) to Creditor. Creditor and Josephine agree that during the ensuing nine months, Josephine will remain in possession of Blueacre, and that if Josephine repays the debt during those nine months, Creditor will tear up the deed and return it to Josephine. By contrast, if Josephine defaults, Creditor will record the deed and institute a summary proceeding to dispossess Josephine. Their agreement to this effect, however, does not appear on the face of the Josephine-to-Creditor deed, which is absolute on its face.

In this situation, Creditor is using the title to Blueacre (as ostensibly conveyed by the absolute deed from Josephine) to secure Josephine's continuing obligation to repay the debt. Notwithstanding the absolute nature of the deed, the intent of the parties to use title to secure Josephine's debt is reflected by their agreement as well as (1) Josephine's retention of possession of Blueacre, (2) the fact that Josephine and Creditor were in a debtor–creditor relationship prior to the execution and delivery of the deed, and (3) the fact that Blueacre is worth two times the amount Josephine owes to Creditor (why, after all, would Josephine have rationally agreed to sell a parcel of land worth $100,000 for a payment of only $50,000?).[132] Under the weight of significant authority, presuming Josephine can demonstrate the true character of the transaction by clear and convincing evidence, courts will exercise their equitable authority to recharacterize the deed as an equitable mortgage.[133] If Creditor attempts after Josephine's default to use summary process to dispossess Josephine, the court will deny this remedy and instead hold that Creditor has only a mortgage lien on Blueacre—and cannot extinguish Josephine's equity of redemption without completing a foreclosure.[134] By declaring the deed to be an equitable mortgage and requiring its enforcement via foreclosure, the court vindicates the equity of redemption.[135]

[131] Burkhart, Freyermuth, Odinet, Nelson & Whitman, Real Estate Transfer, *supra* note 68, at 273.

[132] Freyermuth, Odinet & Tosato, *supra* note 1, at 142 n.302.

[133] Burkhart, Freyermuth, Odinet, Nelson & Whitman, Real Estate Transfer, *supra* note 68, at 273.

[134] Freyermuth, Odinet & Tosato, *supra* note 1, at 142 n.304.

[135] *See* Restatement (Third) of Prop.: Mortgs. § 3.2, reporters' note cmt. a.

(c) The equity pledge

In our hypothetical crypto transaction, Josephine acquires CryptoHome1 LLC and grants Crypto Bank a security interest in the token embodying the ownership interest in the company. Had Josephine acquired title directly and granted a traditional mortgage, she would have extensive mortgagor protections including public auction sales and extended redemption periods. Some states would also require judicial foreclosure and provide post-sale statutory redemption. By contrast, if courts honor the collateralized token transaction, Article 9 permits Crypto Bank to enforce its security interest without these mortgage law protections. But is Crypto Bank's security interest merely a formal device to use land as security while circumventing pro-mortgagor laws? More pointedly, should courts treat this collateralized token transaction as an equitable mortgage to protect the equity of redemption?

In fact, the collateralized token transaction where Josephine grants an Article 9 security interest bears a remarkable resemblance to the equity pledge used in mezzanine financing.[136] In these transactions, property is subject to a senior mortgage with a "mezzanine" lender taking an Article 9 security interest in the entity's ownership interests (an "equity pledge").[137] Mezzanine lenders and senior mortgagees typically enter intercreditor agreements acknowledging the mezzanine lender's subordinate position.[138] While a foreclosure by the senior mortgagee would not extinguish the mezzanine lender's lien under the equity pledge, it would render that lien worthless if the mortgagor is a single-asset real estate entity.

Relatedly, does this equity pledge on a single-asset real estate entity constitute a clog on the equity of redemption or else amount to an equitable mortgage? The entity has no assets beyond real estate and no unrelated obligations. As of this writing, several recent decisions involving single-asset real estate entities show courts' willingness to characterize analogous transactions as creating equitable interests in real property. In *Bayview Loan Servicing LLC v. Fogarty (In re Fogarty)*, the Second Circuit held that a Chapter 7 debtor nearly identical to Josephine held an equitable interest in property based on possession rights, meaning a lender's Article 9 foreclosure sale of her LLC interest willfully violated the automatic stay. Similarly, a New York Supreme Court struck down an oral settlement of a buyout provision in a single-asset real estate corporation as a Statute of Frauds violation, treating the agreement as acquiring an equitable interest in

[136] *See* Brian D. Hulse, *Can a Pledge of Equity Interests Be a Prohibited Clog on the Equity of Redemption?*, 56 Real Prop., Tr. & Est. L.J. 301 (2021).

[137] J. Dean Heller, *Short of Foreclosure: Less Drastic Remedies for the Real Estate Mezzanine Lender*, Prac. Real Est. Law., May 2010, at 51, 51.

[138] *See, e.g.*, Andrew R. Berman, *Risks and Realities of Mezzanine Loans*, 72 Mo. L. Rev. 993, 1018–22 (2007).

real property.[139] The equity pledge arguably enables mezzanine lenders to control real property without the required foreclosure processes. As Brian Hulse has noted, mezzanine lenders customarily advertise UCC sales of loan collateral in commercial real estate publications, thereby reflecting the transaction's true real estate nature.[140]

However, the equity pledge serves important functional purposes in mezzanine loans. First, it enables mezzanine lenders to control the decision-making of defaulting mortgagors before the senior mortgagee foreclosure. Because mezzanine lenders occupy subordinate positions to senior mortgagees, this control is critical for exercising the mortgagor's equity of redemption or taking protective steps, such as negotiating senior mortgage loan modifications.[141] Second, mortgagors effectively cannot obtain junior mortgage financing in commercial transactions. Senior mortgagees can prevent subordinate mortgages by threatening to enforce due-on-encumbrance clauses, which are typically included in senior mortgage documents.[142] Accordingly, equity pledges provide a practical way for landowners to obtain credit against residual land value on a secured rather than unsecured basis. Under these circumstances, courts should not treat mezzanine lenders' mere taking of equity pledges as invalid "clogs" on the equity of redemption, nor automatically recharacterize them as equitable mortgages requiring real estate law foreclosure.

The equity pledge becomes more complicated, however, where the *same* lender takes both a mortgage lien on the real estate and an Article 9 equity pledge—a "dual collateral" loan.[143] If the Article 9 security interest is valid, the lender has a choice of remedies upon borrower default. It can foreclose the mortgage on the real estate, or it can conduct an Article 9 foreclosure sale of the ownership rights in the borrowing entity. While formally distinct remedies, they are practically interrelated. Mortgage foreclosure does not extinguish the equity pledge lien, but it does render both the mortgagor and equity pledge worthless since the mortgagor loses its only asset absent prior redemption. Conversely, if the lender forecloses on the equity pledge under Article 9, that sale does not formally extinguish the mortgage. The buyer acquires control of the mortgagor, which still holds title to the mortgaged land and retains redemption rights by paying off the mortgage debt.

So, does the equity pledge constitute an "end run" around the equity of redemption in a dual collateral loan? Cases involving dual collateral loans have not produced clear consensus. In *HH Cincinnati Textile L.P. v. Acres Capital*

139 Freyermuth, Odinet & Tosato, *supra* note 1, at 145 nn.317, 318.

140 Hulse, *supra* note 145, at 326 n.148.

141 *See id.* at 325.

142 Freyermuth, Odinet & Tosato, *supra* note 1, at 145 n.321.

143 Hulse, *supra* note 145, at 303, 319.

Servicing LLC,[144] the lender held both a mortgage and assignment of rents on two commercial parcels (each owned by separate borrowing entities) and an equity-pledge agreement granting security interests in both mortgagors' equity interests.[145] Seven months after default, the lender announced a UCC public sale of the equity interests, and the borrower sought a preliminary injunction, arguing that the pledge "impermissibly vitiated the Borrowers' equitable right of redemption."[146] The court denied the preliminary injunction, holding that any loss was compensable by money damages.[147] The court explained that the borrowers' equitable right of redemption was not impaired by the operative agreements since they retained a statutory right of redemption under UCC § 9-623, which allows redemption any time before the secured party disposes of collateral at foreclosure sale, provided the borrowers can fulfill their contractual obligations.

This ruling led to premature speculation among commentators that the court had validated the equity pledge's full enforceability. However, the parties stipulated to dismissal without prejudice before any merits ruling. Seven months later, some of the original plaintiffs filed another suit seeking damages, alleging that the equity pledges had clogged the equity of redemption.[148] When the lender moved to dismiss, the court refused to dismiss the clogging claim, noting it " 'had not ruled on the merits' of that claim in the prior case."[149] The parties settled the dispute and entered a stipulation, pursuant to which the court dismissed the complaint with prejudice. Thus, ultimately *HH Cincinnati* provides no definitive confirmation of the full enforceability of an equity pledge in dual collateral loans.

In the 2021 case of *Atlas Brookview Mezzanine LLC v. DB Brookview LLC*, a New York Supreme Court judge ruled on a lender's motion to dismiss a clogging claim on a $65 million dual collateral loan secured by Illinois land and an equity pledge. Following the default, the lender completed an Article 9 foreclosure sale of the equity interests. As in *HH Cincinnati*, the borrower sought a preliminary injunction against the sale, which was denied. Following the sale, the borrower pursued a declaratory judgment to set aside the sale, arguing that providing a pledge agreement with a mortgage loan violates the borrower's equity of redemption.[150] In dismissing the claim, the court emphasized two points. First, approximately eight months passed after default before UCC foreclosure, during which the borrower retained redemption rights under UCC § 9-623 and

[144] No. 652871/2018, 2018 WL 3056919 (N.Y. Sup. Ct. June 20, 2018).
[145] *Id.* at *1.
[146] Verified Complaint ¶ 68, *HH Cincinnati*, No. 652871/2018, 2018 WL 3056919 (N.Y. Sup. Ct. June 20, 2018).
[147] *HH Cincinnati*, 2018 WL 3056919, at *2.
[148] Hulse, *supra* note 145, at 322, 323
[149] *Id.* at 324.
[150] Freyermuth, Odinet & Tosato, *supra* note 1, at 148 nn.335, 336.

could have prevented foreclosure by paying off the loan. Second, it emphasized that accepting the borrower's argument would require the court to hold that the transaction was void despite the fact that the borrower had "entered into the structure voluntarily with this advice of good counsel."[151] The borrower appealed but subsequently renounced the proceedings.[152]

This ruling has again produced great enthusiasm among advocates of the equity pledge, but those advocates exercise caution. Most importantly, the property was located in Illinois, making this a question of Illinois law.[153] Importantly, Illinois is the *only* state that has adopted (by statute) the position that borrowers in commercial real estate transactions may waive the equity of redemption,[154] and the borrower in *Atlas Brookview* expressly waived any and all redemption rights.[155] Thus, the equity pledge could not "clog" an equity of redemption that the borrower had validly waived and that no longer existed. In all other states, including New York,[156] background law clearly prohibits mortgagors from waiving the equity of redemption contemporaneously with the mortgage. Thus, the case cannot be relied on to broadly establish that equity pledges are fully enforceable to permit lenders in dual collateral loans to avoid complying with state mortgage law—except for Illinois land where the mortgagor has validly waived the equity of redemption.

More importantly, *HH Cincinnati* and *Atlas Brookview* oversimplify the clogging principle's nature and nuance. Some legal forms (such as deeds in escrow) are void *ab initio* as clogs on the equity of redemption. Others are not void *ab initio* but remain subject to equitable recharacterization if the borrower establishes by clear and convincing evidence that the form circumvents the borrower's equity of redemption.[157] The courts in *HH Cincinnati* and *Atlas Brookview* appear to have presumed that a successful "clogging" challenge would have required a conclusion that the equity pledge was void *ab initio*. But if so, they are profoundly incorrect.

To demonstrate why, assume Lender makes a dual collateral loan to Borrower, taking both a mortgage and an equity pledge. If Borrower defaults and Lender conducts an Article 9 sale, the buyer's identity matters crucially. If a third party purchases the equity interests, *the distinction between Lender's mortgage and equity pledge is substantive, not purely formal.* The third-party buyer cannot clear title without paying off the mortgage or negotiating a

[151] *Id.*
[152] Atlas Brookview Mezzanine LLC v. DB Brookview LLC, No. 2022-02421, 2022 WL 2924802 (N.Y. App. Div. July 26, 2022).
[153] Freyermuth, Odinet & Tosato, *supra* note 1, at 148 nn.342, 343.
[154] 735 Ill. Comp. Stat. 5/15-1601(b) (2024).
[155] Hulse, *supra* note 145, at 324 n.147.
[156] *See, e.g.*, Mooney v. Byrne, 57 N.E. 163, 165 (N.Y. 1900).
[157] *See* Freyermuth, Odinet & Tosato, *supra* note 1, at 149 nn.348, 349.

release. By contrast, if the mortgagee purchases at the Article 9 sale, *the distinction is purely formal, not substantive.* The mortgagee obtains total dominion without complying with real estate foreclosure processes and pro-mortgagor protections.

Courts should not view dual collateral lenders' taking of equity pledges as invalid *ab initio* clogs. When taken, equity pledges can serve functions separate from real estate mortgages—most obviously if third parties purchase the equity interests. However, mortgagees' purchase of equity interests after default is functionally an end run around redemption rights, particularly if Article 9 sales fail to provide protections required by mortgage law. Rather than asking whether equity pledges are void *ab initio*, courts should focus on whether lenders can exercise equity pledges to acquire real estate control and what protections sufficiently protect borrowers' redemption rights.

* * *

So what are the private law implications of the preceding analysis for our hypothetical crypto transaction in which Josephine acquires a token that embodies ownership of the LLC that owns the home in which she lives, and in which Crypto Bank takes an Article 9 security interest in the token? As discussed previously, if Crypto Bank takes only a security interest in the token, the sale of that token in an Article 9 sale will give the purchaser full dominion and control over the home and place the purchaser in a position to dispossess Josephine from her residence with none of the protections of mortgage foreclosure law. This is, in effect, an end run around Josephine's right of redemption. In a transaction involving Josephine's personal residence, it seems profoundly unlikely that a court in a judicial-foreclosure-only state is going to allow Josephine to be displaced from possession following an Article 9 sale that occurred outside the judicial process.

Furthermore, as discussed above, if Crypto Bank takes only a security interest in the token, Crypto Bank leaves itself subject to the risk that other creditors of Josephine may obtain rights that permit them to lien the land itself, not just the entity rights embodied in the token. The only way Crypto Bank can effectively protect itself against this risk would be for Crypto Bank to structure the loan as a dual collateral loan, with both a mortgage on the land and a security interest in the token. Assuming the mortgage is timely recorded, this would be sufficient (to the extent possible) to give Crypto Bank effective priority vis-à-vis these other creditors. However, in this crypto transaction, the ownership entity is a single-member LLC (with Josephine as the sole member) with a single asset (her personal residence). Under the circumstances, the security interest in the token serves absolutely no purpose not already served by the mortgage, other than to obviate the need to use applicable mortgage foreclosure law to extinguish

Josephine's right to possess the home. Accordingly, it seems likely that courts will recharacterize the security interest in the token as an equitable mortgage, especially in states where the Article 9 disposition process does not accord Josephine with the pro-mortgagor protections of applicable mortgage law.

7.5 Ignoring private law: cascading consequences throughout transaction life cycles

The preceding discussion has shown that the adoption of digital assets and DLT systems in real estate transactions creates legal complications at multiple junctures throughout the life of these transactions. When examined through a private law lens, the promised simplifications and efficiencies prove nonexistent at best and a dangerous mirage at worst. Rather than streamlining property transfers and financing, these digital innovations create cascading legal uncertainties that expose buyers, sellers, and lenders alike to significant and often unforeseen risks.

This final section articulates the private law implications of both models examined in this chapter. First, we demonstrate that while the direct ownership model (Model 1) can achieve certain limited objectives and may possibly yield greater benefits in the future, it falls far short of expectations. In sum, private law constraints fundamentally prevent it from delivering the grandiose promises made by its proponents.

Second, we turn to the indirect ownership model (Model 2). The underlying structure—purchasing real estate through holding companies and subsequently transferring those entities—has long been used in commercial transactions. The innovation, however, lies in using digital assets to embody ownership interests in the holding company. We observe that this approach results in costs and frictions that are demonstrably higher than in traditional real estate transactions for the initial purchase, with potential efficiencies emerging only in subsequent transfers. But even more significant are the implications for financing real estate purchases. This model brings these transactions into the realm of UCC Article 9 and away from mortgage law. While the implications of this shift are well understood in commercial real estate deals, Model 2 threatens to foist upon ordinary consumers a legal framework that is significantly harsher than mortgage law—one they neither anticipated nor bargained for.

Last, the analysis that follows reveals how ignoring or misconstruing private law in complex transactions involving digital assets creates not only immediate risks for individual market participants, but systemic vulnerabilities that can destabilize entire market sectors.

7.5.1 Direct tokenization: digital deeds, not digital title

The direct ownership model (Model 1) promises to tokenize ownership rights in real estate directly, such that the digital asset itself serves as the embodiment of the property interest. Proponents claim that holding the digital asset would confer ownership of the underlying real estate, and that transfers of the token from one digital wallet to another would effectuate legally recognized conveyances. In essence, the goal is to leverage DLT systems to create *de facto* bearer instruments for real estate, thereby enabling fractional ownership, increasing liquidity, and reducing transaction costs. The appeal of this vision lies in its apparent simplicity: Rather than navigating complex recording systems, title searches, and closing procedures, property transfers would occur through straightforward digital asset transfers on distributed ledgers.

Such ambitions, however, collide with the bedrock principles of property law. Despite the bold claims of its proponents, Model 1 cannot and does not overhaul the fundamental regime governing real estate transfers. As examined earlier in this chapter, every American jurisdiction has enacted statutes of frauds requiring conveyances of interests in land to be in writing, with deeds requiring specific formal elements including property descriptions, grantor signatures, and ascertainable grantees. As a result, property law does not allow for the creation of bearer-like instruments for real estate, whether in paper or digital form. Unlike documents of title that can transfer ownership rights in specific goods through mere possession and delivery, real estate interests cannot be embodied in instruments that pass ownership through simple transfer of the physical or digital item itself.

This restriction reflects fundamental policy considerations that distinguish real estate from movable property and financial instruments. The immobile nature of real estate, its substantial value, and its central role in wealth creation and community stability demand formalities, notice requirements, public recording systems, and fraud prevention mechanisms that are incompatible with many of the characteristics of bearer instruments. Despite perhaps being fairly described as archaic and intricate, the current system of written deeds, public recording, and title assurance is a deliberate framework built over centuries and designed to serve critical public functions.

This regime cannot be ignored and sidestepped merely because DLT offers the technical capability to create digital bearer-like instruments. As we have noted many times in this book, while new technology can be readily implemented to facilitate transactions, it cannot be used to rewrite the legal principles that govern property rights. The belief that one can code around mandatory private law rules is a quintessential example of the flexibility fallacy that pervades the digital-asset ecosystem and that we first introduced earlier in this project. Allowing private parties to unilaterally create their own property transfer mechanisms would create legal chaos—third parties would face insurmountable uncertainty and searching costs about ownership, courts would struggle to reconstruct chains of title, and the predictability essential to functioning real estate markets would collapse. As this book argues throughout, market participants need to thoughtfully engage with existing private law—and possibly advocate for statutory reform or judicial recognition—rather than pursue fanciful attempts to disrupt established legal frameworks through new technologies.

Having resisted the siren song of technoabsolutism,[158] we can now safely assess what Model 1 can truly accomplish. While it cannot create the bearer-like instruments envisioned by its most ambitious proponents, it can meaningfully improve the execution of real estate transactions. Building upon existing statutory reforms, particularly E-sign and UETA, it is certainly possible to use digital assets as a medium for conveyance instruments in electronic form. Digital assets maintained on DLT networks offer clear advantages over paper-based systems: They eliminate physical storage requirements, enable instant transmission across vast distances, provide permanent and immutable records that cannot be lost or destroyed, and facilitate automated processing and verification. These benefits alone represent significant improvements over traditional paper-based deed systems.

Moreover, DLT systems offer meaningful improvements even over conventional electronic documents, such as signed PDFs or centralized cloud-based signature services. The underlying distributed ledgers provide tamper resistance, ensuring that once recorded, deed information cannot be altered without detection. The decentralized nature of these networks eliminates single points of failure and reduces dependence on centralized service providers, potentially offering greater long-term reliability and accessibility. These characteristics could address some of the authenticity and integrity concerns that hinder traditional electronic document systems.

The greatest potential benefits, however, lie in future coalescence with electronic land registries. Complete integration between deeds in digital asset form and DLT systems could theoretically yield substantial efficiency gains in execution time, cost reduction, and information accessibility. Such platforms could enable real-time title searches, automated compliance checking, and streamlined transfer processes that genuinely reduce transaction costs and timelines.

However, the practical realization of these benefits faces substantial obstacles. Most fundamentally, adoption of electronic recording systems remains incomplete across American jurisdictions. About 30 percent of the nation's 3,600 have

[158] *See generally* Hilary J. Allen, *Fintech and Techno-Solutionism*, 98 S. CAL. L. REV. 761 (2025).

not implemented e-recording and cannot accommodate electronic deeds of any kind. More significantly, no jurisdiction currently offers an electronic platform that natively integrates digital assets within its system. Therefore, digital asset deeds would create the two-ledger problem identified earlier: The distributed ledger hosting the NFT would exist alongside the county recording system, requiring title reviewers to search multiple systems and potentially increasing rather than decreasing transaction costs.

These limitations reflect deeper systemic challenges inherent in American land recording infrastructure. These systems operate on a county-by-county basis, creating thousands of separate jurisdictions with varying technological capabilities, legal requirements, and administrative procedures. Implementing DLT-based deed systems would require coordinated upgrades, a costly and complex undertaking that would demand policy changes and substantial public investment. While we have not conducted a comprehensive empirical analysis, our suspicion is that the cost-benefit calculus for such systems appears unfavorable when compared to existing electronic document solutions that can achieve many of the same efficiencies without requiring wholesale infrastructure replacement.

It should also be noted that security and fraud concerns present additional barriers that compound the authentication challenges inherent in electronic transactions. As commentators note, "[T]he fact that there is legal support for what we are doing is only part of the battle."[159] Digital asset systems must ensure that signers are correctly identified, that parties understand the documents they are executing, and that the technical infrastructure cannot be compromised or manipulated. Title insurers face expanded exposure to liability, as their policies must cover not only traditional risks but also issues related to improper execution, technical failures, and the validity of electronically created documents. Until these multifaceted barriers are addressed through significant public and private sector coordination, Model 1's benefits remain largely theoretical rather than practically achievable.

7.5.2 Indirect tokenization: uncertain efficiencies and financing complications

The indirect ownership model (Model 2) involves creating a corporate entity that holds title to the real property, with digital assets representing ownership interests in that holding company rather than in the real estate directly.

[159] Palma Collins, *E-mail, E-Sign, E-Notarize? Considerations Surrounding Electronic Real Estate Transactions*, VLTA Examiner (Dec. 18, 2017), https://vltaexaminer.com/2017/12/18/e-mail-e-sign-e-notarize-considerations-surrounding-electronic-real-estate-transactions/.

Purchasers acquire beneficial ownership in the underlying property through their ownership of the digital asset, which embodies their equity interest in the business entity. This approach mirrors traditional real estate investment structures, in which investors hold interests in entities that own property, such as REITs or limited partnerships, but implements this familiar framework through DLT and associated digital tokens.

The structure of Model 2 is neither new nor controversial: Purchasing real estate through holding companies and subsequently transferring ownership of those entities has been a standard practice in commercial real estate transactions for decades. The innovation lies in using digital assets to embody ownership interests in the holding company rather than traditional corporate certificates or membership documents. This digital representation presents legal challenges, as not all state laws clearly authorize the tokenization of corporate ownership interests, thereby placing this approach in relatively untrodden legal territory. However, unlike Model 1's fundamental legal impossibility, Model 2's challenges are primarily matters of business entity law and regulatory compliance.

Additionally, Model 2 can deliver tangible efficiencies, but only under specific circumstances that limit its practical applicability. The model's primary advantage emerges in subsequent transfers: once the corporate structure is established and the initial real estate purchase is complete, transfers of the digital asset representing the equity interest in the holding company can eliminate the need for new title searches, deed preparation, and recording. However, these benefits come at the cost of substantially increased complexity and expense during initial implementation. Compared to standard buyer–seller transactions, Model 2 requires holding company creation, corporate filings, initial title transfers to the entity, and digital asset infrastructure setup—costs that must be absorbed before any efficiencies can be realized. The model therefore reallocates rather than eliminates transaction costs, making its benefits entirely dependent on sufficient subsequent trading activity to justify the upfront investment. For most residential real estate, which changes hands rather infrequently, this cost-benefit analysis remains uncertain at best or unfavorable at worst.

In principle, Model 2 could enable fractionalized real estate investment by allowing multiple investors to hold tokens representing partial ownership interests in the holding entity. Such an approach would be similar to that of REITs. However, any advantages in this context would stem from regulatory frameworks rather than private law benefits, placing such an analysis beyond the scope of our examination in this project.

Nevertheless, Model 2 cannot overcome the inherent structural complexities that arise from layering corporate ownership atop the holding of real property interests. The model requires simultaneous navigation of business entity law, real property law, and emerging digital asset frameworks—creating multiple legal touchpoints rather than simplifying existing processes. These structural limitations persist regardless of technological efficiency, as they stem from the intersection of independently evolved legal frameworks that cannot be harmonized through private ordering alone and may generate coordination failures that actually increase transaction costs.[160]

Beyond the structural complexities in purchasing real estate, Model 2 creates perhaps even more significant complications when we turn to the financing of these transactions. As explained in prior pages of this chapter, financing the direct purchase of real estate provides borrowers with mortgage law's protective provisions including public foreclosure sales, extended redemption periods, and judicial oversight. In contrast, financing the acquisition of ownership interests in a corporate entity that holds real estate subjects the transaction to UCC Article 9 with its faster, harsher enforcement regime that provides significantly fewer safeguards for defaulting borrowers.

This legal shift is well understood and carefully managed in sophisticated commercial real estate transactions, where multiple layers of financing typically involve senior lenders holding first-lien mortgages on the underlying property, mezzanine lenders taking security interests in the equity of the property-holding entity, and providers of various forms of unsecured debt. In this context, all parties are sophisticated actors, represented by experienced legal counsel who understand the different risk profiles and implications of each financing layer. Model 2, however, whether intentionally or more likely inadvertently, given that proponents rarely acknowledge these legal distinctions, threatens to import this financing regime into mass-market residential purchases. Both borrowers and lenders may fail to recognize the fundamental shift from consumer-protective mortgage law to commercial-oriented Article 9 frameworks, potentially exposing themselves to legal uncertainties and risks they neither expected nor bargained for.

The private law implications of Model 2 financing are stark for prospective real estate purchasers. As explained above, in our hypothetical crypto transaction Josephine acquires a token embodying ownership of the LLC and obtains financing from Crypto Bank. While courts in judicial-foreclosure-only states would likely refuse to allow displacement following an Article 9 sale conducted outside the judicial process, such relief is not guaranteed. Moreover, the risk of expedited displacement is even more pronounced in states that permit nonjudicial foreclosures. This is due to the fact that these jurisdictions have already demonstrated a greater willingness to prioritize expedited enforcement over

[160] When one transaction falls under multiple areas of law (a "commercial law intersection"), coordination failures often create gaps, inconsistencies, and higher transaction costs. *See* Giuliano G. Castellano & Andrea Tosato, *Commercial Law Intersections*, 72 HASTINGS L.J. 999, 1020–24 (2021).

borrower protections and may prove more receptive to allowing enforcement over residential homes through the UCC Article 9 framework.

The prospect of homeowners finding themselves subject to UCC Article 9's commercial enforcement when defaulting on their home loans represents a fundamental erosion of consumer protections. These harsh consequences fall most acutely on first-time buyers, who often negotiate from positions of weakness with limited funds and minimal financial sophistication. The loss of a family home through expedited commercial foreclosure procedures inflicts enormous personal harm and disrupts local communities. Systemically, such displacement causes house values to fall throughout neighborhoods, potentially dragging other homeowners into negative equity and precluding their ability to refinance, thereby increasing default risks. Empirical evidence demonstrates that foreclosures disproportionately devastate racial minorities and economically vulnerable populations. During the Great Recession, home foreclosures decimated household wealth in communities of color far more severely than for White families: while White housing equity wealth fell 41 percent, it plummeted 53 percent for Black households and 70 percent for Hispanic households.[161]

Lenders face their own set of complications under Model 2. As previously noted, parties financing the acquisition of equity interests in real estate holding companies expose themselves to the risk that other creditors of the borrower may obtain liens directly on the underlying real estate itself, not merely on the entity rights embodied in the token. In such scenarios, upon default, the token lender might recover nothing after lienholders have satisfied their claims against the property. Additionally, lenders face the risk that courts will recharacterize their security interests in tokens as equitable mortgages, forcing them to comply with mortgage law's procedural requirements and potentially invalidating foreclosure sales that failed to meet those standards. Such interventions could leave lenders with protracted judicial proceedings, extended redemption periods, and significantly diminished recovery prospects. While we are less sympathetic toward lenders, as they should possess the sophistication and legal counsel to understand these risks, we remain mindful that if multiple financial institutions concurrently suffer losses due to widespread judicial recharacterization of these financing structures, the resulting instability could quickly escalate into broader financial crises with painful and far-reaching consequences for society.

In sum, the analysis of both direct and indirect tokenization models reveals that digital asset innovations in real estate create more complications than they resolve. Model 1's promise of bearer-like instruments for real property transfers

[161] *Racial Differences in Economic Security: Housing*, U.S. Dep't of the Treasury (Nov. 4, 2022), https://home.treasury.gov/news/featured-stories/racial-differences-in-economic-security-housing [https://perma.cc/3KBC-UVB9].

founders on centuries-old private law principles that cannot be coded around. Model 2 offers genuine but narrow efficiencies in subsequent transfers, yet it imposes substantial upfront costs and threatens to expose residential borrowers to commercial foreclosure procedures they never anticipated. Both models demonstrate that ignoring established private law frameworks generates cascading risks throughout transaction lifecycles—from initial purchase complexity to financing vulnerabilities that could destabilize communities and markets. Rather than pursuing technological disruption that sidesteps legal foundations, the real estate industry would benefit more from integrating digital innovations within existing private law structures, potentially coupled with targeted statutory reforms that preserve essential consumer protections while enabling genuine gains in efficiency.

8

Stablecoins as private money

8.1 Introduction

We arrive at the final case study, and arguably the most complex.[1] This chapter examines stablecoins, a type of digital asset designed to maintain a stable value relative to a reference asset or basket of assets. These tokens have attracted enormous attention from policymakers, financial institutions, and technology firms for their potential to serve as efficient digital payment instruments that bridge traditional finance and the distributed ledger technology (DLT) world.

The trajectory of stablecoins has been extraordinary: from a negligible market presence in 2014 to over $250 billion in aggregate market supply by mid-2025.[2] Emblematically, Circle, the issuer of the second-largest stablecoin, successfully completed its initial public offering on US exchanges in June 2025, with shares surging 45 percent on the first day of trading as investors clamored for exposure to this burgeoning sector.[3] This meteoric rise has prompted regulatory attention. Over the past two years, the European Union (EU) has operationalized comprehensive stablecoin provisions within the Markets in Crypto-Assets Regulation (MiCAR), while the United States has just (as of this writing) enacted federal legislation through the Guiding and Establishing National Innovation for U.S. Stablecoins Act (GENIUS Act).[4]

For this book, stablecoins merit particular attention because they crystallize two fundamental dynamics that animate our central thesis. First, the conversation surrounding stablecoins has been overwhelmingly dominated by public

[1] Various portions of this chapter are drawn, in whole or in part, from Kara Bruce, Christopher K. Odinet & Andrea Tosato, *The Private Law of Stablecoins*, 54 Ariz. St. L.J. 1073 (2022), and Christopher K. Odinet & Andrea Tosato, *Regulating Stablecoins: Comparing MiCAR and the GENIUS Act*, Notre Dame L. Rev. Reflection (forthcoming 2026), https://papers.ssrn.com/sol3/papers.cfm?abstract_id=5383158. Any reproductions are made with the express permission of the authors.

[2] *See* Jack Caporal, *Which Stablecoins Are the Largest and Most Popular in 2025?*, The Motley Fool (July 15, 2025), https://www.fool.com/research/largest-stablecoins/.

[3] David Zaslowsky, *Circle's IPO and the New Era of Stablecoin Regulation in the U.S.*, Reuters (June 12, 2025), https://www.reuters.com/legal/legalindustry/circles-ipo-new-era-stablecoin-regulation-us-2025-06-12/.

[4] *See* Council Regulation 2023/1114 on Markets in Crypto-Assets, 2023 O.J. (L 150) 4 (EU) [hereinafter MiCAR], https://eur-lex.europa.eu/legalcontent/EN/TXT/PDF/?uri=CELEX:32023R1114; Guiding and Establishing National Innovation for U.S. Stablecoins Act (GENIUS Act), S. 1582, 119th Cong. (2025).

Digital Commercial Law. Christopher K. Odinet and Andrea Tosato, Oxford University Press.
 DOI: 10.1093/9780197758656.003.0011

law approaches and regulatory considerations. To be fair, this attention is not unwarranted given the systemic implications and use cases for these digital assets as payment instruments. However, the near-complete complete disregard for private law considerations is striking and, as we will explain toward the end of this chapter, ultimately undermines regulatory efforts. It is extremely challenging to construct coherent and effective regulatory frameworks without first understanding the significant differences in how various stablecoins are structured from a contracts and property rights perspective as well as appreciating the specific legal rights and obligations that bind both the companies issuing these stablecoins and the people who hold them.

Second, the private ordering structures underlying stablecoins are among the most poorly constructed and problematic across the entire digital assets landscape. As expounded upon in this chapter, our analysis reveals that stablecoin holders have severely limited rights against issuers and maintain only the most tenuous claims to reserve assets in bankruptcy proceedings. More troublingly, we show that in some cases there is no identifiable issuer at all, leaving holders without a contractual counterparty or legal recourse when these systems malfunction or collapse. As we demonstrate throughout our study, all this is exacerbated by a systematic disconnect between marketing representations on the one hand and legal reality on the other.

This chapter proceeds as follows. First we trace the historical evolution of stablecoins, categorizing their diverse architectures, analyzing their business models, and documenting their integration into the broader digital assets and retail payments landscape. Next we conduct a private law examination of the legal frameworks for several leading stablecoins, differentiating between decentralized and centralized models. Our analysis dissects the contractual provisions governing redemption rights, reserve asset custody, liability allocation, and dispute resolution. In this exercise, we also document the systematic discrepancies between the public-facing marketing materials and the operative legal terms. Finally, we assess a range of private ordering and regulatory interventions designed to remedy (or that fail to remedy) the deficiencies we identify.

Before delving into a private law analysis of stablecoins, it is important to understand their structure and economic function in the market. To illuminate the inner workings of these digital assets, we structure our discussion around three central propositions. First, the defining feature of stablecoins is that they are designed to maintain a stable price. Second, there are multiple types of stablecoins, with structural and organizational differences that have significant legal implications. Third, stablecoin issuers pursue a diverse set of business models that markedly affect their operations and, consequently, their legal relationships with their coinholders.

Thereafter, we turn to the market for these digital assets. Data reveal explosive growth in total stablecoin supply, expanding from virtually nothing in 2014 to over $250 billion in mid-2025.[5] We then document how stablecoin use cases are increasing rapidly, extending beyond their original role as niche trading instruments to now encompass decentralized financial infrastructure, cross-border payments, and emerging retail and institutional applications. Our assessment emphasizes not merely current conditions but also the dramatic transformation over the past decade, revealing patterns of boom, contraction, and recovery. This trajectory, in turn, helps illuminate the fundamental dynamics of this sector.

The key challenge for our analysis is the pronounced heterogeneity of the stablecoin landscape. Fully appreciating this diversity is a prerequisite not only for an accurate assessment of the problems that currently exist but also for developing successful solutions, whether through private ordering arrangements or regulatory intervention.

8.1.1 From cryptocurrencies to stablecoins

As we explained in the introduction, the first use case for tokens recorded in DLT networks was digital cash. To be sure, this ambition was not new. Several non-DLT projects—including DigiCash's eCash, Wei Dai's B-money, and Nick Szabo's Bit Gold—had all unsuccessfully attempted to create forms of digital cash.[6] Bitcoin, however, was the first successful implementation, and it was subsequently followed by other DLT-based digital assets such as Litecoin, Zcash, and even Dogecoin.[7] Hence, the moniker "cryptocurrencies" was born to describe digital assets with a payment function. Though the digital assets landscape has since expanded to include other uses, such as Ether and SOL, which run code on their respective networks, and NFTs functioning as unique data objects, the payment function remains persistent and foundational to the whole ecosystem.

Nevertheless, despite capturing the interest of the public and generating enormous hype, it has long been apparent that businesses and consumers

[5] *Stablecoins Offer Another Way to Move Money*, Morgan Stanley (June 16, 2025), https://www.morganstanley.com/insights/articles/stablecoins-change-how-money-moves.

[6] For DigiCash, see David Chaum, *Blind Signatures for Untraceable Payments*, *in* Advances in Cryptology 199 (David Chaum, Ronald L. Rivest & Alan T. Sherman, 1983). For b-money, see *B-Money [1998]*, Wei Dai, http://www.weidai.com/bmoney.txt (last visited Aug. 21, 2025). For Bit Gold, see Nick Szabo, *Bit Gold*, Unenumerated (Dec. 27, 2008), https://unenumerated.blogspot.com/2005/12/bit-gold.html.

[7] For a general overview, see Litecoin, https://litecoin.org (last visited Aug. 21, 2025); Zcash, https://z.cash (last visited Aug. 21, 2025); Dogecoin, https://dogecoin.com (last visited Aug. 21, 2025).

generally do not, in fact, use cryptocurrencies as cash to pay for goods and services in the real world.[8] There is a twofold explanation for this. First, owners of these digital assets primarily acquire them as a store of value investment. They hope the assets will appreciate over time with increased participation in DLT networks. Second, the price of these cryptocurrencies is extremely volatile.[9] For example, Bitcoin was priced at about $29,000 at the end of 2020, surged to almost $57,000 by November 2021, reverted to $20,000 by June 2022, before rocketing to over $100,000 in early 2025.[10] Moreover, this cryptocurrency has exhibited substantial daily volatility throughout its existence, averaging between 4 and 5 percent during 2013 to 2021 (including 4.56 percent in 2021). While this volatility has shown some decline since 2022, it remains significantly elevated compared to traditional currencies.[11] These sharp fluctuations occur because the prices of cryptocurrencies are primarily driven by supply and demand, and are profoundly influenced by market sentiment.[12] As a result, for both consumers and businesses, Bitcoin and similar payment coins are extremely uneconomical, if not outright unworkable, as a currency for pricing goods, services, assets, and liabilities. This is especially true when compared to government-backed currencies, which typically exhibit a minimal volatility of between 0.5 and 1.0 percent.[13]

Stablecoins were designed to overcome these obstacles. They are a digital asset class designed to combine all the technological strengths of DLT networks, such as disintermediation, cryptographic security, and transactional transparency, with the low volatility of traditional, government-backed currencies.[14] Despite variations in type, the cardinal feature that unites all stablecoins is their design with the primary purpose of maintaining a stable price relative to a specified asset or a basket of assets (generally referred to as the *peg*).[15] However, beyond this shared common denominator, there is no generally accepted definition of a stablecoin, largely due to the enormous diversity in their technical

[8] *See* Bruce, Odinet & Tosato, *supra* note 1, at 1088 n.81.

[9] *See* Dirk G. Baur & Thomas Dimpfl, *The Volatility of Bitcoin and Its Role as a Medium of Exchange and a Store of Value*, 61 Empirical Econ. 2663, 2665 (2021).

[10] *See Bitcoin (BTC) Price*, Coindesk, https://www.coindesk.com/price/bitcoin (last visited July 29, 2025).

[11] *See Bitcoin Volatility Index*, Bitbo, https://bitbo.io/volatility/[https://perma.cc/23FQ-A8NG] (last visited July 24, 2025).

[12] Adam Hayes, *What Factors Give Cryptocurrencies Their Value: An Empirical Analysis* 6 (New Sch. for Soc. Rsch., Dep't of Econ., Working Paper No. 06/2014, 2014), https://www.economicpolicyresearch.org/images/docs/research/nssr_working_papers/NSSR_WP_062014.pdf [https://perma.cc/U2LR-328M].

[13] *See generally* Baur & Dimpfl, *supra* note 9; see also *Bitcoin Volatility Index*, *supra* note 11.

[14] Shobhit Seth, *Is Stablecoin the Answer to All Cryptocurrency Problems?*, Investopedia (July 20, 2022), https://www.investopedia.com/tech/stablecoin-answer-all-cryptocurrency-problems/ [https://perma.cc/UK2D-H4HM].

[15] *See* Dirk Bullmann, Jonas Klemm, & Andrea Pinna, *In Search for Stability in Crypto-Assets: Are Stablecoins the Solution?* 9 (Eur. Cent. Bank Occasional Paper Series No. 230, 2019).

implementation, organizational structure, and economic models.[16] For our purposes, this heterogeneity has deep legal implications and must be carefully understood for any meaningful private law analysis.[17]

8.1.2 The variable geometry of stablecoins

The stablecoin landscape is vast and varied. The past five years in particular have witnessed extraordinary growth, with hundreds of projects launching across multiple DLT networks and experimenting with an array of economic models and organizational arrangements. This diversity[18] renders exhaustive classification an exercise better left to economists and computer scientists.[19] Rather, we largely adopt the analytical framework suggested by Amani Moin, Emin Gün Sirer, and Kevin Sekniqi,[20] examining the most economically and conceptually significant stablecoins. We then break them down into three constitutive elements that, in our view, have the most consequences when it comes to private law.

(a) The issuer

The first constitutive element is the *issuer*. In contrast to the ethos of many participants in the DLT ecosystem, the majority of stablecoins are in fact

[16] Institutions provide various definitions. *See* Fin. Stability Bd., Regulation, Supervision and Oversight of "Global Stablecoin" Arrangements 12 (2021), https://www.fsb.org/wp-content/uploads/P071021.pdf [https://perma.cc/LRA7-BNTF]; Erik Feyen, Jon Frost, Harish Natarajan, & Tara Rice, *What Does Digital Money Mean for Emerging Market and Developing Economies?* 1 (Bank for Int'l Settlements, BIS Working Paper No. 973, 2021), https://www.bis.org/publ/work973.pdf [https://perma.cc/X5KF-F7ZG]; Bullmann, Klemm, & Pinna, *supra* note 15, at 1, 10–11; Swiss Fin. Mkt. Supervisory Auth. (FINMA), Supplement to the Guidelines 1–4 (2019), https://www.finma.ch/~/media/finma/dokumente/dokumentencenter/myfinma/1bewilligung/fintech/wegleitung-stable-coins.pdf?sc_lang=en&hash=178A9017323F2FB01B195BA446F41F19 [https://perma.cc/TS5S-WWQQ] [hereinafter FINMA]; Int'l Telecomm. Union, Taxonomy and Definition of Terms for Digital Fiat Currency 10 (2019) (focus group technical report).

[17] This heterogeneity is acknowledged by regulators worldwide. *See* Bd. of the Int'l Org. of Sec. Comm'ns, Global Stablecoin Initiatives: Public Report 3–4 (Mar. 2020), https://www.iosco.org/library/pubdocs/pdf/IOSCOPD650.pdf [https://perma.cc/BR7E-TV8W].

[18] For a census of major stablecoin projects, see Amani Moin, Emin Gün Sirer & Kevin Sekiqi, *A Classification Framework for Stablecoin Designs*, arXiv.org 1, 22–24 app. B (Sept. 18, 2019), https://arxiv.org/pdf/1910.10098.pdf [https://perma.cc/EV8M-6F4E].

[19] The body of scholarship on stablecoin classifications is vast and expanding. *See* Haseeb Qureshi, *Stablecoins: Designing a Price-Stable Cryptocurrency*, Hackernoon (Feb. 9, 2018), https://hackernoon.com/stablecoins-designing-a-price-stable-cryptocurrency-6bf24e2689e5 [https://perma.cc/KB7U-H2Z7]; Ingolf G. A. Pernice, Sebastian Henningsen, Roman Proskalovich, Martin Florian, Hermann Elendner & Björn Scheuermann, *Monetary Stabilization in Cryptocurrencies—Design Approaches and Open Questions*, arXiv.org (May 28, 2019), https://arxiv.org/pdf/1905.11905.pdf [https://perma.cc/RJ5N-5DC7].

[20] *See* Moin, Sirer & Sekniqi, *supra* note 18, at 1–2.

centralized, as they are issued and managed by identifiable corporate entities.[21] Centralized issuers have complete control over the design, operation, minting, and burning of their stablecoins. Crucially, from the perspective of coin holders, these entities constitute identifiable counterparties with which they can interact and, possibly, enter into a contractual relationship with defined rights and obligations.

For example, USDT is issued by Tether International, S.A. de C.V., a company incorporated in El Salvador with several subsidiaries worldwide.[22] The stablecoin USDC is issued by Circle International Financial, a Delaware corporation with multiple subsidiaries and branches that completed its initial public offering in June 2025 on the New York Stock Exchange under ticker CRCL.[23] PAXG and GUSD are issued by the Paxos Trust Company and the Gemini Trust Company, respectively; both are licensed as New York limited trust companies.[24]

Alongside *centralized* stablecoins, there are *decentralized* stablecoins that leverage the distributed computational capabilities of DLT networks, primarily Ethereum. With decentralized stablecoins, a group of software developers, typically collaborating on the basis of an open-source model, deploys a bundle of smart contracts (often collectively referred to as a "protocol") that creates a stablecoin and manages every aspect of its operation, all done automatically pursuant to its code.[25] Updates and modifications to the protocol, and in turn the stablecoin, are effectuated following whatever internal governance arrangement has been adopted by the software developers.[26] This can range from democratic voting by protocol users to technocratic decisions by the project founder. The largest decentralized stablecoins are DAI (recently rebranded to USDS) and Ethena USDe, which are controlled by the MakerDAO (now rebranded

[21] *See* Opeyemi Quadri, *Who Are the Issuers of the Top 20 Stablecoins?*, INFOMEDIANG (June 20, 2025), https://infomediang.com/issuers-of-the-top-20-stablecoins/ [https://perma.cc/V28R-ZDZ5].

[22] The corporate structure behind USDT is opaque and has changed significantly over time. *See* David Yaffe-Bellany, *The Coin That Could Wreck Crypto*, N.Y. TIMES (June 17, 2022), https://www.nytimes.com/2022/06/17/technology/tether-stablecoin-cryptocurrency.html.

[23] *USD Coin: Crypto That's Held to a Higher Standard*, CIRCLE, https://www.circle.com/en/usdc [https://perma.cc/5S7D-49CK] (last visited Sept. 7, 2025); Press Release, Circle Internet Group, Inc., Circle Announces Pricing of Upsized Initial Public Offering (June 4, 2025), https://investor.circle.com/news/news-details/2025/Circle-Announces-Pricing-of-Upsized-Initial-Public-Offering/default.aspx.

[24] *Pax Gold (PAXG)*, PAXOS, https://paxos.com/paxgold/ [https://perma.cc/2JRJ-QDYC] (last visited Oct. 30, 2022); *Gemini Dollar (GUSD)*, GEMINI, https://www.gemini.com/dollar [https://perma.cc/LD4W-DGRX] (last visited Oct. 30, 2022).

[25] *See* WHARTON BLOCKCHAIN & DIGIT. ASSET PROJECT, DEFI BEYOND THE HYPE: THE EMERGING WORLD OF DECENTRALIZED FINANCE 9–10 (2021), https://wifpr.wharton.upenn. edu/wp-content/uploads/2021/05/DeFi-Beyond-the-Hype.pdf [https://perma.cc/E7MH-SGBV] [hereinafter DEFI BEYOND THE HYPE].

[26] *See id.* at 5–6.

as Sky) and Ethena protocols on the Ethereum network, respectively.[27] For example, a person can obtain DAI by transferring certain types of digital assets, such as Ether and other volatile cryptocurrencies, to wallets controlled by the MakerDAO protocol.[28] The governance of this protocol requires that changes to its code must be voted on by holders of another crypto-asset called Maker Token (recently rebranded to Sky token).

Crucially, MakerDAO and similar protocols are, in essence, software programs made available to the public, which individuals use entirely at their own risk. Holders of these stablecoins do not enter into any formal or informal agreements with the software developers in charge of these protocols. Moreover, there are typically express liability disclaimers with respect to claims against the software developers, as is customary with open-source projects.

(b) The peg

The second constitutive element is the *peg*.[29] The choice of the reference asset is one of the most salient for a stablecoin project as it determines its volatility in absolute terms. Because stablecoins are designed to move in unison with their peg, choosing a volatile reference asset results in a volatile stablecoin. At present, almost all stablecoins are pegged to either a currency or a precious metal.[30] In the former group, the US dollar is the most common choice.[31] The largest stablecoins by market capitalization, including USDT, USDC, DAI, Ethena USDe, USD1, FDUSD, PYUSD, and TUSD are all pegged to the US dollar on a 1:1 basis: one

[27] For the market capitalization of DAI, see *Top Stablecoin Tokens by Market Capitalization*, CoinMarketCap, https://coinmarketcap.com/view/stablecoin/ [https://perma.cc/CBR3-MPAQ] (last visited Aug. 15, 2025); Zoltán Vardai, *Maker DeFi Lending Protocol Rebrands to Sky Ahead of USDS Stablecoin Launch*, Cointelegraph (Aug. 27, 2024), https://cointelegraph.com/news/maker-rebrands-sky-launches-usds-sky-token; *Ethena's New Stablecoin Revolution*, Coinrank (June 27, 2024), https://www.coinrank.io/learn/ethenas-new-stablecoin-revolution/ [https://perma.cc/EN5D-XK9C]; Liam Miller, *Ethena Deep Dive: Understand USDe and ENA Token*, NFT Evening (June 11, 2025), https://nftevening.com/ethena-deep-dive-understand-usde-and-ena-token/ [https://perma.cc/KR4X-BLUL]

[28] *See The Maker Protocol: MakerDAO's Multi-Collateral Dai (MCD) System*, MakerDAO, https://web.archive.org/web/20240415212520/https://makerdao.com/da/whitepaper/ [https://perma.cc/32LZ-BMXM] (last visited Apr 15, 2024) [hereinafter *Maker White Paper*].

[29] Bruce, Odinet & Tosato, *supra* note 1, at 1093–94.

[30] *See id.* at 1107 n.113.

[31] As of mid-2025, roughly 99 percent of stablecoin market capitalization remains denominated in US dollars. *See* Christopher J. Waller, *Reflections on a Maturing Stablecoin Market*, Bd. of Governors of the Fed. Reserve Sys. (Feb. 12, 2025), https://www.federalreserve.gov/newsevents/speech/waller20250212a.htm. Nonetheless, there are also stablecoins pegged to other currencies. For example, Tether issues stablecoins pegged to multiple currencies, including the Euro, Chinese Yuan (CNH₮), and Mexican peso. *See Tether Launches Offshore Chinese Yuan (CNH₮) on Tron*, Tether (Dec. 6, 2022), https://tether.io/news/tether-launches-offshore-chinese-yuan-cnht-on-tron/; Sandeep Baghel, *Top Non-USD Stablecoins and Why We Need Them*, AuroBlocks (Sept. 4, 2023), https://www.auroblocks.com/blog/top-non-usd-stablecoins-and-why-we-need-them.

coin equals $1.[32] The reasons for this choice are that the US dollar is presently the world's reserve currency, it has relatively low volatility, and it is commonly used to set reference prices for commodities and other widely traded assets.[33]

In the group of stablecoins tied to precious metals, gold is the favored peg, with PAXG, XAUT, and G-COIN as notable examples.[34] There are also projects that use platinum and silver as their reference assets, yet their market capitalization is significantly smaller.[35] Though precious metals have a history of price fluctuations far exceeding those of fiat currencies, the purported strength of these stablecoins is that they enable their holders both to store value in an asset not linked to a government and to enjoy the technological strengths of DLT.

(c) The stabilization mechanism

The third constitutive element is the *price stabilization mechanism.* To retain a stable price relative to their peg, each stablecoin must implement mechanisms to absorb the volatility caused by holders freely trading their coins in the open market.[36] This component most significantly affects the structure and operation of a stablecoin, exhibits the greatest diversity in approaches to implementation across projects, and, as we discuss below, carries the most far-reaching private law implications.[37]

At present, three stabilization mechanisms are prevalent in the market. The first involves issuers holding reserves of valuable assets and committing both to mint and redeem their stablecoins at a predetermined rate.[38] The two largest stablecoins by market capitalization, USDT (Tether) and USDC (Circle), are built on this kind of price stabilization system.[39] Issuers hold large asset pools and undertake, on the one hand, to supply one of their coins to anyone who tenders $1 and, on the other hand, to allow coinholders to redeem their coins in

[32] Logan Jacoby & Rachel Christian, *World's 6 Largest Stablecoins: Top Cryptocurrencies That Maintain a Stable Price*, BANKRATE (July 11, 2025), https://www.bankrate.com/investing/worlds-largest-stablecoins/[https://perma.cc/GBT3-W8F4].

[33] *See* Paul Krugman, *Wonking Out: Why the Dollar Dominates*, N.Y. TIMES (Apr. 15, 2022), https://www.nytimes.com/2022/04/15/opinion/us-dollar-dominance.html.

[34] *See* Bruce, Odinet & Tosato, *supra* note 1, at 1094 n.117. As of August 2025, the total supply of gold-backed stablecoins reached a record $1.4 billion, with PAX Gold (PAXG) and Tether Gold (XAUt) as the category leaders. *See PAX Gold (PAXG) Price, Market Cap & News*, COINMARKETCAP, https://coinmarketcap.com/currencies/pax-gold/ [https://perma.cc/RPQ6-YWW8] (last visited Aug. 27, 2025); *Tether Gold (XAUt) Price, Market Cap & News*, COINMARKETCAP, https://coinmarketcap.com/currencies/tether-gold/ [https://perma.cc/P4Y5-9AQW] (last visited Aug. 27, 2025).

[35] *See What Are SilverTokens (SLVT)?*, SILVERTOKEN, https://silvertoken.com/silvertokens/ [https://perma.cc/Y249-RFET] (last visited Oct. 30, 2022); *History*, PALLADIUMCOIN, https://palladiumcoin.com/history [https://perma.cc/S52P-24XU].

[36] *See* Moin, Sirer & Sekniqi, *supra* note 18, at 6–8.

[37] *See id.* at 7–12; *see also* Bullmann, Klemm & Pinna, *supra* note 15, at 9–11.

[38] *See* Moin, Sirer, & Sekniqi, *supra* note 18, at 7–8.

[39] *See Top Stablecoin Tokens by Market Capitalization*, *supra* note 27.

return for $1.[40] In principle, this structure uses economic incentives to suppress price fluctuations.[41] If the market price of one of these stablecoins dips below the price at which its issuer offers to redeem it, arbitrageurs will acquire stablecoins in the open market and immediately redeem them with their issuer to make a profit.[42] Vice versa, if the market price of one of these stablecoins ventures above the issuer's fixed minting price, arbitrageurs will obtain coins from the issuer and then sell them at a profit in the open market (once again, making a profit).[43]

This stabilization mechanism is not novel. It can be traced as far back as the seventeenth century, when several prominent European banks issued notes redeemable for precious metal coins,[44] and it also underpinned the Bretton Woods accord, under which the US dollar was pegged to gold.[45] Its viability is dependent on market participants trusting that the issuer has sufficient resources to honor its commitment to mint and, especially, redeem stablecoins at the predetermined rate. It follows, as we describe below, that the contractual terms pursuant to which issuers promise to perform these operations and manage their reserves are of the utmost importance.

For stablecoins adopting this stabilization mechanism, establishing a robust custodial structure for their reserves and choosing which assets to hold are also fundamental design choices that may vary significantly across issuers. Tether serves as a prime example of the complexity of these arrangements. The composition of its reserves has evolved considerably, shifting from a diverse mix of cash, commercial paper, secured loans, and crypto assets to a portfolio now dominated by US Treasury securities.[46] Simultaneously, the company has restructured its custodial arrangements, shifting from financial institutions in the Bahamas and Cayman Islands to the US financial services firm Cantor Fitzgerald for reserve custody. It has also changed the firm responsible for attesting to its reserves from Moore Cayman to BDO Italia.[47]

[40] Notably, Tether has a history of releasing coins in tranches without visibility of whether an equivalent amount of dollars has been tendered. *See* John M. Griffin & Amin Shams, *Is Bitcoin Really Un-Tethered?*, 75 J. Am. Fin. Ass'n 1913, 1918 (2020).

[41] *See* Moin, Sirer & Sekniqi, *supra* note 18, at 7–8.

[42] *Id.* at 7.

[43] *Id.*

[44] *See* Jon Frost, Hyun Song Shin && Peter Wierts, *An Early Stablecoin? The Bank of Amsterdam and the Governance of Money* (Monetary & Econ. Dep't, Bank for Int'l Settlements, BIS Working Paper No. 902, 2020), https://www.bis.org/publ/work902.pdf [https://perma.cc/5TX7-9ZZ9].

[45] James Chen, *Bretton Woods Agreement and the Institutions It Created Explained*, Investopedia (Mar. 21, 2022), https://www.investopedia.com/terms/b/brettonwoodsagreement.asp [https://perma.cc/87NK-HG79].

[46] *See generally Tether Holds $127 Billion in U.S. Treasury Bonds for USDT Stability*, Coin World (July 15, 2025, 11:24 AM), https://www.ainvest.com/news/tether-holds-127-billion-treasury-bonds-usdt-stability-2507/.

[47] David Jeans, *Billions of Tether's Reserves Were Stored at Cantor Fitzgerald, Capital Union and Ansbacher*, Forbes (Feb. 10, 2023), https://www.forbes.com/sites/davidjeans/2023/02/10/tether-reserves-cantor-capital-union-ansbacher/; Hannah Lang & Elizabeth Howcroft, *Tether Is in Talks*

Beyond this centralized fiat-backed model, issuers of stablecoins pegged to precious metals typically hold reserves in-kind, keep their assets with specialized custodians, and may segregate the metals backing the coins of each stablecoin holder.[48] In contrast, decentralized stablecoins deploy software mechanisms that maintain reserves directly through DLT structures, without relying on financial institutions as custodians. MakerDAO illustrates this model: When individuals create DAIs, the reserves backing their stablecoins are held in individual "vaults" (smart contracts) managed by the MakerDAO protocol on the Ethereum network.[49]

Another important aspect for issuers implementing this stabilization mechanism is the ratio of reserves held to stablecoins minted. The industry commonly employs three models, though the terminology used can be misleading. Some projects hold or purport to hold assets sufficient to meet redemptions for all their stablecoins at any moment in time. This model is commonly described as *fully collateralized*.[50] Others hold assets that significantly exceed the value of their stablecoins in circulation. This model is commonly referred to as *overcollateralized*. This model is typically the choice of issuers with reserves that are mostly comprised of volatile assets, especially crypto assets.[51] Still others hold only *fractional reserves*. In this case, the aggregate value of the stablecoins the issuer mints exceeds the value of their reserves.

A second mechanism to stabilize the price of a stablecoin involves a *dual coin structure*.[52] Issuers create a primary coin (the stablecoin) whose price is tied to the peg and, alongside it, create a secondary coin designed to absorb volatility swings in the primary coin. One implementation of this dual coin model is the *seigniorage shares* system.[53] Under this model, if the price of the stablecoin dips below its peg, the issuer auctions the secondary coin in exchange for stablecoins. Thereafter, the issuer withdraws the stablecoins acquired through this auction from circulation, thereby contracting the supply and causing the price to return to the peg.[54] If the price of the stablecoin pushes above that of the peg, the

With 'Big Four' Firm About Reserve Audit, CEO Says, Reuters (Mar. 21, 2025), https://www.reuters.com/technology/tether-is-talks-with-big-four-firm-about-reserve-audit-ceo-says-2025-03-21/.

[48] Notably, this is the structure adopted by G-Coin. *See How G-Coin Tokens Are Unique*, Medium (May 6, 2022), https://gcoin.medium.com/how-g-coin-tokens-are-unique-22030640bd37.

[49] *See Maker White Paper*, *supra* note 28.

[50] *See* Moin, Sirer & Sekniqi, *supra* note 18, at 7–8. Notably, this terminology can be misleading since "collateral" typically implies the granting of a security interest by the issuer to stablecoin holders, which, as we show in in later parts of this chapter, almost invariably does not occur.

[51] *See id.* at 3–6.

[52] *See id.* at 8–10.

[53] *Id.*; Robert Sams, *A Note on Cryptocurrency Stabilisation: Seigniorage Shares*, BitMex Blog 1, 3–4 (Apr. 28, 2015), https://blog.bitmex.com/wp-content/uploads/2018/06/A-Note-on-Cryptocurrency-Stabilisation-Seigniorage-Shares.pdf [https://perma.cc/GMQ9-JD6Q].

[54] Moin, Sirer & Sekniqi, *supra* note 18, at 8.

issuer mints additional stablecoins and distributes them to the holders of the secondary coin. This intervention expands the supply of the stablecoin thereby reducing its price and concurrently incentivizing market participants to hold the secondary coin.

A distinct variation of this system aims to soak up price volatility in the primary coin by linking it to the secondary coin through a mechanism of dynamic, bilateral exchanges. For example, the stablecoin is pegged to the US dollar on a 1:1 basis and its holders can exchange it for $1 worth of the secondary coin at any time by interacting with an automated system (i.e., a smart contract). The issuer allows the price of the secondary coin to float freely based on market demand. In this structure, if the price of the primary coin dips below $1, arbitrageurs will, presumably, acquire it and exchange it for $1 worth of the secondary coin, netting a profit. Conversely, if the price of the stablecoin rises above $1, arbitrageurs will presumably do the opposite: acquire $1 worth of the secondary coin and immediately trade it for the primary coin, thereby expanding its supply and ultimately lowering its price.

Notably, no asset reserves support the primary coin. Rather, the viability of the dual-coin stabilization mechanisms is contingent upon the secondary coin retaining value. Issuers only commit to enable holders of the primary coins to exchange them for secondary coins and, in some cases, to support the price of the secondary coin through economic incentives, including access to services, voting rights linked to the governance of a DLT network, and others. Implicitly, holders accept that a collapse in value of the secondary coin may result in their stablecoin losing its peg. In recent years, multiple projects built on dual-coin stabilization mechanisms have failed catastrophically, with far-reaching implications.[55]

A third price stabilization mechanism relies on algorithms that, operating as a quasi-central bank, absorb market price swings by shrinking and expanding the amount of stablecoins in circulation.[56] This approach is based on the theory that crypto asset volatility can be counteracted by elastically adjusting their supply: "[T]he idea is that an X% change in coin price, followed by an X% change in coin supply, will return coin price to its initial value."[57] For example, Ampleforth (AMPL) is a stablecoin pegged to the US dollar on a 1:1 basis.[58] Every twenty-four hours, the algorithm controlling this crypto-asset readjusts the number of coins of each holder (this process is commonly referred to as

[55] *See* Bruce, Odinet & Tosato, *supra* note 1, at 1117.

[56] *See* Moin, Sirer & Sekniqi, *supra* note 18, at 10; *see also* Ryan Clements, *Built to Fail: The Inherent Fragility of Algorithmic Stablecoins*, 11 Wake Forest L. Rev. Online 131, 136–37 (2021).

[57] Sams, *supra* note 53, at 2.

[58] *See About the Ampleforth Protocol*, Ampleforth Docs, https://docs.ampleforth.org/learn/about-the-ampleforth-protocol [https://perma.cc/Y2Y8-PQK9] (last visited Sept. 6, 2025).

"rebasing"). The software increases or decreases the number of coins of each holder proportionally, depending on whether the price of AMPL has ventured above or below $1 respectively. The rebasing process is elastic and non-dilutive, as it only affects the number of coins of each holder and not their share of the overall supply of AMPL. The challenge for stablecoins implementing this stabilization mechanism is that the only value buttressing these crypto-assets is their scarcity, the stabilization algorithm itself, and possibly economic incentives provided by their issuers. If market participants lose confidence in this value proposition, these stablecoins inevitably collapse, leaving their holders with no recourse against their issuers.

8.1.3 Stablecoin business models

The heterogeneity of stablecoins extends to the approaches adopted by issuers to generate returns. Typically, there are four main revenue strategies.

The first pathway is for an issuer to charge fees for the issuance, redemption, and transfer of its stablecoins.[59] For example, Tether imposes a transaction minimum of $100,000 both for minting and redeeming USDT and charges 0.1 percent as acquisition fee, while the redemption fee is the greater of $1,000 or 0.1 percent, whichever yields a higher amount.[60] Stablecoins pegged to commodities often have particularly high fees due to the significant expenses incurred in maintaining reserves in kind.[61]

It should be noted that issuance, redemption, and transfer fees can have a negative impact on the stability of a stablecoin.[62] As explained above, most stabilization mechanisms, directly or indirectly, rely on arbitrageurs stepping in to take advantage of any price deviation of a stablecoin from its peg. If fees are charged, arbitrageurs will only act when the spread between the stablecoin's price and its peg exceeds the issuer's fees.

Alternatively, a second avenue through which issuers can generate returns is to actively trade their own stablecoin. They can participate in the market as arbitrageurs, profiting when the price of their coins diverges from the peg. Issuers can also act as market-makers by facilitating trades involving their own stablecoin and taking advantage of the bid/ask spread. This can be especially lucrative if issuers operate their own exchange, as is the case with Gemini and Binance.[63] However, these activities are capital-intensive and involve assuming

[59] *See* Bruce, Odinet & Tosato, *supra* note 1, at 1098 n.156.

[60] *See Fees*, TETHER, https://tether.to/en/fees (last visited Aug. 16, 2025).

[61] *See* Bruce, Odinet & Tosato, *supra* note 1, at 1098–99.

[62] *See* Moin, Sirer & Sekniqi, *supra* note 18, at 14–15.

[63] *See* Bruce, Odinet & Tosato, *supra* note 1, at 1100 n.161.

significant trading risks in loosely regulated markets. Indeed, many issuers that have trodden this pathway have incurred substantial losses and even destabilized their own stablecoin.

A third pathway to generate returns involves the use of reserves as investment capital. Issuers that mint and redeem stablecoins at a predetermined rate effectively accept funds with an obligation to return them on demand at an indeterminate future moment.[64] Crucially, issuers typically do not owe interest on the funds they receive from stablecoin holders.[65] Therefore, they can use their reserves as lending capital or to invest in debt securities, equities, commodities, or other digital assets to generate returns.

The risk profile of this strategy, however, has changed dramatically since 2022. Previously, in a decade-long environment of near-zero interest rates, stablecoin issuers faced significant investment risk, essentially operating as portfolio managers seeking profitable investments while facing potential losses that could compromise their ability to cover all outstanding stablecoins. But beginning in 2022, the Federal Reserve raised interest rates from near zero to over 4 percent, thereby fundamentally altering this dynamic. Suddenly, issuers of stablecoins that were pegged to the dollar gained access to a relatively low-risk avenue for generating substantial returns. All they had to do was hold their reserves in short-term US Treasury bills or equivalent cash instruments.

As shown in Figure 8.1 and Figure 8.2, the evolution of Tether's reserve composition vividly illustrates this pivot. In early 2022, US Treasury bills constituted 70 percent of its reserves. By mid-2025, that figure had climbed to over 80 percent as the company shifted its holdings to capitalize on higher yields from government debt. It is noteworthy, however, that even in 2025, approximately 17 percent of Tether's holdings still consist of a combination of precious metals, bitcoin, and secured loans, suggesting a continued pursuit of higher returns despite the accompanying risk of losses.

Circle's recent financial disclosures provide an even starker illustration of this dynamic.[66] The company's S-1 filing reveals a dramatic turnaround from a net loss of over $768 million in 2022 to substantial profitability in 2023 and 2024.[67] This swing was not driven by operational efficiencies or new product adoption, but rather almost entirely by the Federal Reserve's shift in monetary policy. Notably, interest and dividends on its cash and short-term US Treasury securities reserves accounted for 95.3 percent, 98.6 percent, and 99.1 percent of

[64] Sungyu Kwon, *How Do Stablecoins Make Money?*, BENZINGA (Nov. 25, 2024), https://www.benzinga.com/money/how-do-stablecoins-make-money [https://perma.cc/W6WQ-BWU7].

[65] *See* Bruce, Odinet & Tosato, *supra* note 1, at 1100 n.165.

[66] Circle Internet Grp., Inc., Amend. No. 3 to SEC Registration Statement S-1 (Form S-1/A), 156–57 [hereinafter Circle, Form S-1], https://www.sec.gov/Archives/edgar/data/1876042/000119312525126208/d737521ds1a.htm.

[67] *Id.* at 32.

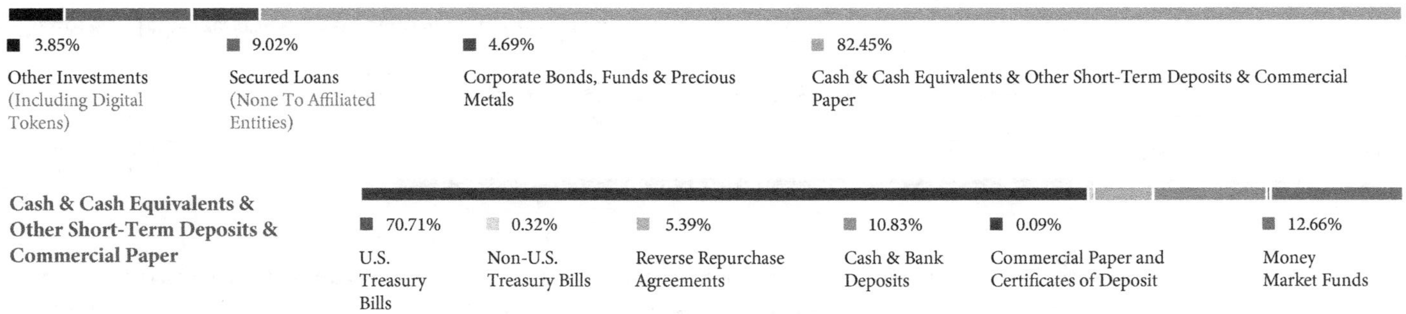

Figure 8.1 Tether reserve asset breakdown as of January 2022.

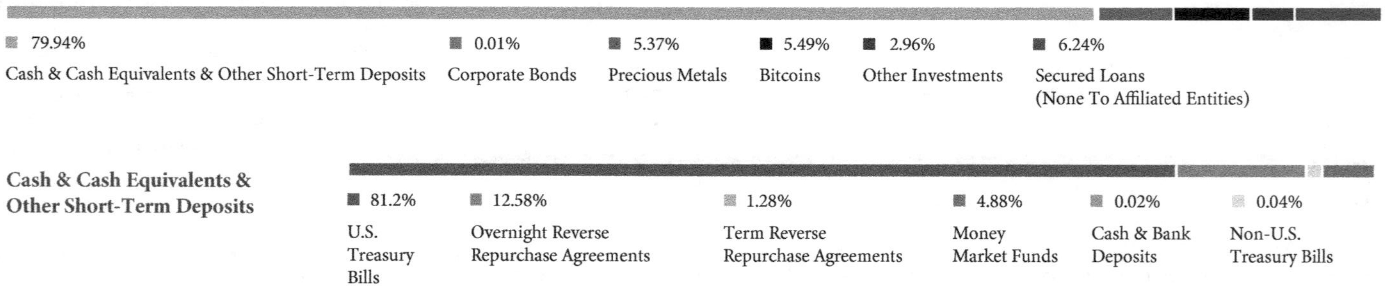

Figure 8.2 Tether reserve asset breakdown as of June 2025.

total revenue for the fiscal years 2022, 2023, and 2024, respectively.[68] In essence, Circle's business model has transformed into that of a non-bank cash management operation, monetizing the collective balance of its stablecoin holders and functioning as a direct proxy for US interest rates.

A fourth avenue for revenue generation involves pursuing a loss leader strategy.[69] Under this model, issuers operate their stablecoin at minimal or no profit to attract users to their broader ecosystem. Instead, revenues are generated through other services, including payment processing, trading and custody fees, and lending. As such, the stablecoins serve as a synergistic entry point that can effectively channel customers and liquidity into the issuer's platform.

This strategy was famously deployed by Binance, which aggressively promoted its BUSD stablecoin by offering zero-fee trading pairs and even autoconverting customer balances from competing stablecoins.[70] While this tactic was highly effective, it also attracted intense regulatory scrutiny, culminating in a 2023 order from New York regulators that halted new issuance of BUSD and effectively began its phaseout.[71] More recent examples of this ecosystem strategy include PayPal's issuance of its PYUSD stablecoin to integrate with its vast payment network.[72]

Thus, the business model adopted by issuers is highly consequential. Different models create vastly different risk profiles, and some introduce an inherent tension between the issuer's pursuit of revenues and the stability of their stablecoin. This risk is compounded by the fact that these profit-seeking strategies are not static. As the rapid pivot following the Federal Reserve's rate hikes illustrates, issuers' approaches can shift rapidly. To make matters worse, issuers often provide limited transparency regarding the strategies deployed to generate those revenues. Given this combination of diverse business models, their potential for rapid transformation, and limited transparency, understanding the contractual and proprietary rights of stablecoin holders becomes crucial.

[68] *Id.* at 57.

[69] *See generally* Attila Ambrus & Jonathan Weinstein, *Price Dispersion and Loss Leaders*, 3 Theoretical Econ. 525, 525 (2008).

[70] *Binance Extends BUSD Zero Maker Fee & Zero Trading Fee Promotion for Seven USD Stablecoin Pairs*, Binance (June 17, 2022), https://www.binance.com/en/support/announcement/detail/9327c312af5e41048756693c46f732ed; *Binance to Auto-Convert USDC, USDP, TUSD to BUSD (Binance USD)*, Binance (Sept. 5, 2022), https://www.binance.com/en/support/announcement/detail/e62f703604a94538a1f1bc803b2d579f.

[71] *See Notice Regarding Paxos-Issued BUSD, Consumer Alert*, N.Y. State Dep't of Fin. Servs. (Feb. 13, 2023), https://www.dfs.ny.gov/consumers/alerts/Paxos_and_Binance.

[72] *See* Aisha Malik, *PayPal Launches PYUSD Stablecoin for Payments and Transfers*, Techcrunch (Aug. 7, 2023), https://techcrunch.com/2023/08/07/paypal-launches-pyusd-stablecoin-for-payments-and-transfers.

8.1.4 Market size

The market for stablecoins was birthed in 2014, when Tether launched USDT.[73] For the next four years, this pioneering digital asset attracted limited capital, remaining little known, little understood, and little used by market participants.[74] Eventually, USDT was joined by new entrants DAI and USDC, with stablecoins pegged to precious metals making their debut in late 2019. Despite these developments, the aggregate float of all stablecoins remained modest, totaling less than US $3 billion by year's end.[75]

The market then entered a period of explosive, chaotic growth between 2020 and early 2022, with a proliferation of new stablecoins launching to capture market share. This boom, however, gave way to a brutal contraction, as the "crypto winter" of 2022 crushed several prominent stablecoins, exposing fundamental design flaws and vulnerabilities. Most notably, the stablecoin TerraUSD collapsed almost overnight, wiping out tens of billions in value in May 2022.[76] But reserve-backed, centrally issued stablecoins also suffered: HUSD experienced damaging de-pegging from which it never recovered,[77] and the undercollateralized Waves-linked USDN was forced into wind-down after repeated liquidity crises.[78] In April 2022, Beanstalk Farms (a credit-based stablecoin protocol) lost approximately $182 million in a flash-loan governance exploit that drained its treasury overnight.[79] After a quieter 2023, the market began a robust recovery in 2024, which accelerated into 2025. This renewed growth has been fueled by increased consumer and institutional interest, clearer regulatory pathways in jurisdictions like the EU, and a more favorable political and legislative outlook in the United States.[80]

[73] *See* Bruce, Odinet & Tosato, *supra* note 1, at 1102 n.173.

[74] For a brief early history, see *The History of Stablecoins: The Reason They Were Created*, OriginStamp, https://perma.cc/2P3M-84GK (last visited Feb. 11, 2023). *See also* Jonathan Bier, *A Brief History of Stablecoins (Part 1)*, BitMEX (July 2, 2018), https://blog.bitmex.com/a-brief-history-of-stablecoins-part-1/ [https://perma.cc/U2XF-SGFW].

[75] Dune & Artemis, The State of Stablecoins 2025: Supply, Adoption & Market Trends 1 (Mar. 2025), https://perma.cc/HE67-NWH2; *see also* Artemis Analytics et al., Stablecoin Payments: From the Ground Up (May 2025), https://reports.artemisanalytics. com/stablecoins/artemis-stablecoin-payments-from-the-ground-up-2025.pdf.

[76] Notably, a similarly structured stablecoin, Iron Finance's IRON, had suffered a similar fate in 2021. *See* Bruce, Odinet & Tosato, *supra* note 1, at 1118–19.

[77] Samuel Haig, *HUSD Stablecoin Delisted After Losing Its Dollar Peg*, The Defiant (Nov. 1, 2022), https://thedefiant.io/news/defi/husd-stablecoin-delisted-after-losing-its-dollar-peg.

[78] Fran Velasquez, *Undercollateralized USDN Stablecoin Needs Tweaking, Waves Founder Says*, CoinDesk (May 11, 2023), https://www.coindesk.com/layer2/2022/06/01/undercollateralized-usdn-stablecoin-needs-tweaking-waves-founder-says.

[79] Corin Faife, *Beanstalk Cryptocurrency Project Robbed After Hacker Votes to Send Themself $182 Million*, The Verge (Apr. 18, 2022), https://www.theverge.com/2022/4/18/23030754/beanstalk-cryptocurrency-hack-182-million-dao-voting.

[80] *U.S. House Sends "Genius Act" Stablecoin Bill to Trump to Sign*, Reuters (July 17, 2025), https://www.reuters.com/legal/government/us-house-sends-genius-act-stablecoin-bill-trump-sign-2025-07-17/; James Morales, *EU Regulation Supports Tokenized Stock Boom, Euro Stablecoins Could Be*

At the time of writing in mid-2025, the market remains dominated by Tether's USDT (approx. $150b) and Circle's USDC (approx. $60b).[81] However, the landscape of challengers is dynamic. MakerDAO's (now Sky) DAI (now USDS) and Ethena's USDe are the leading decentralized players (approx. $5b each), along with newer entrants like World Liberty Financial's USD1 (approx. $2b), First Digital's FDUSD (approx. $2b), and PayPal's PYUSD (approx. $0.9b), which have also gained significant traction.[82] Notably, with the exception of USDT, USDC, and DAI, this "leaderboard" differs markedly from the one we described in 2022, signaling the dynamism and volatility of this quadrant of the digital assets landscape.[83] In contrast, gold-pegged stablecoins have remained steady, with PAXG (approx. $930m) and XAUT (approx. $822m) retaining their leadership positions, likely due to the higher operational hurdles of managing physically backed reserves.[84]

From an overall market perspective, the total supply of stablecoins has exploded from under $6 billion in early 2020 to over $250 billion by mid-2025.[85] As of February 2025, the Ethereum network hosts 55 percent of all outstanding stablecoins; TRON hosts 28 percent, while the Solana and Base networks account for 5.4 percent and 1.8 percent, respectively.[86] However, despite the stablecoin market representing just over 1 percent of the US M2 money supply (which includes all physical currency, checking accounts, savings accounts, and other easily accessible deposits that make up the broader measure of money circulating in the American economy), stablecoins remain a relatively modest component of the overall financial system.[87] By contrast, US money-market funds managed more than $7 trillion in assets as of June 2025.[88] It is noteworthy, however, that stablecoin issuers have become significant players in the Treasury-bill

Next, CCN (July 12, 2025, 11:32 AM), https://www.ccn.com/news/crypto/eu-regulation-supports-tokenized-stocks-euro-stablecoins-could-follow/.

[81] DUNE & ARTEMIS, *supra* note 75, at 1; *Top Stablecoins by Market Capitalization*, COINMARKETCAP, https://coinmarketcap.com/view/stablecoin/ (last visited Aug. 18, 2025).

[82] COINMARKETCAP, *supra* note 81.

[83] *See* Bruce, Odinet, & Tosato, *supra* note 1, at 1102–6.

[84] *PAX Gold (PAXG)*, COINMARKETCAP, https://coinmarketcap.com/currencies/pax-gold/ (last visited Aug. 18, 2025); *Tether Gold (XAUT)*, COINMARKETCAP, https://coinmarketcap.com/currencies/tether-gold/ (last visited Sept. 5, 2025); Nathan Reiff, *Gold-Backed Cryptocurrencies*, INVESTOPEDIA (July 11, 2024), https://www.investopedia.com/tech/goldpegged-vs-usdpegged-cryptocurrencies/.

[85] DUNE & ARTEMIS, *supra* note 75, at 1; ARTEMIS ANALYTICS ET AL., *supra* note 75.

[86] ARTEMIS ANALYTICS ET AL., *supra* note 75; DUNE & ARTEMIS, *supra* note 75, at 1.

[87] Lorenzo Valente, *Stablecoins Could Become One of the US Government's Most Resilient Financial Allies*, ARK INVEST (June 5, 2025), https://www.ark-invest.com/articles/analyst-research/stablecoins-as-a-us-financial-ally.

[88] Press Release, Inv. Co. Inst., Money Market Fund Assets (June 26, 2025), https://www.ici.org/research/stats/mmf.

market, collectively holding in excess of $120 billion, enough to rank them the eighteenth-largest holder of US government debt worldwide.[89]

8.1.5 Use cases and trading volumes

The growth in stablecoin supply reflects their rapidly expanding adoption. The first (and still quantitatively dominant) use case is to serve as the "base currency" for trading other digital assets.[90] As of mid-2025, more than 60 percent of the aggregate supply of outstanding stablecoins sit in accounts controlled by centralized platforms—such as Coinbase, Binance, and Kraken—thereby providing liquidity and serving as collateral for crypto derivatives and margin trading.[91] Individual and institutional digital asset traders avoid keeping their capital in fiat currencies, as these necessitate the use of slow and costly banks, brokers, and clearinghouses, which lack effective interfaces with DLT networks.[92] By contrast, internal ledger transfers at centralized exchanges allow near-instant settlement and, in many pairs, zero-fee execution.[93] The attraction is amplified by the possibility, sometimes the intention, to sidestep *know-your-customer* (KYC) and *anti-money laundering* (AML) obligations, which are almost inescapable when utilizing fiat on-and-off ramps like depository institutions.

While centralized exchanges warehouse the bulk of stablecoin supply, decentralized finance (DeFi) generates the lion's share of transaction volumes.[94] DeFi encompasses financial services accessible through DLT networks and operated through smart contracts, including lending protocols that match crypto asset lenders and borrowers, yield-generating services that offer returns in exchange for deposits of digital assets, and decentralized autonomous organizations (DAOs) that enable pooled investment based on predetermined criteria.[95] For all these transactions, stablecoins have become the preferred settlement asset over volatile cryptocurrencies because their stability eliminates the risk that sharp price fluctuations will erode prospective returns. Consider how

[89] Gertrude Chavez-Dreyfuss, *US Treasuries Face Stablecoin-Driven Demand Surge As Supply Looms*, Reuters (June 25, 2025) https://www.reuters.com/business/us-treasuries-face-stablecoin-driven-demand-surge-supply-looms-2025-06-25/.

[90] *See* Bruce, Odinet & Tosato, *supra* note 1.

[91] Dune & Artemis, *supra* note 75; Artemis Analytics et al., *supra* note 75.

[92] Bank for Int'l Settlements, The Crypto Ecosystem: Key Elements and Risks 18 (2023), https://www.bis.org/publ/othp72.pdf.

[93] *See The Complete Guide to Coinbase Fees*, CryptoPro, https://cryptopro.app/coinbase-fees-guide/ [https://perma.cc/RV4C-PWPF] (last visited Sept. 6, 2025) ("Coinbase waives fees when converting from USD to its native stablecoin USD Coin (USDC).").

[94] Dune & Artemis, *supra* note 75, at 12.

[95] *See generally* DeFi Beyond the Hype, *supra* note 25, at 1–5; Kara Bruce, Christopher K. Odinet & Andrea Tosato, *Bankrupt Crypto Organizations*, N.C. L. Rev. (forthcoming), https://papers.ssrn.com/sol3/papers.cfm? abstract_id=5115277 [hereinafter Bruce, Tosato & Odinet, *Crypto Orgs*].

this preference is clearly reflected in transaction volumes: In the twelve months prior to February 2025, a little over half of all on-chain stablecoin transfers (which were over US $18 trillion) occurred in DeFi through decentralized exchanges, lending pools, and MEV (maximal extractable value) bots.[96] The insight is that users want to participate in DeFi's profit-generating activities but without gambling on crypto price movements that could wipe out their gains. Stablecoins allow them to do just that.

But the most significant development in stablecoin adoption over the past few years has been their emergence as a preferred medium for cross-border payments and remittances.[97] Stablecoins have captured substantial market share by handling approximately $6.3 trillion in payments over the twelve months prior to February 2025, which is equivalent to 15 percent of global retail cross-border payments.[98] The value proposition goes something like this: Stablecoin-based transfers cost between 0.5 and 3.0 percent compared to traditional remittance fees that average around 6.35 percent, while settling in minutes rather than days and while operating continuously across time zones.[99] This transformation has been particularly pronounced in emerging markets. The DLT system TRON dominates the low-value market, processing more than half of all peer-to-peer stablecoin transfers, consisting largely of USDT remittances into Latin America, West Africa, and South-East Asia.[100] In these markets, where access to banking services is limited or expensive, stablecoins serve as both a payment medium and a hedge against local currency depreciation, with money-service businesses now openly exploiting this infrastructure.[101]

Finally, although still at an early stage, both institutional and retail payment adoption are attracting significant interest.[102] On the institutional front, JPMorgan's JPM Coin now supports euro-denominated payments for corporate clients like Siemens, while PayPal has begun using its PYUSD stablecoin for business-to-business transactions. Major banks—including Bank of America, Wells Fargo, and Japan's three largest banks (MUFG, SMBC, and Mizuho)—are either piloting or preparing to launch their own stablecoin initiatives.[103]

[96] Dune & Artemis, *supra* note 75, at 12.

[97] *Id.*

[98] *Id.*

[99] World Bank Grp., Remittance Prices Worldwide Quarterly (Issue 49, Mar. 2024), https://remittanceprices.worldbank.org/sites/default/files/rpw_main_report_and_annex_q124_final.pdf.

[100] Dune & Artemis, *supra* note 75, at 8–9.

[101] *See* Leigh Cuen, *Brazil's Ailing Economy Is Helping Dollar-Pegged Stablecoins Find Traction*, CoinDesk (May 8, 2023), https://www.coindesk.com/business/2020/07/08/brazils-ailing-economy-is-helping-dollar-pegged-stablecoins-find-traction/ [https://perma.cc/6HJP-49KS].

[102] *Why Stablecoins Are Shifting from Crypto Fringe to Corporate Strategy*, Fin. Times (London) (July 3, 2025), https://www.ft.com/content/6a0de463-6915-48d2-abb5-2e59f8e43bf2.

[103] *JP Morgan Rolls Out JPM Coin Blockchain Payments in Euro*, Ledger Insights (June 23, 2023), https://www.ledgerinsights.com/jp-morgan-jpm-coin-blockchain-payments-euro/; *Japan's Big 3 Banks to Use Stablecoins, Swift for Cross-Border Payments*, Ledger Insights (Sept. 18, 2024), https://www.ledgerinsights.com/japans-big-3-banks-to-use-stablecoins-swift-for-cross-border-payments/.

For retail payments, Visa-backed Gnosis Pay lets EU residents spend on-chain USDC or EURC through an ordinary debit-card.[104] PayPal's PYUSD is live across its merchant network and scheduled for small-business bill-pay in the United States by the end of 2025.[105] Stripe has rolled out stablecoin accounts across 101 countries and enables merchants to accept USDC on the Ethereum, Solana, and Polygon DLT networks.[106] Moreover, a growing number of distributed applications (so-called dApps) operating on DLT networks provide services to the general public in return for payments in stablecoins.[107]

8.2 Decentralized stablecoins through the lens of private law

Having examined the overall structure and market function of stablecoins, we now turn to our private law analysis. To do so, we concentrate on three paradigmatic stablecoins: Tether's USDT,[108] Circle's USDC,[109] and MakerDAO's DAI.[110] From a methods perspective, our selection of these stablecoins is deliberate. As the earliest and most enduring stablecoins, they have consistently maintained the largest supply, making them the most economically significant across the entire ecosystem. More importantly, they exemplify the market's core structural and jurisdictional divides. USDT and USDC are issued by centralized entities, one domiciled offshore and the other in the United States, respectively, while DAI is governed by the decentralized protocol MakerDAO (Sky), thereby transcending a conventional jurisdictional analysis. This combination allows us to conduct both a comprehensive and a comparative private law assessment.

In our examination, we draw upon three categories of materials: the public-facing communications these stablecoin projects present through their websites, blog posts, and promotional content; technical white papers and protocol documentation associated with these stablecoins; and the legal agreements stablecoin issuers establish with their coinholders through terms of service/user

[104] Pedro Solimano, *Gnosis Pay Partners with Visa to Expand Web3 Payments*, THE DEFIANT (May 28, 2024), https://thedefiant.io/news/defi/gnosis-pay-partners-with-visa-to-expand-web3-payments.

[105] Emily Mason, *PayPal Plans to Ramp Up Adoption of Its Stablecoin Through 2025*, BLOOMBERG (Feb. 25, 2025), https://www.bloomberg.com/news/articles/2025-02-25/paypal-plans-to-ramp-up-adoption-of-its-stablecoin-through-2025?embedded-checkout=true.

[106] John Egan, *Introducing Stablecoin Financial Accounts in 101 Countries*, STRIPE (May 20, 2025), https://stripe.com/blog/introducing-stablecoin-financial-accounts.

[107] *See* Bruce, Odinet & Tosato, *supra* note 1, at 1107.

[108] *Legal: Terms of Service*, TETHER, https://tether.to/en/legal/#terms-of-service [https://perma.cc/YXU8-G7KU] (last updated Sept. 2, 2022) [hereinafter *Tether ToS*].

[109] *Legal & Privacy: USDC Terms*, CIRCLE, https://www.circle.com/en/legal/usdc-terms [https://perma.cc/7JJY-5GQL] (last updated Oct. 4, 2024).

[110] *Terms of Service*, SKY, https://docs.sky.money/legal-terms [https://perma.cc/6LFL-2KLX] (last updated July 11, 2022).

agreements. We aim, first, to delineate the mutual rights and obligations between issuers and coinholders, with particular attention to redemption mechanisms and the extent to which coinholders possess proprietary claims to the relevant, underlying reserve assets. Second, we aim to assess the degree of alignment between the representations made in these public-facing materials and the actual legal commitments contained in the formal terms of service/user agreements.

At the outset, we must acknowledge that the following analysis reflects a temporal snapshot of sources available as of July 2025, which are often (if not always) transient and subject to change. Nonetheless, the private law issues we identify are of lasting significance as they reveal challenges that we believe are ontologically inherent to the relevant stablecoin category itself (be it centralized or decentralized).

Having established this comparative framework, we begin with DAI, the most prominent decentralized stablecoin. Our analysis proceeds in five parts. First, we detail the DAI protocol's unique operational scheme, identifying the key actors and the mechanics of DAI's minting and redemption. Second, we examine the significant consequences of the absence of contractual relationships within this ecosystem. Building on this foundation, the third, fourth, and fifth parts of our analysis explore the limited and uncertain legal recourse available to users through property, tort, and fiduciary law, respectively.

8.2.1 Legal documentation and operational mechanics

Assembling the legal documentation governing MakerDAO presents immediate and revealing challenges. The relevant materials are dispersed across multiple websites and refer to different entities. There are legal terms regarding the role of the Dai Foundation as a steward for the intellectual property of MakerDAO, there are separate agreements that apply to the various interfaces through which users can access the protocol, and there are residual documents pertaining to the now-dissolved Maker Foundation.[111] Further complication stems from this stablecoin's recent rebranding initiative.[112] More broadly, this fragmentation does not reflect mere organizational inefficiency, but rather it is a direct consequence of the distributed nature of MakerDAO.

Crucially, unlike with centralized stablecoins, there are no terms of service specifically addressing the issuance, holding, and use of DAI. Instead, the cardinal document is MakerDAO's technical white paper. This text, however, is not

[111] *See Terms of Service*, THE DAI FOUND., https://daifoundation.org/terms-of-service/ [https://perma.cc/P3WY-ZJNY] (last updated Mar. 8, 2021); *Terms*, MAKER FOUND., https://foundation.app/terms [https://perma.cc/5PJQ-FNZB] (last updated May 30, 2024).

[112] *See Introducing Sky*, SKY, https://sky.money/ (last visited Sept. 7, 2025).

a contractual instrument. Rather, this is a descriptive explanation of the technological mechanics underpinning this stablecoin. The private law consequences of this unconventional design are best understood by first examining the protocol's operational scheme.

The Maker Protocol's operations, as detailed in its white paper, involve several distinct groups of actors all interacting with the MakerDAO smart contracts. The first group consists of DAI end users, divided into two types: *DAI Holders* and *Vault Owners.*[113] The former comprises persons who obtain DAI in secondary market transactions, such as those who purchase DAI on cryptocurrency exchanges or who receive DAI as payment. Vault Owners, on the other hand, are the persons who originally mint (create) DAIs. The process is initiated by depositing an approved digital asset into a smart contract known as a Maker Vault.[114] Each Vault is noncustodial and segregated, thereby avoiding the commingling of assets among users. From these locked-in assets, the Maker Protocol allows the Vault Owner to generate DAI up to a specified percentage of the value of the deposited digital asset. The threshold for this percentage varies by digital asset type and is set by the protocol's governance scheme.[115] For example, a person depositing $1,000 worth of the digital asset *Ether* might be able to generate up to $750 worth of DAI.[116]

Beyond end users, the protocol also relies on two other key groups of actors: *Governors* and *Maintainers.* The Governors are primarily the holders of the MKR token (the MakerDAO governance coin), who vote on and directly control the Maker system's parameters, such as which assets are accepted, the rates for Stability Fees, and other critical risk variables.[117] They can also authorize Emergency Shutdown procedures of the entire MakerDAO system. The Maintainers (of which there are multiple subgroups) are a range of independent, economically incentivized actors who perform essential services related to the continued upkeep and operation of the MakerDAO system.[118] As to this subgroup, so-called "Keepers," for example, are market participants who help maintain DAI's price stability by participating in the automated asset auctions.[119] "Oracles" provide the trusted, real-time price feeds that the protocol needs to value assets and trigger the automated disposal of risky Vaults, while developers contribute to the underlying open-source code.[120] "DAO teams" consist of

[113] *Maker White Paper*, *supra* note 28, at 7, 12.
[114] *Id.* at 7.
[115] For a complete list of MakerDAO compatible assets, see *A Guide to Dai Stats*, MAKERDAO (Dec. 15, 2020), https://blog.makerdao.com/a-guide-to-dai-stats/.
[116] *See Maker White Paper*, *supra* note 28, at 14–15.
[117] *Id.*
[118] *Id.* at 19.
[119] *Id.* at 9.
[120] *Id.* at 3, 10–11.

individuals and service providers who may be contracted through governance to provide specific services to the protocol.[121] The Maintainers thus form an umbrella category, encompassing various actors who work collectively to ensure the MakerDAO system's continued operation and stability.

At any moment in time, Vault Owners can redeem DAIs. This is achieved by transferring stablecoins to their Vault along with a "Stability Fee."[122] When they do so, they receive in return the digital assets originally deposited. Importantly, if the dollar value of deposited digital assets falls below a predetermined threshold, the MakerDAO protocol automatically seizes and disposes of those assets through an internal auction mechanism.[123] The protocol then retains proceeds sufficient to cover the outstanding DAI, thereby ensuring that DAI remains pegged to the dollar.[124] This is how its stability mechanism works.

This auction system is the protocol's first line of defense against instability, but its ultimate backstop is the Emergency Shutdown procedure.[125] As a last resort in the face of a severe market event or technical attack, the protocol can trigger a system-wide settlement.[126] When this occurs, the entire protocol freezes, preventing further vault creation or manipulation, and price feeds lock at their last known value. The shutdown process unfolds in three phases: First, vault owners can withdraw digital assets that do not actively support outstanding DAI.[127] Second, any pending asset auctions are completed. And third, DAI holders can claim proportional shares of the remaining asset portfolio at fixed rates based on the DAI target price. If the total value of deposited digital assets in the system is less than the total DAI supply at the time of the shutdown, DAI holders will receive less than one dollar's worth of assets per DAI token.[128] In this way, with the peg being broken, the system begins a sort of liquidation process.

8.2.2 The absence of contractual relationships

The contract law implications of this structure are profound. Most fundamentally, users who mint, hold, or redeem DAIs do not enter into contractual arrangements. Contracts require agreements between two or more parties,[129]

[121] *Id.* at 11.
[122] *Id.* at 7.
[123] *Id.* at 8–9.
[124] *Id.*
[125] *Id.* at 19; *Maker Protocol 101*, Maker Protocol Tech. Docs (Dec. 8, 2020), https://drive.google.com/file/d/1VtGV8Ct2iBO8WjWsjFYLg5DnwlGmetSp/view?pli=1.
[126] *Maker White Paper*, *supra* note 28, at 19; *Maker Protocol 101*, *supra* note 126, at 13.
[127] *Maker Protocol 101*, *supra* note 125, at 63.
[128] *Maker White Paper*, *supra* note 28, at 20.
[129] *See generally* 1 Williston on Contracts § 1:1 (4th ed., May 2025 update), Westlaw WILLSTN-CN § 1:1.

yet no such bilateral or multilateral relationships exist in the MakerDAO landscape. Despite the complex ecosystem involving Vault Owners, DAI Holders, MKR Governors, and various Maintainers, these actors interact directly with autonomous smart contracts rather than entering into agreements with identifiable legal persons. The protocol itself possesses no legal personhood and cannot enter into contractual relationships.[130] This comprehensive absence of contractual counterparties extends across all participant categories, distinguishing MakerDAO fundamentally from traditional financial arrangements.

The MakerDAO white paper and technical document employ terminology that imprecisely, if not misleadingly, suggests bilateral contractual relationships where none exist. The protocol consistently uses terms such as "collateral," "debt," "collateralized debt positions," and "liquidation"—all of which typically denote secured lending arrangements between identifiable parties.[131] This wording confusingly implies that someone is lending DAI to users pursuant to agreed terms, with digital assets serving as security held by a lender. However, in law, this characterization is plainly and unquestionably wrong. While the vault mechanics may functionally echo the dynamics of loans and secured transactions, no such private law relationships exist. There is no lender, there is no borrower, there is no loan agreement, and, importantly, there is no security interest in the conventional legal sense.

The private law reality is that DAI end users engage with the protocol entirely at their own risk, using open-source software made available without any contractual counterparty or protection.[132] This is explicitly and repeatedly acknowledged in the protocol's foundational documents. Vaults are described as "inherently noncustodial" where "each user has complete and independent control over their deposited collateral."[133] Users are warned that they "understand and accept that the software, technology, and technical concepts and theories applicable to the Maker Protocol are still unproven and there is no warranty."[134] The white paper further acknowledges the "inherent risk that the technology could contain weaknesses, vulnerabilities, or bugs causing, among other things, the complete failure of the Maker Protocol."[135]

Thus, the absence of contractual relationships has stark implications for DAI end users. Should the MakerDAO protocol behave in ways that defeat user

[130] *See generally Maker White Paper*, *supra* note 28, at 1.

[131] *See generally id.* (using terms such as "collateral," "debt," and "liquidation" throughout); *see also Maker Protocol 101*, *supra* note 125, at 6, 8.

[132] The Maker Protocol is an "open-source project." The core smart contracts are available under an open-source license. *See, e.g.*, *Dai in Smart Contracts*, SKY-ECOSYSTEM, https://github.com/sky-ecosystem/developerguides/blob/master/dai/dai-in-smart-contracts/dai-in-smart-contracts.md (last visited Aug. 8, 2025).

[133] *Maker White Paper*, *supra* note 28, at 7.

[134] *Id.* at 18.

[135] *Id.*

expectations or should the system suffer an outright technical malfunction, users lack contractual recourse against any identifiable party. We see these risks as manifesting across several categories. Technical failures could render vaults unresponsive, thereby preventing DAI redemption. Or exploitation of the system's smart contracts could compromise the underlying code infrastructure. Security breaches might enable the unauthorized withdrawal of assets from vaults or allow governance attacks where malicious actors acquire sufficient MKR governance tokens to control the protocol. There are also system-wide risks. These could include scenarios where DAI loses its peg due to compromised vaults, if faulty Oracle feeds trigger improper asset seizures,[136] if emergency shutdowns result in haircuts for DAI holders, or if overall digital asset market crashes render the system insolvent.[137]

Across all these scenarios, Vault Owners and DAI Holders have no contractual remedies. Of course, this is not to say that DAI end users cannot seek protection elsewhere. A sophisticated Vault Owner might secure private insurance, or a DAI holder who acquires tokens on a centralized exchange may negotiate limited recourse against the exchange itself based on its specific terms of service. These arrangements, however, are entirely separate from the Maker Protocol, and they would not impose any duty or liability on the protocol's decentralized community of actors.

We note that beyond these immediate limitations for recourse, the absence of contractual relationships creates deeper structural vulnerabilities. Specifically, users have no protection against unilateral protocol modifications that could adversely affect their positions; they have no disclosure rights regarding system risks or governance decisions; and they have no procedural protections such as notice periods or dispute resolution mechanisms. More fundamentally, the implied covenant of good faith and fair dealing that permeates contractual relationships (for whatever one may wish to say about its modern efficacy) is entirely absent, leaving users vulnerable to governance decisions that may prioritize the interest of MKR governance coinholders over protecting MakerDAO users.

8.2.3 Ownership, control, and proprietary interests

The property law implications for DAI end users follow directly from the absence of contractual counterparties that we established above. For Vault owners, whatever property rights existed in the digital assets they deposited continue unaltered. Since no contractual transfer occurs when assets enter a vault, and the

[136] *See id.* at 10–11.
[137] *See id.* at 16–17 (describing "black swan" event risk).

protocol lacks legal personhood to acquire ownership of them or anything else, Vault Owners retain their proprietary interests throughout the process. Similarly, Vault Owners acquire full ownership of any DAI they generate, all as consistent with our analysis in Chapter 2 regarding property rights in digital assets. And finally, the subsequent commercial circulation of DAI would be governed by the general principles established in Article 12 of the UCC.

A more complex scenario arises, however, when stolen digital assets are deposited into Maker Vaults in order to generate DAI. While the original owner indubitably retains proprietary rights in the misappropriated digital assets even when they are held within the Maker vault, the status of any DAI generated using such assets presents novel questions. Drawing on established equity principles, we tentatively suggest that an argument can be made whereby the wrongdoer should be deemed to hold the generated DAI on constructive trust for the rightful owner of the stolen, deposited digital assets.[138] In similar contexts involving tangible assets, courts have consistently held that when stolen property is used to acquire new assets—whether through sale proceeds, investment returns, or other transformations—the original owner may trace their interest into the substitute property.[139] The doctrinal foundation for such claims typically rests on a constructive trust arising from knowing receipt, where the wrongdoer deals with stolen assets (which they hold on constructive trust for the original owner) in a manner inconsistent with that trust, supported by established property-tracing principles.[140] The underlying principle is that allowing the wrongdoer to retain proceeds from stolen property would provide positive incentives for theft while unjustly enriching criminals at the expense of victims.

However, this analysis faces several practical and doctrinal challenges. Unlike traditional tracing scenarios where stolen property is directly converted into substitute assets, DAI generation involves an intervening algorithmic process. Here, the wrongdoer does not directly exchange stolen assets for DAI but rather uses them as inputs to an automated protocol that creates new tokens while leaving the original assets intact within the vault. Algorithmic intermediation creates a degree of separation between the wrongdoer's actions and the resulting DAI, and, arguably, this separation distinguishes this scenario from more traditional cases involving direct conversions of tangible property. A further challenge would arise when wrongdoers combine stolen assets with their own legitimate holdings within the same Maker Vault. In these circumstances, the fractional generation of DAI relative to total asset value would create complexities

[138] *See* George P. Costigan, Jr., *The Classification of Trusts as Express, Resulting, and Constructive*, 27 Harv. L. Rev. 437 (1914).

[139] *See* Restatement (Third) of Restitution and Unjust Enrichment § 58 (Am. L. Inst. 2011).

[140] Adam J. Levitin, *Not Your Keys, Not Your Coins: Unpriced Credit Risk in Cryptocurrency*, 101 Tex. L. Rev. 877, 910–11 (2023).

in establishing the precise quantum of the constructive trust, thereby requiring courts to apply established mixed-fund tracing principles to determine proportional entitlements.[141]

More fundamentally, the practical utility of any constructive trust remedy would be severely limited by the operation of the qualified purchaser rule under UCC Article 12.[142] Once DAI tokens enter general circulation, acquirers who obtain the tokens in good faith, for value, and without notice of competing proprietary claims would take free of any constructive trust. And, given the rapid circulation that one typically sees in digital asset markets, this qualified purchaser protection would effectively limit any constructive trust remedy to only DAI under the wrongdoer's control. Conversely, virtually all subsequent holders who acquired the tokens through normal market transactions from the wrongdoer would be shielded by the qualified purchaser protection.

8.2.4 Tortious and criminal remedies

In the absence of contractual claims, DAI end users' remaining avenues for recourse would lie in tort or criminal law. Such actions against identifiable external attackers who, for example, hack Maker Vaults or otherwise compromise the MakerDAO protocol would clearly be actionable and would present no conceptual difficulties, although there would likely be significant practical challenges in identifying and prosecuting the perpetrators. We think that the more complex scenario would involve losses caused by internal protocol malfunctions, design flaws, or unforeseen economic events. In these cases, there may well be no person to actually sue/prosecute. Thus, our takeaway is this: Although the ultimate viability of tortious and criminal claims would depend heavily on specific facts and the particular jurisdiction's approach to these novel issues, DAI end users would face formidable obstacles in pursuing recovery.

A claim in negligence specifically would likely face a substantial initial barrier: establishing the all-important *duty of care*.[143] A plaintiff would have to convince a court that a diffuse, pseudonymous, and ever-changing group of global actors (think back to our discussion earlier of the Governors who vote on risk parameters or the Maintainers who contribute to the open-source code) owes a specific legal duty to prevent economic harm to every anonymous user of the protocol. Courts have traditionally been reluctant to impose such expansive

[141] *See* Austin W. Scott, *The Right to Follow Money Wrongfully Mingled with Other Money*, 27 Harv. L. Rev. 125 (1913); *see also* Commodity Futures Trading Comm'n v. Walsh, 712 F.3d 735, 748 (2d Cir. 2013).

[142] *See* U.C.C. 12-102(a)(2) (Am. L. Inst. & Unif. L. Comm'n 1977).

[143] *See* Restatement (Second) of Torts § 282 (Am. Law Inst. 1965).

duties between parties with no direct relationship, especially in the context of open-source projects where the underlying software licenses explicitly disclaim liability.[144] Additionally, many jurisdictions apply economic loss doctrines that further restrict negligence recovery for pure financial losses absent special relationships.[145] Even if a duty were established, proving a *breach* of that duty would require demonstrating that a specific governance vote or line of code fell below an undefined standard of *reasonableness* for a decentralized protocol—a task that would be both technically onerous and legally novel.[146]

The tort of *conversion* may also be ill-suited to address most failure scenarios.[147] Conversion requires proof of an intentional act of exercising dominion over another's property without their consent. If the protocol automatically seized and sold the assets in a Vault due to a bug or a legitimate, if harsh, execution of its coded rules, it would be difficult to identify a specific human actor with the requisite *intent* to convert the assets in question at that moment. Indeed, a court may find that the user's initial decision to deposit the assets into the smart contract and the protocol's automated nature to be sufficient factors to negate the element of wrongful intent that is a hallmark of this tort.

A claim in deceit or fraudulent misrepresentation would also be challenging.[148] A plaintiff would have to prove they justifiably relied on a false statement. While one could argue that language in many of MakerDAO's front-facing materials describing DAI as "stable" constitutes a misrepresentation, such claims would likely be negated by the numerous and explicit disclaimers in the white paper. As noted previously, the foundational documents warn users of "inherent risk," the possibility of "complete failure," and that the technology is provided with "no warranty."[149] In light of such extensive risk disclosures, many courts would likely find that it was not justifiable for a user to rely solely on marketing slogans, thereby causing the claim to fail.

8.2.5 Fiduciary liability

Beyond the bounds of contract, tort, and criminal law, a final avenue of recourse for DAI end users might be found in the principles of *fiduciary law*.[150] In the

[144] *See generally* Carla Reyes, *(Un)Corporate Crypto-Governance*, 88 FORDHAM L. REV. 1875, 1907–8 n.235 (2020).
[145] For a discussion of some of these doctrinal limitations, see Christopher K. Odinet, *Modernizing Mortgage Law*, 100 N.C. L. REV. 89, 141–42 (2021).
[146] RESTATEMENT (SECOND) OF TORTS § 285, cmt. d.
[147] *Id.* § 222A.
[148] *Id.* § 525.
[149] *See Maker White Paper*, *supra* note 28, at 18.
[150] *See generally* TAMAR FRANKEL, FIDUCIARY LAW (2011).

event of a protocol failure that results in various losses, users could possibly argue that the Governors of MakerDAO breached fiduciary duties owed to them. This line of reasoning moves the analysis away from specific actions connected to discrete acts and toward the nature of the underlying relationship between the architects of a protocol and its users.

The theory that DLT software developers should be treated as fiduciaries has been a subject of intense academic debate. It was first comprehensively articulated by Angela Walch in 2019.[151] In this work, Walch argues that despite their "decentralized" reputation, public blockchains like Bitcoin and Ethereum are actually controlled by identifiable groups of "core developers" who exercise significant powers over these systems.[152] Drawing on the influential writings of Tamar Frankel, Walch contends that these developers bear a strong resemblance to traditional fiduciaries.[153] She bases this on multiple factors. First, she argues that the developers provide socially desirable expert services requiring specialized technical knowledge. Second, they also exercise control over property and power entrusted to them. Additionally, they create vulnerability to misuse among those who rely on their decisions. Finally, she argues that the developers operate in contexts where users lack adequate self-protection mechanisms or market safeguards. From this analysis, Walch reaches the normative conclusion that this power should be matched with the corresponding legal duties of care and loyalty, ensuring accountability for those who effectively act as stewards of these novel systems.[154]

More recently, this issue was considered by the High Court and Court of Appeal of England & Wales in *Tulip Trading v. Van der Laan* (*Tulip Trading*).[155] In the High Court, Lady Justice Falk summarily dismissed the claim that DLT software developers were fiduciaries, concluding that this proposition was simply not arguable.[156] However, while the court of appeal accepted that no developer fiduciary obligation currently exists under English law and also acknowledged that Tulip's claim would require a "significant development of the common law on fiduciary duties," it nonetheless allowed the appeal on the basis

[151] Angela Walch, *In Code(rs) We Trust: Software Developers as Fiduciaries in Public Blockchains*, *in* Regulating Blockchain: Techno-Social and Legal Challenges 58 (Phillip Hacker, Ioannis Lianos, Georgios Dimitropoulos & Stefan Eich eds., 2019).

[152] *Id.* at 58.

[153] *Id.* at 64–65.

[154] *Id.* at 69.

[155] [2022] EWHC 667 (Ch), [2022] 2 All ER (Comm) 624 (Eng.); Tulip Trading v. Van der Laan [2023] EWCA Civ 83, [2023] 4 WLR 16 (Eng.). For an insightful analysis of these cases, see Peter Hunn, Matthew Kimber & Sarah Worthington, *Developers of Software Code as Fiduciaries: Whatever Next for Cryptoassets and Bitcoin*? (Dec. 4, 2024), https://papers.ssrn.com/sol3/papers.cfm?abstract_id=5060411.

[156] Tulip Trading v. Van der Laan [2022] EWHC 667 (Ch) at [171].

that the proposition was at least arguable and raised a serious issue to be tried.[157] In particular, Lord Justice Birss stated:

> Pulling all this together . . . there is, it seems to me, a realistic argument along the following lines. . . . Viewed objectively the developers have undertaken a role which involves making discretionary decisions and exercising power for and on behalf of other people, in relation to property owned by those other people. That property has been entrusted into the care of the developers. The developers therefore are fiduciaries.[158]

We believe that an argument to impose fiduciary duties on the Governors of the MakerDAO protocol would face a steep uphill battle, with a very uncertain path to success. In our view, this argument is particularly unlikely in the case of DAI holders who acquire their stablecoin in secondary market transactions. This is because these persons have no direct interaction with the protocol, they do not deposit digital assets into its care, and they do not delegate any authority to the Governors. Their relationship to the protocol's participants is indeed quite remote and impersonal. The fact that there is no act of entrustment of property makes, to our minds, the argument that the Governors owe a fiduciary duty to every anonymous holder of DAI on the open market conceptually difficult (if not impossible).

The analysis is admittedly more complex for Vault Owners, who actually deposit digital assets into the protocol's smart contracts, with Governors exercising power affecting those assets through risk parameter adjustments. On its face, this appears closer to the entrustment that underpins traditional fiduciary relationships. Nevertheless, beneath the surface, this resemblance breaks down.

Applying Walch's framework to this assessment,[159] considering the first element, one might argue that Governors provide socially desirable expert services requiring specialized technical knowledge. Specifically, they continuously calibrate complex risk parameters, including stability fees, liquidation ratios, and debt ceilings, ensuring that DAI retains its soft peg and that the protocol remains solvent. This technical expertise in decentralized financial risk management could be characterized as analogous to the specialized knowledge traditionally provided by investment advisors. However, we think that this similarity obscures some fundamental distinctions. Governors operate impersonally within a decentralized system, setting general rules for protocol operation rather

[157] Tulip Trading v. Van der Laan [2023] EWCA Civ 83 at [86]–[91].

[158] *Id.* at [86]. But contrast Tulip Trading v. Van der Laan [2022] EWHC 667 (Ch) at [73].

[159] Note that even among common law jurisdictions there are differences in how fiduciary relationships are theorized and the precise elements required for their establishment. We apply Walch's framework as representative of the leading academic analysis in the context of digital assets and DLT software developers.

than providing personalized services to individual Vault Owners.[160] Moreover, scholars like Carla Reyes offer that the Governors often act for ideological and reputational reasons, rather than in furtherance of service relationships with users.[161] Their governance function resembles legislative rule-making more than the individualized professional services that characterize traditional fiduciary relationships.[162]

Regarding the second element, the entrustment of property and power, Vault Owners do deposit valuable digital assets into smart contracts, and Governors possess the power to trigger involuntary liquidations through parameter changes. In practical terms, depositing assets into a Vault might be seen as a mandate to Governors to determine when collateral may be forcibly sold, potentially satisfying entrustment requirements. However, we see there being an important distinction between the power to affect another's property and the power to act on their behalf. The critical element of a fiduciary relationship is generally described as the delegation of the principal's own autonomous decision-making power.[163] That does not happen in this context. Governors cannot access or dispose of assets within noncustodial Vaults. Users do not appoint Governors as their agents; rather, they voluntarily opt into a system with a preexisting governance structure. In this way, the powers wielded by Governors are a feature of the protocol itself, not a power entrusted to them by users in the typical sense.

Turning to the third element—vulnerability to misuse—Vault Owners are arguably vulnerable to Governor misconduct through incompetent risk assessments and conflicts of interest. Yet, we think that this vulnerability is unlikely to arise from a relationship of entrustment, which, as demonstrated above, is foundational and also absent in these cases. Furthermore, the protocol's foundational documents explicitly place the risk of technical failure or incompetence on users. Rather than being owed protection, users are arguably put on notice that they are interacting with experimental, open-source software on a caveat emptor basis. Indeed, the decentralized system is designed to replace relational trust with trust in autonomous mechanisms, and one might argue that users implicitly accept the risks inherent in that design. Moreover, as explained previously, the protocol incorporates a Governance Module, which imposes a twenty-four-hour delay on the execution of governance decisions. This mechanism provides Vault Owners with advance notice of parameter changes and a window of opportunity to exit their positions before potentially adverse modifications take effect.[164]

160 *See* Hunn, Kimber & Worthington, *supra* note 155, at 15–16.
161 Reyes, *supra* note 144, at 1920–25.
162 *Id.* at 1901.
163 *See* Hunn, Kimber & Worthington, *supra* note 155, at 21.
164 For details, see *Maker Protocol 101*, *supra* note 125.

Finally, regarding the elements of the unavailability of self-help remedies and market constraints, there is good reason to find that Vault Owners retain meaningful exit options. For instance, they may close their Vaults and withdraw from the system if they disagree with governance directions. We do admit that market volatility might make such an exit costly, but this reflects underlying economic dynamics rather than a legal barrier. The Governance Security Module's delay mechanism facilitates such exits by providing the advance warning of governance changes described above.

8.3 Centralized stablecoins through the lens of private law

Turning now to the other category, in the discussion that follows we dissect the private ordering of the two largest and most systemically important *centralized* stablecoins: Tether's USDT and Circle's USDC. In stark contrast to the decentralized architecture of MakerDAO, these stablecoins are issued and managed by identifiable corporate entities that exercise complete control over their design and administration. For our purposes, this centralized structure creates a more conventional private law landscape, one in which traditional contractual relationships between issuers and coinholders can, at least theoretically, be established and enforced.

Our analysis proceeds in four parts. First, we examine the legal documentation and operational mechanics of Tether and Circle. Second, we scrutinize the general conditions/terms of service, with particular attention paid to disclaimers, exculpatory provisions, and the assignment of rights and obligations. Building on this foundation, the third part examines the all-important redemption mechanisms. Here, we assess the legal nature of the redemption right and the conditions that govern its availability. Finally, we investigate a critical but often overlooked risk: whether coinholders possess proprietary claims to the reserve assets that ostensibly back these stablecoins, as well as their related position in the event of the issuer's bankruptcy.

8.3.1 Legal documentation and operational mechanics

The legal materials governing USDT and USDC are available through dedicated legal sections of their issuers' websites.[165] However, this ready accessibility is

[165] *Legal*, Tether, https://tether.to/en/legal/ (last updated Jan. 27, 2025); *Legal & Privacy: Circle Mint User Agreement*, Circle, https://www.circle.com/legal (last updated Aug. 7, 2025).

impaired by significant fragmentation and complexity. Rather than consolidating their legal obligations into unified agreements, both issuers fragment their terms across multiple interconnected documents. Tether distributes its contractual framework among six distinct instruments: terms of service, privacy statement, anti-spam policy, law enforcement requests, cookies notice, and risk disclosure statement,[166] alongside important supplementary information in its "Knowledge Base" and "Relevant Information Document."[167] Circle takes a similar approach, compartmentalizing its terms across multiple interconnected agreements.[168]

Consistent with standard industry practice, these documents are lengthy, drafted in dense legal language, and replete with internal cross-references that obscure, rather than clarify, the parties' respective rights and obligations. A notable distinction, however, is that Circle pays greater attention to the requirements of different jurisdictions than Tether, providing distinct terms of service for each jurisdiction.[169]

The operational mechanics underlying these stablecoins mirror their legal complexity, as we demonstrate below by examining Tether's structure first, followed by Circle's alternative approach.

(a) Tether

Tether has historically maintained an opaque corporate structure that has undergone multiple reorganizations over the years. The primary contracting party, as stipulated in the Terms of Service updated January 27, 2025, is Tether International, S.A. de C.V.,[170] following a recent corporate migration from the British Virgin Islands, where it was known as Tether International Limited, to the Republic of El Salvador.[171] In El Salvador, the company has obtained authorization as both a Stablecoin Issuer and Digital Assets Service Provider under the regulatory framework of the National Commission of Digital Assets of El Salvador (CNAD).[172]

166 *Legal: Risk Disclosure Statement*, TETHER, https://tether.to/en/legal/?tab=risk-disclosure-statement (last updated Jan. 27, 2025) [hereinafter *Tether Risk Disclosure Statement*].

167 *See Knowledge Base*, TETHER, https://tether.to/en/knowledge-base (last visited Aug. 24, 2025); *Relevant Information Document*, TETHER (Jan. 27, 2025), https://tether.to/public/Relevant_Information_Document_-_Tether_International,_S.A._de_C.V.pdf [hereinafter *Tether RID*].

168 *See Legal & Privacy: Circle Mint User Agreement*, *supra* note 165.

169 Circle has bespoke terms for both the European Economic Area and Singapore customers. *See Legal & Privacy: Singapore Addendum*, CIRCLE, https://www.circle.com/legal/singapore-addendum (last updated May 30, 2025); *Legal & Privacy: Circle Mint User Agreement*, *supra* note 165.

170 *See Tether ToS*, *supra* note 108, pmbl.

171 *See id.* (documenting a formal novation and assignment of rights effective January 27, 2025, whereby Tether Limited assigned all its rights, duties, and obligations to the new Salvadoran entity, Tether International, S.A. de C.V.).

172 *Tether RID*, *supra* note 167, at 1.

However, this corporate move is coupled with a critical legal stipulation that substantially complicates the jurisdictional picture and reveals Tether's strategic bifurcation between its regulatory compliance and private law governance. The Terms of Service explicitly stipulate that the agreement "shall be governed by and construed and enforced in accordance with the Laws of the British Virgin Islands" and "shall be interpreted in all respects as a British Virgin Islands contract."[173] Moreover, any disputes are subject to mandatory, confidential, binding arbitration conducted in the British Virgin Islands before a sole arbitrator who must be a legal practitioner in that jurisdiction.[174] This structure suggests that Tether seeks to benefit from El Salvador's crypto-friendly regulatory framework while simultaneously leveraging the more developed, English-based common law system of the British Virgin Islands for contractual governance and dispute resolution.

We note that Tether employs a highly restrictive gatekeeping approach that creates substantial barriers to entry for prospective customers, implemented through a multilayered screening system. The process begins with procedural requirements whereby prospective customers must first create an account through Tether.to, enable two-factor authentication, and choose between an "individual" or "corporate" account.[175] Thereafter, applicants must complete a verification process entailing compliance checks related to anti-money laundering, counterterrorist financing, and sanctions. All of this must be accompanied by a nonrefundable verification fee of 150 USDT,[176] with Tether retaining sole discretion to approve or reject applications. The financial barriers are also significant, with successful applicants facing minimum transaction thresholds of $100,000 for both purchases and redemptions.[177] Finally, Tether imposes comprehensive geographic exclusions, categorically prohibiting access to individuals from the United States, Canada, and Singapore.[178]

Consistent with this stringent client selection framework, Tether's minting, referred to as "acquiring," and redemption process operates as a highly structured six-step process.[179] For minting operations, preapproved customers must initiate the process through the Tether.to platform by submitting an acquisition

[173] *Tether ToS*, *supra* note 108, § 1.4.

[174] *Id.* § 7.1; *Tether RID*, *supra* note 167, at 24 (confirming arbitration seat "will be Road Town, Tortola, BVI").

[175] *Knowledge Base: How to Verify an Account on Tether.to*, TETHER, https://tether.to/ru/verify-your-account/ (last visited Aug. 25, 2025).

[176] *Tether RID*, *supra* note 167, at 14; *Fees*, *supra* note 60.

[177] *Tether RID*, *supra* note 167, at 14; *see also Knowledge Base: Transacting Supported in Tether.to*, TETHER, https://tether.to/ru/transactions-supported-in-tether (last visited Sept. 8, 2025).

[178] *Tether ToS*, *supra* note 108, § 1.1.30. For US persons, only a narrow discretionary exception exists for "eligible contract participants": entities with total assets exceeding $10 million incorporated outside the United States.

[179] *Tether RID*, *supra* note 167, at 22.

request, selecting their preferred blockchain protocol for token delivery, and specifying the destination wallet address.[180] This request must also include "travel rule" information, detailing whether the destination wallet is custodial or noncustodial and identifying the ultimate beneficiary. Once the request has been reviewed and approved (subject to Tether's discretion), Tether instructs the client to wire funds to their account. All incoming transfers must originate exclusively from preverified bank accounts and must be in the specified fiat currency. Upon receipt of funds, Tether incorporates these assets in its reserves and issues the corresponding amount of USDT to the customer's designated digital wallet address.

The redemption process follows a parallel but reverse operational structure. Preapproved customers must first transfer USDT into their account on the Tether.to platform. Notably, the company explicitly states that its platform is not "a wallet service" and that deposits should only be made with the intent to redeem.[181] Thereafter, the customer can initiate a redemption request, specifying the amount of USDT to be redeemed and selecting the verified bank account to which the fiat currency should be sent.[182] All redemption requests require two-factor authentication and are subject to Tether's internal review.[183] Upon processing a redemption request, Tether removes the corresponding tokens from circulation and uses a proportional amount from its reserves to facilitate the transfer of fiat currency to the customer's designated bank account.[184] Notably, both acquisitions and redemptions are subject to identical minimum thresholds of $100,000 and a 0.1 percent transaction fee.[185]

Given these barriers to entry, it is unsurprising then that, as of January 2025, Tether reports having only 882 approved customer accounts worldwide.[186] We observe that this is an extraordinarily small client base considering that USDT commands the largest market capitalization among all stablecoins, with billions of tokens in circulation. Tether's operational model appears designed to insulate the issuer from the millions of individuals and institutions that hold and trade USDT. They do this through a contractual firewall, in essence making sure

[180] *See Knowledge Base: How to Acquire Tether Tokens*, TETHER, https://tether.to/ru/how-to-acquire-tether-tokens (last visited Sept. 8, 2025).

[181] *Knowledge Base: Deposits of Unsupported Tokens to Tether.to*, TETHER, https://tether.to/ru/deposits-of-unsupported-tokens-to-tether-to (last visited Sept. 8, 2025); *Tether RID*, *supra* note 167, at 19.

[182] *Knowledge Base: Redeem Tether Tokens to Fiat Currency*, TETHER, https://tether.to/ru/redeem-tethers-to-fiat-currency (last visited Sept. 8, 2025).

[183] *Tether RID*, *supra* note 167, at 22 ("Tether may freeze, burn, or block the transfer of Tether Tokens, in accordance with the Terms . . . ."); *Tether ToS*, *supra* note 108, § 9.

[184] *Tether RID*, *supra* note 167, at 22–23.

[185] *Id.* at 15.

[186] *Id.* at 14. Tether designates customers with approved accounts as "KYC Verified Customers." No updated figures appear in quarterly attestations through Q1 2025, suggesting continued limited primary market access.

that they only have privity (through the creation of a customer account) with individuals that they preapprove. The result is a chasm: an exclusive, wholesale primary market of rarified customers on one side, and an unconstrained secondary market of disconnected USDT holders on the other.

This opacity is significant. Tether does not publicly disclose its client list, nor does it reveal whether it has special commercial arrangements with any of its key customers. Consequently, the mechanisms through which USDT supply flows from Tether to the major exchanges that provide global liquidity to the crypto markets are not transparent. The lack of information is particularly pronounced with respect to US markets, where Tether's categorical exclusion of US persons necessitates the existence of offshore intermediaries that bridge Tether's issuance of its stablecoins with American trading platforms and users. We see this structure as a patently deliberate exercise in regulatory arbitrage on a global scale. Specifically, Tether minimizes its direct exposure to multiple jurisdictions by maintaining formal contractual relationships only with a carefully curated set of clients. In doing so, Tether effectively externalizes regulatory compliance costs and risks to its customers that serve as intermediaries to end markets worldwide. What is perhaps underappreciated is that this strategy also has profound private law reverberations. The millions of end users who hold USDT do not have any direct relationship with Tether. This lack of a legal connection not only severely compromises their ability to enforce contractual rights associated with USDT, but it also undermines proprietary and tortious claims against the issuer.

(b) Circle

Circle has a relatively linear and transparent corporate structure, coupled with notable attentiveness to jurisdictional idiosyncrasies.[187] In the United States, the sole issuer of USDC is Circle Internet Financial, LLC, a Delaware limited liability company that completed its initial public offering on the New York Stock Exchange in June 2025.[188] As a publicly traded company, this entity is subject to oversight by federal regulators, including the Office of Foreign Assets Control (OFAC) and FinCEN for anti-money laundering compliance.[189] Moreover, it holds licenses as a money transmitter in forty-seven US states,[190]

[187] In addition to the United States, European Economic Area, and the Singaporean frameworks discussed below, in February 2025, Circle also obtained a Bermuda Digital Assets Business Act license. *See* Circle, Form S-1, *supra* note 66.

[188] *See Legal & Privacy: Circle Mint User Agreement*, *supra* note 165. Regarding Circle's IPO, see also *Circle Announces Pricing of Upsized Initial Public Offering*, Business Wire (June 4, 2025), https://investor.circle.com/news/news-details/2025/Circle-Announces-Pricing-of-Upsized-Initial-Public-Offering/default.aspx.

[189] *Legal & Privacy: Circle Mint User Agreement*, *supra* note 165, § 35 (Applicable Law; Legal Compliance).

[190] *Id.* § 39 (State-Specific Disclosures).

as well as a BitLicense from the New York State Department of Financial Services.[191]

The Circle Mint User Agreement stipulates that it is governed by the "laws of the State of Delaware and applicable United States federal law."[192] Any disputes are subject to mandatory, binding individual arbitration under Judicial Arbitration and Mediation Services (JAMS) rules, which generally entails a waiver of the right to a jury trial and to join in a class action.[193] For claims not subject to arbitration, the parties agree to the exclusive jurisdiction of courts located in Boston, Massachusetts.[194] Similarly, the USDC Terms explicitly stipulate that the agreement shall be governed by the laws of "the State of Delaware and applicable United States federal law, including the Federal Arbitration Act as specified herein."[195]

For the European Economic Area (EEA), in July 2024, the company established Circle Internet Financial Europe SAS (Circle SAS) in France as a second issuer designed specifically to comply with the EU MiCAR.[196] Circle SAS is a licensed "Electronic Money Institution" and a registered Digital Assets Services Provider in France, subject to the French Autorité de Contrôle Prudentiel et de Résolution (ACPR).[197] Under this regime, the public offering of USDC within the EEA is governed by and interpreted in accordance with the laws of France. For Singaporean operations, customers contract with Circle Internet Singapore Pte. Ltd. under a distinct set of terms governed by Singaporean law.[198] The company operates under Singapore's regulatory framework for digital asset services, and disputes are resolved through arbitration administered by the Singapore International Arbitration Centre under SIAC Rules.[199] Given this book's focus on American private law, our subsequent analysis concentrates on Circle's US operations, but we do draw comparative insights from its EEA and Singapore structures where they are analytically relevant.

While not as restrictive as Tether's approach, Circle nevertheless exercises a substantial gatekeeping function that limits access to its primary issuance services. The Circle Mint platform is designed exclusively for institutional clients

[191] *Circle Granted First BitLicense*, FINEXTRA (Sept. 22, 2015), https://www.finextra.com/newsarticle/27884/circle-granted-first-bitlicense.

[192] *Legal & Privacy: Circle Mint User Agreement*, *supra* note 165, § 36 (Governing Law; Venue).

[193] *Id.* § 26 (Arbitration).

[194] *Id.* §§ 26, 36 (Arbitration; Governing Law; Venue).

[195] *Legal & Privacy: USDC Terms*, *supra* note 109, § 36 (Governing Law; Venue).

[196] *Legal & Privacy: USDC White Paper*, CIRCLE, https://www.circle.com/legal/mica-usdc-whitepaper (last visited Sept. 6, 2025).

[197] *Id.*

[198] *Legal & Privacy: Circle Mint User Agreement*, *supra* note 165, § 40 (Singapore Terms); *Legal & Privacy: USDC Terms*, *supra* note 109, § 34 (Singapore Terms).

[199] The Singapore Addendum is available at *Legal & Privacy: Singapore Addendum*, *supra* note 169.

in supported jurisdictions.[200] The target market comprises corporations, partnerships, limited liability companies, and other business organizations, provided they are "duly organized and validly existing under the applicable laws of the jurisdiction of its organization."[201] Circle's documentation indicates that such institutional clients typically include cryptocurrency exchanges, institutional traders, wallet providers, banks, and consumer application companies operating in supported jurisdictions.[202] These clients access not merely the typical issuance and redemption services but also Circle's comprehensive suite of digital asset infrastructure. This includes hosted wallets, multichain capabilities, and payment processing tools. However, the terms of service categorically prohibit access for any "restricted person" or entities in "restricted territories." This includes individuals and entities named on sanctions lists maintained by US and other governmental authorities, as well as persons located in comprehensively sanctioned jurisdictions.[203] Such individuals seeking to acquire USDC are otherwise directed to the secondary market.[204]

In our study of the relevant materials, we found that to understand Circle's operational model, it is critical to grasp the intricate web of strategic partnerships—a web that reaches far beyond the conventional issuer–client relationship. Recent SEC filings show that Coinbase, the largest US-based crypto-asset exchange, is Circle's seminal partner in the distribution and promotion of USDC.[205] Having cofounded the CENTRE Consortium that first launched USDC in 2018, the two firms replaced that structure with a collaboration agreement executed in August 2023. The agreement establishes a revenue-sharing mechanism for all interest, dividend, and realized-gain income earned on the reserves backing USDC. After Circle deducts portfolio management fees, capital costs, and its own tiered retention fee, the remaining income is allocated in two stages. First, each party receives a share proportional to the USDC held on its platform. Second, Coinbase receives a specified percentage of income from all USDC held elsewhere—whether on other exchanges, in private wallets, or within DeFi protocols. The arrangement thus incentivizes Coinbase not only to deepen USDC balances on its own products/accounts but also encourages Coinbase to expand USDC adoption across the wider ecosystem, since its revenue increases with every dollar of USDC that circulates anywhere in the world. Remarkably, the agreement provides that if regulatory actions prevent Circle from making

[200] *Legal & Privacy: Circle Mint User Agreement*, *supra* note 165, § 1 (Eligibility; Limitations).
[201] *Id.*
[202] *See Who Is Eligible for a Circle Account?*, CIRCLE HELP, https://help.circle.com/s/article/Who-is-eligible-for-a-Circle-Account (last visited Sept. 6, 2025).
[203] *Legal & Privacy: Circle Mint User Agreement*, *supra* note 165, § 35 (Applicable Law; Legal Compliance); *Legal & Privacy: USDC Terms*, *supra* note 109, § 3 (Applicable Laws and Regulations).
[204] *Legal & Privacy: USDC Terms*, *supra* note 109, § 2 (Scope of USDC and Key Terms).
[205] Circle, Form S-1, *supra* note 66, at 13, 72, 96–108.

these payments to Coinbase as contemplated in the agreement, Coinbase may demand assignment of the USDC trademark itself. We think that this provision underscores both the partnership's depth and the perceived regulatory fragility of the stablecoin business model more broadly.

Beyond Coinbase, Circle has pursued partnerships with other major digital asset platforms to ensure global liquidity. After Binance, the world's largest crypto exchange, was forced to wind down its own stablecoin in 2023,[206] it entered into a partnership with Circle to promote USDC across its services.[207] And indeed, this led to a significant increase in USDC's share of stablecoins on Binance, growing from roughly 10 percent in mid-2024 to approximately 20 percent by April 2025.[208] Circle also relies on a network of institutional market makers and liquidity providers, including firms like Cumberland, Galaxy Digital, and Wintermute, to distribute USDC and ensure it can be readily traded for local fiat currencies in global markets.[209]

Signaling a strategy to bridge crypto-native assets with mainstream financial markets, Circle entered into a memorandum of understanding with Intercontinental Exchange (ICE), the parent company of the New York Stock Exchange, in February 2025.[210] While still nascent, the partnership outlines plans to explore integrating USDC and other Circle products into traditional trading and clearing infrastructure, potentially for use as collateral in trades and settlements.

Circle is also actively embedding USDC in global payment ecosystems by partnering with leading regional fintech platforms. Recent alliances include Grab (a Southeast Asian "super-app"), Mercado Libre (Latin America's e-commerce giant), and Nubank (a major Brazilian digital bank), which are introducing USDC to millions of users in their respective markets.[211] Circle has also teamed up with major payment companies like Visa, Mastercard, and MoneyGram to test USDC for network settlements and to enable USDC-funded remittances that can be cashed out in local currency.[212] These moves have the potential to extend Circle's reach into the conventional payment system.

From a customer perspective, the procedural requirements begin with online registration through the Circle Mint platform. Applicants must provide

[206] Helene Braun, *Binance Will Cease Support for Its BUSD Stablecoin on Dec. 15*, CoinDesk (Mar. 8, 2024), https://www.coindesk.com/business/2023/11/29/binance-will-cease-support-for-its-busd-stablecoin-on-dec-15.

[207] Circle, Form S-1, *supra* note 66, at 143–44.

[208] *USDC Trading Volume Doubles in 2025, Driven by Binance Partnership and Regulatory Compliance*, Ainvest: Coin World (May 19, 2025), https://www.ainvest.com/news/usdc-trading-volume-doubles-2025-driven-binance-partnership-regulatory-compliance-2505/.

[209] Circle, Form S-1, *supra* note 66, at 23.

[210] *Id.* at 13.

[211] *Id.* at 126.

[212] *Id.* at 22.

comprehensive organizational information, including full legal entity names, jurisdictional details, and designated administrator credentials.[213] Regulatory compliance requires completion of extensive due diligence procedures, encompassing anti-money laundering, counterterrorist financing, and sanctions screening processes, though Circle does not impose verification fees.[214] From a substantive perspective, applicants must demonstrate a legitimate business purpose and agree to refrain from prohibited activities, while Circle reserves discretionary authority to approve or reject applications and may require additional documentation through its "Enhanced Due Diligence" process.[215] Circle operates a flexible fee structure that does not impose minimum transaction charges for basic services, although specific charges may apply for particular operations.[216]

Circle's minting (misleadingly termed "tokenizing" USD into USDC[217]) and redemption processes operate through its hosted digital currency wallet service.[218] Notably, unlike Tether's transient redemption platform, Circle's hosted wallets enable clients to maintain USDC balances indefinitely. The company emphasizes integration with banking systems and multichain functionality, though all operations remain subject to internal review for compliance and security.[219] For USDC issuances, clients who have been successfully approved for a Circle Mint account initiate the process by depositing US dollars via bank wire transfer to Circle's designated segregated accounts.[220] All incoming funds must originate from preverified bank accounts in the client's name and be denominated in USD to avoid currency conversion fees or delays.[221] Upon receipt and confirmation of funds, Circle incorporates the assets into its reserves and automatically issues an equivalent amount of USDC (at a 1:1 ratio) to the client's hosted wallet on the selected blockchain.[222] Beyond basic issuance, clients can leverage Circle's multichain swapping to move USDC seamlessly between supported blockchains, access treasury yield products for idle balances, and use payment processing services for commercial transactions. Circle

[213] *Legal & Privacy: Circle Mint User Agreement*, *supra* note 165, § 1 (Registration Process; Identity Verification).

[214] *Id.* § 35 (Applicable Law; Legal Compliance).

[215] *Id.* § 1.

[216] *Id.* § 10 (Fees).

[217] See *Tokenizing and Redeeming USDC*, Circle Help, https://help.circle.com/s/article/Tokenizing-and-redeeming-USDC (last visited Sept. 6, 2025).

[218] *Legal & Privacy: Circle Mint User Agreement*, *supra* note 165, § 2.4 (Wallet Services).

[219] *Id.* § 2.6 (Multichain Swapping); *Legal & Privacy: USDC Terms*, *supra* note 109, § 9 (USDC Supported Blockchains and Smart Contract Modifications).

[220] *Legal & Privacy: USDC Terms*, *supra* note 109, §§ 1–2 (Scope of USDC and Key Terms); *see also Tokenizing and Redeeming USDC*, *supra* note 217.

[221] Non-USD wires are converted by Circle's banking partners at prevailing rates, with potential additional charges, before USDC issuance. *Legal & Privacy: USDC Terms*, *supra* note 109, § 16 (Currency Conversion); *Legal & Privacy: Circle Mint User Agreement*, *supra* note 165, § 10 (Fees).

[222] *Legal & Privacy: USDC Terms*, *supra* note 109, § 2 (Scope of USDC and Key Terms); *Legal & Privacy: Circle Mint User Agreement*, *supra* note 165, § 2.1 (USDC-related Services).

customers can also opt for services like "USDC Express," whereby incoming fiat wires transiently settle as USDC in the Circle Mint account before being subsequently transferred to an external wallet address of the client's choice.[223]

The redemption process mirrors that of minting but with additional checks and safeguards

Clients first transfer USDC to their Circle Mint account, from either their Circle-hosted wallet or other external wallet.[224] Circle then conducts an internal review to verify the request and to ensure compliance with applicable regulations.[225] Upon approval, Circle burns the corresponding USDC coins, thereby permanently removing them from circulation, and initiates a fiat wire transfer of the equivalent USD amount (less any applicable fees) to the client's preverified bank account.[226] Unlike with Tether, redemptions are processed without explicit minimum thresholds, though the agreement notes potential delays for compliance checks, technical issues, or high volumes.[227] Circle explicitly disclaims responsibility for bank-imposed fees or processing times, and it reserves the right to suspend redemptions if necessitated by illiquidity, regulatory orders, or suspected misconduct.[228] Notably, the USDC terms of service reinforce the idea that redemption is conditional on maintaining a Circle Mint account in good standing, with no direct recourse for non-account holders.[229] We see this as underscoring the platform's institutional focus and limited retail accessibility.

Data from Circle's S1 securities filing quantifies the scale of this operational model. Cumulatively, over $1 trillion of USDC had been minted and redeemed since the stablecoin's inception. More recently, between January 1, 2021, and March 31, 2025, Circle minted over $558 billion and redeemed over $502 billion in USDC. The on-chain transaction volume is even more striking, with USDC facilitating more than $25 trillion in transactions during this period. To measure adoption, Circle tracks "Meaningful Wallets," which are addresses holding at least $10 of USDC.[230] These numbered approximately 4.9 million by the end of the first quarter of 2025.

Taking a step back, we offer a point of comparison. Although Tether's USDT and Circle's USDC share a nearly identical architecture as centrally-issued,

[223] *Legal & Privacy: Circle Mint User Agreement*, *supra* note 165, § 11 (USDC-Specific Terms).

[224] *Id.* § 2.5 (Digital Currency Transfers).

[225] *Id.* § 1 (Registration Process; Identity Verification); *id.* § 16 (Right to Change/Remove Features or Suspend/Delay Transactions).

[226] *Legal & Privacy: USDC Terms*, *supra* note 109, § 2 (Scope of USDC and Key Terms); Circle, *Tokenizing and Redeeming USDC*, *supra* note 218.

[227] *Legal & Privacy: Circle Mint User Agreement*, *supra* note 165, § 16 (Right to Change/Remove Features or Suspend/Delay Transactions).

[228] *Id.* § 10 (Fees); *id.* § 16 (Right to Change/Remove Features or Suspend/Delay Transactions).

[229] *Legal & Privacy: USDC Terms*, *supra* note 109, § 2 (Scope of USDC and Key Terms).

[230] Circle, Form S-1, *supra* note 66, at 100.

dollar-pegged stablecoins reliant on a reserve-backed stabilization mechanism, their operational models present a study in contrasts. Where Tether maintains a narrow focus on wholesale issuance and redemption with minimal client touchpoints, Circle sees itself as a hybrid of a payments company, a financial market infrastructure, and an internet platform, benefiting from the network effects of broad adoption.[231] It seeks to serve a broad institutional ecosystem, actively building the "Circle stablecoin network" through multiple distribution channels and partnerships, as well as by providing extensive developer tools, APIs (application programming interfaces), and a wide suite of products and services.[232]

Nevertheless, much like Tether, Circle creates a fundamental bifurcation between its verified account holders and the wider universe of USDC holders. Clients with a Circle Mint account (User Type A) have a direct contractual relationship with Circle, governed by a comprehensive user agreement that grants them full access to minting, redemption, and custody services. According to Circle's S1 filing, there were 1,834 Type A Users, as of March 31, 2025. Non-account holders (User Type B), by contrast, are relegated to secondary markets and are expressly excluded from primary issuance and redemption services. Circle estimates there are over 600 million end user wallet products with access to USDC globally, the vast majority of which belong to individuals. While the divide between these user types is not as stark as with Tether due to Circle's extensive partnerships with exchanges and fintech platforms that serve as intermediaries, a critical legal gap remains. Perhaps most remarkably from a private law perspective, Circle asserts that all USDC holders are bound by its terms of service merely by "obtaining and using USDC."[233] This proposition raises foundational questions regarding contractual formation and enforceability—all of which we examine more deeply in the following sections.

8.3.2 Determining contractual counterparties

A threshold issue that must be resolved before analyzing the substantive terms of Tether's and Circle's contractual scheme concerns the identification of the parties who are actually bound by these agreements. Regarding Tether, there is no doubt that its contractual framework binds only its select group of verified/

[231] *Id.* at 98.

[232] *Legal & Privacy: Circle Mint User Agreement, supra* note 165, § 2.8 (Payment Processing Services); *id.* § 2.7 (Treasury Services); *see also* Circle, Form S-1, *supra* note 66, at 136–38; *Legal & Privacy: Circle Mint User Agreement, supra* note 165, § 11 (USDC-Specific Terms, Bridged USDC-Specific Terms and EURC-Specific Terms).

[233] *Legal & Privacy: USDC Terms, supra* note 109, pmbl.

preapproved customers, and it does not extend to USDT holders that obtain these stablecoins in the secondary market.

Regarding Circle, the issue is more complex. While Circle's Mint User Agreement and USDC Terms clearly govern the relationship between Circle and its customers who have opened a Mint account (User Type A), Circle's USDC Terms assert broader application over a much wider universe of potential counterparties.

Specifically, as we noted above, the USDC Terms provide that "to the extent you do not have a Circle Mint account but hold USDC, these Terms still apply to your holding and use of USDC" (User Type B).[234] Circle's position is therefore that its contractual terms govern not only direct customers but also secondary market holders who have never interacted with the company, certainly do not have Mint accounts, and indeed have never accessed Circle's services. This raises the fundamental question whether, in law, such persons (the User Type B group, to be specific) are actually bound by these terms. As we see it, this issue turns on consent.

The debate over consent in the context of nonnegotiated, standard-form contracts has a long history in contract law.[235] Throughout the twentieth century, as these "contracts of adhesion" became ubiquitous, a scholarly thesis emerged contending that they sit uneasily with the classical paradigm of contractual consent.[236] Their argument stemmed from the empirical observation that individuals rarely read the fine print, and indeed, the companies providing the terms do not expect them to. Proponents of this view have argued that one cannot truly consent to terms whose content is unknown, leading some to question the enforceability of such agreements.[237]

Despite this persistent unease, the prevailing view in courts and academia is that standard form contracts are, in fact, binding (at least most of the time).[238] This conclusion is typically justified by one of two theories. The first posits that an individual who objectively manifests their assent, by signing a document or clicking an "I Agree" button, is deemed to have consented to the terms, whether they read them or not.[239] The second, articulated by Karl Llewellyn, suggests that an individual gives "blanket assent" to any reasonable terms that

[234] *Id.*

[235] *See generally* Todd D. Rakoff, *Contracts of Adhesion: An Essay in Reconstruction*, 96 HARV. L. REV. 1173 (1983).

[236] *Id.* at 1177–78.

[237] *Id.* at 1179–80.

[238] For a US perspective, see W. David Slawson, *The New Meaning of Contract: The Transformation of Contracts Law by Standard Forms*, 46 U. PITT. L. REV. 21, 31–44 (1984); Michael I. Meyerson, *The Reunification of Contract Law: The Objective Theory of Consumer Form Contracts*, 47 U. MIAMI L. REV. 1263, 1264, 1274–81 (1992).

[239] *See* RESTATEMENT (SECOND) OF CONTRACTS § 19 (AM. L. INST. 1981).

do not undermine the core, "dickered" aspects of the transaction.[240] This debate intensified with the rise of "clickwrap" licenses in the digital age, which magnified the consent dilemma due to their peculiar formation process.[241] Nevertheless, even critics of these digital formation mechanisms ultimately accept that the presence of consent in these agreements cannot be universally called into question,[242] though they advocate for the introduction of special rules regulating either precontractual negotiations or substantive terms, particularly when consumers are involved.[243]

In our view, Circle's position offers another example of the flexibility fallacy, which, as we have shown throughout these many chapters, pervades the digital assets ecosystem. Here, it manifests itself as an audacious attempt to reshape foundational, mandatory, nonamendable rules of contract formation. The legal analysis supporting the binding of contracts of adhesion presupposes at least some action that can be construed as a manifestation of assent, however thin. It is untenable, however, to suggest that a person, merely by holding and using USDC, can be deemed to have consented to terms they have never been presented with (even in the most illusory way). If the opposite were true, it would create an absurd scenario where a person could, for example, unknowingly receive USDC in a digital wallet as a payment from a third party, and become unwittingly bound by a complex web of contractual obligations that they do not know exist and were never presented with. As Nancy Kim has written, online contracting at least requires that the assenting party be given notice of the terms, and "[n]otice means that some terms were visible that indicated legal terms applied to the activity that was being undertaken by the adhering party."[244] Circle's approach would thus reduce contract formation to a mere fiction, where the fundamental requirement of notice vanishes entirely, leaving users vulnerable to a labyrinth of obligations that exist only in the imagination of the contract drafter. This is a bridge too far, even for the most expansive interpretation of contracts of adhesion. While it is certainly possible for a person acquiring USDC

[240] Karl N. Llewellyn, The Common Law Tradition: Deciding Appeals 370 (1960); K. N. Llewellyn, Book Review, 52 Harv. L. Rev. 700 (1939) (reviewing O. Prausnitz, The Standardization of Commercial Contracts in English and Continental Law (1937)); Colin K. Kaufman, *The Resurrection of Contract*, 17 Washburn L.J. 38, 70–72 (1977) (supporting Llewellyn's submission and exploring its corollaries).

[241] Nancy S. Kim, Wrap Contracts: Foundations and Ramifications (2013) (providing a systematic account of this topic); Robert A Hillman & Jeffrey J. Rachlinski, *Standard-Form Contracting in the Electronic Age*, 77 N.Y.U. L. Rev. 429, 442–45 (2002).

[242] Notably, there are a number of instances where courts have refused to enforce online contracts on account of a lack of consent. *See, e.g.*, Nguyen v. Barnes & Noble Inc., 763 F.3d 1171, 1177 (9th Cir. 2014); *see also* Specht v. Netscape Commc'ns Corp., 306 F.3d 17, 20 (2d Cir. 2002); Berkson v. Gogo LLC, 97 F. Supp. 3d 359, 385 (E.D.N.Y. 2015) (citing Nancy Kim's work as authority).

[243] Margaret Jane Radin, Boilerplate: The Fine Print, Vanishing Rights, and the Rule of Law 218–25 (2013).

[244] *See* Kim, *supra* note 241, at 109–11.

on a crypto exchange to be bound if that platform incorporates Circle's terms via a click-wrap agreement, the mere use and holding of USDC cannot, in itself, constitute consent.

Circle's approach also fails under general principles governing tortious liability disclaimers. Liability waivers and disclaimers are generally only effective against parties who have actual or constructive notice of their existence and consent to them.[245] American courts have consistently held that tort disclaimers must be conspicuous and brought to the attention of the affected party through reasonable means and must be accompanied by some manifestation of consent, even if not of the nature typical of contracting.[246] The doctrine of assumption of risk, which underlies many tort disclaimers, requires that the plaintiff have knowledge of the specific risk and voluntarily consent to it.[247] Similarly, exculpatory clauses in tort cases are strictly construed and will not be enforced unless the parties had a clear understanding of their scope.[248] Circle's assertion that mere possession of USDC constitutes agreement to its terms would therefore fail to satisfy even these minimal notice and consent requirements applicable to tort disclaimers.

8.3.3 General conditions of service

We now turn to the substantive contractual terms under which Tether and Circle offer their services. These terms establish the foundational legal relationship between issuers and their direct customers. The analysis that follows focuses on the general conditions that define the parties' respective rights and obligations, with particular attention to exculpatory provisions, disclaimers of warranties, and limitations of liability that serve to allocate risk between the issuers and coinholders.

(a) Tether

The legal framework governing the relationship between Tether and its approved clients is acutely asymmetric, with the issuer being granted far-reaching powers while simultaneously disclaiming nearly all liability. The Tether Terms of Service (Tether ToS) and "Incorporated Materials"[249] establish a comprehensive shield through layered disclaimers, releases, and risk-shifting mechanisms

[245] *See* Restatement (Second) of Torts § 496B cmt a (Am. Law Inst. 1965).

[246] *See id.*

[247] *See id.* § 496A cmt. c; *see also id.* § 496E.

[248] *See id.* § 496B cmt. d.

[249] *Tether ToS, supra* note 108, pmbl. (defining "Incorporated Materials" as the "Terms by reference: the Risk Disclosure Statement; the Anti-Spam Policy; the Law Enforcement Requests Policy; and the Fee Schedule").

coupled with grants of broad discretionary authority. Section 12 of the Tether ToS establishes the foundational disclaimer, providing that "Tether makes no representations, warranties, covenants or guarantees to you of any kind" and that "the Site and the Services are offered strictly on an as-is, where-is basis."[250] Beyond these core warranty disclaimers, Tether specifically disclaims responsibility for any third-party software security and warns that beta features may contain bugs, remain incomplete, or never launch commercially.

Section 15 of the Tether ToS functions as the centerpiece of Tether's liability shield, transcending mere damage limitations to create a comprehensive preemptive release.[251] Clients irrevocably agree and acknowledge that neither Tether nor its "Associates"[252] assumes any liability or responsibility for any "losses," encompassing virtually any claim, cost, or damage.[253] This expansive release covers seventeen enumerated and wide-ranging categories of potential losses, composed of user breaches, Site and Service use, legal noncompliance of any kind, the accuracy of information, Tether Token value fluctuations, operational failures, security breaches, unauthorized account usage, third-party insolvency, government seizures, blockchain forks, ownership disputes, and third-party software failures.[254]

Paired with these broad exclusions from liability, Tether reserves extraordinary unilateral powers to modify, suspend, or terminate user services without prior notice. Specifically, Section 6 grants Tether discretionary authority to delay or suspend access to its platform and services.[255] This extends to blockchain support decisions, where Section 4.4 disclaims all liability for supporting or withdrawing support for particular protocols.[256] The company further disclaims responsibility for the irreversible nature of blockchain transactions, stating that users accept all associated risks.[257]

These provisions are reinforced by the Risk Disclosure Statement, which is explicitly incorporated by reference into the ToS.[258] This document enumerates potential perils, including market risk, settlement risk, liquidity and listing risk, risk related to Tether's reserves, and risk related to the redemption of Tether tokens.[259] By accepting the Tether ToS, clients are deemed to have acknowledged and accepted responsibility for these dangers, effectively transforming them from operational liabilities of the issuer into known and assumed risks of the client.

[250] *Id.* § 12.
[251] *Id.* § 15.
[252] *Id.*; *see also id.* § 1.1.4 (defining associates to include a wide variety of parties and individuals).
[253] *Id.* § 1.1.24.
[254] *Id.* § 15.1 to 15.17.
[255] *Id.* § 6.
[256] *Id.* § 4.4.
[257] *Id.* § 5.
[258] *Id.* pmbl.
[259] *Tether Risk Disclosure Statement*, *supra* note 166, §§ 1–5.

Moreover, the Relevant Information Document (RID) contains additional disclaimers, including warnings that registration with El Salvador's CNAD does not imply certification of quality or solvency,[260] that forward-looking statements are subject to risk,[261] and that Tether and its associates disclaim responsibility for the document's accuracy and completeness.[262] Remarkably, in a final flourish of self-preservation, the RID explicitly provides that in the event of any inconsistency between the RID and the Tether ToS, the latter prevails, ensuring that even in the unlikely event of a conflict between two sets of exculpatory provisions, the more restrictive terms will govern.[263]

Beyond the core disclaimers, Tether's comprehensive contractual shield is buttressed by ancillary clauses that further shift risk and compliance burdens onto clients while expanding the company's enforcement powers. The force majeure provision excuses Tether from performance under exceptionally broad circumstances, extending beyond traditional Acts of God to include events that are actually quite central to the operational risks of a stablecoin issuer.[264] The explicit inclusion of "bank failures" and "Digital Token market collapse" is particularly striking, as it insulates Tether from the very systemic and counterparty risks that are most acute in its business model.

The most striking contractual asymmetry appears in Section 8's enforcement powers, granting Tether virtually unlimited discretion to punish suspected violations. Based merely on suspicion, Tether may impose sanctions at will, including asset confiscation/freezing, account termination, and government reporting, all to be done without notice.[265] Section 9 further enables transaction blocking, enhanced due diligence, or service termination for any reason.[266]

Complementing this is the extensive set of representations and warranties demanded from the clients, which transfers the entire burden of legal and regulatory compliance onto them.[267] Each client must warrant, on an ongoing basis, that they are not a "prohibited person," are in full compliance with all applicable anti-money laundering (AML) and counterterrorist financing (CTF) laws, and will not use the services for any prohibited purpose.[268] This transfer of responsibility extends beyond regulatory matters, requiring the client to also warrant their legal capacity to contract, their understanding of the associated risks, that their funds are legally obtained, and that they will employ reasonable measures

260 *Tether RID*, *supra* note 167, at 1.
261 *Id.* at 3.
262 *Id.* at 2.
263 *Id.* at 1.
264 *Tether ToS*, *supra* note 108, § 17.
265 *Id.* § 8.
266 *Id.* § 9.
267 *Id.* § 11.
268 *Id.* §§ 11.2, 11.5, 11.7. The definition of and restrictions on "prohibited use" are detailed in section 8.

to protect their own accounts.[269] Any breach of these warranties, whether intentional or inadvertent, provides Tether with a contractual basis to deny liability and take punitive action, including property seizure and asset freezing.[270]

The lopsided nature of the relationship is further reinforced by Tether's explicit disclaimer of fiduciary duties in Section 14.[271] This disavowal, combined with the comprehensive disclaimer that Tether "does not provide any investment, portfolio management, legal, accounting, tax or other advice,"[272] creates a relationship where clients bear all risks. Mandatory arbitration provisions, including jury trial waivers, further limit recourse through confidential proceedings favoring institutional repeat players.[273]

Finally, on two important issues for traditional financial institutions, Tether's legal posture is defined by an interesting combination of strategic silence and unambiguous denial. None of the company's contractual documents contain provisions governing unclaimed property, escheatment, or dormant accounts. This omission is highly unlikely to be an oversight for an entity managing assets on the scale of Tether, which has contemplated so many other matters in its extensive documents. Rather, we see this omission as representing a deliberate choice—and one that creates a significant legal vacuum. In the absence of a contractual or statutory duty to escheat, the fate of the reserve assets notionally backing unredeemable USDT in lost wallets is undefined. This suggests a potential internal policy where, after some period, the assets backing such "zombie" USDT effectively become unencumbered property of Tether and are absorbed into the company's corporate treasury.

Second, on the matter of government-backed insurance, Tether's position is unequivocal. The Tether ToS makes clear that "Tether Tokens are not legal tender and are not backed by any Government" and, crucially, "are not subject to Federal Deposit Insurance Corporation or Securities Investor Protection Corporation protections, or to analogous protections in other jurisdictions."[274] The Risk Disclosure Statement reinforces this, stating, "neither Tether Tokens nor the Reserves are insured by a private company or Government."[275]

(b) Circle

Like Tether, Circle's legal framework establishes a marked relational asymmetry between the issuer and its clients. However, Circle's contractual architecture reflects its more expansive business model. As we detailed earlier in this

[269] *Id.* §§ 11.1–2, 11.4, 11.12.
[270] *Id.* § 16.
[271] *Id.* § 14.
[272] *Id.*
[273] *Id.* § 7.6.
[274] *Tether ToS*, *supra* note 108, § 4.1.
[275] *Tether Risk Disclosure Statement*, *supra* note 166, § 9.

chapter, while Tether operates almost exclusively as an issuance and redemption platform, Circle provides a wide suite of services including hosted wallets, multichain swapping, treasury yield products, payment processing, and more. As such, this expanded operational scope necessitates a more complex contractual apparatus. Yet, as we will explain, the resulting relationship remains equally lopsided with Circle retaining unilateral control while disclaiming virtually all possible liability.

Section 23 of the Circle Mint User Agreement serves as the foundational disclaimer, providing that the services are offered "as is" without any representation or warranty—whether express, implied, or statutory.[276] Circle specifically disclaims implied warranties of title, merchantability, fitness for a particular purpose, or noninfringement. Beyond these core warranty disclaimers, Circle expressly rejects any guarantees regarding service requirements, uninterrupted access, security, error-free operation, or the quality of products, services, information, or materials obtained through the platform. This extends to educational content about digital currencies, which Circle clarifies does not constitute investment, tax, or legal advice.[277] The USDC Terms reinforce this protection by mirroring the "as is" language and disclaiming all representations, warranties, covenants, or guarantees related to USDC, as well as incorporating the Mint Agreement's limitations.[278]

Sections 23 of the Circle Mint User Agreement and 24 of the USDC Terms also combine to create a comprehensive preemptive release. Circle disclaims all liability for indirect, incidental, special, consequential, exemplary damages, or damages for loss of profits, including losses of goodwill, use, data, or other intangible losses.[279] This sweeping exclusion covers liability arising in contract or tort due to use or inability to use services; procurement of substitute goods and services; unauthorized access or data alteration; and any other matter relating to Circle's services. Section 22 compounds this protection by requiring users to indemnify Circle, its affiliates, and service providers from any claims arising from Agreement breaches, legal violations, or service use, which explicitly includes attorneys' fees and any regulatory penalties.[280]

Supplementing these liability limitations, Circle reserves extraordinary unilateral modification powers. For example, Section 16 of the Circle Mint User Agreement grants the company the right to "change, suspend, or discontinue any aspect of the Services at any time, including hours of operation or

[276] *Legal & Privacy: Circle Mint User Agreement*, *supra* note 165, § 23.
[277] *Id.* § 5.
[278] *Legal & Privacy: USDC Terms*, *supra* note 109, § 24 (incorporating Mint Agreement limitations by reference for User Type A).
[279] *Legal & Privacy: Circle Mint User Agreement*, *supra* note 165, § 23.
[280] *Id.* § 22.

availability of any feature, without notice and without liability."[281] This extends to declining any issuance or redemption without prior notice and limiting or suspending services "in our sole discretion."[282] Section 19 grants Circle extensive rights following USDC issuances, including retroactive cancellations, deductions from future issuances, account suspensions, and cross-account setoffs.[283] Section 15 further reserves Circle's right to "change the deposit, withdrawal, storage, transfer, and velocity limits" and establish "individual or aggregate transaction limits" at its discretion.[284] Section 9 similarly authorizes account suspension or termination "without liability to you or any third party" for various reasons, including account inactivity, failure to respond to requests, or agreement violations.[285] Circle may also "delay any transaction if we believe that such transaction is suspicious, may involve fraud or misconduct, violates applicable laws or payment network or ACH rules, or violates any term of this Agreement."[286] Additionally, Circle retains sweeping authority over the underlying blockchain infrastructure. In Section 9, Circle reserves the right to migrate USDC to different blockchains at its discretion, accompanied by a provision requiring users to facilitate such migrations or otherwise risk incompatibility with their accounts.[287]

This arsenal of protective provisions is reinforced through incorporated risk disclosures. While Circle does not maintain a separate risk disclosure statement comparable to Tether's, the USDC terms contain detailed risk factors addressing price stability on third-party platforms, operational challenges, and regulatory uncertainties.[288] Users are deemed to accept these risks by using the services effectively, as with Tether, turning what are otherwise operational hazards into inherent risks assumed by customers.

Circle's framework also includes ancillary clauses that further insulate the company while expanding its powers. The force majeure provision in Section 30 of the Circle Mint User Agreement excuses performance for conditions "beyond our reasonable control," including governmental action, terrorism, pandemics, natural disasters, labor conditions, power failures, equipment failures, and "Internet disturbances."[289] While less explicitly tailored to stablecoin risks than Tether's provision, this broad language encompasses many operational failures central to Circle's business model.

[281] *Id.* § 16.
[282] *Id.*
[283] *Id.* § 19.
[284] *Id.* § 15.
[285] *Id.* § 9.
[286] *Id.* § 16.
[287] *Id.* § 9.
[288] *Legal & Privacy: USDC Terms*, *supra* note 109, § 13.
[289] *Legal & Privacy: Circle Mint User Agreement*, *supra* note 165, § 30.

Circle's enforcement powers, while perhaps less draconian in tone than Tether's, grant similarly broad discretion. Section 19 of the Circle Mint User Agreement authorizes Circle to "block" certain addresses and to freeze associated digital currency that it determines "may be associated with illegal activity or activity that otherwise violates the terms of this Agreement."[290] This determination rests "in its sole discretion," and may result in account termination and asset forfeiture.[291] The subsequent Section 25 grants comprehensive setoff rights, authorizing Circle to apply user funds against any liabilities, including the right to "convert and/or exchange any Supported Digital Currency" at prevailing rates.[292] The blocking and forfeiture mechanisms extend further through the USDC Terms, which establish Circle's right to freeze assets based on sanctions compliance and report to law enforcement.[293]

Circle's transfer of compliance burdens mirrors Tether's approach through extensive user representations and warranties. Circle users must warrant ongoing compliance with all applicable laws, including tax, AML, and CTF provisions.[294] They must represent that they are not restricted persons, that funds are not criminal proceeds, and that they will not use services for prohibited activities.[295] Section 35 of the Circle Mint User Agreement reinforces that continued service access is "conditional on your continued compliance at all times with this Agreement and all applicable laws and regulations."[296] Any breach, whether intentional or inadvertent, provides Circle with contractual grounds to deny liability and take punitive action, including asset freezing and forfeiture.[297] Notably, Circle does provide limited protections for unauthorized transactions under Section 24: users who report within two business days face maximum losses of $50, while those who delay face up to $500 in losses, provided they notify Circle within sixty days.[298] Notably, such a consumer-oriented provision is entirely absent from Tether's contracts.

Circle's explicit disclaimer of any potential elevated duties parallels Tether's approach. Section 3 of the Circle Mint User Agreement emphatically states that Circle "is not a trust company nor do we maintain a trust company charter" and "is not a fiduciary, and Circle does not provide any trust or fiduciary services."[299] This agreement further clarifies that custody references relate solely to money transmission authority, not in any way related to Circle's status as a qualified

290 *Id.* § 19.
291 *Id.*
292 *Id.* § 25.
293 *Legal & Privacy: USDC Terms*, *supra* note 109, § 13.
294 *Legal & Privacy: Circle Mint User Agreement*, *supra* note 165, § 35.
295 *Id.*; *Legal & Privacy: USDC Terms*, *supra* note 109, § 4.
296 *Legal & Privacy: Circle Mint User Agreement*, *supra* note 165, § 35.
297 *Id.* §§ 19, 35.
298 *Id.* § 24.
299 *Id.* § 3.

custodian. Section 5 reinforces that Circle "does not provide investment, tax, or legal advice, nor does Circle broker trades on your behalf."[300] Combined with mandatory arbitration provisions and class action waivers, these disclaimers create a relationship where users bear all risks while surrendering traditional legal remedies.[301]

Finally, on critical institutional issues, Circle demonstrates more transparency than Tether while reaching similar substantive positions. Regarding unclaimed property, Section 34 of the Circle Mint User Agreement acknowledges potential escheatment obligations but reserves the right to "deduct a dormancy fee or other administrative charges from such unclaimed funds, as permitted by applicable law."[302] This provision, while more transparent than Tether's silence, still permits Circle to reduce its obligations through administrative fees. On insurance, Circle's position precisely mirrors Tether's: assets "are not subject to deposit insurance protection," including FDIC, SIPC, or international equivalents.[303]

In order to more fully appreciate the differences in core and salient terms across these two centralized issuers, Table 8.1 sets forth the relevant provisions and related corporate and contractual information side by side.

8.3.4 Redemption

The redemption mechanisms of Tether and Circle lie at the heart of their price stabilization systems and, thus, constitute the cornerstones of their overall operations. As detailed above, USDT and USDC maintain their peg through a structure whereby the issuers hold reserves of valuable assets and commit to mint and redeem their stablecoins at a predetermined rate. The viability of this stabilization approach depends fundamentally on market participants trusting that the issuer has both the capacity and the obligation to honor redemption requests. Indeed, the promise of redemption prevents price deviations through arbitrage opportunities. Without it, these stablecoins would lose their fundamental value proposition and their ability to maintain price stability. We explore the redemption rights for Tether and Circle as follows.

(a) Tether

First, Tether's public-facing materials depict redemption as a straightforward and reliable process. The company's website prominently features claims that

[300] *Id.* § 5.
[301] *Id.* § 27.
[302] *Id.* § 34.
[303] *Id.* § 14.

Table 8.1 Comparative overview of key legal and contractual features of Tether (USDT) and Circle (USDC) Terms of Service.

Feature	Tether (USDT)	Circle (USDC)
Governing law & dispute resolution	British Virgin Islands (BVI) laws; interpreted as BVI contract. Mandatory confidential binding arbitration in BVI before sole arbitrator.	For US clients, Delaware law and US federal law. Mandatory binding individual arbitration under JAMS rules; jury trial and class action waiver.
Provision of services and warranty disclaimers	Services provided "as-is, where-is"; no representations, warranties, covenants, or guarantees; disclaims third-party software security and beta features.	Services provided "as-is"; no express, implied, statutory warranties; disclaims merchantability, and fitness; no guarantees on availability, security, error-free operation; denies advice.
Liability limitations and releases	Irrevocable release from all losses across 17 categories.	No liability for indirect, special, consequential damages, lost profits, and goodwill; covers contract/tort.
Force majeure provisions	Excuses for broad events, including bank failures and digital asset market collapse.	Excuses for events beyond control, including governmental action, pandemics, disasters, failures, and internet issues.
Unilateral powers (modification/ suspension/ termination)	Discretion to modify, suspend, terminate, delay all services, without notice, as well as supported blockchains.	Change/suspend/discontinue services without notice/liability; decline issuances; alter limits; suspend/terminate accounts.
Enforcement Powers (e.g., Sanctions, Freezing, Set-Off)	Suspicion-based sanctions (e.g., confiscation, termination, reporting); blocking/seizure/ freezing.	Block/freeze for illegal activity/ violations; set-off rights with conversion; termination/ forfeiture.
User Representations, Warranties, and Assumption of Risks	Ongoing warranties (e.g., not prohibited, AML/CTF compliance, capacity, account protection); breaches enable actions; assumes enumerated risks via ToS.	Ongoing compliance warranties (e.g., tax/AML/CTF, not restricted, no criminal funds/ prohibited uses); conditional access; assumes all risks via use.
Disclaimer of Fiduciary Duties	Explicit no fiduciary duties; no investment/legal/tax advice.	Not trust company, qualified custodian; no fiduciary duties.
Treatment of Unclaimed Property	Silent; implies potential absorption into treasury.	Escheatment possible; deduct dormancy/admin fees as permitted.
Deposit Insurance	No deposit insurance (e.g., FDIC/SIPC equivalents).	No deposit insurance (e.g., FDIC/SIPC equivalents).

USDT holders enjoy "unparalleled liquidity," suggesting seamless convertibility between tokens and fiat currency.[304] The knowledge base reinforces this narrative, describing redemption as simply depositing your USDT to Tether.to and "receiving their values in fiat currencies . . . into a verified bank account."[305] Redemptions are presented as a routine three-step operation: sign in, fill in the redemption amount, and receive confirmation.[306] This description, coupled with Tether's emphasis on being "100 percent backed" by reserves, creates a perception of simplicity and low friction that would reassure any reasonable holder of USDT tokens.[307]

However, the contractual reality reveals that USDT's redemption mechanism is far more fragile and restricted than these representations suggest. Most fundamentally, only "KYC Verified Customers" with a Tether.to preapproved account can redeem directly from Tether. As described previously, this is a small and hard-to-join constituency that represents a minuscule fraction of the global user base of USDT.[308] This limitation means that the overwhelming majority of holders, numbering in the millions, have no direct redemption avenue whatsoever. These many individuals must rely instead on secondary market transactions and indirect access to Tether. While USDT's market success suggests that this structure has functioned adequately for the time being, this systemic lack of direct recourse against Tether for the vast majority of USDT holders creates a critical vulnerability. It concentrates system-wide risk in a small number of secondary market intermediaries, whose own liquidity and operational capacity may become constrained or fail during periods of acute market stress, volatility, or panic. Indeed, this became apparent during the May 2022 crypto market turmoil following TerraUSD's collapse, when, at a time of panic, USDT temporarily lost its peg, falling below $0.96, and forced Tether to issue a press release emphasizing it was honoring redemptions.[309]

Even for the select few verified customers, the right to redeem is legally circumscribed and heavily constrained. Starting with the legal nature of the right itself, the Tether ToS generally describe access to all "Services," including redemption, as "a personal, restricted, non-exclusive, non-transferable, non-sublicensable, revocable, limited licence."[310] This proposition is reinforced by a

[304] TETHER, https://tether.to/en/ (last visited Aug. 25, 2025) (claiming "unparalleled liquidity").

[305] *Knowledge Base: Redeem Tether Tokens to Fiat Currency*, TETHER, https://tether.to/en/redeem-tethers-to-fiat-currency/ (last visited Aug. 25, 2025).

[306] *Id.*

[307] TETHER, *supra* note 304 (stating USDT is "backed 100% by Tether's reserves").

[308] *Tether RID*, *supra* note 167, at 14.

[309] Press Release, Tether, Tether Continues to Honour All Redemptions from Verified Customers During Market Volatility on Track to Process $2bn Today (May 12, 2022), https://tether.io/news/tether-continues-to-honour-all-redemptions-from-verified-customers-during-market-volatility-on-track-to-process-2bn-today/.

[310] *Tether ToS*, *supra* note 108, § 2.

further characterization of redemption as "a contractual right personal to [the client]," employing language that echoes the general anti-assignment provisions in Section 18, which prohibit the transfer of any right "without prior written consent of Tether."[311] This restrictive framing stands in stark contrast to Tether's marketing materials. It also establishes the legal foundation for the extensive restrictions that follow.

Crucially, the contractual documents reveal extensive limitations on the exercise of redemption rights that fundamentally undermine their reliability. Even under normal circumstances, the redemption process involves multiple layers of review and approval, with Tether maintaining discretion at each stage.[312] Beyond these routine controls, the Tether ToS affords Tether broad discretionary authority to "delay or suspend your access to the Site or the Services (including in respect of purchases and redemptions)" for numerous reasons, including suspicion of violations, legal concerns, government directives, or unacceptable risk.[313] Moreover, Tether reserves the right to delay the redemption or withdrawal of USDT "if such delay is necessitated by the illiquidity or unavailability or loss of any Reserves held by Tether to back the Tether Tokens."[314] This provision, which is also repeated in the Risk Disclosure Statement, fundamentally contradicts its marketing promise of "unparalleled liquidity."[315] Operating as a contractual escape hatch, it allows Tether to suspend performance unilaterally at the very moment its stability function is most critical and thereby shift the risk to the stablecoin holders that reserve assets cannot be sold for cash by the issuer quickly enough to meet demand.

Finally, clients attempting to enforce their redemption rights face formidable procedural and substantive obstacles. As described above, the Tether ToS mandate that all disputes be resolved through confidential, binding arbitration in the British Virgin Islands under the law of that jurisdiction. This choice of a remote, offshore jurisdiction and a confidential arbitral process is a strategic decision designed to deter litigation by increasing its cost and complexity. Simultaneously, the confidentiality requirement prevents the formation of adverse public precedent and shields Tether's conduct from public scrutiny. Last, Tether can rely on its comprehensive liability disclaimers and the force majeure provisions that specifically excuse performance for "bank failures" and "digital token market collapse," as we analyzed in the preceding sections.[316]

[311] *Id.* § 4.1 (describing redemption as "a contractual right personal to you"); *id.* § 18 ("These Terms of Service, and any of the rights, duties, and obligations contained herein, are not assignable by you without prior written consent of Tether").

[312] *Knowledge Base: Redeem Tether Tokens to Fiat Currency*, *supra* note 305.

[313] *Tether ToS*, *supra* note 108, § 6.

[314] *Id.* § 4.1.

[315] *Tether Risk Disclosure Statement*, *supra* note 166, § 5.

[316] *Tether ToS*, *supra* note 108, § 17.

(b) Circle

Moving along, Circle adopts a public posture that is comparable to Tether's, framing USDC redemption in the language of certainty and reliability. The company's website prominently states that USDC is "[a]lways redeemable 1:1 for U.S. dollars" and that holders can easily convert back to local fiat currencies.[317] The USDC Terms reinforce this commitment, declaring that "when Circle redeems USDC for USD, it will always redeem such USDC at a rate of one USD ($1) per one (1) USDC, less fees where applicable."[318] This framing suggests an unconditional right to redemption at par value, fostering expectations of immediate accessibility, continuity of service, and resilience in the face of challenging market conditions.

Yet, here again, a careful examination of the contractual reality reveals a landscape fraught with caveats and constraints. As with Tether, the direct redemption of USDC with Circle is limited exclusively to institutions that have a Circle Mint account, with the USDC Terms explicitly stating: "[Y]ou may not redeem USDC with Circle unless and until you open a Circle Mint account."[319] While Circle describes itself as the "redeemer of last resort,"[320] millions of USDC holders who obtain tokens on secondary markets have no direct redemption rights whatsoever.[321] We acknowledge that Circle's redemption architecture does appear more institutionally developed than Tether's, with a larger client base, no blanket geographic exclusions, and a number of strategic partnerships such as its arrangement with Coinbase. Nevertheless, the structural reliance on intermediation remains a salient risk.[322] During periods of severe market stress and volatility, USDC holders without direct access to Circle accounts may still face significant challenges redeeming through intermediaries. This intermediated structure also creates vulnerability to contagion effects, whereby distress at either Circle or a major partner like Coinbase could cascade through the redemption infrastructure, potentially freezing access when it is most needed.

Looking past the challenge of direct access, for those that do hold Circle Mint accounts, the redemption right presents a complex and confusing legal construction. The Circle Mint User Agreement characterizes access to all Services, including redemptions, as "a limited, non-exclusive, non-sublicensable, and non-transferable license, subject to the terms and conditions of this Agreement."[323]

[317] *See USDC Now Available Natively on Base*, Circle (Sept. 5, 2023), https://www.circle.com/blog/usdc-now-available-natively-on-base; *see also USDC: The World's Largest Regulated Stablecoin Powering Global Finance*, Circle, https://www.circle.com/en/usdc (last visited Sept. 5, 2025).

[318] *Legal & Privacy: USDC Terms*, *supra* note 108, § 13.

[319] *Id.* § 2.

[320] *See* Circle, Form S-1, *supra* note 66, at 8–9.

[321] This characterization applies primarily to the United States. Under EU MiCAR, stablecoin issuers must provide direct redemption rights to all holders, regardless of the source of acquisition.

[322] *See* Circle, Form S-1, *supra* note 66, at 141.

[323] *Legal & Privacy: Circle Mint User Agreement*, *supra* note 165, § 33.

Yet this description sits uneasily alongside Circle's simultaneous qualification of redemption as an assignable right. The USDC terms contain a perplexing provision that appears three times, stating that "sending USDC to another address automatically transfers and assigns to that Holder, and any subsequent Holder, the right to redeem USDC for USD with us so long as the Holder is eligible to, and does, register a Circle Mint account."[324]

We think that this provision unveils two critical insights. First, Circle acknowledges that the right to redeem and the USDC token itself are distinct assets: the token being personal property, while the redemption right remains a contractual claim (evidenced by the license description). Second, and more problematically, Circle purports to create an automatic assignment mechanism whereby the transfer of USDC tokens supposedly effects a simultaneous transfer of redemption rights. This is another crisp example of the flexibility fallacy. A contractual provision cannot override fundamental principles of assignment law. Circle cannot unilaterally impose a universally applicable, blanket "automatic transfer and assignment" through mere contract terms; if a USDC holder does not actually assign their redemption rights, Circle's only recourse would be a breach of contract claim, not an enforceable assignment.

The confusion deepens with Circle's assertion that "USDC does not itself generate any interest or return for holders of USDC and only represents your right to redeem USDC for an equivalent amount of USD through your account with Circle."[325] This provision suggests that USDC tokens somehow embody or "tokenize" the redemption right itself. Yet, as explained in Chapter 3, such tokenization of contractual rights cannot be achieved through private ordering alone. The creation of property rights is governed by the numerus clausus principle, which limits the forms of property interests that private parties can create. No property law rule permits the tokenization of contractual redemption rights in the manner Circle's terms suggest. The result is a fundamental legal incoherence. On the one hand, Circle's contractual framework treats redemption as a non-transferable license, separate and apart from the USDC itself. On the other, it characterizes redemption as an automatically assigned contract right that travels together with the USDC token, as if it were an inherent attribute that needs no separate assignment or legal act to transfer .

Beyond these conceptual difficulties, Circle's discretionary powers over redemption mirror those of Tether, though articulated through slightly different mechanisms. Section 27 of the Circle Mint User Agreement provides that Circle may "change, suspend, or discontinue any aspect of the USDC Services at any time . . . without notice and without liability."[326] More specifically, Circle reserves

[324] *Legal & Privacy: USDC Terms*, *supra* note 108, §§ 2, 13, 27.
[325] *Id.* § 2.
[326] *Legal & Privacy: Circle Mint User Agreement*, *supra* note 165, § 27.

the right to "decline to process any issuance or redemption without prior notice and may limit or suspend your use of one or more USDC Services at any time, in our sole discretion."[327] The USDC Terms layer on additional conditions for redemption, such as "(i) your possession of a corresponding amount of USDC associated with a registered Circle Mint account, (ii) no violation of these Terms or your Circle Mint account User Agreement, and (iii) no action, pending or otherwise, by a regulator, law enforcement or a court of competent jurisdiction that would restrict redemption."[328] Here, as with Tether, these conditions create numerous avenues through which redemption rights may be denied or delayed precisely when market conditions might make their exercise most critical.

Finally, the enforceability of redemption rights faces procedural and substantive hurdles reminiscent of those found in Tether's agreements, albeit less prohibitive. The Circle Mint User Agreement mandates binding arbitration conducted in accordance with JAMS rules, with proceedings taking place in the US county of the user's physical address or, absent such location, in Suffolk County, Massachusetts.[329] While this certainly represents a more accessible forum than Tether's required arbitration in the British Virgin Islands, the confidentiality requirements and class action waivers still limit collective action and public accountability.[330] Combined with the comprehensive liability disclaimers and force majeure provisions analyzed in preceding sections, Circle's contractual framework significantly undermines the practical enforceability of a coinholder's redemption rights. Thus, while Circle's redemption system may be broader and its dispute resolution forum more accessible, the fundamental disconnect between its marketing promises and the contractual reality remains just as pronounced as with Tether. Table 8.2 sets forth a side-by-side comparison of redemption rights between Circle and Tether.

8.3.5 Stablecoin holders' property rights and bankruptcy implications

This section delves into the crucial (yet often overlooked) question of the property rights of holders of centralized stablecoins. The analysis encompasses four primary issues: the property rights stablecoin holders have in the tokens themselves, the nature of their interests in tokens held within issuer-hosted wallets, their interests in the issuer-held reserves backing the right to redemption, and their ultimate position in the event of the issuer's bankruptcy. Following the

[327] *Id.*
[328] *Legal & Privacy: USDC Terms*, *supra* note 108, § 13.
[329] *Legal & Privacy: Circle Mint User Agreement*, *supra* note 165, § 26.
[330] *Id.* § 27.

Table 8.2 Comparison of redemption mechanism for Tether (USDT) and Circle (USDC).

Feature	Tether (USDT)	Circle (USDC)
Public Representations	Straightforward process with "unparalleled liquidity"; routine three-step redemption to verified bank account; emphasizes "100% backed" reserves.	"Always redeemable 1:1 for U.S. dollars"; easy conversion to fiat; unconditional at par value less fees.
Eligibility for Direct Redemption	Limited to KYC Verified Customers with Tether.to account (882, as of Jan 2025); no direct redemption for USDT holders.	In the U.S., limited to institutions with Circle Mint account (1834, as of Mar 2025); no direct redemption for USDC holders.
Nature of redemption right	Access to redemption service described as a "personal, restricted, non-exclusive, non-transferable, revocable limited license". Redemption described as a non-assignable right "personal to you."	Access to redemption service described as a limited nonexclusive/nontransferable license. ToS describes redemption as a right represented by USDC tokens, in contrast with *numerus clausus* principle. ToS also purports that the right to redeem is automatically assigned on USDC token transfer, but this is untenable in private law.
Issuer's discretionary powers and limitations	Retains broad authority to "delay or suspend . . . access to the Site or the Services (including in respect of . . . redemptions)" for numerous reasons at its discretion, including "illiquidity or unavailability or loss of any Reserves."	Reserves the right to "change, suspend, or discontinue any aspect of the USDC Services at any time . . . without notice and without liability." Can decline to process any redemption without prior notice

analytical schema established in the preceding sections, we consider Tether and Circle in turn, distinguishing between holders who maintain direct contractual privity with these issuers and those who acquire their stablecoins through secondary markets.

(a) Tether

First, we look to Tether. Holders of a Tether.to account own, control, and dispose of the USDT tokens they acquire and hold directly in unhosted wallets pursuant to the general principles of property law that we discussed in Chapter 2. That part is dealt with easily enough.

A more complex question, however, is whether they retain said ownership of the USDT held for them in their Tether.to accounts. As explored in Chapter 4, the custody of digital assets may, under certain circumstances, give rise to a bailment, where the custodian (bailee) holds the asset for the benefit of the owner (bailor), who retains title. The alternative is a debtor–creditor relationship, where the holder transfers title to the asset to the firm and retains only a contractual claim for the return of the specific or an equivalent asset. This distinction is of course critical in an insolvency proceeding. A bailor can reclaim their specific property from a bankrupt bailee, whereas a mere creditor must stand in line with all other unsecured creditors to receive only a pro rata share of the bankruptcy estate according to insolvency law.

The Tether ToS and ancillary documents strongly indicate a debtor–creditor dynamic rather than a custodial bailment. Indeed, we think that multiple provisions converge to support this conclusion. Tether explicitly disclaims providing wallet or custodial services. The knowledge base states unequivocally: "Tether.to is not a wallet service" and instructs users to deposit USDT only "if you are planning to redeem TETHER tokens to fiat currency."[331] We find that the transient nature of these deposits is legally significant, as it suggests Tether does not undertake the custodial obligations typically associated with bailment.

Moreover, the risk disclosure statement establishes that deposits are commingled upon receipt, providing that "[a]ny Tether Tokens transferred to Tether to enable redemptions may be commingled with the Tether Tokens of other users of the Site and with the Tether Tokens of Tether and its Affiliates."[332] As analyzed in Chapter 4, while the commingling of fungible assets does not categorically preclude bailment; it significantly complicates the bailee's redelivery obligation and suggests that the parties did not intend a bailment relationship at all.

Most significantly, Section 11 of the Tether ToS requires account holders to acknowledge that "Fiat, Digital Tokens or other property reflected in your Tether Tokens Wallet are not segregated assets held in your name or for your benefit but reflected only in the books and records of Tether."[333] This language, particularly the emphasis on book entries rather than segregated assets, strongly indicates a debtor–creditor relationship where Tether owes a debt rather than holds specific property. This arrangement closely resembles the depositing of money in a retail bank account—in other words, a debtor–creditor relationship.

A similar analysis applies to the question of whether Tether.to account holders possess proprietary claims to Tether's reserve assets proportional to their token

[331] *Knowledge Base: Deposit Tether Tokens to Tether Account*, TETHER, https://tether.to/ru/deposit-tethers-to-your-account (last visited July 16, 2025).

[332] *Tether Risk Disclosure Statement*, *supra* note 166, § 11.

[333] *Tether ToS*, *supra* note 108, § 11.

holdings. While Tether's contractual documents do not explicitly address this issue, we think that several provisions provide compelling evidence in favor of a negative answer. First, and most fundamentally, the legal framework grants Tether complete and unilateral control over the reserve assets. The RID states unequivocally that "the composition of Reserves is subject to change at Tether's sole discretion."[334] This unfettered power is simply incompatible with the rights of a beneficiary, as beneficiaries of assets held in trust or bailment typically have enforceable interests that limit the holder's discretion over the bailed property.

Second, the characterization of redemption rights reinforces this conclusion. The terms of service define redemption as "a contractual right personal to you."[335] The risk disclosure statement further clarifies that "your right to request redemption of your Tether Tokens is a contractual right and does not represent security in favour of a holder of Tether Tokens," adding that "[p]ost sale, Tether's only obligation is to redeem Tether Tokens through the Site subject to the Terms."[336] This language explicitly positions the relationship in contract rather than property law, pointing toward the treatment of Tether.to account holders as unsecured creditors rather than beneficial owners.

Third, nothing in Tether's legal structure or contractual labyrinth suggests that reserve assets are ring-fenced or otherwise protected from general creditor claims. In fact, the absence of structural protections is underscored by explicit warnings about potential loss. The risk disclosure statement warns that reserves "could be subject to unexpected diminution in value" and that "neither Tether Tokens nor the Reserves are insured by a private company or Government."[337] Most starkly, this document cautions Tether.to account holders that "any loss you may experience as a holder of Tether Tokens would not be offset by any insurance payment."[338] These disclaimers effectively acknowledge that reserve assets are exposed to operational risks and Tether's creditor claims, all of which are fundamentally incompatible with a trust or bailment structure that would shield the bailed assets for the benefit of token holders.

Taken together, these provisions paint a clear picture: Tether.to account holders do not have a proprietary interest in Tether's reserves. The legal relationship is one of unsecured debtor and creditor. As such, absent the imposition of a constructive trust or similar form of equitable relief,[339] the reserve assets would likely be treated as general corporate property and, upon an insolvency filing, constitute property of the bankruptcy estate. This would make the reserve

[334] *Tether RID*, *supra* note 167, at 17.
[335] *Tether ToS*, *supra* note 108, § 4.1.
[336] *Tether Risk Disclosure Statement*, *supra* note 166, § 4.
[337] *Id.* § 4.5.
[338] *Id.*
[339] *See* Bruce, Odinet & Tosato, *supra* note 1, at 1132–33 (explaining the difficulties coinholders face in establishing constructive trusts under such circumstances).

assets available for distribution to all of Tether's creditors according to the priority scheme established by bankruptcy law.

The proprietary position of the millions of USDT holders who do not have a direct contractual relationship with Tether is even more precarious. These holders acquire their tokens on secondary markets, and, as established, they have no standing to redeem their USDT directly with Tether. Their relationship with the issuer is attenuated to the point of nonexistence, mediated entirely by the exchanges and platforms on which they trade. These holders have no plausible claim to a proprietary interest in Tether's reserves. Their legal rights are confined to the USDT tokens themselves, which they own as personal property. In the event of Tether's insolvency, we see these holders as having no direct claim against the bankruptcy estate at all. Their only potential recourse might be against the secondary market counterparties from whom they acquired their USDT, and the success of any such claim would depend entirely on the terms of the relevant agreement. The ultimate result is that these holders bear the full, unmitigated market risk of Tether's potential collapse.

(b) Circle

The proprietary rights of Circle's USDC holders present a more intricate (and at times contradictory) legal picture than those of Tether. Circle Mint account holders, like their Tether.to counterparts, own, control, and dispose of the USDC tokens they hold in their unhosted wallets according to general principles of property law and UCC Article 12—as we explained in Chapter 2.

The analysis becomes more complex for USDC tokens that Circle Mint account holders keep in Circle's "hosted wallet." The Circle Mint User Agreement is inexplicably ambiguous on this matter. On one hand, it clearly states that "you own the Digital Currencies held in your Hosted Wallet."[340] This statement is reinforced by a provision stating that "the title to all of your Supported Digital Currency will remain with you at all times. As the beneficial owner of Supported Digital Currency in your Hosted Wallet, you shall solely bear the risk of loss of such Supported Digital Currency."[341] This language would suggest either a trust or bailment relationship whereby account holders retain ownership of the tokens and Circle merely has control of them.

However, Circle definitively rules out the possibility of a trust through explicit disclaimers: "we are not a trust company nor do we maintain a trust company charter in any U.S. state or territory."[342] Even clearer, the agreement further emphasizes that "Circle is not a fiduciary, and Circle does not provide

[340] *Legal & Privacy: Circle Mint User Agreement*, *supra* note 165, § 2.4.
[341] *Id.* § 4.
[342] *Id.* § 3.

any trust or fiduciary services to any User."[343] Surprisingly, the alternative argument for a bailment is also severely weakened by the agreement's own terms. The Circle Mint User Agreement includes the startling admission that "in the event of a Circle bankruptcy we make no representations or warranties as to whether all Supported Digital Currencies held in your Hosted Wallet will be successfully returned to you."[344] Moreover, the Circle Mint User Agreement also explicitly states that: "Circle is not a Qualified Custodian pursuant to 17 C.F.R. § 275.206(4)-2."[345] This disclaimer is highly consequential, as the regulatory regime for qualified custodians (which is part of the larger legal framework for federally regulated investment advisors) is specifically designed to protect client assets by requiring strict segregation from the custodian's own property, thereby shielding them from the custodian's creditors in an insolvency.

Therefore, despite express statements that title and ownership of tokens in hosted wallets remain with clients, Circle's own various contract terms create significant doubt about the legal nature of this relationship. We believe that this inconsistency leaves open the possibility that account holders are in a debtor-creditor relationship with Circle. Consequently, there is a material risk that these tokens could be treated as part of Circle's estate in a bankruptcy proceeding. If this ambiguity is uintended, it is particularly regrettable. As explained in Chapter 4, had Circle wished to provide its clients with unequivocal property rights, it could have done so by opting into the UCC Article 8 framework. This established legal regime would have granted clients clear, enforceable, and bankruptcy-remote property interests in their custodied tokens.

This lack of clarity extends beyond hosted wallets to the equally important question of whether Circle Mint account holders possess proprietary claims to Circle's reserve assets. The USDC Terms provide superficially reassuring language that reserves are held in "Segregated Accounts . . . on behalf of, and for the benefit of, Users."[346] However, this apparent beneficiary designation must be evaluated against Circle's comprehensive disclaimers and actual reserve structure. Three lines of reasoning strongly suggest that Circle Mint account holders do not possess proprietary claims to the reserves.

First, the nature of the redemption right undermines any claim to proprietary interests. As discussed above, Circle's legal characterization of redemption rights is fundamentally incongruous, with terms ranging from describing it as a revocable license to a contractual right to an obligation somehow tokenized into the USDC coins themselves. Yet, regardless of this conceptual confusion,

[343] *Id.*

[344] *Id.* §§ 3, 4. This means investment advisers cannot use Circle to meet their legal custody requirements, as Circle lacks the regulatory safeguards required for holding client assets.

[345] *Id.* § 3.

[346] *Legal & Privacy: USDC Terms*, *supra* note 108, § 1.

the redemption right is never framed as a proprietary interest. This positions Circle Mint account holders not as owners demanding their property but as counterparties seeking performance of a contractual obligation from Circle.

Second, the structure of the reserves, while professionally managed, does not grant holders any kind of direct claims. As of early 2025, approximately 90 percent of USDC reserves were held in the Circle Reserve Fund, which is a government money market fund managed by BlackRock, with BNY Mellon serving as custodian.[347] While this "outsourced trust" model provides operational security, the legal ownership structure is determinative of the issue under consideration. According to SEC filings, the only entity permitted to purchase shares in the fund, and thus the only party that would seem to have a direct legal claim to the fund's assets, is Circle—*not* the Circle Mint account holders.[348]

Third, while Circle could theoretically hold these fund shares in trust for its users, its own legal agreements foreclose this interpretation. As explained earlier, the categorical statements in the Circle Mint User Agreement that Circle is not a trust company, not a fiduciary, and not a qualified custodian would seem to apply to all of its operations, including its management of the reserves. These disclaimers, when combined with the structure of the reserve fund and the contractual nature of the redemption right, lead us to what seems to be the unavoidable conclusion that Circle Mint account holders possess only contractual claims against Circle rather than proprietary interests in the underlying reserves.

Turning to the secondary market acquirers, the legal status of USDC holders who are not Circle Mint account holders presents an even starker reality. As detailed above, the USDC Terms state that these secondary market participants "are not customers of Circle" and that they "may not redeem USDC with Circle unless and until [they] open a Circle Mint account."[349]

This absence of a direct relationship, combined with the structure analyzed above, renders any claim of a proprietary interest in the reserves legally untenable. If even Circle Mint account holders with contractual agreements cannot assert such a claim, then non-account holders certainly have no reasonable legal basis for such a claim. Their rights are confined to the ownership of the USDC tokens as personal property, with legal recourse limited to whatever arrangements exist with the exchanges, wallet providers, or other third-party platforms through which they acquired or hold their USDC.

As with the secondary market acquirers in the case of Tether, in the event of a Circle bankruptcy, these millions of holders would have no standing to file claims against the bankruptcy estate. They would be entirely dependent on

[347] Circle, Form S-1, *supra* note 66.
[348] *See* Bruce, Odinet, & Tosato, *supra* note 1, at 1133–34.
[349] *Legal & Privacy: USDC Terms*, *supra* note 109, pmbl., § 2.

whether their respective platforms, themselves likely to be unsecured creditors of Circle, can recover and distribute any available funds according to their own terms of service. Stepping back, we find that this multilayered, intermediated structure creates a troubling paradox: Circle benefits from the widespread circulation and use of USDC by non-account holders (which increases reserves, drives adoption, and enhances network effects), while bearing no direct legal obligations to these users. The vast majority of USDC holders thus bear the full credit risk of Circle's solvency without any corresponding rights or protections.

The position of USDC holders who acquired their tokens through or maintain them with Coinbase warrants particular mention, given this platform's unique partnership with Circle. As a founding partner in USDC and a party to revenue-sharing arrangements regarding income generated from reserve assets, Coinbase occupies a distinct position in the Circle ecosystem. Whether this special relationship might give rise to claims against Coinbase, rather than Circle, in the event of Circle's insolvency presents complex questions of agency, third-party beneficiary rights, and the specific terms of Coinbase's user agreements. As we see it, crucial questions include whether Coinbase's revenue participation creates duties to USDC users and whether its role in distributing this stablecoin establishes it as more than a mere intermediary. While these issues merit careful consideration, their resolution depends on factual and legal analyses beyond the scope of our examination here.

8.4 Private law and regulatory interventions

The preceding analysis of decentralized and centralized stablecoins revealed flaws and vulnerabilities that expose holders to significant risks without adequate legal protection. These deficiencies stem not from technical failures or market volatility but from the underlying private law architecture or, in some cases, the absence thereof.

For holders of *decentralized* stablecoins, the promise of automation and disintermediation proves to be a siren's call: irresistible in its appeal, fatal in its consequences. Fundamentally, the problem is that there are no contractual counterparties. Unlike traditional financial relationships, users interact either directly or indirectly with autonomous smart contracts that possess no legal personhood. Consequently, if the software in question malfunctions, fails, or simply fails to meet expectations, there is generally no party to be held accountable. This void forces holders to seek remedies through tort, property, or fiduciary law. Yet, as we explained in this chapter, these offer scarcely more than a scintilla of hope. Moreover, this predicament is compounded by the cavalier use of familiar financial terminology, which creates the false impression of traditional bilateral arrangements where none exist, widening the chasm between user expectations and legal reality.

Centralized stablecoins, on the other hand, present a different but equally troubling set of challenges. First, only a small cadre of verified institutional clients maintains direct relationships with issuers, while millions of retail holders remain entirely outside the contractual framework, despite bearing identical economic risks. Second, even for those privileged few with direct access, the contractual terms are extraordinarily one-sided, granting issuers sweeping discretionary powers while disclaiming virtually all liability. Third, redemption rights, the cornerstone of the stabilization mechanism of these stablecoins, are heavily conditional and revocable, subject to suspension for reasons as broad as "unacceptable risk" or reserve illiquidity. Fourth and perhaps most alarmingly, stablecoin holders possess no proprietary interest in reserve assets. In bankruptcy, holders with contractual relationships would stand as mere unsecured creditors, while the vast majority without such relationships would likely have no standing whatsoever to assert claims against the estate.

These structural deficiencies demand systematic intervention. The following sections examine potential solutions through two complementary lenses: private ordering mechanisms and regulatory interventions. Given the distinct architectures of decentralized and centralized stablecoins, we analyze each separately, recognizing that effective solutions must be tailored to their fundamentally different operational and legal structures.

8.4.1 Private ordering mechanisms

This section explores a menu of private ordering mechanisms that could address the stablecoin vulnerabilities identified earlier in this chapter. Unlike regulatory mandates, we acknowledge that these solutions rely on discretionary implementation by issuers and protocol developers seeking to build durable and trustworthy offerings. Our purpose here is twofold. First, we demonstrate that superior private law structures—providing clearer contractual relations, stronger proprietary claims, and more balanced risk allocations—are achievable within established principles of contract, property, and corporate law. Equally important, by illuminating these possibilities, we hope to catalyze a market dynamic where issuers compete on the quality of their legal frameworks and users demand higher standards.

Second, we acknowledge that voluntary approaches face inherent constraints. Current structures reflect rational business decisions under existing incentives: issuers naturally minimize legal obligations while users often lack the sophistication to demand better terms. Yet a number of forces may shift this equilibrium. Sophisticated institutional users are increasingly demanding stronger protections, creating market segmentation. New entrants may seek a competitive advantage through superior legal design. And the prospect of regulatory intervention has the potential to create incentives for proactive reform.

Our discussion below reflects the fundamental differences between centralized and decentralized stablecoins, offering distinct strategies for each.

(a) Decentralized stablecoins

Proposing private law mechanisms to remedy the deficiencies of decentralized stablecoins may appear unrealistic and even naive, given that these systems are deliberately built to operate without counterparties or recourse. These software projects embody the core tenets of the cypherpunk and crypto-anarchist movements that have so profoundly shaped the DLT landscape.[350] In their ideologically purest form, decentralized protocols aim to achieve financial sovereignty by providing tools that are autonomous, disintermediated, and privacy-preserving, enabling individuals to transact without reliance on governments or regulated entities. From this perspective, the absence of identifiable counterparties represents not a design flaw but a fundamental feature, as the elimination of trusted intermediaries is the very purpose of the technology. That users bear all risks of failure or malfunction without legal recourse is understood by adherents not as an unfortunate gap but as the necessary price of true financial autonomy.

Despite these philosophical constraints, however, we think at least one private ordering mechanism offers meaningful improvement over the status quo without encroaching on this ethos: *decentralized insurance.*

Decentralized insurance emerged as a market-driven response to early, catastrophic smart contract failures, with projects like Etherisc pioneering parametric coverage via smart contracts.[351] The sector gained significant traction with Nexus Mutual's launch in 2019 as the first discretionary mutual for Ethereum risks.[352] In principle, users purchase coverage through pseudonymous transactions, claims are assessed by decentralized governance (e.g., token-holder voting), and payouts occur automatically through smart contracts, all while preserving anonymity and automation. As of 2025, these projects have demonstrated practical viability, offering community-pooled protection against

[350] *See* Bruce, Odinet & Tosato, *Crypto Orgs*, *supra* note 95.

[351] *Core Contracts*, ETHERISC, https://docs.etherisc.com/gif/core-contracts [https://perma.cc/UX4Q-RE9F].

[352] NEXUS MUTUAL, https://nexusmutual.io/ [https://perma.cc/GM73-RC7N] (last visited Sept. 7, 2025); *Decentralized Insurance*, MKT. RSCH., https://www.marketresearch. com/Global-Industry-Analysts-v1039/Decentralized-Insurance-41255273/ [https://perma.cc /V5Y5-ZVUC] (last visited Sept. 7, 2025).

smart contract failures, hacks, and oracle manipulations. Notably, InsurAce has expanded coverage to include DeFi risks such as stablecoin depegging events.[353]

The application of decentralized insurance could directly mitigate the financial consequences of several vulnerabilities we identified.[354] Coverage could be tailored to address stablecoin risks, such as smart contract bugs that cause unintended liquidations, oracle manipulation that triggers erroneous liquidations, or verifiable governance attacks that maliciously exploit protocol code. However, its scope would necessarily be limited. While it would not create a legal counterparty for a breach of contract claim, decentralized insurance would provide a functional substitute: direct financial recourse for specific, verifiable technical failures, without requiring reliance on a centralized entity.

Coverage, though, would necessarily be narrow. Crucially, these policies would not, and likely could not, cover losses stemming from inherent economic design flaws (such as death spirals in algorithmic mechanisms), poor-but-legitimate governance decisions that prove detrimental, complete protocol abandonment, or losses from user error. These risks, rooted in subjective human judgment and economic modeling, lack the objective, verifiable trigger events that are generally required for underwriting and create intractable moral hazard problems.

We believe that decentralized stablecoin protocols should integrate insurance mechanisms either as native features or through formal partnerships with established coverage providers. By making insurance purchasing seamless, perhaps even automated based on user-defined risk parameters, protocols could offer their users a robust, market-based protective layer that significantly improves upon the current decentralized stablecoin landscape.

Beyond decentralized insurance, though, we see limited scope for substantive interventions acceptable to those who embrace decentralization as a philosophical imperative. Our only other meaningful recommendation concerns transparency. Protocol developers should abandon terms borrowed from traditional financial transactions that falsely imply bilateral counterparties and enforceable obligations. The MakerDAO white paper's use of "collateral," "debt," and "liquidation" exemplifies this problem. Instead, all relevant materials accompanying decentralized stablecoins should unequivocally explain that there are no legal counterparties, no recourse beyond what insurance might cover, and that all

[353] *Stablecoin De-Peg Cover*, InsurAce Protocol, https://docs.insurace.io/landing-page/documentation/cover-products/stablecoin-de-peg-cover [https://perma.cc/252U-NZ3W] (last visited Sept. 7, 2025).

[354] *See* Gina Alsdorf & Jason Berkun, *Is Blockchain the Next Big Thing for Insurance Companies?*, Reuters (Oct. 9, 2024), https://www.reuters.com/legal/legalindustry/is-blockchain-next-big-thing-insurance-companies-2024-10-09/ (describing how a decentralized insurance smart contract functions).

economic and governance risks rest entirely with users. Such clarity would align expectations with reality and deter the inadvertent participation of those unprepared for the uncompromising nature of these systems.

Yet, we posit that purists are not the only ones interested in decentralized stablecoins. A different constituency exists: "DLT-pragmatists." These are individuals who approach decentralized stablecoins less ideologically, seeking to escape the frictions and costs of traditional financial institutions, as well as the opaque, asymmetric terms of centralized stablecoin issuers, while remaining unwilling to accept the all-or-nothing risks of total self-reliance. As the user base matures, transaction values grow, and use cases extend beyond mere speculative trading, we expect this pragmatic orientation to become increasingly prevalent.

We hypothesize that these DLT users would evaluate private ordering mechanisms not ideologically but pragmatically. While introducing counterparties or recourse for failures would inevitably encroach upon disintermediation, automation, and privacy, their calculus would be to assess whether the added protections represent an acceptable trade-off. This requires identifying the precise point where legal protection becomes meaningful without triggering the institutional overhead that these users explicitly reject.

While many private ordering mechanisms could serve DLT pragmatists, one is particularly intriguing to us: a DAO with legal personhood issuing the stablecoin. Such an entity could leverage "contractware,"[355] embedding terms directly into the protocol's code, using metadata within each stablecoin token to record rights and obligations, or implementing programmable electronic instruments that execute contractual provisions automatically. As a result, users could opt into legally enforceable relationships through their interactions with the protocol, all without requiring traditional paper agreements or otherwise compromising the system's automated nature. Notably, this approach would fundamentally differ from existing decentralized stablecoins like DAI. While MakerDAO operates as a protocol without legal personhood, leaving users without a counterparty for contractual relationships, our proposed structure would establish a DAO that has legal capacity to enter into binding agreements with stablecoin users.

The implementation of this idea could leverage the growing array of legal frameworks recently enacted in states like Wyoming and Tennessee.[356] These new laws generally grant DAOs limited liability protection, recognize smart contracts as legally binding instruments, and enable tokenized voting systems,

[355] Jason Grant Allen, *Wrapped and Stacked: 'Smart Contracts' and the Interaction of Natural and Formal Language*, *in* Smart Legal Contracts: Computable Law in Theory and Practice 23 (Jason Grant Allen & Peter Hunn eds., 2022).

[356] *See* Bruce, Odinet & Tosato, *Crypto Orgs*, *supra* note 95 (manuscript at 15–20).

all done in such a way as to preserve the flexibility necessary for decentralized governance structures. A DAO organized under such laws could address the specific vulnerabilities identified in decentralized stablecoins. It would provide users with an identifiable legal counterparty for recourse when technical failures or governance decisions cause losses, it would create enforceable contractual rights beyond mere code-based mechanisms, it would establish legal obligations for critical functions like oracle operations and liquidation procedures, and it would offer dispute resolution pathways that extend beyond the limitations of decentralized insurance. Furthermore, such a DAO could also address vulnerabilities common to centralized stablecoins by holding reserve assets in custody and structuring transactions to provide proprietary rights to stablecoin holders. All these capabilities would be achieved while preserving the decentralized decision-making and automated operations that distinguish DAOs from traditional corporate forms.

(b) Centralized stablecoins

In principle, the private law deficiencies plaguing *centralized* stablecoins admit fairly straightforward solutions, largely through amendments to terms of service and accompanying structural adjustments grounded in contract, property, and corporate law. Unlike their decentralized counterparts, where the underlying intellectual foundations and absence of legal counterparties create fundamental obstacles, centralized issuers have complete authority to restructure their legal frameworks however they wish.

The first three vulnerabilities identified arise from contractual design and yield to relatively simple revisions. To expand direct contractual privity, issuers could enlarge their client base through graduated access tiers. While operational concerns may justify some gatekeeping, it is difficult to describe the current extremes as anything other than an artificial insulation through selective curation of customers. Issuers could easily implement differentiated onboarding tracks for various user categories, or even more expansively replicate the inclusive models pioneered by investment trading platforms like Robinhood and eToro, which have successfully balanced accessibility with regulatory compliance.

Similarly, redressing the startling asymmetries seen in issuer terms of service would require only modest recalibration. At minimum, issuers could eliminate the most egregious provisions, including unlimited discretion to suspend services at any moment without notice or reason. They could also implement graduated response mechanisms, such as temporary processing delays during high-volume periods and thus protecting operational stability without eviscerating the rights of token holders. More ambitiously, balanced drafting could impose mutual obligations: mandatory reserve disclosures, advance notice for material modifications, and liability for gross negligence. Such negligence-based standards, replacing blanket disclaimers, would align with current norms in regulated industries such as banking and utilities.

The redemption right could also be improved with minimal effort. Rather than the current confused characterization as an amalgam of revocable license, personal right, and token attribute, it could be reframed as a coherent contractual duty. The core of this obligation would be unambiguous: each token embodies an enforceable claim to receive one dollar from the issuer, exercisable by any holder who completes reasonable verification requirements. While we admit that operational limitations may be necessary, redemption quantity thresholds and processing delays should be designed to ensure minimal disruption to the redemption function. Any temporary suspensions should be accompanied by advance notice, transparent criteria, and defined resolution timelines.

The fourth vulnerability, the absence of proprietary interests in the reserve assets, presents greater complexity but, to our minds, remains eminently addressable. In previous work, we examined three such approaches in detail.[357] Issuers could establish reserves in bankruptcy-remote special purpose vehicles, with independent trustees managing assets exclusively for the benefit of token holders. Alternatively, particularly for commodity-backed stablecoins, tokens could be structured as electronic warehouse receipts under UCC Article 7, creating negotiable documents of title that embody proprietary claims to the reserved assets. Or issuers could adopt specialized corporate forms such as limited purpose trust companies or Wyoming special purpose depository institutions that impose fiduciary obligations and regulatory oversight that supports the custodial treatment of reserves. A fourth approach involves the UCC Article 8 opt-in framework described in Chapter 4. Issuers could agree with direct clients to treat reserves as "financial assets" in "securities accounts," granting those clients security entitlements that protect their interests from the issuer's creditors. While secondary market holders would lack proprietary claims absent contractual privity, institutional clients with direct relationships would benefit from Article 8's comprehensive protections.

We admit that, despite the relative simplicity of these private ordering solutions, market leaders have not implemented them. After nearly a decade of operation, spanning market bubbles and crashes, regulatory scrutiny, and global economic turbulence, Tether and Circle (commanding over $210 billion in combined market capitalization) maintain their highly problematic contractual frameworks, with all the deficiencies we detailed above. This persistence demands explanation.

While we cannot definitively ascertain or ascribe motivations, it seems highly unlikely that institutions of the size and sophistication of Tether and Circle

[357] *See* Bruce, Odinet & Tosato, *supra* note 1, at 1149–58.

remain unaware of these deficiencies or their potential legal solutions. In our assessment, certain provisions betray doctrinal confusion rather than strategic design. For example, the incoherent characterization of redemption rights and Circle's attempt to impose blanket, automatic assignment through contractual fiat appear to reflect technological enthusiasm overriding legal precision. Our hypothesis, as we explained in Chapter 1 and will return to more directly in the Conclusion, is that there are deficiencies that reflect a lack of good private law lawyering. Nevertheless, the overall architecture of these agreements—with their comprehensive liability shields, conditional redemption mechanisms, and exclusion of proprietary interests—suggests that maintaining these frameworks represents a deliberate strategy.

In our view, one reason this choice likely persists is that market dynamics currently reward network effects over private law quality. Tether and Circle have successfully leveraged first-mover advantages, strategic partnerships, and platform integration to dominate the stablecoin market despite offering lackluster legal protections to their customers and token holders. Their continued growth demonstrates that users prioritize liquidity, accessibility, and ecosystem integration over robust rights and insolvency safeguards.

Historical evidence reinforces this hypothesis. As we noted in previous work, by 2022, stablecoins with superior private law architectures already existed in the market.[358] Gemini USD and Paxos USD, both issued by New York limited-purpose trust companies with stronger custodial frameworks, offered holders more balanced contractual terms, more robust redemption rights, and better protection against issuer insolvency. Yet these projects have remained marginal players, collectively capturing less than 1 percent of the stablecoin market. Their failure to gain traction suggests that private ordering alone cannot overcome the market's preference for liquidity over security. The market has spoken clearly: In the absence of external pressure, problematic legal structures backed by superior market position will prevail over superior legal structures lacking network effects.

This dynamic tentatively suggests that the stablecoin market may be experiencing a form of market failure. When competition fails to drive improvements in fundamental legal protections, when network effects entrench inferior structures, and when millions of users bear risks that, we believe, they neither understand nor can effectively price, the conditions that typically justify regulatory intervention begin to emerge. Indeed, the persistence of these private law deficiencies despite readily available solutions may ultimately provide the strongest argument for the regulatory frameworks currently under consideration in multiple jurisdictions.

[358] *Id.* at 1091–93.

8.4.2 Regulatory interventions

Having established that private ordering mechanisms have proven insufficient to remedy the core legal deficiencies of stablecoins, we now turn our analysis to regulatory interventions. Unlike other segments of the digital assets ecosystem where regulatory approaches remain fragmented and tentative (or even non-existent), stablecoins have attracted targeted legislation in both the European Union and the United States.[359] This prioritization reflects both the explosive growth of stablecoins and their emerging role as systemically important payment instruments that bridge traditional finance and digital assets.

To be clear, we welcome these developments, albeit with a significant and familiar qualification that is central to the thesis of this book. As we have argued, particularly in Chapter 1, regulatory/public law interventions in the digital assets space are essential, but they must be built upon a complete and sophisticated understanding of the underlying private law reality. Our concern is that regulation is too often enacted without a full appreciation for the intricate and often precarious web of contractual and proprietary relationships, or the stark absence thereof, that defines these assets and gives rise to the very risks that regulation seeks to mitigate. The analysis that follows examines the MiCAR in the EU and the GENIUS Act in the United States. In these pages we do not aim to provide a comprehensive assessment of these regimes. Rather, we want to assess the extent to which and the manner in which these efforts address the specific private law vulnerabilities that we have identified throughout this chapter. It bears noting that both regulatory frameworks are extremely recent (indeed, the GENIUS Act was passed as we were finalizing the draft of this final chapter of the book). Thus, our considerations are necessarily preliminary.

(a) Decentralized stablecoins

The regulatory challenges posed by decentralized stablecoins mirror and magnify the private law difficulties analyzed earlier in this chapter. As we established, protocols like MakerDAO operate without legal personhood, leaving users with no contractual counterparties, no identifiable parties to hold accountable, and no recourse beyond the autonomous operation of smart contracts. This fundamental absence of legal persons creates a corresponding regulatory void: There is, quite simply, no entity to regulate. The software exists, the tokens circulate, and billions of dollars in value move through these systems. As such, regulators

[359] *Fiat-Backed Stablecoin Regulation Compared: UK, EU, Hong Kong, and US*, Morgan Lewis (June 12, 2025), https://www.morganlewis.com/pubs/2025/06/fiat-backed-stablecoin-regulation-compared-uk-eu-hong-kong-and-us [https://perma.cc/29LW-QR6Y].

are left to confront an architecture deliberately designed to evade any centralized oversight.

From a theoretical perspective, regulators confronting decentralized stablecoins have three primary avenues for intervention, each presenting distinct challenges. First, regulators could target the software developers and core maintainers who create and modify the protocol code. This might include imposing functional requirements on smart contract design, mandating certain protective features, or even criminalizing the deployment of noncompliant protocols. This approach is technically feasible: Although often pseudonymous, developers are identifiable individuals subject to jurisdiction under the law.[360]

Second, regulators could focus on users themselves by restricting who may hold decentralized stablecoins or by imposing quantity limits. Lawmakers could also create burdensome tax regimes that discourage adoption of decentralized stablecoins (a pathway that would echo broader restrictions on digital assets pursued in some jurisdictions). This strategy is also relatively straightforward in terms of feasibility, although it risks driving activity offshore or into more opaque systems, potentially exacerbating rather than mitigating risks.

Third, public law efforts could concentrate on the interfaces between decentralized protocols and both the wider digital assets landscape and traditional financial system. Under this approach, regulators would target the exchanges, hosted wallet companies, and other service providers that enable most users to acquire, hold, and transfer decentralized stablecoins. Although this approach simply cannot reach users who interact directly with protocols (as in the case of holding stablecoins in unhosted wallets), it can significantly constrain mainstream adoption by leveraging existing regulatory relationships with identifiable entities. This strategy has been deployed in other contexts, such as the pressure on major exchanges that led to the delisting of privacy-enhancing coins.[361]

The EU's approach to decentralized stablecoins under MiCAR appears to exemplify this approach of focusing on intermediaries. This law establishes a regime that avoids direct regulation of autonomous protocols, choosing instead to exercise oversight through the access points that most users depend upon to interact with these systems. On one hand, Recital 22 explicitly excludes digital assets with "no identifiable issuer" from the core regulatory framework

[360] As shown by recent enforcement actions, in the United States. *See* United States v. Storm & Semenov, No. 1:23-cr-00430 (S.D.N.Y. filed Aug. 23, 2023); *see also In re* Universal Navigation Inc. d/b/a Uniswap Labs, CFTC Docket No. 24-25 (Sept. 4, 2024); United States v. Rodriguez & Hill, No. 1:24-cr-00082 (S.D.N.Y. filed Feb. 14, 2024).

[361] For example, exchanges like Binance and Kraken have delisted privacy coins (Monero, Zcash, Dash) in various jurisdictions due to regulatory pressure and AML/KYC compliance difficulties with obscured transaction data.

for issuers,[362] thereby seemingly cutting out decentralized stablecoins such as DAI.[363] On the other hand, the same recital immediately clarifies that while the protocols themselves are not in scope, "crypto-asset service providers (CASPs) providing services in respect of such crypto-assets should, however, be covered by this Regulation."[364]

In practice, MiCAR operationalizes this approach through specific requirements that transform CASPs into quasi-issuers for decentralized crypto assets (which is the term MiCAR uses for digital assets). When crypto assets have no identifiable issuer, CASPs that wish to offer such assets must draft and publish a white paper describing the asset's characteristics, functionality, and risks, while also performing enhanced due diligence and suitability assessments.[365] The CASP assumes full responsibility for the accuracy of these representations, creating liability exposure for any assets that they cannot control. This places both the regulatory burden and legal risk on intermediaries, who must determine whether listing such assets is worth the exposure to claims arising from any autonomous systems that are beyond their influence. The result is a framework that may constrain mainstream access to decentralized stablecoins not through direct prohibition, but through the allocation of potentially unmanageable or at least difficult to manage risks to market intermediaries.

Yet the application of MiCAR's framework to decentralized stablecoins reveals unresolved tensions. The regulation establishes special rules for e-money tokens (EMTs), which are crypto assets that purport to maintain stable value by referencing an official currency.[366] For EMTs, MiCAR presupposes the presence of an issuer that must, among other things, obtain preapproval for their white paper from designated regulatory authorities,[367] and the issuer must grant holders a direct right of redemption backed by a reserve of assets held in custody.[368] Decentralized stablecoins like DAI appear to satisfy the functional definition of an EMT (since they purport to maintain stable value), yet they lack the centralized issuer necessary to comply with MiCAR's mandatory requirements. This creates a regulatory conundrum: Can a CASP legally offer an

[362] MiCAR, *supra* note 4, recital 22 ("Where crypto-assets have no identifiable issuer, they should not fall within the scope of Title II, III or IV of this Regulation.").

[363] *See* Matthias Lehmann, *MiCAR–Gold Standard or Regulatory Poison for the Crypto Industry?*, at 4 (EBI Working Paper Series No. 160, 2024), https://papers.ssrn.com/sol3/papers.cfm?abstract_id=4692743; *see also MiCAR & Unidentifiable Issuers of Crypto Assets*, Axis Advisory (Sept. 10, 2023), https://axisadvisoryxyz.substack.com/p/mica-unidentifiable-issuers-of-crypto.

[364] MiCAR, *supra* note 4, recital 22.

[365] Council Regulation 2023/1114, *supra* note 4, arts. 4(3), 6 (requiring CASPs to prepare the white paper and comply with content requirements for crypto assets without an identifiable issuer).

[366] MiCAR, *supra* note 4, art. 3(1)(7) (defining "e-money token" as "a type of crypto-asset that purports to maintain a stable value by referencing the value of one official currency").

[367] *Id.* art. 51 (requiring competent authority approval of EMT white papers before publication).

[368] *Id.* art. 48(1).

asset that functionally qualifies as an EMT but structurally cannot satisfy EMT obligations? Or must such tokens be excluded from EU markets entirely? To date, no EU-based CASP has, as of the time of writing, listed a major decentralized stablecoin under the MiCAR regime, although whether this reflects a regulatory prohibition or mere market caution remains to be determined.[369] Moreover, it should be noted that Article 146 of MiCAR requires the European Commission to present, within forty-eight months of the regulation's effective date, a comprehensive assessment of decentralized finance and recommendations for its adequate regulatory treatment.[370]

Traveling across the pond, the United States appears to be adopting a fundamentally different approach through the recently enacted GENIUS Act.[371] Unlike MiCAR's broad definitional scope, this legislation focuses exclusively on centralized stablecoins. In fact, the Act's definition of a "payment stablecoin" requires an identifiable "issuer," thereby excluding decentralized protocols that lack such entities.[372] This exclusion is reinforced through explicit carveouts in Section 2(7)(B) that exempt distributed ledger protocols, self-custodial software interfaces, and liquidity pools from the definition of "digital asset service provider."[373] The result is a regulatory perimeter that acknowledges but explicitly does not capture decentralized stablecoins.

However, in our study of the legislation, the GENIUS Act certainly has its own uncertainties. While decentralized protocols themselves escape regulation, the GENIUS Act remains silent on whether digital asset service providers may list or facilitate trading in decentralized stablecoins. This creates potential market access questions similar to those under MiCAR. Notably, the Act's approach appears deliberately provisional. Section 14 mandates a Treasury Department study specifically examining "endogenously collateralized payment stablecoins"—a category that would appear to encompass tokens such as DAI—while Section 9(e)(1)(E) requires recommendations regarding the application of digital asset service provider definitions to decentralized finance.[374] This

[369] *See Interim MiCA Register-Other Crypto-Assets*, ESMA (Dec. 2024) (on file with author) (showing no white papers published for major decentralized stablecoins such as DAI).

[370] MiCAR, *supra* note 4, art. 146.

[371] GENIUS Act, S. 1582, 119th Cong. (2025).

[372] *Id.* § 2(22)(A)(ii) (requiring that payment stablecoins have an "issuer" that "is obligated to convert, redeem, or repurchase for a fixed amount of monetary value").

[373] *Id.* § 2(7)(B) (excluding from the definition of "digital asset service provider" any "distributed ledger protocol," "immutable and self-custodial software interface," and participation in "liquidity pool[s] or other similar mechanism[s] for the provisioning of liquidity for peer-to-peer transactions").

[374] *Id.* § 14 (mandating study of "endogenously collateralized payment stablecoins" defined as digital assets that rely "solely on the value of another digital asset created or maintained by the same originator"); *id.* § 9(e)(1)(E) (requiring recommendations on "the scope of the term 'digital asset service provider' and the application of that term to decentralized finance").

regulatory sequencing and study-first approach suggests that the United States recognizes that decentralized stablecoins may require different regulatory tools than their centralized counterparts. What that different treatment might be remains an open question pending further study.

(b) Centralized stablecoins

Centralized stablecoins present a fundamentally different regulatory proposition than their decentralized counterparts, since their issuers are readily identifiable legal entities that can be easily subjected to conventional oversight. This structural difference enables the deployment of the full arsenal of financial regulatory tools, such as entry requirements, ongoing supervision, safety and soundness rules, and operational standards.

MiCAR addresses centralized stablecoins through two distinct categories: asset-referenced tokens (ARTs) and EMTs. ARTs are defined as crypto-assets that "purport to maintain a stable value by referencing another value or right or a combination thereof, including one or more official currencies."[375] This category captures stablecoins pegged to commodities (such as gold), baskets of currencies, or other assets, provided they do not reference a single official currency. EMTs, by contrast, are crypto-assets that "purport to maintain a stable value by referencing the value of one official currency."[376] This category encompasses only stablecoins pegged to a single fiat currency, such as the US dollar or euro.[377] The GENIUS Act adopts a different categorical approach, establishing a single "payment stablecoin" classification defined as digital assets "designed to maintain stable value relative to a reference asset and are readily redeemable for fiat currency."[378] Unlike MiCAR's distinction based on the nature of the reference asset at issue, the GENIUS Act focuses on the functional requirement of fiat redeemability, thereby potentially capturing within a single category stablecoins that MiCAR would separate into ARTs or EMTs.

Regarding the first vulnerability (that being the limited direct contractual relationships between issuers and token holders), neither MiCAR nor the GENIUS Act mandates the formation of a traditional agreement with every holder. Both laws permit the continuation of market structures where many holders acquire stablecoins on secondary markets without a direct agreement with the issuer. Instead, both laws create statutory rights and obligations that produce a direct legal nexus between the issuer and any of the holders of its stablecoin. Through this regulatory architecture, MiCAR and the GENIUS Act

375 MiCAR, *supra* note 4, art. 3(1)(6).
376 *Id.* art. 3(1)(7).
377 *Id.* recital 16.
378 GENIUS Act § 2(22).

also address, to varying degrees, the asymmetrical power dynamics that have historically characterized issuer-holder relationships. This is accomplished by establishing baseline standards that constrain issuer discretion and protect holder interests, regardless of the contractual arrangements at play.

MiCAR addresses the profound imbalance of power in issuer-holder relationships through a multi-pronged approach that combines principles-based duties, specific prohibitions, and a robust liability regime. For both ARTs and EMTs, the regulation imposes a fundamental duty on issuers to act in a manner that is honest, fair, and professional and to communicate in a way that is "fair, clear and not misleading" under Articles 27 and 44, respectively.[379] MiCAR also mandates extensive disclosure requirements through detailed white papers under Articles 19 (ARTs) and 51 (EMTs), ensuring transparency about holder rights and issuer obligations.[380] Significantly, a strict liability regime is introduced for any misleading information that is contained in crypto asset white papers. Articles 26 (for ARTs) and 52 (for EMTs) hold issuers and their management liable for any loss incurred by holders due to information that is "not complete, fair or clear, or that is misleading."[381] Crucially, Articles 26(2) and 52(2) render any contractual clause attempting to exclude or limit this civil liability as "deprived of legal effect."[382] This, in effect, directly invalidates the broad liability disclaimers we discussed above and that are so prevalent in current market practice.[383] Issuers must also establish internal complaint-handling procedures and must cooperate with competent authorities in resolving disputes.[384] Additionally, Recital 29 explicitly confirms that existing EU consumer protection legislation (including the Unfair Terms Directive) continues to apply alongside all of MiCAR's specific provisions, thus creating multiple layers of stablecoin

[379] MiCAR, *supra* note 4, arts. 27(1), 44, 53(1). For issuers of EMTs, the obligation to act honestly, professionally, and fairly comes from the imposition of special standards of conduct by EU member states who, under the Electronic Money Directive, authorize these issuers to operate. *See id.* art. 48(1) (requiring issuer of e-money tokens to be "authorized as a credit institution or an electronic money institution."); *see also* Council Directive 2009/110, art. 3(1), 2009 O.J. (L 267) 7 (EC) (requiring that those seeking authorization as an electronic money institution follow Article 5 of the Payment Services Directive); Council Directive 2007/64, art. 5, 2007 O.J. (L 319) 1 (EC) ("For authorisation as a payment institution, an application shall be submitted to the competent authorities of the home Member State"). Notably, Member States of the EU have generally required that authorized electronic payment institutions act professionally, fairly, and honestly, in the best interests of their customers, or some variation thereof. *See, e.g.*, Consumer Protection Code 2012, § 2.1 (Central Bank of Ireland 2012) (rev. 2015), https://www.centralbank.ie/regulation/consumer-protection/consumer-protection-code; *see also* Code monétaire et financier [C. mon. fin.], art. L519-4-1 (Fr.), https://www.legifrance.gouv.fr/codes/article_lc/LEGIARTI000032297612/2016-07-01.

[380] MiCAR, *supra* note 4, arts. 19, 51. Notably, ARTs require white paper approval before issuance (Arts. 17(1)(a), 21(1)), while EMTs need only notify competent authorities before publication (Art. 51).

[381] *Id.* arts. 26, 52.

[382] *Id.* arts. 26(2), 52.

[383] *See* Bruce, Odinet & Tosato, *supra* note 1, at 1092–93.

[384] MiCAR, *supra* note 4, art. 34.

holder protection.[385] However, the fourteen-day right of withdrawal found more broadly in the Consumer Rights Directive does not apply to purchases of any stablecoins, per Article 13.

The GENIUS Act, in comparison, provides a significantly more limited set of rights and obligations governing the issuer-holder relationship. The focus here is primarily on operational requirements rather than on addressing the fundamental power imbalances that characterize current market practice. Section 4(a)(9) prohibits deceptive naming or marketing that would lead a "reasonable person" to believe the stablecoin is issued, guaranteed, or approved by the US government.[386] Without imposing either fiduciary duties or principles-based conduct standards comparable to MiCAR, Section 6(c) simply states that nothing in the Act may be construed to "modify or otherwise affect any right or remedy under any Federal consumer financial law."[387] Section 7(f)(4) further clarifies that the Act does not "preempt State consumer protection laws, including common law, and the remedies available thereunder," thereby maintaining state-level protections.[388] Possibly recognizing the statute's limited prescriptive content regarding issuer conduct and holder rights, the GENIUS Act delegates broad authority for rulemaking that could potentially introduce additional rights for stablecoin holders, such as disclosure requirements or standards of issuer conduct. Notably, Section 3(d) empowers the Secretary of the Treasury to "issue regulations to implement Section 3 of the Act, including to define terms," while Section 4(b) mandates that primary federal payment stablecoin regulators "shall issue such regulations relating to permitted payment stablecoin issuers as may be necessary to administer Section 4."[389]

Addressing one of the most critical private law deficiencies currently affecting centralized stablecoins, both law substantially strengthen redemption rights. They do so, however, through quite different legal mechanisms.

MiCAR establishes redemption as an unconditional statutory right that cannot be contractually limited or suspended except in very narrow regulatory circumstances. For ARTs, Article 39(1) mandates that holders "shall have a right of redemption at all times against the issuers," with Article 39(2) specifying that issuers must redeem either by paying funds equivalent to market value

[385] *Id.* recital 29 ("Even though some offers of crypto-assets other than asset-referenced tokens or e-money tokens are exempt from various obligations of this Regulation, Union legislative acts that ensure consumer protection, such as Directive 2005/29/EC . . . or Council Directive 93/13/EEC . . . remain applicable to offers to the public of crypto-assets where they concern business-to-consumer relationships.").

[386] GENIUS Act, S. 1582, 119th Cong. § 4(a)(9) (2025).

[387] GENIUS Act § 6(c).

[388] GENIUS Act § 7 (f)(4).

[389] GENIUS Act §§ 3(d), 4(b). Under the Act, the "Primary Federal Payment Stablecoin Regulator" is the federal agency supervising payment stablecoin activities, determined by the issuer's chartering authority.

or by delivering the referenced assets themselves.[390] For EMTs, Article 49(1) requires issuers to "redeem, at any moment and at par value, the monetary value of the e-money tokens held."[391] Both provisions explicitly prohibit redemption fees under Articles 39(3) and 49(5).[392] While MiCAR does permit temporary suspensions of redemption under Article 46(4) in circumstances threatening financial stability, such acts require regulatory approval and must be "justified having regard to the interests of the holders."[393]

The GENIUS Act takes a different approach. This law defines a "payment stablecoin" as a digital asset "the issuer of which is obligated to convert, redeem, or repurchase for a fixed amount of monetary value."[394] This provision centers on the digital asset and its issuer. Though terse, this language appears to constitute a form of "tokenization, from a private law perspective ." As we explain in Chapter 3, that is to say that the digital asset is deemed to evidence and embody the issuer's legal obligation to convert, redeem or repurchase. The counterargument would rest on the premise that the stablecoin token and the right to redeem are distinct assets; that holding the digital asset does not, without more, make one the beneficiary of the issuer's obligation to "convert, redeem, or repurchase." However, read systematically and in light of its declared objectives, the Act's structure suggests the opposite: that the redemption right is merged into the digital asset itself. To be sure, the GENIUS Act does not use this exact language, does not employ the word tokenize or a derivative, and does not include any additional description or elaboration about who can and who cannot enforce the redemptive right in respect of the stablecoin. More specifically, as to this last point, the Act does not explicitly address to whom this obligation is owed—whether to the owner of the stablecoin or the person in control of it. We would favor the latter interpretation, which would align the regulatory category of payment stablecoins with controllable payment intangibles under Article 12 of the UCC. As we explained in Part I of this book, under Article 12, control (rather than ownership) determines who can enforce the underlying monetary obligation.

Building on this structure, Section 4(a)(1)(B) operationalizes the redemption right by requiring issuers to establish and publicly disclose "clear and conspicuous procedures for timely redemption" with all fees disclosed in "plain language" and changeable only with "not less than 7 days' prior notice to consumers."[395] Critically, the GENIUS Act removes an issuer's power

[390] MiCAR, *supra* note 4, art. 39(1)–(2).
[391] *Id.* art. 49(1).
[392] *Id.* arts. 39(3), 49(5).
[393] *Id.* art. 46(4).
[394] *See* GENIUS Act § 2(22)(A)(ii)(I).
[395] GENIUS Act § 4(a)(1)(B).

to unilaterally suspend redemption, providing that "any discretionary limitations on timely redemptions can only be imposed by a State qualified payment stablecoin regulator, the Corporation, the Comptroller, or the Board."[396]

Finally, regarding stablecoin holders' absence of proprietary interests in reserve assets, MiCAR and the GENIUS Act pursue comparable objectives through markedly different legal mechanisms. Under MiCAR, the regulation establishes comprehensive requirements for reserve asset management, including mandatory segregation from the issuer's own assets under Article 36(3), custody with authorized credit institutions or crypto asset service providers under Article 37, and investment restrictions limiting reserves to highly liquid, low-risk assets under Article 38.[397] MiCAR also requires that reserve assets be segregated from the estate of the issuer and requires that custody arrangements ensure reserves are insulated from claims of creditors of the issuer.[398] However, MiCAR stops short of granting token holders direct proprietary rights or security interests in the reserve assets. The regulation's approach creates a form of quasi-proprietary protection through operational and legal segregation requirements, but in an insolvency scenario, holders would likely remain unsecured creditors, albeit with claims against a segregated asset pool whereby they would ostensibly face no competition from other creditors. This approach likely reflects the EU's constrained legal authority when it comes to harmonizing insolvency law across member states, thereby leaving the ultimate treatment of token holder claims to national bankruptcy laws.[399]

The GENIUS Act similarly imposes strict reserve management requirements, though with a characteristically American regulatory approach. Section 4(a)(1)(A) mandates that payment stablecoin issuers maintain reserves on a one-to-one basis, composed exclusively of specified low-risk assets, including US currency, Treasury securities, central bank reserves, and repurchase agreements collateralized by Treasury securities, all held with certain qualified financial institutions acting as custodians.[400] Section 4(a)(2) categorically prohibits rehypothecation of reserves except for limited liquidity management purposes, while Section 10(c) requires that payment stablecoin reserves be segregated from the custodian's own assets and separately accounted for, though omnibus

[396] GENIUS Act § 4(a)(1)(B).

[397] MiCAR, *supra* note 4, arts. 37(2), (3), 38(1), 54.

[398] *Id.* arts. 36(3), 54 (requiring EMT issuers to comply with article 7(1) of Council Directive 2009); *see* Council Directive 2009/110, *supra* note 379, art. 7 (requiring "safeguarding" of funds received in exchange for electronic money under Article 9(1) and (2) of Directive 2007/64/EC); Council Directive 2007/64, *supra* note 379, art. 9(1)(a) (prohibiting commingling and requiring insulation from the issuer's insolvency).

[399] Consolidated Version of the Treaty on the Functioning of the European Union art. 114, Oct. 26, 2012, 2012 O.J. (C 326) 47 (limiting the EU's competence to approximation of laws necessary for the functioning of the internal market).

[400] GENIUS Act § 4(a)(1)(A).

accounts holding multiple issuers' reserves are permitted.[401] The Act extends protection even in the event of the custodian holding the reserve assets becoming insolvent, with Section 10(c)(3) granting stablecoin holders priority claims over other creditors of the custodian with respect to the reserves.[402]

Beyond these reserve management requirements and special priority rules, the GENIUS Act directly amends the US Bankruptcy Code to create unprecedented insolvency protections for stablecoin holders. Section 11(e)(3) excludes reserves from the debtor's estate, stating that required reserves "shall not be considered . . . property of the estate."[403] This creates complete bankruptcy remoteness, ensuring that the issuer's general creditors cannot reach the reserve assets. Moreover, there is no possibility for the debtor to obtain credit based on the reserves, nor can these assets be surcharged under Section 506(c) for estate preservation expenses.[404] Even more radically, Section 11(a) establishes a comprehensive priority scheme for stablecoin holders. First, Section 11(a)(2) ensures that "any person holding a payment stablecoin issued by the permitted payment stablecoin issuer shall be deemed to hold a claim," thereby guaranteeing standing in bankruptcy proceedings regardless of contractual arrangements.[405] Second, Section 11(a)(1) provides that "the claim of a person holding payment stablecoins . . . shall have priority, on a ratable basis with the claims of other persons holding such payment stablecoins, over the claims of the permitted payment stablecoin issuer and any other holder of claims against the permitted payment stablecoin issuer, with respect to required payment stablecoin reserves."[406] Third, Section 11(a)(3) clarifies that "the priority under paragraph (1) shall not apply to claims other than those arising directly from the holding of payment stablecoins," ensuring that only legitimate holders benefit from these protections.[407] Most strikingly, Section 11(d) creates a "super-priority" for any shortfall in reserves, granting stablecoin holders priority over all other Section 507 claims, including the administrative expenses necessary to operate the bankruptcy proceeding itself.[408]

[401] GENIUS Act §§ 4(a)(2), 10(c).
[402] GENIUS Act § 10(c)(3).
[403] GENIUS Act § 11(e)(3).
[404] GENIUS Act § 506 (c).
[405] GENIUS Act § 11(a)(2).
[406] GENIUS Act § 11(a)(1).
[407] GENIUS Act § 11(a)(3).
[408] GENIUS Act § 11(d). For an early analysis of these provisions, see Adam Levitin, *Forcing Bank Deposits to Subsidize Stablecoins: the GENIUS Act*, Credit Slips (May 7, 2025), https://creditslips.org/2025/05/07/the-genius-acts-insolvency-provisions-crypto-investors-come-ahead-of-bank-depositors/; *see also* Edwin Smith, Penelope Christophorou, Stacie Hartman, Stacy Hrdy & David Wake, *Lawflash: The Proposed GENIUS Act Raises Concerns over Insolvency Provisions*, Morgan Lewis (July 2, 2025), https://www.morganlewis.com/pubs/2025/07/the-proposed-genius-act-raises-concerns-over-insolvency-provisions.

While these GENIUS Act provisions clearly address the current market reality where stablecoin holders lack meaningful claims to the relevant reserve assets, the law's solution of providing maximum protection for stablecoin holders gives us pause. We question whether these provisions risk, ironically, creating yet a new private law flaw. The subordination of administrative claims to any shortfall claims of the stablecoin holders dramatically increases the likelihood of an administratively insolvent debtor. This means that the debtor lacks sufficient assets to cover the administrative expenses of the bankruptcy case itself, such as trustee fees, attorney costs, and other case administration expenses. As such, this potentially makes a bankruptcy reorganization unfeasible. The Act's approach effectively grants stablecoin holders something approaching absolute priority in the reserves, but at the potential cost of undermining the bankruptcy system's ability to actually function effectively. We suggest that a more measured approach might have treated stablecoin holder claims as secured claims with super-priority status over other secured creditors. This would preserve both stablecoin holder protection and bankruptcy functionality. As currently drafted, the provisions may inadvertently harm the very holders they seek to protect by creating unworkable insolvency proceedings that destroy value for all the stakeholders.

Conclusion

As we reach the end of our journey, one conclusion stands clear: the digital asset economy is mired in legal disequilibrium. As we see it, two great imbalances are responsible for this condition. First, the legal community's engagement with distributed ledger technology (DLT) has been overwhelmingly channeled through a public law lens. An intense focus on financial regulation has overshadowed the private law tenets upon which all commercial relationships are built. Second, when private law enters the conversation, the discussion is nearly always confined to contract law. Foundational rights and duties defined by property, tort, and other areas of private law are swept aside. This is the flexibility fallacy: the misguided belief that private agreements are omnipotent, capable of overriding the fundamental boundary separating rights enforceable only between the parties and those enforceable against the world, as well as the line separating default and mandatory rules. As described in the preceding chapters, this delusion prospers in good times but inevitably collapses in litigation or bankruptcy.

As a normative matter, we believe that restoring equilibrium requires coordinated action from three distinct but interconnected communities, each of which plays a crucial role in shaping how the law adapts to technological change. First, we turn to lawmakers, encompassing judges, legislators, and regulators. These actors must recognize that effective public policy in the digital asset space requires a sophisticated wedding of regulation and private law, where the former is carefully constructed upon the foundation of the latter.

Second, we turn to the members of the bar who counsel clients in deploying emerging technologies. We argue that these individuals must abandon the flexibility fallacy. Instead, they must recognize that contractual agreements, however sophisticated their drafting, operate within defined boundaries that cannot be transgressed. Equally important, they must develop genuine expertise in property, bailment, secured transactions, and the other branches of private law, understanding both what these frameworks make possible and what limits they impose.

Third and last, we turn to a group all too familiar to the two of us: the legal academy. Collectively, we must confront the diminished role of private law in both our curricula and research. And, in doing so, we must recommit to

Digital Commercial Law. Christopher K. Odinet and Andrea Tosato, Oxford University Press.
 DOI: 10.1093/9780197758656.003.0012

providing students with all the tools they need to navigate an increasingly complex legal and economic landscape.

The stakes of this rebalancing extend far beyond the digital asset ecosystem itself. As we have seen repeatedly throughout the preceding chapters, attempts to circumvent fundamental private law principles through technological solutions or creative contractual arrangements inevitably lead to confusion, litigation, and overall market dysfunction. The spectacular failures we have documented, from the collapse of major exchanges to the illusory promises of nonfungible tokens (NFTs) and the faulty mechanisms for stablecoin redemption, do not trace their primary origins to technological deficiencies or market manipulation. Instead, they find their roots in fundamental misunderstandings about the interface between public and private law and the inherent limits of contract.

To lawmakers: coordinated public–private law governance

Turning to our first group (the lawmakers), we start with *judges*.

Judges occupy a unique position as the primary architects and guardians of the common law. In the digital asset space, this role is more critical than ever, as they face a two-pronged challenge from private parties seeking to operate outside established legal constraints. The first challenge is the flexibility fallacy, through which contract law is wielded to trample over the distinct and mandatory private law principles. A second, subtler challenge often reinforces this: the misconception that whatever technology makes possible, the law must recognize as permissible and enforceable.

Faced with these pressures, we recommend that judges embrace two essential responsibilities. They must preserve the distinct scope and competence of each branch of private law, resisting attempts to use contract to achieve what the law otherwise either forbids or governs within strict parameters. In parallel, they must also reaffirm that law, not technology, is the legitimate source of rights and obligations. As Professor Lawrence Lessig observed, code can shape behavior through its architectural constraints. However, as lucidly theorized by H.L.A. Hart and other legal positivists, it is the law alone that determines what is legally permissible and how relationships are to be governed.

To implement these recommendations, judges need both the sword and the shield. They must wield the sword to slice through complex arrangements, severing genuine innovation from inadmissible artifice. Common law judges have a long and storied history of accommodating novel business practices. That vital tradition must continue. However, it must be paired with an equally strong commitment to striking down provisions designed not for true innovation but either to artfully sidestep mandatory legal duties or negate third-party rights.

Consider, for example, the dubious tokenizations involving real estate assets or the assertions that ownership of NFTs is mediated soley by technological systems.

But the sword alone is not enough. A judge also needs the shield to observe and understand the effects of technology. The goal is not to become programmers but to understand how systems operate to avoid conflating technological capabilities with legal validity. Too often, courts allow themselves to be overwhelmed by seemingly impenetrable technical intricacies, leading them to defer uncritically to industry-preferred explanations or to accept oversimplified metaphors that obscure rather than illuminate the true nature of the relationships. As Carla Reyes observes, authorities often fabricate intermediaries to shoehorn peer-to-peer systems into frameworks designed for intermediated relationships. The result is a judicial tendency to mischaracterize fundamental technological realities, treating software as entities or smart contracts as traditional contracts, rather than grappling with the actual nature of decentralized systems.

This functional understanding of technology is essential to overcome any technological intimidation and to scrutinize the narratives presented by litigants. Digital asset firms and their lawyers have become adept at deploying self-serving characterizations, such as describing themselves as mere "platforms" or "intermediaries" that provide standardized services without assuming responsibility for outcomes. Concurrently, they often argue that technological advancement necessarily implies legal novelty, and that their innovative systems create completely new categories of relationships entirely outside traditional law.

Judges should treat such claims with a healthy degree of skepticism. To penetrate these narratives, they should ask probing, operational questions: How do users actually interact with the system? Who makes decisions about system modifications? What happens when things go wrong, and who bears the consequences? These questions reveal the true nature of legal relationships far more clearly than abstract discussions of technology. This analytical process is the ultimate payoff of functional understanding: It allows a judge to look past the technology and identify whether an arrangement is, in substance, a bailment, a trust, or some other established legal relationship. For instance, in a custody dispute, this method allows a judge to determine whether one party has truly transferred control of an asset to another for safekeeping or if a person has merely acquired a software service to manage their own assets. From that core determination, the parties' rights and duties inevitably flow.

By wielding both the sword and the shield, judges can fulfill their essential duty: ensuring that digital asset transactions operate within, not outside, established private law. Structures that respect the distinction between contractual obligations and property rights deserve judicial recognition. Those that attempt to create rights without duties or to operate outside private law's fixed categories merit no judicial recognition.

The importance of judges fulfilling these responsibilities extends far beyond individual disputes. If judges fail to maintain private law's boundaries or are paralyzed by technological sophistication, the systemic consequences are severe. The most immediate casualty is the coherence of private law itself. If contract law is allowed to eclipse all other branches, the predictability of commercial relations vanishes, and the principles that undergird market stability are compromised. This legal uncertainty, in turn, facilitates highly problematic business practices that lead to systemic market failures and consumer harm. The stakes, however, are higher still. By insisting that code must operate within the law, judges affirm the primacy of our legal and democratic order over purely technological capabilities. In doing so, they preserve the law's role as the guardian of society's normative prescriptions. This judicial engagement serves a vital democratic function: It ensures that the development of commercial law remains within the bounds of established institutional processes, rather than being captured by private parties with superior technical knowledge and resources. When courts defer uncritically to industry-provided technological explanations and contractual arrangements, they effectively delegate legal decision-making to the very parties whose interests are at stake in the litigation.

The common law has always adapted to technological change, from the printing press to the postal system to the telegraph. This adaptation, however, has never been a capitulation. It has always proceeded through the principled application of established legal concepts to new facts. Digital assets, however sophisticated, are simply the latest chapter in this long story of legal evolution.

Next, we turn to *legislators* and to the administrative *regulators* they empower.

In the United States, legislators have been grappling with the challenges posed by the digital asset ecosystem for over a decade. At the state level, this has led to a fragmented patchwork of regulations from comprehensive licensing regimes in New York and California to Wyoming's recognition of decentralized autonomous organizations as legal entities and Texas's enactment of "proof of reserves" legislation for digital asset custodians. At the federal level, a multiplicity of bills has been proposed to address various aspects of this fast-evolving landscape, yet these initiatives have often proved contentious and failed to garner sufficient support. This long-standing impasse, however, was broken in early 2025. As this book was being finalized, Congress enacted the GENIUS Act, establishing a federal framework for stablecoins.

With the notable exception of state enactments of the 2022 Amendments to the UCC, which proved surprisingly divisive, the overwhelming majority of this legislation has concentrated on financial regulation issues. Legislators have focused on classification issues (whether digital assets should be treated as commodities, currencies, or securities), licensing requirements for digital asset businesses, anti-money laundering compliance, sanctions enforcement, market manipulation prohibitions, customer asset protection rules, cybersecurity standards, and money transmission regulations at the state level. This focus on measures designed to reduce systemic risk, govern market participants' conduct, and protect consumers is both understandable and warranted. Yet this near-exclusive attention to public law matters has left the private law underpinnings of the digital assets world dangerously understudied, creating the risk of a regulatory superstructure that may collapse under market stress.

To understand the problem, we must recognize how private law and public law interact regarding commercial transactions. Private law establishes the bedrock: It defines the breadth of property rights and the mechanisms for their transfer, determines tortious and contractual rights and obligations, apportions risks between parties, establishes the priority of claims, and provides remedies for breaches. Public law then intervenes atop this foundation, imposing gatekeeping requirements and standards of conduct, shifting default risk allocations, and, in some cases, even altering the parties' duties or introducing additional remedies, all in service to broader normative goals. But public law cannot succeed without a thorough understanding of the private law substratum it seeks to modify.

Consider how this dynamic plays out in the custody of traditional financial assets. The private law bedrock is governed by long-standing common law principles of bailment and agency together with the body of rules established by UCC Article 8. This framework realizes a coherent regime that defines a customer's unique property interest (the "security entitlement"), codifies the core duties of the intermediary, and includes powerful rules that insulate customer assets from the intermediary's insolvency. Because this private law foundation is clear and well-understood, financial regulation can effectively be built upon it. Agencies like the Securities and Exchange Commission (SEC) and the Office of the Comptroller of the Currency (OCC) can focus on supervisory issues like net capital requirements, reporting obligations, and conduct rules for financial institutions, confident in their understanding of the customer–property–intermediary nexus. This entire structure is further reinforced by statutory backstops, like the Securities Investor Protection Corporation (SIPC) insurance, which provides an additional layer of customer protection.

Understanding the interplay between private law and public regulation is not an academic exercise. It is an indispensable condition for crafting effective and durable legislative frameworks for digital assets. Regulatory interventions that ignore the private law bedrock are destined to be ineffective or worse, to create unintended and pernicious consequences. It is with this principle in mind that we offer the following recommendations for legislators.

First, as with the judiciary, legislators should develop a working, functional knowledge of digital asset technologies. While the required skill is the same, its objective is distinct. A judge uses this knowledge to correctly adjudicate the relationship between specific litigants. A legislator, in contrast, must comprehend the technology to craft rules that govern how society uses these systems.

Second, the legislative process must begin with a thorough due diligence of the existing private law landscape. Before proposing a new regulatory regime, lawmakers must investigate and understand how the current rules of property, contract, and commercial law apply to the activity under consideration. As our analysis of stablecoins demonstrated, this assessment can be extremely complex and multifaceted, unearthing a range of heterogeneous issues that require careful consideration. To conduct this assessment, legislators need not start from scratch. They can and should formally engage with nonpartisan, expert bodies dedicated to this work, including the Uniform Law Commission and the American Law Institute.

Third, the findings from this due diligence should inform a crucial strategic choice: whether a legislative response is necessary and, if so, what form it should take. A new layer of regulation should not be the default solution. In some cases, the most efficient and effective remedy is to clarify or update the private law itself. For example, as we suggested in Chapter 4, extending common law bailment principles to digital asset custody could resolve major market uncertainties more elegantly than a complex licensing regime. This strategic choice is further complicated by American federalism, as private law is primarily the domain of the states while major financial regulation is federal. This division can create significant friction, hindering the path to coherent reform.

Finally, if a public law solution is chosen, its implementation requires careful design to ensure that public regulation and private law do not operate as noncommunicating silos. To the contrary, they must be designed to be consistent and synergistic, with new regulations constructed as a superstructure that is carefully placed upon the private law foundation. This task is further complicated by the federal-state division discussed above.

This model of building public law upon a clear private law foundation has a proven record of success in other areas. The regulation of electronic payment systems, for example, has succeeded largely because it built upon well-established private law concepts governing money, contracts, and banking relationships.[1] Payment system regulations work effectively because they operate within a legal framework where the property and contract rights associated with electronic account balances, the contractual obligations between payment processors and

[1] *See* Mark Edwin Burge, *Emerging Payment Systems and the Primacy of Private Law*, CLS Blue Sky (Feb. 11, 2016), https://clsbluesky.law.columbia.edu/2016/02/11/emerging-payment-systems-and-the-primacy-of-private-law/; *see also* Christopher K. Odinet, Andrea Tosato & Yesha Yadav, *The Moneyness of Stablecoins*, Yale L.J. (forthomcing 2026).

users, and the liability rules for unauthorized transactions are relatively clear and stable.[2]

The arguments outlined above have equally important implications for regulatory and enforcement agencies that implement legislative directives and oversee day-to-day market operations. These agencies often possess greater technical expertise and more detailed industry knowledge than judges and legislators. Moreover, unlike judges and legislators, who come into contact with the world of digital assets only periodically, regulators operate in this environment continuously. This places them in a unique position not merely to identify but also to address situations where regulatory effectiveness depends on clarifying underlying private law relationships.

Regulatory agencies should recognize that their traditional tools (rulemaking, supervision, and enforcement[3]) may be insufficient to address problems stemming from uncertain private law foundations. When market participants exploit legal uncertainty to avoid traditional obligations, regulatory responses that focus solely on public law requirements may fail to address the root causes of problematic behavior. Indeed, several of the market failures documented throughout this book, from custodial arrangements that collapsed into unsecured debt to tokenization schemes that conveyed no property rights, stemmed not from a simple lack of regulation, but from a disregard of private law principles. Agencies should also consider how their regulatory initiatives interact with private law principles and should advise state legislators when statutory clarifications would enhance regulatory effectiveness.

To navigate this complex interface, we propose three core recommendations for regulators. First, as with judges and legislators, regulators should acquire a functional understanding of the technologies they oversee. However, the objective for regulators is distinct. A judge's technical understanding is retrospective, aimed at resolving a specific past dispute. A legislator aims to craft broad, prospective rules for society. A regulator's understanding must be operational and continuous, sufficient to assess the ongoing risks posed by a given system's architecture. The perplexing lack of technical sophistication displayed in actions ranging from government white papers to recent cases against major platforms demonstrates a critical gap in this operational capacity.

Second, regulators should develop greater private law competency. Just as financial regulators maintain economists, data scientists, and technologists on staff to understand market dynamics and technological systems, they need

[2] U.C.C. §§ 4, 4A (Am. L. Inst. & Unif. L. Comm'n 2022); Electronic Funds Transfer Act (EFTA), 15 U.S.C. §§ 1693–1693r (2018 & Supp. V 2023); 12 C.F.R. § 1005 (2025); 12 C.F.R. § 210, subpt. B (2025); 31 C.F.R. § 210 (2025).

[3] *See* Adam J. Levitin, Consumer Finance Law: Markets and Regulation 85–157 (2022).

private law specialists who can assess whether novel business models and contractual arrangements are sound. For example, a prudential regulator examining a decentralized lending protocol would benefit greatly from an expert in secured transactions who can both determine whether the protocol creates legally perfected security interests under UCC Article 9 and distinguish proprietary rights from mere contractual claims. This expertise is critical for supervision, as it enables examiners to probe beyond surface compliance and scrutinize terms that create hidden insolvency risks.

Third, regulators should make private law assumptions explicit in their regulations and guidance. Too often, regulations operate on unstated assumptions about underlying legal relationships, assuming, for example, that customer assets are held in bailment or that digital tokens constitute property or confer certain rights against determinate persons. When these assumptions prove false, the entire regulatory structure is compromised. By embedding these private law baselines directly into the text of regulations, agencies would shift the burden of proof, requiring firms to demonstrate that their operations rest on sound private law foundations to achieve regulatory compliance. A custody rule, for instance, should define a compliant arrangement as one that opts into the UCC Article 8 framework, compelling firms to build their practices on sound legal ground. Likewise, enforcement actions should be framed with precision, articulating how a public law violation resulted from a specific private law failure. This approach clarifies legal expectations for all market participants and turns enforcement from a blunt instrument into a surgical tool.

In sum, the ultimate goal of the approaches outlined above is to create frameworks that provide stable, predictable foundations for long-term market development while preserving the flexibility to accommodate technological innovation.

To the lawyers: counseling clients within private law constraints

Next, we turn to the members of our profession—the *lawyers*. Lawyers practicing in the digital asset space find themselves in a uniquely difficult position. The technology evolves at a relentless pace, while clients, eager to capitalize on emerging opportunities, demand rapid and definitive legal solutions in areas where the law is often unsettled. In this high-pressure environment, lawyers have understandably gravitated toward their most familiar tool: contracts. This response, however, has led to two fundamental issues that must be resolved.

The first is the now all-too-familiar flexibility fallacy: an overreliance on contractual agreements to solve all novel problems. To be sure, contract law allows parties to allocate risks, specify performance obligations, and create procedures for enforcement. Yet, as we have explored throughout these chapters, this truth has metastasized into the conviction that private ordering possesses a boundless capacity to reshape both the legal relations between parties and the foundational principles that govern them.

The second issue is the spread of the seductive but misguided notion that "code is law." Besotted by the novel capabilities of DLT and smart contracts, many practitioners have succumbed to a form of technological determinism: the assumption that if code makes an outcome possible, the law must recognize it as enforceable. This is a profound error. The validity of law, as jurists across theoretical traditions have long recognized, is determined by the legal system and the normative principles that sustain it, not from the architectural constraints of a software program. Code can create powerful behavioral constraints, but it cannot conjure legal obligations out of thin air.

These misconceptions have produced devastating consequences, both for individual clients and for the digital asset market as a whole. Regarding the former, lawyers who embrace the flexibility fallacy have created structures that appear robust in calm markets but collapse catastrophically under stress. As we explained in Chapter 4, the customers of FTX and Celsius discovered too late that their "custodial" arrangements were nothing of the sort when bankruptcy proceedings revealed that they were merely unsecured creditors. Similarly, as we showed in Chapters 5 and 6, NFT purchasers discovered they had no rights in the artwork linked to their tokens, while investors in blockchain-based real estate ventures learned that direct tokenization of real property is legally impossible and that tokenizing equity interests in property-holding companies creates a labyrinth of financing complications.

At the systemic level, these failures have contributed to market dysfunction and crisis. Each major collapse in the digital asset space—from the implosion of dual-coin stablecoins, whose automated mechanisms proved powerless against market forces, to the failure of decentralized finance protocols built on legally unsound assumptions about collateral and liquidation—can be traced, at least in part, to fundamental misunderstandings about the interface between technology and law.

Against this backdrop, we offer two recommendations for lawyers. First, attorneys must rediscover private law in all its facets. They must reconnect with all its branches and, most critically, reengage with the core principles of property law. Indeed, in writing this book, we spoke to many lawyers who candidly admitted that their property law knowledge was a hazy memory from law school, often limited to estates in land. These professionals ought to regain an appreciation for the *numerus clausus* principle, which establishes that parties cannot invent new forms of property rights at will. As such, lawyers must relearn the crucial distinction between personal claims enforceable only against a counterparty and property rights enforceable against the world. This includes relearning the core principles and key tenets governing commercial transactions, including the rights and duties of bailees and agents; the framework for attachment, perfection, and priority of security interests; the regime applicable to holdings and transfers of intermediated securities; and the requirements for a valid assignment.

Second, lawyers must cultivate a sophisticated understanding of the difference between code and law and the interface between them. Code is architecture; it governs the realm of the possible through technical constraints. Law, by contrast, is normative; it governs the permissible through rights and duties recognized by the legal system. As we see it, the trouble is that code's extraordinary effectiveness in controlling behavior creates a dangerous illusion. Its regulatory power can seem indistinguishable from the law's normative force. Yet code, standing alone, cannot constitute law. It requires formal investiture through the legal system's sources of law. A smart contract can automatically transfer a digital asset from one wallet to another, but only the law can determine whether that transfer constitutes a valid conveyance of title, a fraudulent transfer, or an act of conversion. The lawyer's role is not to assume that technology can overcome legal obstacles but rather to ensure that an arrangement rests on sound legal foundations before it is implemented through technological means.

Actualizing these recommendations requires a collective effort. Professional organizations are uniquely positioned to lead this initiative. Groups such as the American College of Commercial Finance Lawyers and the American Bar Association's Business Law Section possess the necessary institutional credibility, substantive expertise, and professional networks to spearhead this undertaking. Their mandate should be to facilitate the collaborative development of best practices and professional guidelines, convening sustained dialogues among practitioners, judges, and academics. This effort must be aimed at fostering a shared understanding of how foundational private law principles apply to digital asset transactions. In doing so, they will significantly equip lawyers to structure innovative solutions that are not only commercially effective but also legally sound.

To the law professors: foundational private–public law education

Last, we turn to our colleagues in the *legal academy*.

American legal education stands at a critical crossroads. The decisions law schools make in the coming years will determine whether future generations of lawyers possess the foundational knowledge necessary to navigate a commercial landscape increasingly transformed by DLT, digital assets, automated systems, and the novel business models they enable. More specifically, the choices regarding pedagogical priorities, curriculum design, and faculty hiring will shape the profession's capacity to address the crucial legal questions explored throughout this book that arise when technological innovation intersects with private law.

Paradoxically, we (alongside other commercial law scholars and professional organizations) have witnessed a systematic erosion of private law education over the past two decades. This retreat represents one of the most significant but underappreciated challenges facing the legal profession. The evidence is stark: Some law schools have eliminated property law from the required first-year curriculum; others have relegated essential commercial law courses like sales, secured transactions, and bankruptcy to adjunct faculty; moreover, critical subjects including agency law, private international law, remedies, payments, and UCC Article 8 have all but vanished. Corporate law remains the sole private law subject still receiving robust coverage. Faculty hiring and curriculum design now prioritize almost exclusively the study of constitutional law, administrative law, criminal law, and other domains where individuals encounter state power.

This decline extends equally to scholarship. The most prestigious law reviews rarely publish private law articles, and young scholars quickly learn that career advancement comes through constitutional theory, not commercial law doctrine. This is uniquely American. In other common law jurisdictions, including Australia, Canada, Singapore, and England, private law scholarship remains central to the academic enterprise. Civil law countries find our neglect of private law bewildering, given that it forms the core of their legal science. For an academy that prides itself on being a broader church than what one finds in other jurisdictions, the tendency to underappreciate doctrinal private law scholarship is somewhat unexpected.

While the specific mechanisms driving this shift are complex, we surmise that they appear rooted in a series of institutional incentives that are understandable yet ultimately counterproductive. A tacit assumption seems to have taken hold that private law subjects impart no more than practical knowledge, which is best acquired through practice rather than academic study. Furthermore, academic prestige flows disproportionately to scholars who tackle constitutional and other public law controversies rather than to those who study and develop the doctrinal foundations of commercial life. Accordingly, this prestige differential drives faculty hiring committees to favor candidates who can contribute to the school's research reputation in these high-profile areas. The same pressure can also lead curriculum committees to prioritize courses that align with faculty research agendas. These factors tend to create a self-reinforcing cycle whereby law schools gradually reduce their investment in private law courses, making it more difficult to attract and retain faculty expertise in these areas, which in turn makes it easier to justify further reductions in curricular requirements. As this dynamic accelerates, entire fields of private law risk becoming extinct in the academy.

Whatever the institutional causes, the consequences of this public law tilt in American legal academia are profound. Without a solid grounding in private law principles, new attorneys lack the analytical tools necessary to identify the fundamental legal relationships that underpin their clients' activities. They emerge from law school fluent in regulatory compliance, able to mount constitutional challenges, parse administrative guidance, and navigate enforcement regimes, yet they are unable to answer threshold questions about the nature of the rights and obligations the law purports to regulate. This deficiency may remain hidden when lawyers operate within well-established commercial frameworks where centuries of precedent have settled the private law foundations. But when innovation disrupts settled practice, regulatory knowledge alone proves dangerously inadequate.

Consider how this manifests in digital asset practice. As the case studies in Parts II and III illustrate, lawyers must regularly address questions about whether a particular token constitutes property or only gives rise to a contractual claim, how custody relationships should be structured, what contractual arrangements effectively transfer ownership and create enforceable security rights, and whether automated protocols can substitute for traditional legal intermediaries. These are private law, not regulatory, questions, that require mastery of personal property law, bailment, agency, and commercial law principles. When a client asks whether smart contract execution creates an enforceable obligation or whether tokenization confers actual ownership, knowledge of securities regulations, anti-money laundering requirements, and money transmission rules provides no answer. The lawyer stands mute on the very question that determines whether the regulatory framework even applies.

We believe that law schools bear the primary responsibility for remedying this crisis. They serve as gatekeepers to the profession and provide the only opportunity for comprehensive and systematic instruction in fundamental legal principles. When law schools fail in this mission, they create gaps in competence that are difficult and expensive to remedy through later training. Breaking the cycle of private law's decline, therefore, requires law schools to undertake a fundamental rebalancing of public and private law in both teaching and research.

On the teaching front, law schools must restore private law to the mandatory curriculum. This begins with ensuring that property returns to the required first-year course, taught by full-time faculty members who can provide students with a complete understanding of its concepts and applications across legal practice. While the elimination of mandatory property instruction currently affects only a small number of institutions, we raise this warning here and now in hopes of preventing its spread to other law schools that often follow their lead. Moreover, contract and property law, once year-long courses at most institutions, should be expanded beyond their current formats. Just as many schools offer constitutional law I and II to cover its complexities, contract and property law deserve similar treatment, allowing for instruction that moves beyond key tenets to address the intricacies of these subjects and their application to contemporary commercial arrangements.

This commitment must also extend to the upper-level curriculum, where schools must achieve some level of parity between public and private law offerings, not only in the number of courses but also in staffing equity. Courses in sales, secured transactions, bankruptcy, and remedies should not be rarities but regular offerings that students can reliably access. Moreover, these commercial law electives deserve the same institutional commitment as their public law counterparts. If courses on administrative law or federal courts merit tenure-track professors, so too should secured transactions and bankruptcy, subjects that form the backbone of commercial practice. While adjunct faculty bring valuable practical experience, their role should be understood as complementing, not substituting for, the expertise of full-time faculty who advance these fields through research and law reform.

Beyond these structural changes, pedagogical reform is also necessary. The interface between public and private law must become an explicit focus across the curriculum. For example, courses on financial regulation should be mindful of the private law foundations upon which they are based. Coextensively, private law courses should acknowledge how public and administrative law frameworks modify and constrain private ordering. Equally important, private law instruction must address twenty-first-century challenges. Students need grounding in established doctrine alongside the skills to navigate uncharted legal territory. For instance, property law courses should cover not only the traditional doctrines that govern real estate and tangible personal property but also grapple with the conundrums created by emerging forms of intangible assets.

The legal academy can continue on its current path. Or, it can commit to the principle that a deep grounding in private law and a sophisticated understanding of its interplay with public law are the essential prerequisites for governing innovation wisely. The digital asset economy has exposed the costs of the current imbalance; the choice of which path to take will determine the legal profession's ability to steward society in the complex commercial world of the future.

* * *

We began this book by identifying two fundamental problems plaguing the digital asset landscape: the overwhelming dominance of public law approaches at the expense of private law foundations and the flexibility fallacy. These interlocking pathologies have affected every corner of this emerging commercial sphere, from the most basic questions about whether digital assets constitute property to the legal architecture of their custody, tokenization, and the complex arrangements that underpin stablecoins.

The case studies in Parts II and III revealed the devastating consequences of these misconceptions. NFT purchasers found that their tokens conveyed no rights in the associated artworks because a contract cannot create property rights where none exist. Real estate tokenization projects collapsed into expensive redundancies because property law's mandatory rules cannot be sidestepped through coding. Stablecoin holders learned that dual-coin mechanisms provide no substitute for an actual counterparty. And throughout the crypto winter's cascading bankruptcies, customers of FTX, Celsius, and other platforms confronted the harsh reality that entrusting digital assets to a platform, outside bailment and the UCC Article 8 framework, is merely an unsecured loan dressed in technological jargon. Each failure traced back to the same source: attempting to build commercial relationships while ignoring the private law tenets upon which they are founded.

As we have argued, the path forward requires coordinated action. Lawmakers must resist the siren call of purely regulatory solutions and recognize that effective public law requires sound private law underpinnings. Lawyers must abandon the misguided belief in the omnipotence of private ordering, whether expressed through contract or code, and develop genuine expertise in the private law branches that govern these transactions. And the legal academy must recommit to teaching the core subjects that provide the analytical framework for all commerce, especially in an age of technological disruption.

The importance of this rebalancing extends far beyond the digital asset landscape. As we move deeper into an economy where artificial intelligence converges with DLT and digital assets, the questions explored in this book will only grow in urgency and significance. The digital asset economy is merely the first wave of a broader technological transformation that will test whether our legal system can maintain commercial order through principled doctrinal analysis, rather than reactive regulation. A robust private law framework is not a barrier to innovation but rather its essential infrastructure. A digital economy built on legal quicksand will inevitably fail, but one grounded in private law provides the stability necessary for genuine innovation to flourish.

Index

For the benefit of digital users, indexed terms that span two pages (e.g., 52–53) may, on occasion, appear on only one of those pages.

Tables and figures are indicated by an italic *t* and *f*.

E